EFFORTLESS FLEX 4 DEVELOPMENT

LARRY ULLMAN

Effortless Flex 4 Development
Larry Ullman

New Riders
1249 Eighth Street
Berkeley, CA 94710
510/524-2178
510/524-2221 (fax)
Find us on the Web at: www.newriders.com
To report errors, please send a note to: errata@peachpit.com

New Riders is an imprint of Peachpit, a division of Pearson Education.

Editor: Rebecca Gulick
Production Coordinator: Myrna Vladic
Compositor: Debbie Roberti
Copy Editor: Elle Yoko Suzuki
Proofreader: Patricia Pane
Cover and Interior Design: Terri Bogaards
Indexer: Valerie Haynes Perry
Technical Editor: Ryan Stewart

ISBN 13: 978-0-321-70594-5
ISBN 10: 0-321-70594-7
9 8 7 6 5 4 3 2 1

Printed and bound in the United States of America

With eternal gratitude to all the doctors, nurses, and staff at Fresenius, CMSA, and Johns Hopkins, most especially to Dr. Fine, who has gone well above the call of duty time and again.

SPECIAL THANKS

Bucketsful of thanks to everyone at Peachpit Press/New Riders for their assistance, patience, and hard work, particularly:

My favorite-est editor ever, Rebecca Gulick. Thanks, thanks, and thanks!

Elle Suzuki and Patricia Pane, for the extra coat of polish on my writing.

Myrna and Deb, who can magically take a Word doc and some images and turn that into an actual book.

Valerie Haynes Perry, the indexer, for making sure readers can find what they're looking for amongst all those pesky pages and words.

Everyone else at Peachpit for doing what's required to create, publish, distribute, market, sell, and support these books. And thanks for sparing the extra pages when you can!

Jason Batten, for taking the time and putting in the effort to read through the chapters and provide feedback. The input, and the votes of confidence, really helped!

Ryan Stewart at Adobe, who provided the technical review, making the book accurate.

And lots of thanks to Mike Potter at Adobe, who got me interested in Flex in the first place (well, more interested), and did what he could to make this book happen. Big thanks for all the support, too!

CONTENTS

INTRODUCTION

The Rich Internet Application (RIA) has been a driving force online for the past several years. RIAs provide an improved user experience compared to what's possible using HTML alone and the somewhat clunky interface that is the Web browser. A good RIA turns the Web experience into something much closer to what users have become accustomed to with desktop applications: easy to use, without too many overt server requests, and clearly the work of a professional Web developer.

RIAs can be created using a handful of technologies, but the top two choices are certainly Flash and Ajax ("Ajax" being the name often given to the combination of HTML and JavaScript). People commonly think of Flash as an animated, timeline-driven thing designers use to create games and advertisements, but there's an entirely different side to Flash, based upon the Flex framework.

This book is intended as a programmer's guide to Flex. As I have practically no design skills, you won't see the *best-looking* Flash content, but you will discover and master the best techniques for creating *functional* Flash content. In short, this book is the perfect guide to learning an excellent technology for making today's exemplary Web applications.

WHAT IS FLASH?

Flash is talked about a lot, but there's still quite a bit of misunderstanding about what, exactly, Flash is. Flash, in its broadest sense, is a platform of software and technologies created by Adobe for the purpose of presenting dynamic content. The content itself can range from basic text to forms to multimedia and games. In a narrow sense, Flash is another medium for communication, like HTML, PDFs, or video. However you prefer to think of Flash, it all starts with the development tools and ends with the user's environment.

Adobe has created three programs for generating Flash content:

- Flash Professional
- Flash Builder
- Flash Catalyst

Flash Professional is the current version of the original program used to generate Flash. It provides graphic designers a way to create content that plays out over time, like animation and games. In many ways, Flash Professional is what people generally associate with Flash: a tool for designers.

tip

Flash Builder was named Flex Builder in previous versions.

Flash Builder is an Integrated Development Environment (IDE) for creating Flash content using the Flex framework. Flex will be discussed next in the chapter, but just know that Flex provides a programmatic, event-driven approach to Flash development. Just as Adobe's Dreamweaver application makes Web development faster and easier, Flash Builder makes Flex development faster and easier. I will add that although the book discusses Flash Builder, it really focuses on Flex itself, so you aren't required to have Flash Builder to follow along.

Flash Catalyst is a new product in the Adobe family and acts as an agent between graphical applications like Flash Professional or even Photoshop and the programming tool Flash Builder.

No matter how you develop Flash content, the output will be a Flash file, with an *.swf* extension (pronounced "swiff"). Flash content can then be run in one of three ways:

- In a Web browser that has a Flash Player plug-in installed
- Outside of a Web browser, using the standalone Flash Player
- Outside of a Web browser, using Adobe AIR

tip

Adobe AIR provides a way to create desktop applications using Web technologies.

Generally speaking, Flash content run in a Web browser through the Flash Player plug-in is the most common use of Flash. And, towards that end, most of this book is written with that in mind, although you'll encounter some information about developing for Adobe AIR, too.

WHY USE FLASH?

Flash is one way to present dynamic content but certainly not the only way. Whether you're making an interactive Web site or a standalone desktop application, you have your choice of technologies to use. But before making a comparison, let's look at the argument for Rich Internet Applications as a whole.

The Case for RIAs

Over the course of the Internet's relatively short history, it has already gone through several unique phases. At first, the Web used just HTML and images to present information statically. Then, JavaScript and plug-ins added the ability to run animations, display video, and create (often annoying) effects. Splash pages, pop-ups, and blinking text were not the Internet's high point! But static HTML, with or without adornment, is of limited value and far too impractical to maintain. To make a better Web for end users and developers alike, several server-side technologies arose for generating HTML content on the fly. The most common of these include Microsoft's ASP, Adobe's ColdFusion (originally by Macromedia), Java Server Pages (JSP), and my personal favorite, PHP.

Server-side technologies made dynamic sites possible, but still relied upon the classic client-server model, where the client (aka, the browser) makes a request of the server, the server returns its response, and the client redraws itself accordingly. For each user action, a separate request and another redrawing of the browser was required. It was time for something new...

Over time, through technologies such as Flash and Ajax, the client-server model has been significantly altered. What Flash and Ajax have in common is that both can make server requests behind the scenes, unbeknownst to the user, and then update the client in a more seamless manner. The end result is a better user experience, akin to that of a desktop application. Some call this "Web 2.0" (I prefer not to), but whatever you call it, the fact is that the best, most popular, and certainly the most useful Web sites around, all qualify as Rich Internet Applications.

The Case for Flash

Why should you use Flash to develop your next RIA then, instead of HTML and JavaScript, the most logical alternative? First of all, thanks to Flex, developing Flash applications can be really quick. And I mean really, really quick. With a fair understanding of Flex, you can complete projects in a day that would take you a week to do using HTML and JavaScript alone. And as your RIAs become more complex, this is even truer. Achieving simple effects and interactivity using JavaScript is not that hard, but anything of moderate to advanced complexity gets to be really difficult to do in JavaScript, even if you use a framework.

A second reason to use Flash is that the content will look and function the same in all browsers regardless of type, version, or operating system. If you've done any Web development at all, you know that getting a site to look and work the same in various browsers can be a tedious chore: in Internet Explorer 6, 7, and 8 on Windows; Firefox and Safari on Windows and other operating systems. Flash will always run through the Flash Player plug-in, so there's a consistent experience regardless of the browser or operating system in use.

But what if the user doesn't have the Flash Player plug-in installed? That would actually be surprising, as there's a nearly 98% adoption rate of the plug-in! And if the user doesn't have a current enough version of the player, they'll be prompted to upgrade. Conversely, well-written Ajax sites should degrade smoothly, but the responsibility is on you, the developer, to make sure that's the case. And, again, you have to test the degradation on multiple browsers, with multiple JavaScript settings.

Finally, another benefit to using Flash is that the Flash platform changes quickly with the times and expectations of users. Being a proprietary technology isn't always a bad thing. Adobe regularly improves upon the Flash platform to reflect what people want to be able to do. Conversely, JavaScript evolves over the course of years, not months, so JavaScript developers often have to play catch-up.

The Case Against Flash

It wouldn't be honest or credible to argue why you should use Flash without mentioning the valid reasons not to. First, you'll need to learn a new technology, in this case, Flex. I personally like learning new things, but not everyone wants to be bothered. If you've already mastered HTML and JavaScript, then maybe you don't have a compelling need to learn Flex. Second, although the Flash Player plug-in is installed on practically every browser, if it's not, then the Flash content will not be shown at all; there is no "degrade nicely" option.

The third reason you may not want to use Flash is because of its incomplete support on mobile devices. While some phone companies are specifically working with Adobe to allow Flash content to be viewed using their devices, Apple is famously resistant, meaning that iPod, iPhone, and iPad users won't be able to see your Flash work. (As I write this, Apple and Adobe are in the middle of a public fight over this very issue, but this could change in time, too.)

Finally, although you can develop Flash content without spending a dime (without even using any of Adobe's tools, in fact), you're likely to spend some money if you embrace the Flash platform at all. For example, the Flash Builder application is excellent, but is a commercial product (see Adobe's site for specific pricing).

note

As a minor point, printing Flash content is less than ideal, but I personally hardly ever consider printing out online content.

All that being said, if you're looking at this introduction, then I assume you're at least curious about Flex (and therefore Flash), so I'd recommend you at least give it a quick spin around the block. This book shouldn't set you back much, Flex is an open source technology, and Flash Builder is available in a 60-day free trial, so you can decide for yourself if it is worth your while, without a significant financial investment.

WHAT IS FLEX?

note

The first chapter discusses Flex, MXML, ActionScript, and Flash Builder in more detail.

As I already said, Flex is a framework for creating Flash content. Most people think of Flash as a graphic design technology, and think they need those skills for Flex, but Flex is for programmers. Trust me on this: I have absolutely no design skills whatsoever, but that hasn't hindered my Flex development at all.

The Flex framework consists of two pieces: MXML and ActionScript. MXML defines the elements you'll use in an application, and the primary application file will be an MXML document. MXML is very similar in both syntax and usage to HTML. ActionScript is an object-oriented programming language used to add logic to an application. ActionScript is very similar in both syntax and usage to JavaScript. But, simply stated, Flex is a framework: an easy means to an end.

If you're using the Flash Builder IDE to develop in Flex, it comes with the Flex framework, along with all the tools needed to turn Flex into Flash (called *compilers*). If you're not using Flash Builder, you'll need to download the free Flex Software Development Kit (SDK). Along with the Flex framework itself, the Flex SDK contains the compilers, code templates, examples, and more.

Flex has been around since 2004 and is currently in version 4, released in 2010. That's the version this book uses exclusively.

tip

Flex 4-generated Flash content will run on Flash Player version 10 and later.

ABOUT THIS BOOK

To understand this book, you should know a little about me. I'm a programmer and developer by occupation, entirely self-taught and with a complete lack of aesthetic skills, as previously mentioned. As with all my books—this is my 18th—it's written under the principle of "If I were learning this subject for the first time, what kind of book would I want?" Largely this means

- Real-world examples
- No fluff, filler, or esoteric examples that you'd never actually use
- Minimal expectations of the reader
- Crystal-clear explanations

Technical writing is largely a matter of making choices about what you need to know and what you don't need to know. Hopefully, I've done a good job of that. By the end of the book you should have a sound understanding not just of how to use Flex but how to use it well. Everything you *need* to know about Flex is covered including, most importantly, how you go about learning more when your knowledge and needs have eclipsed the parameters of this text.

I should also point out that I have a strong aversion to spending any money at all. I say that because I generally use open source software and free applications whenever possible. Still, I find Flex to be a strong enough tool that I use it—and willingly pay for Flash Builder. But this book is not for the purpose of making money for Adobe, and so I'm not going to assume you're necessarily using Flash Builder. The book is really about Flex. Still, Flash Builder is an excellent tool that most Flex developers are in fact using, so the book does discuss some Flash Builder-specific topics. And now that I'm talking more about the book and less about me, I'll point out that the book doesn't spend much time dwelling on how Flex 4 differs from Flex 3 or earlier versions. If you already know Flex 3, you'll see a few notes that X or Y has changed, but that's about it. Flex 3 is Flex 3 and Flex 4 is Flex 4 and this here book is about Flex 4.

A lot of the talk surrounding Rich Internet Applications goes into how you can create a great user interface. And while that's both true and valid, I'm of the opinion that the *data* used by an RIA is the real star of the show. It's the data that gives users the reason to be at a Web site in the first place and it's the data that will give them reason to return. Accordingly, the meat of the book can be found in Part 2, "Data and Communications." The five chapters there cover everything you need to know about displaying, manipulating, and transmitting data, including three chapters on the client-server relationship. For those chapters, I exclusively use PHP as the server-side technology. Although I explain the purpose of every line of PHP code, if you're not familiar with PHP, you may have difficulty with two of those chapters. In such a case, I could recommend my *PHP for the Web: Visual QuickStart Guide* (Peachpit Press, 2009) book, or any of the available PHP tutorials to be found online. Similarly, MySQL will be used as the database application in those chapters.

So what else do I expect of you, the benevolent reader? I expect many readers will be like me, having used PHP and MySQL but now accepting the need to also know a powerful client-side technology. I expect you probably have done some Web development, having dirtied your hands with HTML even the slightest. If this is true and you have even minimal familiarity with JavaScript, learning Flex will not be a problem. Flex is easy to learn and not even that hard to master.

If you do have problems along the way, you can turn to the book's corresponding Web site: *www.DMCInsights.com/flex4/*. There you can download all of the code from the book, find supplemental material (I also write about Flex, PHP, and other topics on my blog), and get assistance through my online forum.

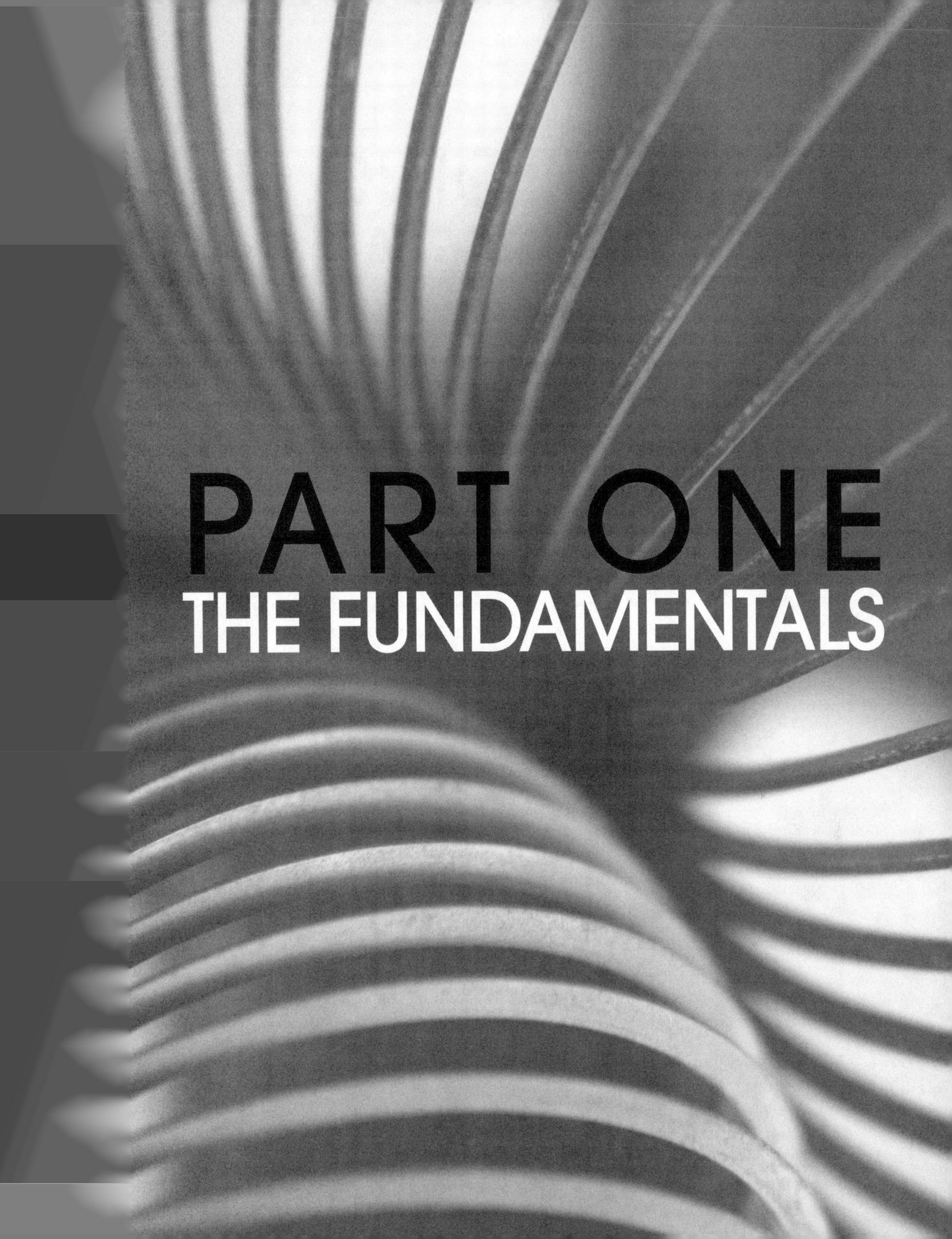

PART ONE
THE FUNDAMENTALS

1 BUILDING FLEX APPLICATIONS

The focus in this chapter is simple: how to create and deploy Flex-based applications. You'll learn two ways of generating Flex content—one fast but commercial, the other free but requiring more effort—and two ways of using that content: on the Web and as a standalone application. Just as important, though, the chapter begins with an overview of the technologies and tools involved, and ends with your best resources for getting help as you learn Flex. Along the way, you'll also see some tips, tricks, and best practices for working as a Flex developer.

Before getting into the specifics, one last note: The images shown in this chapter, as will be the case in other chapters, were taken on both Windows and Mac OS X. However, all of the concepts and most of the steps are platform-neutral. I'll be certain to highlight any specific platform disparities, when they occur.

A SURVEY OF THE LAND

If you're entirely unfamiliar with Flex, it's easy to be confused by all the terminology and parts involved. You'll frequently see these words and acronyms: Flex, MXML, ActionScript, Halo, Spark, Flash Builder, Flash Catalyst, Flash Professional, Flash Player, SWF, etc. And that list doesn't even include the common data-related acronyms XML, JSON, and AMF (the second part of the book focuses on integrating data with Flex and will go into these in great detail). Before doing any actual coding, let's get a survey of the Flex world you're about to enter into.

The Flex Framework

Flex is simply a framework for creating Flash content and Flash is simply a tool for making interactive applications. The Flex framework has two key parts: MXML and ActionScript (MXML is not officially an acronym, by the way). Although they are not literally equivalent, you may find it easiest to think of MXML and ActionScript as being like HTML and JavaScript. If you have some experience creating Web pages, the concepts behind Flex won't be totally foreign to you.

tip

See the book's Introduction for more on what Flash is capable of and how it can be used.

MXML, like HTML, is based upon XML (eXtensible Markup Language), which means that they have similar syntaxes. In HTML, a text input is created using

```
<input type="text" id="address"/>
```

In MXML, a text input is created using

```
<s:TextInput id="address"/>
```

Remarkably similar, right? MXML, like HTML, is used for creating the body of an application, plus the elements that a user sees and interacts with, like text inputs.

While I'm talking about MXML, you should know that Flex 4 has added something called *Spark*. Ever since Flex 1, all of the available components—things you'd use in an application, like the text input above—were part of the same core definition. These were called *Halo* components, and they all had the same general look, usage, and behavior. But the Halo components had their limitations, particularly when it came to changing their look to better fit in with the aesthetic of your application. The solution in Flex 4, then, was to create a new series of components, called *Spark*, which don't have these issues. At the same time, the Spark series defines new components that were missing from the Halo collection.

Now you could just program using only the new Spark pieces, but in order to make Flex 4 more compatible with older Flex code, and because not everything has yet been re-implemented in Spark, the older Halo components are also still available. The result is that your MXML code, as of Flex 4, will contain two representative abbreviations: *s* and *mx*—*Spark* and *Halo*, respectively. So the above code creates a Spark text input, whereas this code creates a Halo text input:

```
<mx:TextInput id="address"/>
```

Throughout the course of the book you'll see me frequently mention that a component is defined in Halo or Spark. When I do so, it's an indicator of both the initial abbreviation for that component—*s* or *mx*—as well as where you can find more information about it, and what you'll be able to do with it once you get into aesthetic issues such as skinning and styling.

You'll also come across the *fx* abbreviation in this book. It represents the Flex core components, also a new designation as of Flex 4.

Along with MXML, Flex applications make heavy use of ActionScript. ActionScript, like JavaScript, is based upon ECMAScript. You don't have to know what that is; the important thing is that ActionScript and JavaScript are similar in both usage and syntax. As with JavaScript in a Web page, ActionScript primarily acts as the brains of an application. Chapter 3, "ActionScript You Need," provides an introduction to the language. To be absolutely clear, ActionScript is not restricted to just Flex programming: It's an established language that's been used with Flash for years.

The Software

Just as you can create a Web page in any number of applications, you can create Flex-based applications using any text editor or Integrated Development Environment (IDE). Adobe has made the Flex framework open source as of version 2, and its Software Development Kit (SDK) has been free as of version 3. By taking these free tools, and the software you already have, you can begin creating Flex applications at no additional cost (and you will see how in this chapter). That being said...

Just as an IDE like Adobe Dreamweaver facilitates Web development, Adobe's Flex-based IDE, Flash Builder, is a *significantly better* alternative to the text editor/IDE-SDK route. And I'm not saying that because I have to promote Adobe: I overwhelmingly prefer free or cheap software to commercial products, but some things are worth spending money on, and Flash Builder is definitely one of them. Admittedly, Flash Builder isn't cheap, but it's well worth the money in my opinion (see Adobe's Web site for applicable pricing). Don't take my word for it though; find out for yourself: Adobe has a very generous 60-day free trial of it available at *www.adobe.com/go/flex*. Sixty days should be more than enough time to get through this book, grasp Flex, and see if spending the extra money makes sense for you.

Along with Flash Builder, Adobe has two other applications for creating Flash content: Flash Professional and Flash Catalyst. Flash Professional is the current version of the original program used to generate Flash, and provides graphic designers a way to create content that plays out over time, like animation and games. By comparison, Flex development is primarily about programming an application to respond to events. Adobe Flash Catalyst is the newest software package on the block and is intended as an intermediary between the designer-centric Flash Professional and the developer-centric Flash Builder. I do not discuss either Flash Professional or Flash Catalyst in this book, as both warrant their own books. Plus, if you were to list whatever talents I may have, design skills would not be among them!

Deployment

Once you've used whatever software to create an application that does what you want it to, you can then make it available to the world at large. This process involves using the Flex compiler to turn all of the MXML and ActionScript into a compiled SWF (pronounced "swiff") file. If you're going the free route, a compiler is included in Adobe's free SDK; you'll just need to go through a command-line interface to use it. If you're using Flash Builder, the compiler is built into the program, so you just click a button.

To deploy the application, which is the SWF file, online, an HTML page needs to be created that embeds the file. This page will then be loaded by the Web browser, so that the SWF file can be executed using the browser's Flash Player plug-in. The Flash Player plug-in is extremely common (installed on around 98% of all browsers) and you can take great comfort in knowing that users will be asked to update their Flash Player should they run across incompatible content (**Figure 1.1**).

Figure 1.1

If you want to create a cross-platform desktop application, you can do that too, thanks to Adobe AIR. AIR is a runtime engine that allows you to develop an application once, and have it be executable on Windows, Mac OS X, and even Linux. Because AIR applications run like regular desktop applications, AIR application programming is a bit more complicated than Web application programming and has its own security considerations.

As Flash content is much more widely used online than on the desktop, this book is geared towards applications intended for the Web. Still, much of the knowledge and techniques covered also constitute the foundation of Flex-based AIR programs. This book cannot go into the AIR-specific knowledge in any great detail, but you will be introduced to the main points of AIR application development with Flex, both in this chapter and later on.

BASIC MXML

Before getting into the tools and how you go about building an application, let's examine the shell of a plain Flex program. The basis of a Flex application is just MXML. When developing for the Web, you start with the following:

```
<?xml version="1.0" encoding="utf-8"?>
<s:Application xmlns:fx="http://ns.adobe.com/mxml/2009"
    xmlns:s="library://ns.adobe.com/flex/spark"
    xmlns:mx="library://ns.adobe.com/flex/mx">
</s:Application>
```

You cannot have any spaces or characters before the ***<?xml*** on the first line of the MXML file!

MXML is valid XML, so the first line of code indicates that this file contains XML (version 1.0 is fine; this is a different thing than the version of Flex in use). The first line also indicates the encoding used in this file, *UTF8* by default. Encoding is a big subject beyond what I could explain here, but if you're not familiar with it, you can get away with just knowing the following:

- UTF8 is the perfect choice, unless you know you have reasons to choose another encoding.
- The actual encoding used by the application creating the MXML file must match the declared encoding.

You can normally change the file's actual encoding in your application's preferences or when you save the file. In Flash Builder, you set the encoding under Preferences > General > Workspace (**Figure 1.2**).

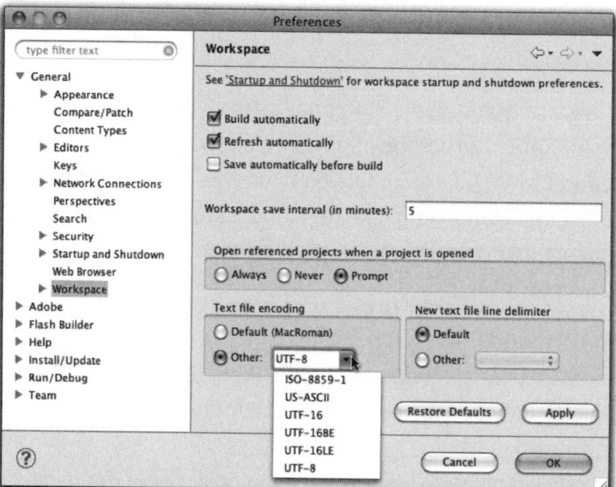

Figure 1.2

The next line of code is the opening **Application** tag. Everything that is the application will go between the opening and closing **Application** tags, just as everything on a Web page goes between the opening and closing **HTML** tags. The opening **Application** tag can have several properties, such as **width** and **height**. The only required property is **xmlns**, which stands for *XML namespace*. You'll see the word *namespace* occasionally; in layman's terms, a namespace is just where something is defined. For example, the namespace declaration in the **Application** tag indicates that every use of *fx* will represent components defined at *http://ns.adobe.com/mxml/2009*.

Three namespaces are identified in the above code: *fx*, *s*, and *mx*. I've introduced these abbreviations already: They represent the Flex core components (*fx*), the Spark components (*s*), and the legacy Halo components (*mx*).

You may also note that the opening **Application** tag is written over several lines. Not only is this perfectly acceptable, it's also a standard technique for making code more legible.

And that's all there is for a very basic Flex application destined for the Web. Such an application neither does nor displays anything but is syntactically valid. In a desktop Flex application that will run using Adobe AIR, everything in the basic shell is the same except that the opening and closing **Application** tags become **WindowedApplication**.

tip

To save space, the code in this book will be kept compact. Feel free to space out your code to make it easier to read and edit.

Before expanding upon this shell, there are a few things you should know about MXML:

- **MXML is case-sensitive.**

  Application is a valid tag, whereas *application* or *APPLICATION* is not. You'll need to pay attention to exactly how things are written in the book and in various other resources you use.

- **All tag property values must be quoted.**

  For example, in the **Application** tag, the **xmlns** property's value (that which comes after the equals sign) is in quotes.

- **All tags must be formally closed.**

  XML, and therefore HTML and MXML, allow you to close open tags using one of two formats. The first requires both an opening and a closing tag, as with **Application**: **<s:Application></s:Application>**. The second format does not have a closing tag, instead concluding the opening tag with a slash before its closing angle bracket. The Flex **TextInput** component is an example of this:

  ```
  <s:TextInput id="address"/>
  ```

  Normally elements that won't encompass other elements (e.g., no other tag would be put within a **TextInput**) are closed in this manner. For aesthetic purposes, you can place a space before the slash, if you prefer:

  ```
  <s:TextInput id="address" />
  ```

- **All tags must be properly nested.**

  This only applies if you're using opening and closing tags. What is meant is that if you open element A, then open element B (so that element B is contained within A), you must then close B before closing A. In HTML, this would be an example of an *improperly* nested pair of tags:

  ```
  <div><p>Some text.</div></p>
  ```

Breaking any of these rules will break your application, but the rules are easy enough to understand and follow. As you'll find, Flash Builder goes a long way towards helping you in this regard, as it quickly and obviously flags such problems for you.

USING FLASH BUILDER

Flash Builder is Adobe's IDE for creating Flex 4 applications (in earlier incarnations, it was known as Flex Builder). It's based upon the popular and open-source Eclipse IDE (*www.eclipse.org*), and can be installed either on its own or as an Eclipse plug-in (if you're already using Eclipse, that would be a logical route to take). Flash Builder is available in both standard and professional editions, with the professional version primarily adding extra performance and testing tools to facilitate development (see Adobe's Web site for a full breakdown of the two versions). Flash Builder is a commercial product that requires a license to use in the long run, but is available as a free 60-day trial (yes, 60!). I would strongly, strongly, strongly (insert 57 more "stronglys") urge you to download the trial and begin your Flex life using Flash Builder. You'll learn so much more, so much faster, if you do.

Flash Builder is available for Windows and Mac OS X operating systems. I'll assume you know how to download, install, and open an application on your computer, so I'll just skip ahead to using Flash Builder. The application does require the Java Runtime Engine (JRE), so you'll be prompted to download and install that if it's not already available on your machine (or if a current-enough version isn't present).

A Quick Tour of Flash Builder

Flash Builder is an extremely smart and mature IDE, thanks to its Eclipse foundation. It's one of those tools that reward taking the time to learn its features and customizing it to your needs. Some of that can be done within the application's preferences, but first I want to discuss the *workbench*, which is the combination of open windows, tabs, and panels in Flash Builder (i.e., everything you see when you open the program, **Figure 1.3**).

Front and center in Flash Builder is the Editor. This window takes up most of the space and is where you'll most often do your design and programming. The Editor has tabs representing each open file, with the file's name on the tab itself. Double-click a tab to view that Editor in a near-fullscreen mode; double-click again to return to the previous size.

The Editor runs in two modes: Source (Figure 1.3) and Design (**Figure 1.4**). The former shows the raw source code; the latter how that code is visibly rendered, much like the difference between viewing HTML code and viewing how a browser interprets that code.

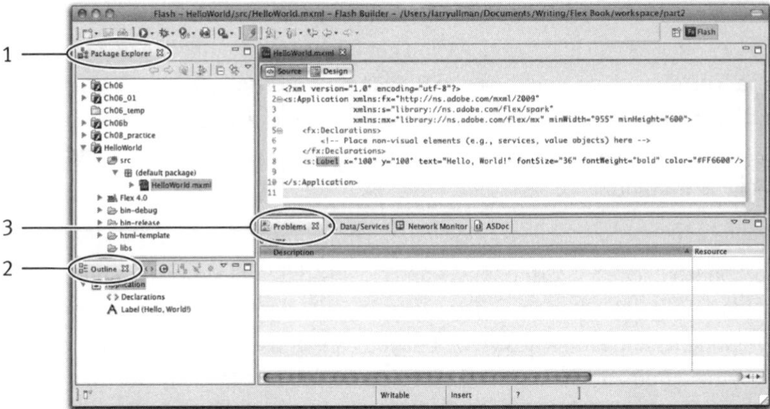

Figure 1.3

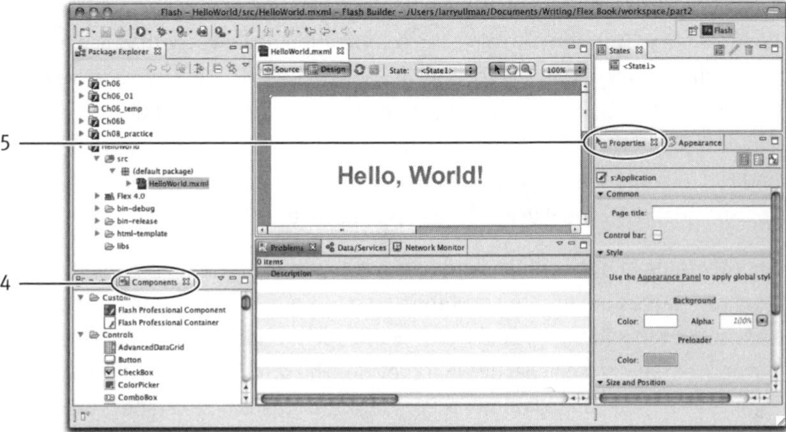

Figure 1.4

The rest of the workbench is comprised of panels called *views*. Each view represents a single concept or aspect of the development process. Some key views include

- **Package Explorer,** for navigating through files, directories, and projects (Figure 1.3, 1)
- **Outline,** which lists the components in a file (Figure 1.3, 2)
- **Problems,** where errors and warnings are listed (Figure 1.3, 3)
- **Components,** a list of Flex elements (Figure 1.4, 4)
- **Properties,** for editing a selected component's attributes (Figure 1.4, 5)

There are almost a dozen more views available, but those listed above are the key ones as you just begin. As you get further on and need to do more advanced debugging, you'll use the **Breakpoints, Console, Debug, Expressions,** and **Variables** views. Other views are used to interact with data services or assist in profiling an application. I'll discuss these other views throughout the book, as warranted.

You'll see that as you switch Editor modes (between Source and Design), the workbench itself changes: opening and closing different views as appropriate (compare Figures 1.3 and 1.4). For example, in Design mode you can use the Components and Properties views but you cannot use them in Source mode. Also, the automatic closing of several views provides a larger Editor for working with the source code, which is a logical change.

A view can be closed by clicking the X on the view's tab, rearranged by grabbing its tab and moving it elsewhere, and opened by selecting it from the Window menu. You can also alter the combination of views (both which ones are open and where they are located in the workbench) using *perspectives*. A perspective is a memorized setup defined to correspond to certain tasks. Flash Builder ships with three perspectives already defined—Flash, Flash Debug, and Flash Profile—and you can define your own (or edit the predefined ones). For the most part, you'll use the Flash perspective.

Another thing to notice in the workbench is that the most important choices from the various menus are also represented as quick-access icons in the toolbars at the top and the bottom of the workbench window. Allow your cursor to hover over them to see exactly what they do. The toolbar options are also customizable by selecting Windows > Perspective > Customize Perspective. And, as with most desktop applications, Control-clicking or right-clicking in various areas creates useful contextual menus.

More of Flash Builder's behavior and appearance is controlled within the application's Preferences area. There are too many options to walk through here, and most are self-explanatory, so I'll leave it to you to investigate those when you feel the time is right. Note that I have refrained from tweaking most of the preferences and perspectives for the pictures in this book in order to keep the images as consistent as possible with what you should see.

Over the course of this chapter, and throughout the rest of the book, you'll learn lots more about how you can use Flash Builder to effortlessly create your Flex applications. In particular, the last section of this chapter highlights some of the help tools built into this one program.

Creating a Simple Application

Creating any Flex application using Flash Builder is stunningly simple, as these next few steps will show.

1. Open Flash Builder, if it is not already.

2. Select File > New > Flex Project.

Each application you build will likely be its own project, at least until you start making much more elaborate software.

3. In the New Flex Project window (**Figure 1.5**), do the following:

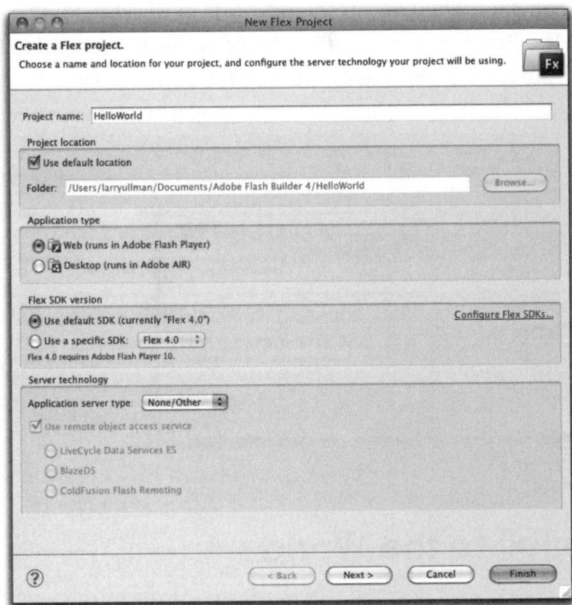

Figure 1.5

1. Enter a name for the project. The name should be both descriptive and unique, but can only contain numbers, letters, and a space. Conventionally, one uses CamelCase for the project's name, without spaces: *HelloWorld*, not *Hello World*, *helloworld*, or *helloWorld*.

2. Choose the project's location. Flash Builder will store all projects in a default location unless you override the behavior.

3. Select the application type. This is where you indicate whether the output will be for the Web (i.e., run in the Flash Player) or for desktops (run in Adobe AIR). For almost every example in the book, except where explicitly stated otherwise, I'll be creating Web applications.

The MXML template the Flash Builder uses includes opening and closing ***fx:Declarations*** tags. We'll get to their meaning and usage later in the book but you can ignore them in the interim. They have no effect on the rendered content as is.

You can customize the default templates in Preferences > Flash Builder > File Templates.

You'll most likely find that the best way to use Flash Builder, particularly as you are just learning Flex, is to drag components from the Components view onto the application, then edit the component using the Properties view. You'll create programs much faster and have fewer errors by starting out this way.

4. Determine which SDK you'll use. Here you can choose to use older versions of Flex (which would allow you to create applications that run in older versions of the Flash Player or Adobe AIR) or newer, beta versions, if you want to test forthcoming releases. For every example in this book, I'll be using Flex 4.0.

5. Ignore the server type for now. In Part 2, "Data and Communications," you'll learn to play with this setting.

4. Click Finish.

As you'll see, Flash Builder will create an organized project directory (as shown in the Package Explorer view in **Figure 1.6**), the exact particulars of which will depend upon whether you selected Web or Desktop for the application type. The ***ProjectName.mxml*** file, found within the **src/default package** folder, is the primary document you'll edit to customize what the application does. Flash Builder will automatically open this file for you in the Editor.

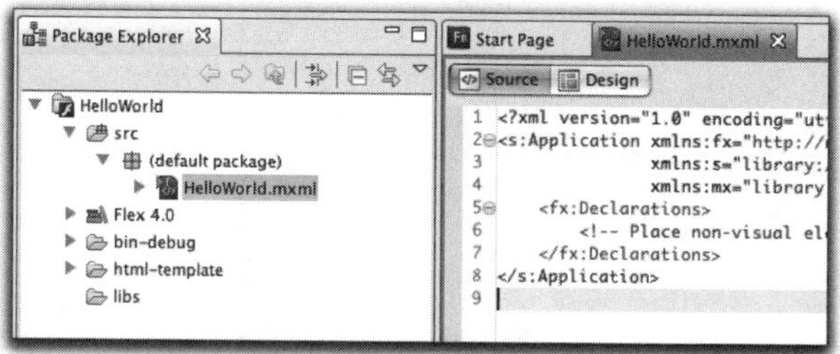

Figure 1.6

Saying "Hello" to the World

If you use Design mode to look at the plain application auto-generated by Flash Builder, you'll see that there's nothing there. So before compiling and running it, let's add a little code so that it does *something*. In keeping with standard book conventions, we'll make a classic "Hello, World!" example. Of course, it's a terrible use of Flash's power but is easy to follow and unlikely to have problems. Let's add some text to the existing, plain application, and then run the whole thing to see the result.

1. Open **HelloWorld.mxml** in Flash Builder, if it's not already.

2. Before the closing **Application** line, add the following:

```
<s:Label x="100" y="100" text="Hello, World!" fontSize="36"
color="#FF6600" fontWeight="bold"/>
```

That code creates a **Label** element, which is the simplest way to add text to an application. The initial **s:** indicates that this is a Spark component, not available in versions of Flex prior to 4. The x- and y- coordinates position the top-left corner of the element within the window (where the top-left corner of the window is at 0, 0, **Figure 1.7**). The **text** attribute is where you put the actual text to be displayed. The **fontSize**, **color**, and **fontWeight** attributes format the text as 36 point in size, orange in color, and bold.

There are two ways you might enter this code in Flash Builder:

- Use the Source mode and the Editor to type in all that code. As you'll see once you start typing, Flash Builder has code hinting (**Figure 1.8**): it'll provide lists of possible values as you type; use the arrow keys, or continue typing, to further select an option; then press Enter or Return once you've found the right choice.

Figure 1.7

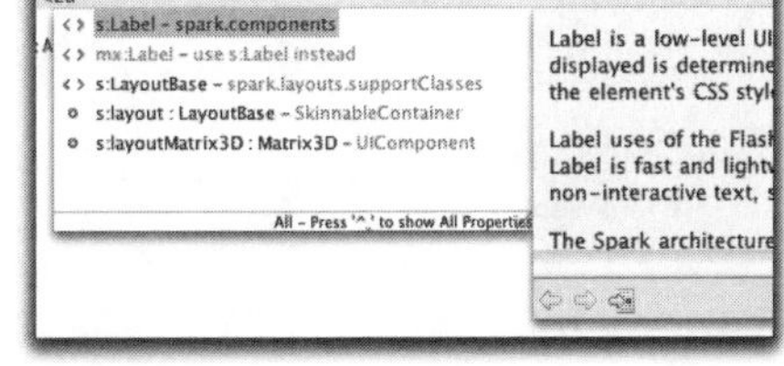

Figure 1.8

- Alternatively, make sure you are in Design mode, then drag the **Label** element from the Components view (**Label** is listed under Controls) onto the Editor window. This will create, and select, the **Label** element. Next, use the Properties view to alter the component's various attributes (**Figure 1.9**).

3. Save the file.
4. Select Run > Run *ProjectName* to test the application.

   You can also click the Run icon in the toolbar at the top of the workbench or use the keyboard shortcut (shown in the Run menu). If you've been creating an application for the Web, it'll run in your default browser. If you've been creating a desktop application, it'll run in *adl*, the Adobe AIR Debug Launcher.

   Because this application just has static text, the running version will look exactly like that in the Editor's Design mode (this will not be the case for more sophisticated applications).

tip

If you select "Always" under Save required dirty editors before launching in the Preferences > Launching window, Flash Builder will automatically save your edited file prior to running it.

note

In order to run the project, you'll see that Flash Builder will have generated several files, placed in the project's **bin-debug** folder. These are not to be used to deploy your application.

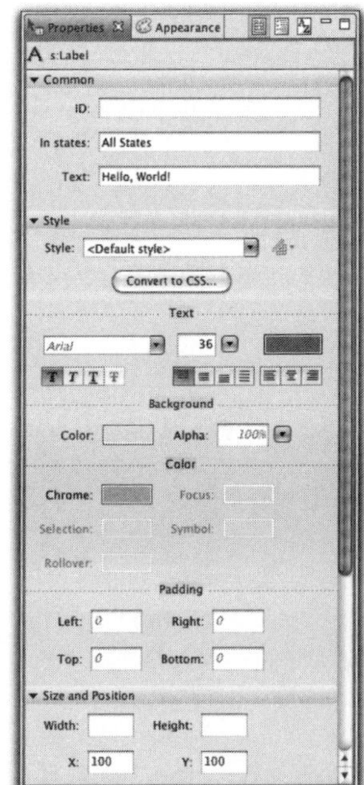

Figure 1.9

Deploying Web Applications

Once you've tested your application and have it both looking and behaving as you want it to, it's time to deploy the application, which is to say release it into the wild and make it available for others to see. Start by selecting Project > Export Release Build (or File > Export > Release Build). This begins the Export Release Build wizard.

If exporting a Web application, there's just one window of options (**Figure 1.10**):

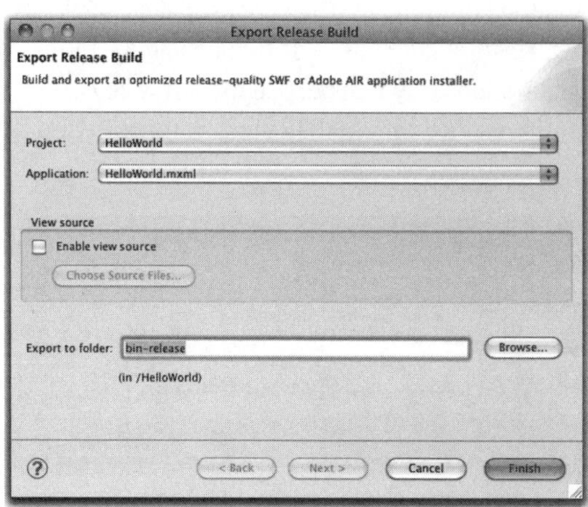

Figure 1.10

1. Select the project to export (you can export a project without opening it).

   You'll see that Flash Builder auto-selects the corresponding primary application file for you.

2. If you want, check the Enable view source box.

   Unlike Web pages, where anyone can view the underlying HTML and JavaScript, compiled Flash code is not readily accessible. Most likely you won't want to change this, but if you do want the viewer to be able to see the work itself, you can check this box, then click the Choose Source Files button to select the specific source files that are viewable.

3. Select where you want the output to be generated.

   By default, the exported files go into the project's **bin-release** (binary release) folder.

4. Click Finish.

   In the folder selected in Step 3 (**Figure 1.11**), you'll now find all sorts of goodies, the most important of which being the ***ProjectName*.swf** file, the compiled application. ***ProjectName*.html** is the HTML page that embeds the SWF file, and is what the browser would directly view (you can load it in your browser locally to confirm this for yourself).

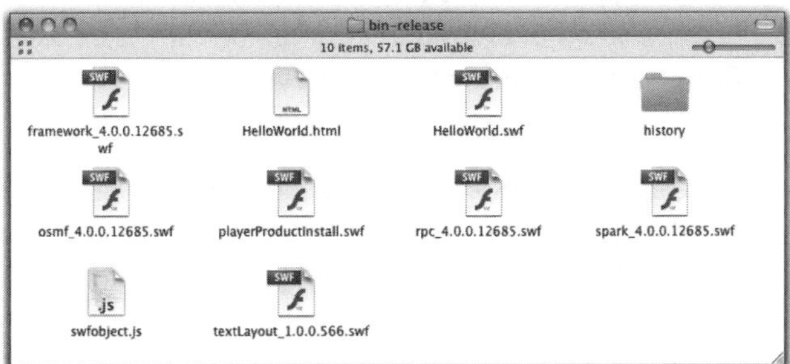

Figure 1.11

There are many other required files found in the folder. To start, the code libraries used by the application (e.g., the Flex required components) will be stored in several SWF files with odd names like **framework_4.0.0.12685.swf**. These are essentially backup libraries that will only be sent to the user's computer if the user's browser doesn't already have them available, thereby saving bandwidth and improving the download speed. There is also **swfobject.js**, an important JavaScript file used by the HTML page to embed the Flash content into the Web page in a cross-browser-safe way. And **playerProductInstall.swf** will come into play if the user's browser doesn't have the proper Flash Player plug-in installed.

5. Copy all of the files found in the project's **bin-release** directory to your Web site.

   By putting all these files on your Web server, users can now execute your Flash application by loading the ***ProjectName*.html** page in their browsers. To incorporate the application into an existing Web page, just copy the HTML and JavaScript out of ***ProjectName*.html** and put it in the proper places in your other HTML file. The HTML file is fairly well documented, making it sufficiently simple to copy out the parts you'll need.

tip

Many of the output settings are adjustable by going to Project > Properties. In particular, see the Flex Compiler section.

THE OPEN SOURCE ALTERNATIVE

To be absolutely frank, using Adobe's Flash Builder makes Flex development so much faster that I personally wouldn't consider creating Flex applications any other way. And I say that as a person who is really rather cheap, and way more likely to use a free alternative to commercial software whenever feasible. Still, Flash Builder does cost some money, and it doesn't run on Linux, so I'll acknowledge that there are some valid reasons why you might not be using it. That being said, as a final plea, at least *try* the 60-day free trial of Flash Builder while you work your way through this book (which will have an admitted bias for Flash Builder, as if you couldn't tell). Then, after the book or 60 days, whichever comes first, you can decide for yourself if Flash Builder is worth the money. Moving on...

The Flex Software Development Kit (SDK) is available for free, allowing you to develop Flex applications using any text editor or IDE and a command-line interface. Before downloading and setting up the SDK, you should make sure you have the following tools:

- A decent text editor or IDE
- An interface for command-line interactions
- The Java Runtime Environment

tip

FlashDevelop (*www.flashdevelop.org*) is a free IDE that runs on Windows.

The emphasis here is really a *decent* text editor or IDE (i.e., not Notepad). If you don't have a preferred development tool already, a quick search online will easily turn up several great possibilities, in a range of prices. If you prefer an IDE to a text editor, you should really consider Eclipse (*www.eclipse.org*), which is the standard-bearer for IDEs everywhere, runs on most operating systems, and is available at no cost.

If you don't know how to access your computer from a command-line interface, you'll just want to use the Terminal application on most variants of Linux and on Mac OS X (found within the **Applications/Utilities** folder). On Windows, you can find the command-line interface (called the console window or DOS prompt, **Figure 1.12**) by

1. Clicking Start.
2. Selecting Run.
3. Entering **cmd** in the Run prompt (**Figure 1.13**).
4. Clicking OK.

note

I've changed the settings in my console window to be black text on a white background, which looks better in a book than the default white text on a black background.

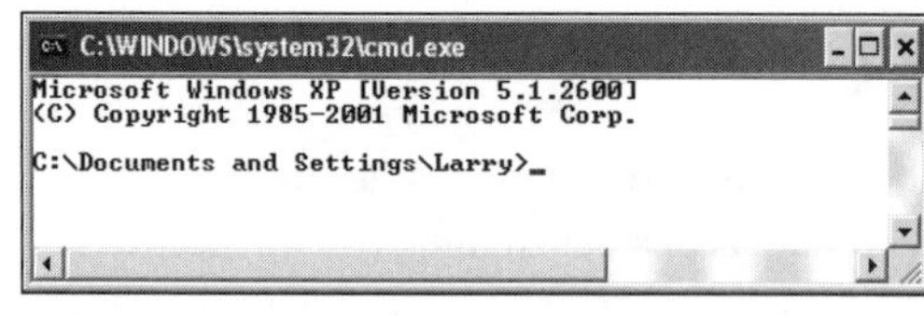

Figure 1.12

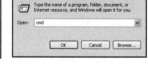

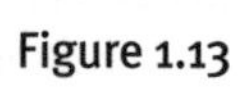

Figure 1.13

The Java Runtime Environment is required to run the Flex compiler. It may already be installed on your computer, but if not, is available for free at *http://java.sun.com* (at the time of this writing, there is a "Get Java For Your Desktop" link, which is what you want).

Installation and Setup

Once your computer has the minimum requirements, the first step is to download the SDK from Adobe's Web site. Start by heading to *www.adobe.com/go/flex*, then click the link that says something like "Get the Free Flex SDK."

The downloaded file will be in ZIP format that you'll need to expand. The resulting folder has lots of goodies in it. Copy this entire directory somewhere that'll be easy to find and makes logical sense. This may be the root of your computer (like **C:\flex4sdk**) or your desktop or wherever.

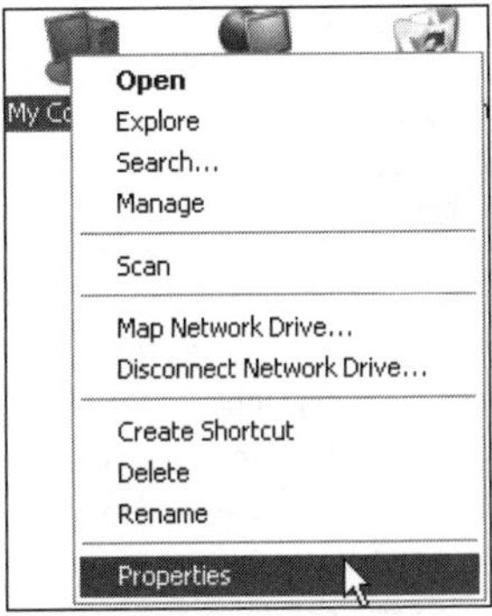

Figure 1.14

Next, you'll need to add the location of the compiler to your *path*. The path, if you're not familiar with it, is a list of places that contain executables. When you enter, say, **someCommand** at a command-line prompt, the system needs to know where to find the **someCommand** program. That's what we're going to do next. The particular steps are very much operating system-specific. I discuss Windows and Mac OS X specifically; if you're using Linux, search online to find out how to change your path, if you don't already know.

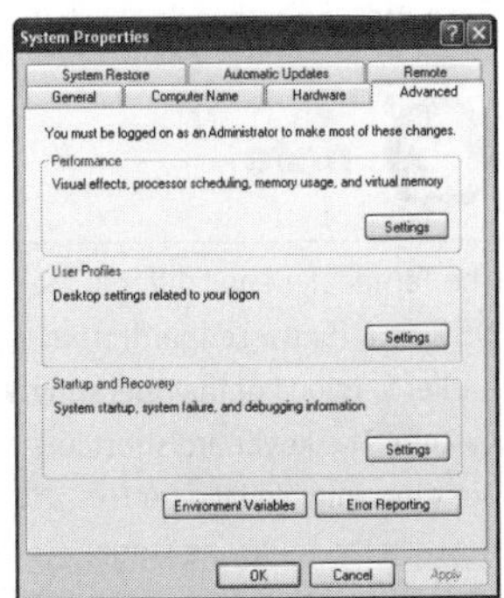

Figure 1.15

UPDATING YOUR PATH ON WINDOWS

1. Close any open console windows.

   The path change you're about to make takes effect for any console windows (aka DOS prompts) opened *after* making the change. To avoid confusing problems later, close any open console windows prior to changing the path.

2. Bring up the System Properties dialog.

   One way to do this is by right-clicking My Computer and selecting Properties (**Figure 1.14**).

3. Within the System Properties dialog, click the Advanced tab (**Figure 1.15**).

4. Click the Environment Variables button at the bottom of the Advanced tab (see Figure 1.15).

5. In the Environment Variables dialog, click Path in the System variables listing (**Figure 1.16**).

6. Click Edit to bring up the Edit System Variable dialog.

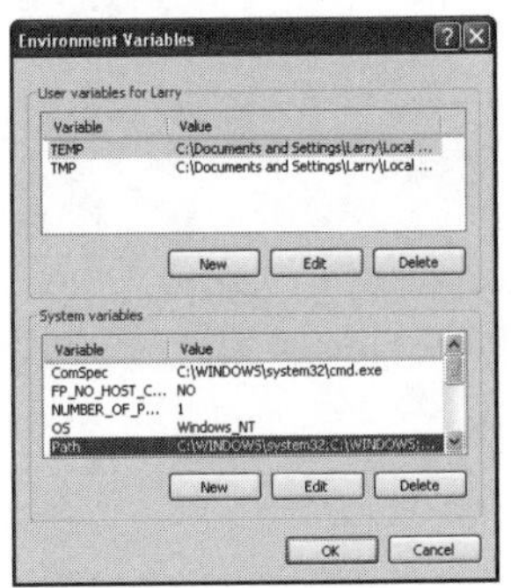

Figure 1.16

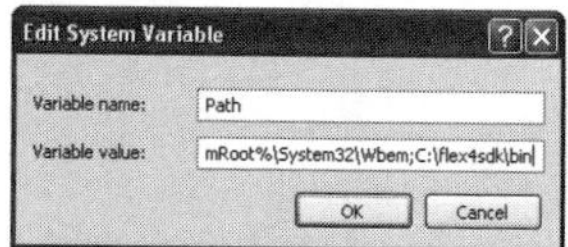

Figure 1.17

tip

You don't technically need to modify the path to use the command-line tools. But if you don't, when it comes time to invoke them, you'll need to type something like **C:\"Documents and Settings"\"Larry Ullman"\Desktop\flex4\bin\mxmlc** instead of just **mxmlc**. Changing the path is a worthwhile shortcut.

note

The Terminal menus differ in Mac OS X 10.6 (Snow Leopard) from earlier versions of the operating system. The keyboard shortcuts are the same, so I'll refer to those in the following steps.

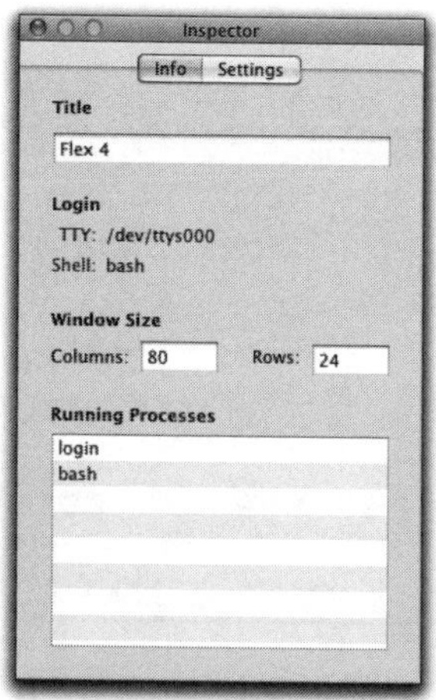

Figure 1.19

7. At the end of Variable value, add a semicolon plus the full path to the SDK's **bin** directory (**Figure 1.17**).

   It's very important that you *add* the SDK path to the existing value; you should not replace the existing value with just the Flex SDK path.

   To confirm the correct full path, you can open the SDK folder in an Explorer window (**Figure 1.18**) and copy the address. Make sure that what you're adding to the Variable value includes the final **\bin**, because that's the most important part here.

Figure 1.18

8. Click OK in all three dialogs to close them.

UPDATING YOUR PATH ON MAC OS X

1. Open a Terminal window using Command+N, if one is not already open.

2. Confirm what shell you are using by pressing Command+I to bring up the Terminal Inspector (**Figure 1.19**).

   How you change the path depends upon what shell you're using (if you're really curious about what shells are, search the Web for "Unix shell"). The Terminal Inspector names the shell in use. The most common shells (with the program's actual name in parentheses) are:

   - Bourne (sh)
   - Bourne Again Shell (bash, and I'm not making that up)
   - C shell (csh)
   - T shell or T C shell (tsch)
   - Korn shell (ksh)

The most recent versions of Mac OS X are pre-set to use the bash shell (as indicated in Figure 1.19). For these instructions, I'm going to assume you are using the bash shell. If your Terminal Inspector says otherwise, you'll need to do an online search for how to change that particular shell's path.

3. Close the Inspector by clicking the red button at the top-left corner.

4. Within a Terminal window, move to your home directory by typing **cd** and pressing Return.

   This shouldn't be necessary since you're likely in your home directory when you create a new Terminal window, but follow this step just to be safe. The **cd** command is used to change the directory. Invoking it without any following values (like naming a directory) will move you into your home directory.

5. List all the current files by typing **ls -a** and pressing Return (**Figure 1.20**).

   The **ls** command lists the contents of a directory; the **-a** option says that all the files should be listed, including hidden ones, like what we're looking for.

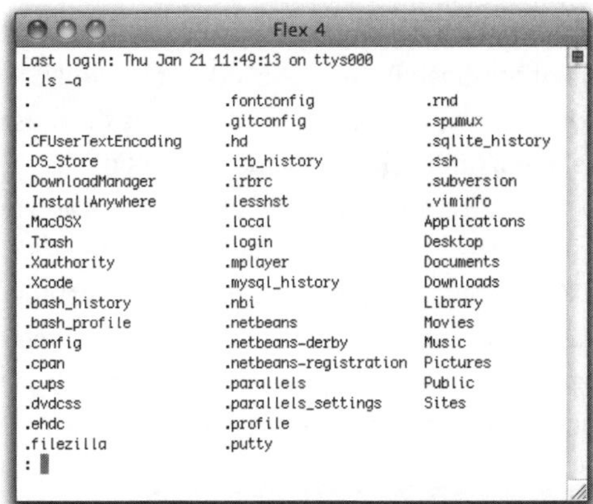

Figure 1.20

6. If there is not a file called **.bash_profile** in the directory listing (Figure 1.20), create one by entering **touch .bash_profile**.

   Files that begin with a period are normally special, hidden files. This particular file, **.bash_profile**, is used to affect how the bash shell behaves. If the file does not already exist, the **touch** command will create it.

7. Open the **.bash_profile** file in any text editor.

   I prefer the popular (and most excellent) TextMate text editor, so I can open the file by typing **mate .bash_profile** from the command line. You can also use Bare Bones' BBEdit (*www.barebones.com*) for this purpose, or one of the many command-line editors: vi, vim, emacs, pico, and so on.

tip

In many Mac OS X programs you can insert the full path to a folder into a file by dragging that folder onto the file. For example, if you grab the SDK's **bin** folder in the Finder and drag it into the **.bash_profile** file in BBEdit, the full path to **bin** will be inserted into **.bash_profile** wherever you release the mouse button.

tip

You don't technically need to modify the path to use the command-line tools. But if you don't, when it comes time to invoke them, you'll need to type something like ***/Users/larryullman/Desktop/flex4/bin/mxmlc*** instead of just ***mxmlc***. Changing the path is a worthwhile shortcut.

8. In the **.bash_profile** file, add this line:

   export PATH="$PATH:*/path/to/Flex/SDK*/bin/"

   The **export PATH** command changes the path for the bash shell. The value of the path should be the current path (represented by **$PATH)** plus the full path to the SDK **bin** directory (you'll need to use the actual path in place of */path/to/*; see the related tip). Each directory in the path is separated by a colon.

   If your **.bash_profile** document already has an **export PATH** line, just add the colon, plus the full path, to the current value.

9. Save and close the file.

10. Close the Terminal window.

    The change to the path will take effect the next time a Terminal window is opened.

THE FLASH PLAYER

To finish setting up your computer for Flex development, you'll need to make sure you have the latest version of the Flash Player installed. In fact, you'll actually want to install a *debug* version of the player. You may have the most current Flash Player already installed, but likely not the debug version. If you're using Flash Builder, it'll install the proper Flash Player for you. If you're going the manual route, you'll find installers for the Flash Player in the SDK's **runtimes/player** folder. The SDK will contain versions of the Flash Player for Windows, Mac OS X, and Linux. For each operating system, you'll find standalone players and browser plug-ins. For Windows, there's one ActiveX plug-in installer for Internet Explorer and another for other browsers (**Figure 1.21**).

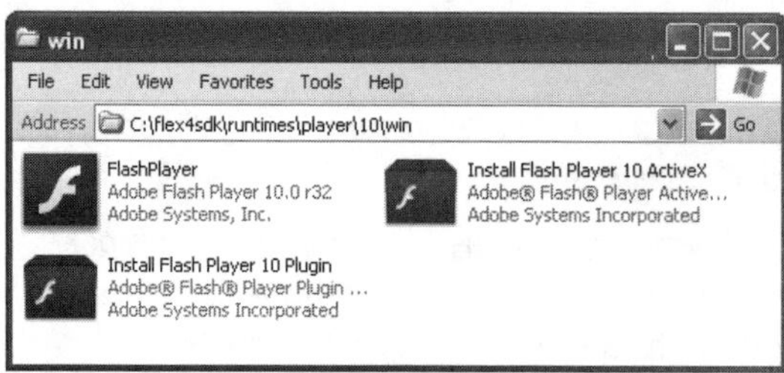

Figure 1.21

Creating a Simple Application

Once you've downloaded, installed, and configured everything, you're ready to begin the coding and compiling process. Let's start by creating the shell of a Flex project.

1. Create a new folder for your project.

   You should put each project in its own folder, and all the projects within their own parent folder. By doing so, you'll have all your Flex code in one place. I'll call this project, and the folder, *HelloWorld*. Conventionally, one uses CamelCase for the project's name: *HelloWorld*, not *Hello World*, *helloworld*, or *helloWorld*.

2. Using your text editor or IDE, create a new, blank plain-text file.

3. Add the shell of an MXML application to the text file:

   ```
   <?xml version="1.0" encoding="utf-8"?>
   <s:Application xmlns:fx="http://ns.adobe.com/mxml/2009"
      xmlns:s="library://ns.adobe.com/flex/spark"
      xmlns:mx="library://ns.adobe.com/flex/mx">
   </s:Application>
   ```

   This code was first shown and discussed earlier in the chapter. It creates an empty Flex application destined for the Web.

4. Save the file as **HelloWorld.mxml**.

   The primary application file should have the same name as the project, plus the **.mxml** extension.

Saying "Hello" to the World

Before executing the simple shell of a Flex application, let's add a little code so that it does *something*. In keeping with standard book conventions, we'll make a classic "Hello, World!" example. Of course, it's a terrible use of Flash's power but is easy to follow and unlikely to have problems. Let's add some text to the existing, plain application, and then run the whole thing to see the result.

1. Open **HelloWorld.mxml** in your text editor or IDE, if it's not already.

2. Before the closing **Application** line, add the following:

   ```
   <s:Label x="100" y="100" text="Hello, World!" fontSize="36"
   color="#FF6600" fontWeight="bold"/>
   ```

   That code creates a **Label** element, which is the simplest way to add text to an application. The initial **s:** indicates that this is a Spark component, not available in versions of Flex prior to 4. The x- and y- coordinates position the top-left corner of the element within the window (where the top-left corner of the window is at 0, 0, see Figure 1.7). The **text** attribute is where you put the actual text to be displayed. The **fontSize, color**, and **fontWeight** attributes format the text as 36 point in size, orange in color, and bold.

   Make sure you type the code precisely, following the case of the various words and all of the syntax.

tip

If you get a "could not find JRE" or "could not find Java 2 Runtime Environment" error when you invoke the ***mxmlc*** command, that means you haven't yet installed the Java Runtime Engine.

3. Save the file.
4. Access your computer from a command-line interface.

   Earlier instructions indicate how to do this.
5. Move into the project directory by entering **cd /*path*/*to*/HelloWorld**.

   The **cd** command moves you from one directory to another. You'll need to change the /*path*/*to* part so that it's accurate for your setup. For example, on Windows this may be **C:\"Documents and Settings\Larry\flex4\HelloWorld"** and on Mac OS X it may be **/Users/larryullman/Documents/flex4/HelloWorld**.
6. Enter **mxmlc HelloWorld.mxml** and press Enter or Return (**Figure 1.22**).

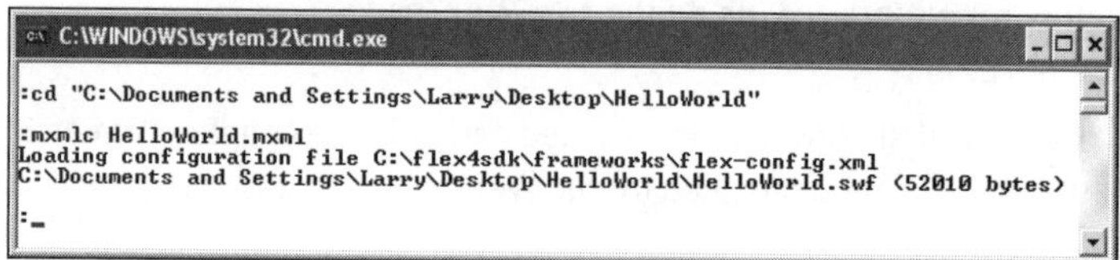

Figure 1.22

   The **mxmlc** application, found in the SDK's **bin** folder, is the compiler that does all the hard work. It'll take a moment or two, but hopefully you'll see the results like those in the figure.
7. Run the program by double-clicking the SWF file in Windows Explorer (Windows) or the Finder (Mac OS X).

   Double-clicking the generated SWF file should open it in the standalone Flash Player (**Figure 1.23**).

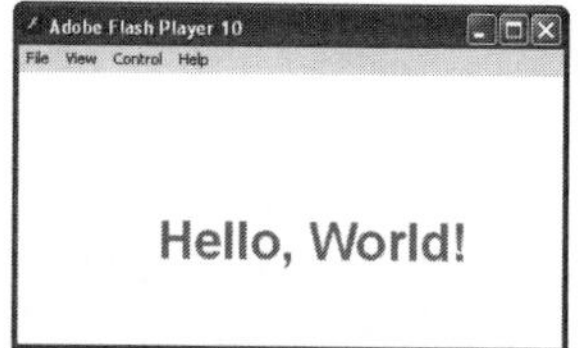

Figure 1.23

Deploying Web Applications

Once you've tested your application and have it both looking and behaving as you want it to, it's time to deploy the application, which is to say release it into the wild and make it available for others to see. As Flash content runs within a Web page in a browser, you'll need to create an HTML document that embeds the generated SWF file. Fortunately, Adobe provides an HTML template, plus the appropriate JavaScript code, to properly place your Flash content within a Web page.

1. If you have not yet done so, compile the completed Flex project as a SWF file using the steps just outlined.

2. Open the *Flex 4 SDK*/**templates/swfobject/index.template.html** file in your text editor or IDE.

   This is the HTML template that ships with the SDK. It's quite easy to edit and use for your own content.

3. Edit the file accordingly, being certain to replace instances of **${*var*}** with an actual value.

   The template contains placeholders for values you should insert. This includes everything from the page's title (**${title}**) to the size of the Flash content (**${width}** and **${height}**, each in multiple places). Just search for instances of **${** and edit what you find. For example, you might turn

   <title>${title}</title>

   into

   <title>My Great Flash Page</title>

   I want to highlight the most important of these placeholders:

   - **${version_major}.${version_minor}.${version_revision}** should be replaced with the minimum version of the Flash Player required to view the content. For Flex 4, this is 10.0.0.
   - **${expressInstallSwf}** should be replaced with the name of the SWF file that will handle the Flash Player plug-in express installation. The **playerProductInstall.swf** file, also found in the SDK's **templates/swfobject** directory, can serve this purpose.
   - **${application}** should be the project's name, like *HelloWorld*.
   - **${swf}** is to be replaced with the actual SWF file, **HelloWorld.swf**.

4. Save a copy of the file, changing its name in the process.

   So as not to overwrite the template, be certain to save the file as a copy.

5. Copy all of the required files to your Web site.

   By putting all these files on your Web server, users can now execute your Flash application by loading the ***whatever*.html** page in their browsers. To incorporate the application into an existing Web page, just copy the HTML and JavaScript out of ***whatever*.html** and put it in the proper places in your other HTML file. The HTML file is fairly well documented, making it sufficiently simple to copy out the parts you'll need.

   You'll need to make sure that you also copy the **swfobject.js** file to your Web site, as it's used by the HTML page for browser detection. And if you use the **playerProductInstall.swf** file to handle installation of a compatible Flash Player plug-in, that'll need to go online as well.

tip

You may want to test the HTML page locally (i.e., on your computer) in a browser before putting it online.

CREATING DESKTOP APPLICATIONS

Thanks to Adobe AIR, you can create true cross-platform desktop applications using Flex, Flash, or even HTML and JavaScript. Because these are desktop applications, as opposed to those that run in a Web browser, there's much more that they can do, like interact with the user's file system, store data locally, open other applications, and so forth. AIR applications also have a slightly different security model than Web-based ones, because of the broader powers. While this book won't cover AIR development exhaustively, I do want to provide enough of an introduction to the fundamentals so that you can start playing with it, should you have the interest. Here I will demonstrate the absolute basics of creating AIR applications using the Flex framework.

A Word on Certificates

Unlike Flash content destined for the Web, as a security measure, every AIR application requires a *digital signature certificate*. This is intended to prove the authenticity of a program, thereby reassuring the end user that it's safe to install the application.

tip

A self-signed certificate will be valid for five years from the time it was created.

There are two kinds of certificates you can use. The first is purchased from an accredited company like Thawte or VeriSign. These certificates imply the highest level of security because those companies will verify your credentials. The second option is a self-signed certificate: something you create that allows you to build installable AIR applications but offers no real assurance to the application's end users. This option is free but essentially means that you're the one telling end users that you are legitimate. If they don't know you, that's not worth much. But for testing purposes, creating a self-signed signature makes sense.

There are two ways you can generate your own certificate: using Flash Builder or using the command-line tools. I'll discuss both in the corresponding sections for deploying desktop applications.

Desktop Applications in Flash Builder

Here's what you need to do to create a Flex-based desktop application in Flash Builder:

1. Open Flash Builder, if it is not already.
2. Select File > New > Flex Project.

3. In the New Flex Project window (**Figure 1.24**), do the following:

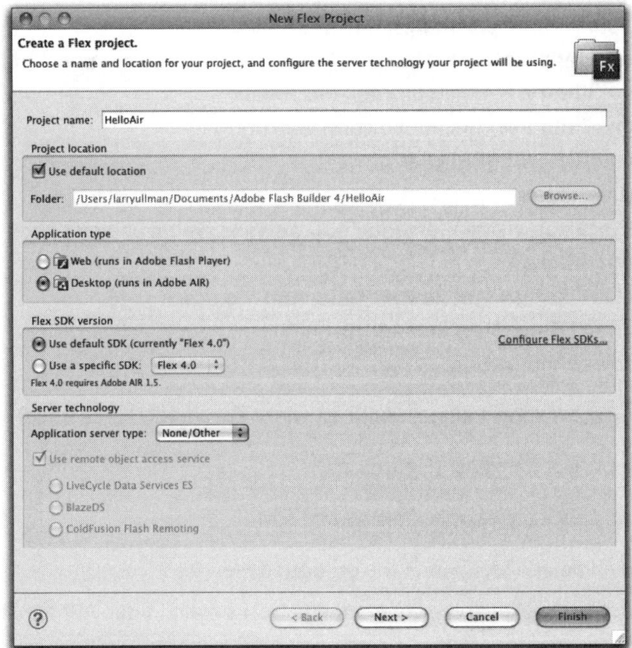

Figure 1.24

1. Enter the project's name.
2. Choose the project's location.
3. Select **Desktop** for application type.
4. Determine which SDK you'll use.
5. Ignore the server type for now.

4. Click Finish.

There are more options if you click Next, but they won't make much sense to you now and you can get away with the default values when you first start.

5. Create and complete the application in Flash Builder.

For a quick example, I first changed the application's background color. To do so, I switched to Design mode and then used the Properties view with no element selected. You'll see that the Properties view shows the element being manipulated at the top (**Figure 1.25**).

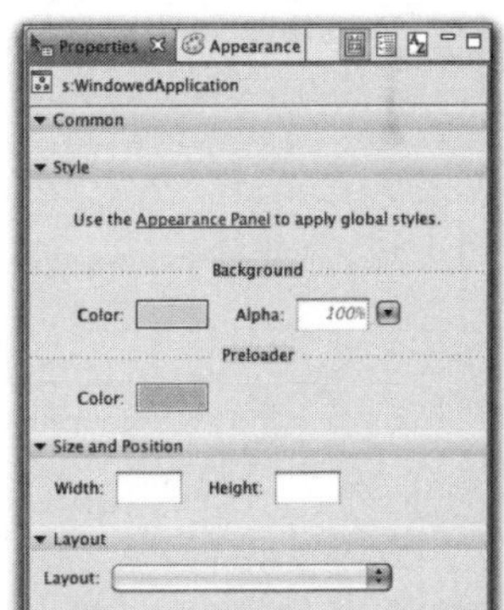

Figure 1.25

Next I added and tweaked a **Label** component. The final code for my dummy AIR application is

```
<?xml version="1.0" encoding="utf-8"?>
<s:WindowedApplication xmlns:fx="http://ns.adobe.com/mxml/2009"
  xmlns:s="library://ns.adobe.com/flex/spark"
  xmlns:mx="library://ns.adobe.com/flex/mx"
  backgroundColor="#EAF388">
  <fx:Declarations>
    <!-- Place non-visual elements (e.g., services, value objects) here -->
  </fx:Declarations>
  <s:Label x="50" y="50" text="Hello, AIR!" fontSize="36"
  fontFamily="Times New Roman"/>
</s:WindowedApplication>
```

6. Select Project > Export Release Build (or File > Export > Release Build).
7. Select the project to export (**Figure 1.26**).
8. If you want, check the Enable view source box.
9. Select the name and location of the outputted file.

   By default, the exported files go into the project's main folder. AIR applications are packaged together as a single **.air** file.
10. Click Next.
11. On the next page, add a digital signature to the file (**Figure 1.27**).

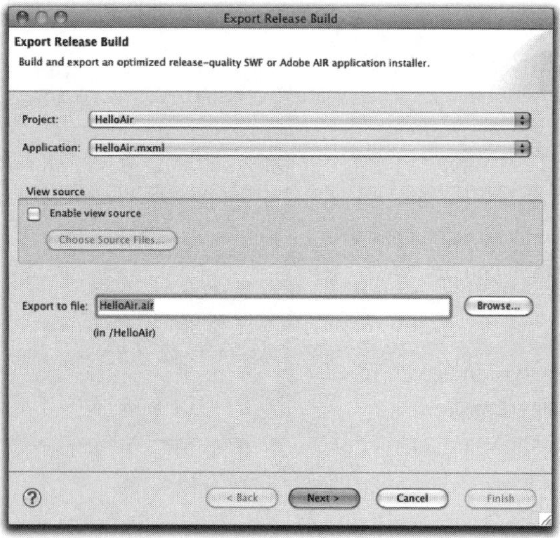

Figure 1.26

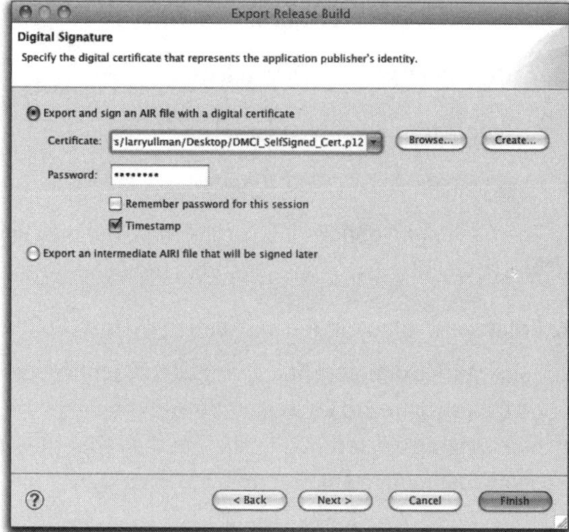

Figure 1.27

If you have purchased or created your own certificate already, you can browse to select it, then enter the corresponding password. If you don't already have a certificate, click Create to make one now. In the corresponding window (**Figure 1.28**), do the following:

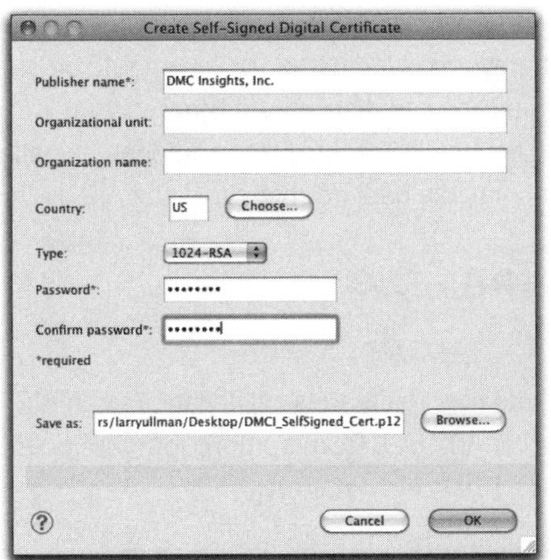

Figure 1.28

- Enter you or your company as the Publisher name. This identifies the creator of the certificate, and therefore, the authenticator of the application.
- Enter the same password for the certificate twice.
- Select where to save the certificate file on your computer.

That's all you have to do to create a valid self-signed certificate! After you click OK, the previous window will be populated with the new certificate's information (see Figure 1.27).

12. Click Next.

13. On the last page, you can check which files should be included (**Figure 1.29**).

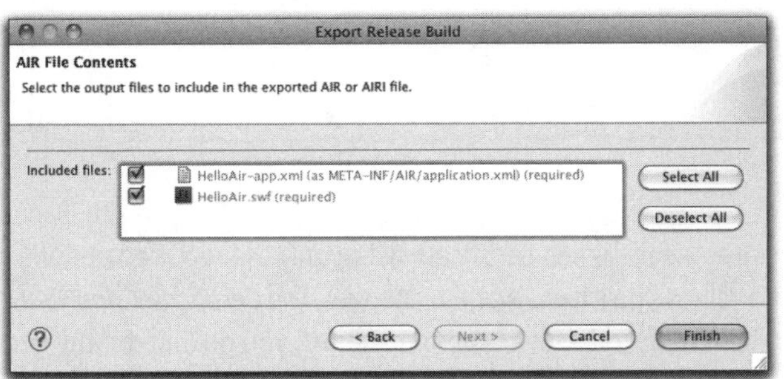

Figure 1.29

When you're just starting, you likely won't have to do anything here. In time, as projects become more complex, you may have used resources during the development process that shouldn't be packaged in the final product. You could exclude those at this step.

14. Click Finish.

    In the project's folder, or wherever you indicated the file should be outputted, you'll find the new AIR file. You can distribute it through your Web site, on a CD or flash drive, or even by e-mailing it to someone. Installation of the program begins as soon as the user double-clicks the AIR file.

Desktop Applications the Open-Source Way

In these next steps, I'll demonstrate how to create a certificate and an AIR application using the command-line ADT (AIR Development Tool) utility. This program can be found in the Flex 4 SDK's **bin** directory.

CREATING AN AIR CERTIFICATE

1. Access your computer via a command-line interface.

   I go through the specific operating system steps for both Windows and Mac OS X earlier in the chapter.

2. Move to an obvious directory by typing **cd *path/to/wherever*** and pressing Enter/Return.

   It'd be best to create the certificate somewhere that'll be easy to find, like your desktop or your Flex 4 code directory.

3. Type the following and press Enter/Return (**Figure 1.30**):

   adt –certificate -cn *CertificateCommonName* 1024-RSA *certName*.pfx *somePassword*

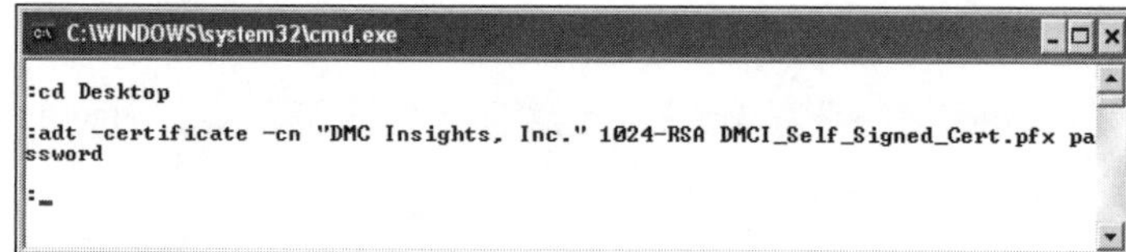

Figure 1.30

This line creates a self-signed certificate using only the required options (and I've italicized values you'll likely want to change). The *CertificateCommonName* string should be replaced with a "common name" you provide for the certificate. This might be your company's name or something else useful and indicative of you, the creator of the application that will use this certificate. If your common name has spaces or special punctuation, wrap it in quotes.

The *certName.pfx* is the name of the generated certificate file. Again, give this a meaningful name (like *MySelfSignedCert*) but you must use a **.pfx** extension. Finally, the *somePassword* text will be the password associated with this certificate. You'll need to provide this when building the application (in the next series of steps).

The 1024-RSA text indicates the type of key used for this certificate (which impacts how "tough," security-wise, it is). A tougher alternative is to use 2048-RSA.

4. Check the folder's contents for the newly created certificate (**Figure 1.31**).

Figure 1.31

CREATING AN AIR APPLICATION

1. Create a new folder for your project.

   I'm going to call this project *HelloAir*, so I'll name the folder that as well.

2. Using your text editor or IDE, create a new, blank plain-text file.

3. Add the shell of an MXML application to the text file:

```
<?xml version="1.0" encoding="utf-8"?>
<s:WindowedApplicaiton xmlns:fx="http://ns.adobe.com/mxml/2009"
   xmlns:s="library://ns.adobe.com/flex/spark"
   xmlns:mx="library://ns.adobe.com/flex/mx"
   backgroundColor="EAF388">
</s:WindowedApplication>
```

   This is a variation on the standard MXML application in two ways. First, the primary tag is **WindowedApplication**, not **Application**, which is required for desktop applications. Second, I added a **backgroundColor** property to the tag to change the background color.

4. Add a visual element.

```
<s:Label x="50" y="50" text="Hello, AIR!" fontSize="36"
fontFamily="Times New Roman"/>
```

   This is another **Label** component. It displays the words *Hello, AIR!* in a large, Times New Roman font.

5. Save the file as **HelloWorld.mxml**.

   The primary application file should have the same name as the project, plus the **.mxml** extension.

6. Open the ***Flex 4 SDK*/templates/air/descriptor-template.xml** file in your text editor or IDE.

   AIR applications use an application descriptor file to identify metadata (information about the program) for an application. The SDK comes with a template that you can edit accordingly.

7. Edit the XML file as needed.

   The template file is well documented and there are only a couple of required fields:

   - **id**, a unique identifier for the program
   - **filename**, the name the application will have in the user's computer
   - **version** (self-explanatory)
   - **content**, the compiled SWF file

   The *id* is an identifier that will not be seen by the end user, but each application on the user's computer must have its own unique *id*. Conventionally one uses a reverse-domain name system. For example, my company's Web site is *www.dmcinsights.com*, so my *id* for this application might be *com.dmcinsights.air.HelloAir*. Another program I might write would have an *id* of *com.dmcinsights.air.Pong*.

   Along with the four elements listed above, you'll want to change the optional *visible* element, found under *initialWindow*. For some reason, the default value is false, meaning you'll create an application whose primary window is invisible. Assuming you want the end user to actually see your work, you'll need to set this value to true.

   A minimal but valid application descriptor file might therefore be:

```
<?xml version="1.0" encoding="utf-8" ?>
<application xmlns="http://ns.adobe.com/air/application/1.5.2">
    <id>com.dmcinsights.HelloAIR</id>
    <filename>HelloAIR</filename>
    <name>Hello, AIR!</name>
    <version>1.0</version>
    <initialWindow>
        <content>HelloAir.swf</content>
        <visible>true</visible>
    </initialWindow>
</application>
```

   There's much more you can do in the descriptor file, but this will do for now.

8. Save the application descriptor file as **application.xml** in the same project directory as **HelloAir.mxml**.

   You can name the application descriptor file anything, but you'll normally see either just **application.xml** or ***ProjectName*.xml** (e.g., **HelloAir.xml**).

9. Access your project directory from a command-line interface.

   I go through the specific operating system steps for both Windows and Mac OS X earlier in the chapter.

10. Compile the MXML file as a SWF by entering **amxmlc HelloAir.mxml** (**Figure 1.32**).

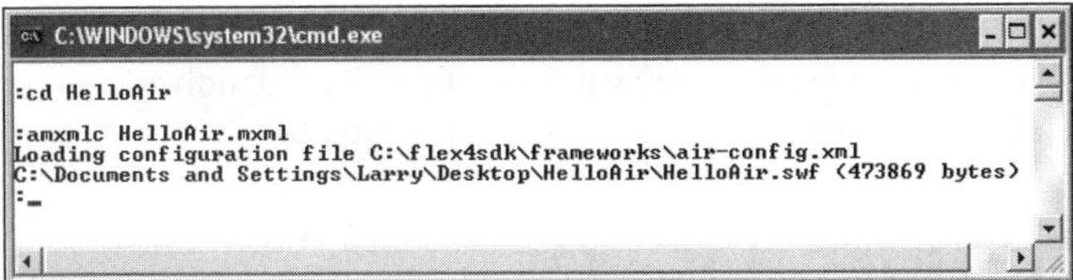

Figure 1.32

When creating AIR applications, you use **amxml** (AIR MXML compiler) instead of **mxmlc**, although both applications have the same syntax and usage. The result will be a file named **HelloAir.swf**. This name must be the same as the *content* value used in the application descriptor file (see Step 7).

11. Compile the AIR application itself by entering the following (**Figure 1.33**):

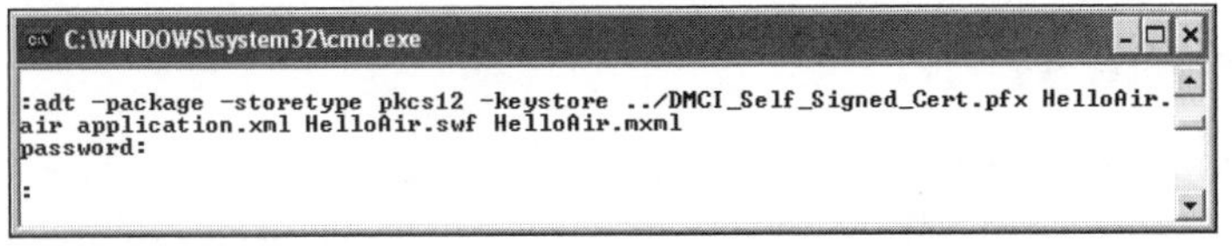

Figure 1.33

adt -package -storetype pkcs12 -keystore */path/to/certName*.**pfx HelloAir.air application.xml HelloAir.swf HelloAir.mxml**

The **-package** argument specifies that you want to build a packaged application. The **-storetype pkcs12 -keystore *certName*.pfx** identifies the certificate to use for this application (as created using the previous steps). The next argument is the name of the **.air** file that should be generated. You then list the XML file, the base SWF file, the base MXML file, and every other asset that needs to be packaged together. To be clear, every file,

Enter ***mxmlc --help*** at the command-line to learn more about how to use both ***mxmlc*** and ***amxmlc***.

tip

For a full list of certificate generation options, type ***adt --help*** or see the Adobe AIR official documentation for all the details.

folder, or resource that an application uses needs to be mentioned on the **adt** line. For this simple example, there's nothing else to include.

You'll need to change the */path/to/certName*.pfx part of this command to correspond to the actual location of your self-signed certificate, relative to this folder. The only other caveat is that this entire command needs to be entered on one line (i.e., you can't hit Enter or Return midway through).

After typing in all this and pressing Enter or Return, you'll be prompted for the certificate's password.

12. Confirm the success of the operation by looking for the new **HelloWorld.air** file in the application's folder (**Figure 1.34**).

    You can distribute the AIR application through your Web site, on a CD or flash drive, or even by e-mailing it to someone. Installation of the program begins as soon as the user double-clicks the AIR file.

Figure 1.34

GETTING HELP

No matter the language in use, becoming a good programmer always involves learning where and how to get help when you have questions and problems. Here are a few resources and tips that will be useful now and the rest of the book will continue to expand on these with specific recommendations when attempting certain things. I can say, not to belabor the point, that the best thing you can do to minimize errors (and therefore your frustration) is use Adobe's Flash Builder application. It just does so much for you! (But my apologies for the hard sell.)

On the Web

There are plenty of useful Flex-centric resources available online, but you'll likely want to start with the copious resources Adobe has made available:

- *www.adobe.com/go/flex*, Adobe's official site
- *www.flex.org*, another Adobe site
- *www.adobe.com/devnet/flex*, the Flex Developer Center
- *www.adobe.com/support/flex*, Flex Help and Support
- *www.adobe.com/devnet/flex/learn*, the Flex Learning Paths
- *http://forums.adobe.com/community/flex*, Adobe's Flex support forums
- *http://feeds.adobe.com*, click Flex to see feeds from various blogs

From any one of those sites you can quickly get to tons of tutorials, videos, sample applications, and much, much more.

In time, you'll find that Adobe's own documentation for the framework will become quite useful, too. You can find it at *www.adobe.com/support/documentation/en/flex/*. I say "in time" because when you're just getting going, detailed documentation like the Adobe Flex Language Reference won't be very meaningful.

One of my favorite Flex resources is Tour de Flex, *www.adobe.com/devnet/flex/tourdeflex/web/*. Also available as a desktop AIR application, Tour de Flex provides a simple interface for learning more about the available components. Use the navigation on the left to select a component, and then see what it looks like and check out sample code for its usage (**Figure 1.35**).

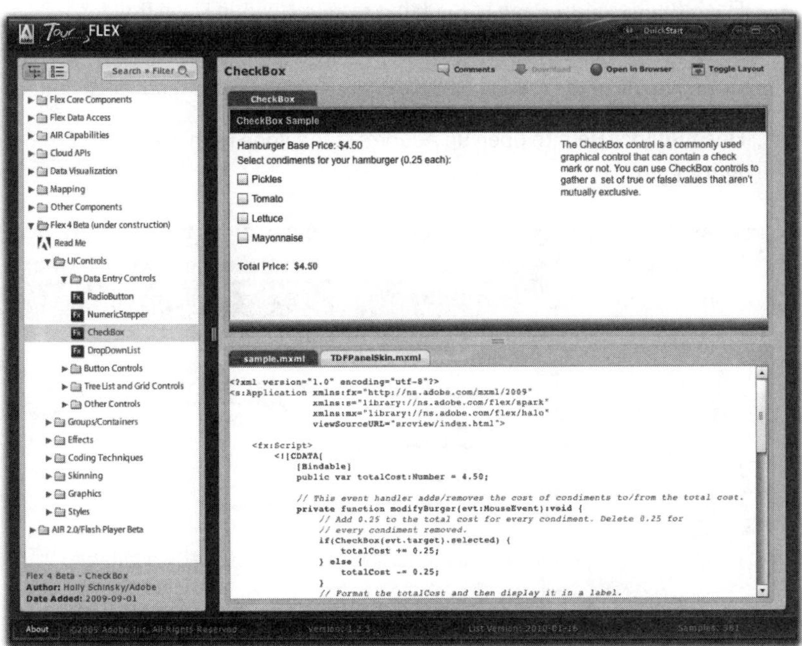

Figure 1.35

There are lots of third-party sites worth your while, as well. A search will turn up plenty, but I want to recommend Community Flex (*www.cflex.net*), Community MX (*www.communitymx.com*), and the Flexcoders Yahoo! Group (*http://tech.groups.yahoo.com/group/flexcoders/*) first. And if you need to hunt for something, you can try FlexSearch (*www.flexsearch.org*), a search engine for just Flex material.

I have also found, as a person who came to Flex from other programming languages and Web technologies, that sites without a specific Flex bent can often be the most informative. Consider the following:

- *www.dzone.com*, Dzone
- *www.sitepoint.com*, Sitepoint
- *http://devzone.zend.com/tag/Flex*, Zend

Within Flash Builder

If you're using the Flash Builder application for your Flex development, there are ample resources available starting in this same tool. Open the Help menu, then select

tip

The front page of Flash Builder Help provides the quickest access to lots of documentation, explanations, tutorials, and more.

- ...**Flash Builder Start Page** to load that resource within Flash Builder.

  This page can display anything Adobe deems useful, including links to tutorials and many of the resources on Adobe's site that I've already highlighted.

- ...**Flash Builder Help** to open up Adobe's standalone Help application (**Figure 1.36**).

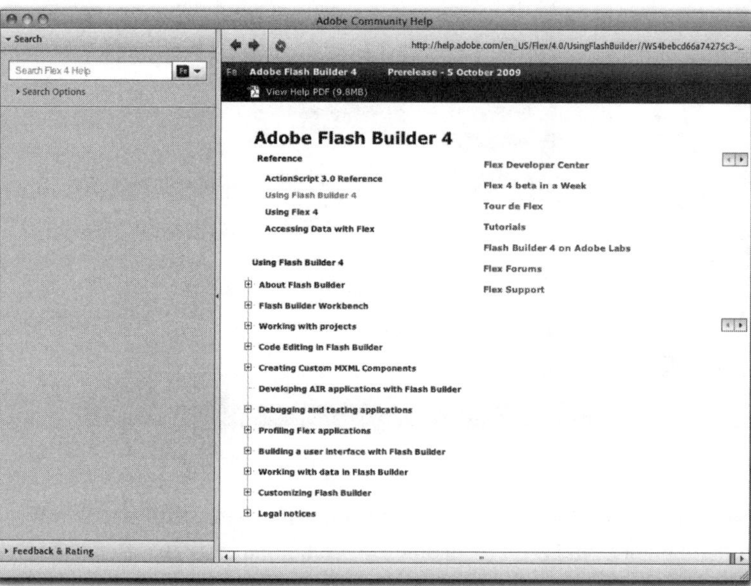

Figure 1.36

The interface is searchable, has tons of links, and provides quick access to the raw documentation.

- ...**Key Assist** to view command keyboard shortcuts (**Figure 1.37**).

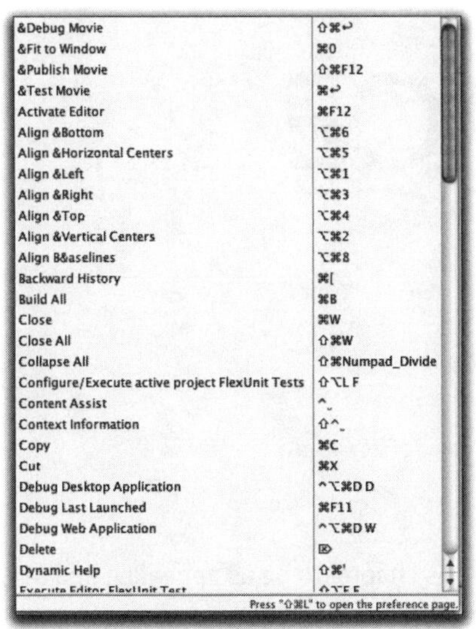

Figure 1.37

- ...**Dynamic Help,** which opens in a view panel within Flash Builder.

  The Dynamic Help is extremely useful as it's, um, dynamic. This means that the content shown in the window changes to reflect what's going on in the Editor. Select an element in your application and you'll see information specifically about that element.

You can also put the cursor on an element in the Editor's Source mode and press F2 (Mac OS X) or Shift+F2 (Windows) to see a pop-up window describing that element in some detail (**Figure 1.38**).

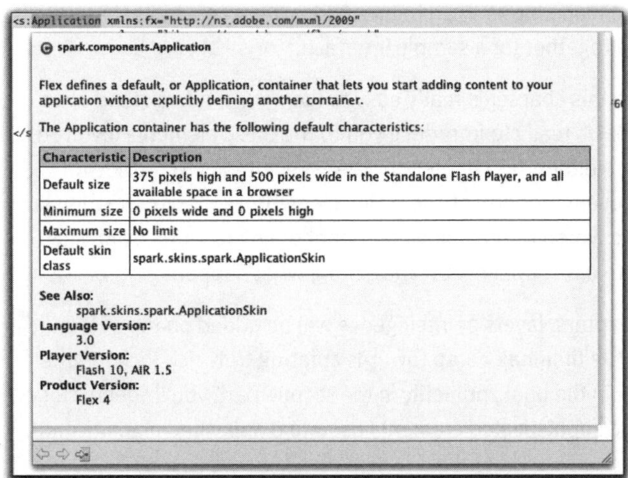

Figure 1.38

2 USER INTERFACE BASICS

I hope that you'll find the material in this chapter to be as appealing and as easy to grasp as I do. In it, you'll learn how you can create an attractive user interface for your applications in mere moments.

The chapter begins with a few development tips and some background know-how. I also discuss how to minimize errors when applying the information covered. Finally, a brief section discusses some of the basic terminology, so as not to lose you amongst the jargon.

In the second part of the chapter, I take a slightly longer look at the base **Application** tag and how you might tweak it to customize the look of your Flex software. The remainder of the chapter discusses elements you'll use to create a user interface, how you can control the positioning and sizes of those elements, and how to make forms. The chapter ends with an example that ties all of the information together for a sample interface.

The information in this chapter is really easy to learn, use, and expand upon. To be clear, the goal is really to introduce you to the basic elements involved in user interfaces. Neither this chapter nor the book intends to provide an exhaustive list of every property of every Flex element, as that information is easily enough discovered through any number of online resources or by just adding elements to a test application and seeing what happens.

In the next two chapters, layers of intelligence will be added on top of this content, which is the first major step towards creating truly rich Rich Internet Applications. Later in the book, primarily in the second part, you'll spend a lot of time with the more sophisticated elements used to display and manage data.

THINGS TO KNOW

Before getting into the meat of the chapter, let's go through a few things that'll help ease the learning process.

Comments within MXML

I often learn best by taking notes as I go, and good programmers place their notes right alongside the code itself. To do that in MXML, you can create comments using the same tags as you would in HTML: **<!--** and **-->**. Anything within those tags, even over multiple lines, will be invisible to the user and have no effect on the application itself. Note the following example:

```
<?xml version="1.0" encoding="utf-8"?>
<s:Application xmlns:fx="http://ns.adobe.com/mxml/2009"
   xmlns:s="library://ns.adobe.com/flex/spark"
   xmlns:mx="library://ns.adobe.com/flex/mx">

   <!-- Label components are the simplest way of displaying text. -->
   <s:Label x="50" y="50" text="Hello, World!"/>

</s:Application>
```

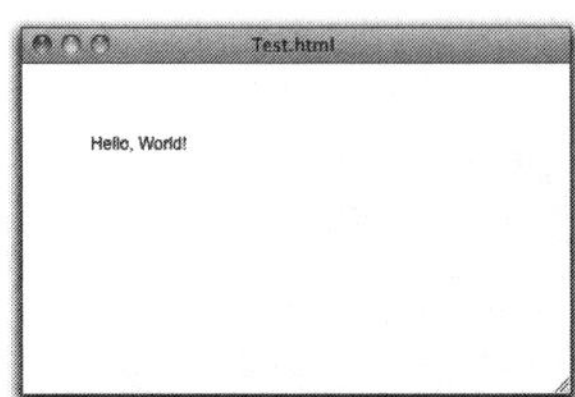

Figure 2.1

As you can see in **Figure 2.1**, the comment does not appear on the screen.

The only caveat is that you cannot put a comment before the initial **<?xml** as nothing can come before those five characters in your MXML file.

note

The default MXML code created by Flash Builder when you create a new project includes the ***fx:Declarations*** tag. It has no effect if present, but I'll be removing it from my examples in this chapter, as it's not yet necessary.

Adding Components

MXML is a relatively simple language, so problems will primarily occur because of syntax errors (as applications become more complex, the problems will become that much harder to find and fix). Preventing syntax errors is largely a matter of making the most of your development tools.

If you're using Flash Builder for Flex development, there are two reliable ways to add code to an application. Design mode is nearly foolproof and is probably the fastest way to add elements to an application, or tweak their properties, when you're just learning. To use it, do the following:

1. Find the element you want in the Components view.
2. Drag the element onto the application, dropping it where you want it to go.
3. Use the Properties view to adjust the component as needed.

tip

The Properties view indicates the selected tag (i.e., the element whose properties are being adjusted) near the top of the panel, just under the word "Properties."

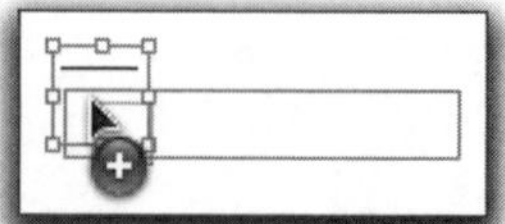

Figure 2.2

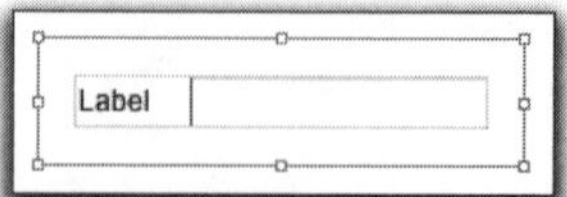

Figure 2.3

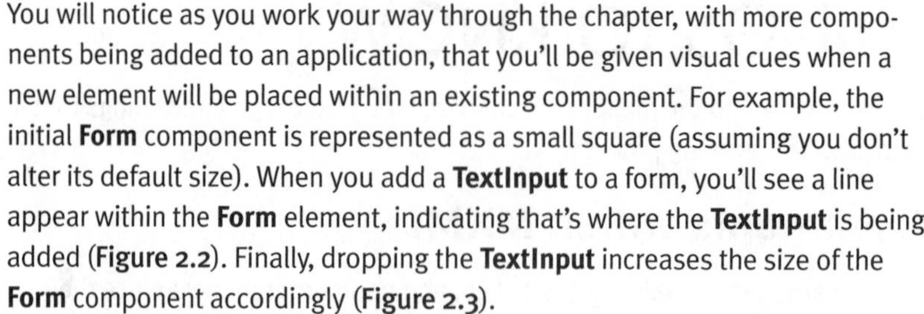

You will notice as you work your way through the chapter, with more components being added to an application, that you'll be given visual cues when a new element will be placed within an existing component. For example, the initial **Form** component is represented as a small square (assuming you don't alter its default size). When you add a **TextInput** to a form, you'll see a line appear within the **Form** element, indicating that's where the **TextInput** is being added (**Figure 2.2**). Finally, dropping the **TextInput** increases the size of the **Form** component accordingly (**Figure 2.3**).

I should also point out that Flash Builder takes some steps to limit clutter. This includes showing common options in many situations. The Components view lists recommended components by default; click the down arrow at the top of the Components view and deselect Only Show Recommend Components (**Figure 2.4**) to see more. Keep in mind that there's probably a reason Flash Builder isn't showing you some options, however, so you may want to keep things simple, especially as you're just beginning.

note

There are Flex components defined within both the mx and s (Halo and Spark) namespaces. For components defined in both, like ***TextInput***, you should use the Spark version. The only exception would be if you wanted to support older Flash Players or versions of Adobe AIR.

Figure 2.4

Similarly, the Properties view has three ways to list the available properties (**Figure 2.5**). The default Standard shows the most common properties grouped by kind. You can click the second icon on the right side of the Properties view to switch to Category listing. In this mode, every available property for the given component is listed, but still grouped by kind. The third icon represents Alphabetical listing, which lists every available property for the selected component in alphabetical order. This particular view is most useful if you know a particular property exists but you're not certain under what category it'd be filed. Assuming you're using Design mode, that is...

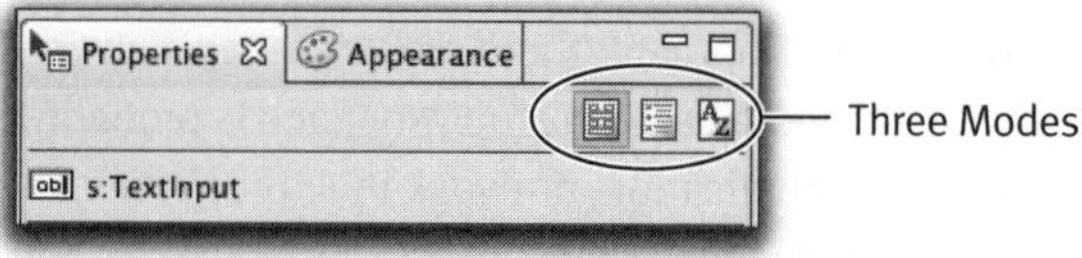

Figure 2.5

tip

Many of the properties associated with a component have to do with events, effects, styles, and other topics not yet discussed.

You can also develop applications in Source mode, where you're looking at the actual code behind an application. Which mode you prefer is really up to you, but you're almost guaranteed to use both modes to some degree. In Source mode you don't have the drag-and-drop convenience that Design mode offers, but you do have *code hinting* and *code completion*. To make use of these features, take the following steps:

1. Start by typing the opening angle bracket (<).
2. Next, enter the first couple of letters for the component to be added.

   Flash Builder will present a logical list of components (**Figure 2.6**).

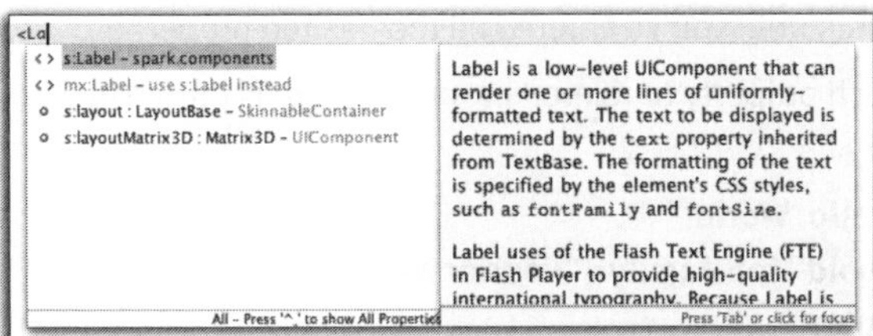

Figure 2.6

3. To select the intended component from the list, you can
   - Keep typing until the proper option is selected, then press Enter or Return.
   - Use the up and down arrow keys to navigate the list, then press Enter or Return. You can even use the up arrow from the top of the list to quickly go to the bottom.
   - Click the correct element.

   At this point, Flash Builder will insert the start of the opening tag into the application.
4. Press the spacebar to see a list of available attributes (**Figure 2.7**).

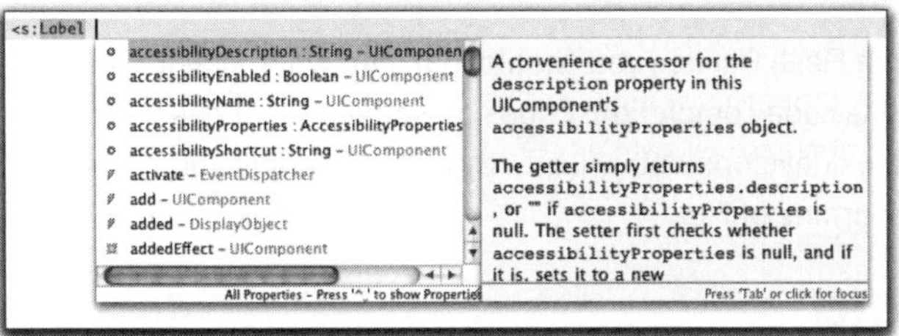

Figure 2.7

   A component's attributes will include properties such as **x** or **text**, events, effects, and styles. You'll be introduced to all of these in the course of this book.
5. Use the same options as in Step 3 to narrow down and select a property.

   The attribute will be appended to the opening tag, along with the equals sign and a pair of double quotation marks with the cursor between them, ready for you to enter the property's value.

tip

To use code hinting, you do have to type the opening angle bracket, but you don't have to type the namespace abbreviation: s, mx, or fx.

tip

Recommended components will be displayed in bold. Alternative components that match your typing but aren't recommended will appear in gray. This will include legacy components since replaced by newer versions.

tip

You can always press Control+Space while the cursor is within an element to see the available attributes for that element. Continue to press Control+Space to limit the displayed attributes by type: properties, events, effects, and styles.

If the property is restricted to certain possible values, those will be displayed. For example, the **enabled** property takes a Boolean value (**Figure 2.8**).

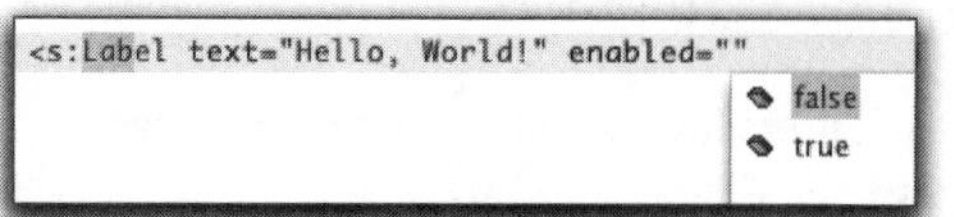

Figure 2.8

6. Repeat Steps 4 and 5 until you've entered all the desired properties.

   Conventionally, each property or related property group is placed on its own line:

   ```
   <s:Label text="Hello, World!"
      fontWeight="bold" fontFamily="Courier New"
      textAlign="center"
      paddingLeft="5" paddingRight="5" paddingTop="5"
      paddingBottom="5"
      width="125" height="200"/>
   ```

   Although spreading out the code over multiple lines makes it easier to read, I won't always do so in this book in order to save space.

7. Type /> to close the element or just > to have Flash Builder close the opening tag and automatically create a closing tag.

   In XML, and therefore MXML, you can close tags using either the slash at the end of the opening tag or by using a separate closing tag. Generally speaking, developers use the later syntax only for elements that may contain other elements. Regardless, if you type a closing angle bracket without a slash first, Flash Builder will always create the pair of tags.

If you're not using Flash Builder, you should look into whether your development software has code completion. Choosing software that has this feature, specifically for Flex development, will greatly expedite application development and your learning of Flex.

Debugging

Debugging, when it comes to MXML, is largely a matter of fixing the syntax when it's wrong. Again, there are a few things you can do to make this debugging easier.

If you're using Flash Builder, make sure that the Project > Build Automatically option is checked. With this enabled, Flash Builder will build the project, thereby checking all of the syntax, as the files are saved. Any problems found will be indicated by a red X on the Editor tab for the file with the problem (this becomes more useful as your projects contain more than a single file). Within the file that has the problem, you'll see a red circle with a white X inside on the line next to where the problem was found. The Problems view, at the bottom of the workbench, will show a description of every error, including the file in which it occurs and on what line (**Figure 2.9**).

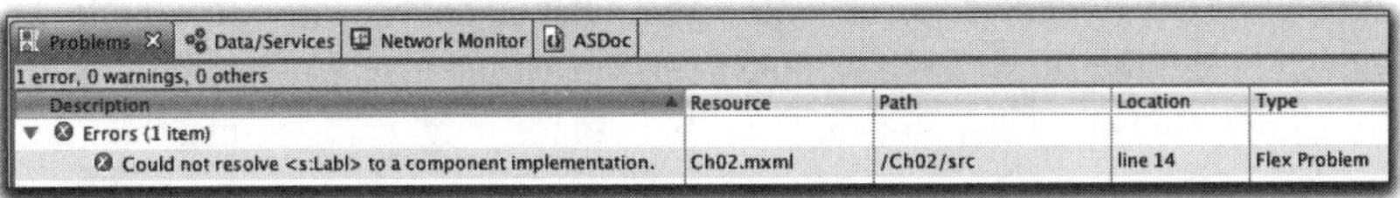

Figure 2.9

The particular problem in that image is that I misspelled **Label** as *Labl*, so Flash Builder didn't recognize it as a defined component.

Sometimes where a problem is found isn't truly reflective of where it starts. For example, in the following, the problem will be reported as having an unmatching closing tag:

```
<s:RchText id="oops">
</s:RichText>
```

However, the real culprit is the invalid opening tag. Still, generally speaking you should trust the error messages you see.

tip

To restore previous versions of code, right-click or Control+click within an MXML file, and then select Compare With > Local History. This will bring up a window that shows previously saved versions of the code.

If you're not using Flash Builder as your development tool, you'll need to figure out the best way to catch potential errors. If using a plain-text editor, you'll only find out about problems when you go to compile the application. You'll quickly tire of this approach. A step up would be to use an editor that can check XML syntax for you as you type. That will catch some problems, like invalid closing tags or missing quotation marks. The next step up would be an editor that recognizes MXML, such as Flash Develop (*www.flashdevelop.org*), which is also available for free.

Component Types and Terminology

tip

For a quick, visual reference for any component—*what it looks like and how it's used—check out Tour de Flex (online or as a standalone application) or the Flex Component Explorer. A quick search online will turn up either.*

In order to create working user interfaces, you need to be familiar with the available elements. Just as HTML includes definitions for elements like a text input, the Flex framework defines elements in MXML (more formally called *components*). In the first chapter I made use of the **s:Label** component, which is used to display a bit of text and is defined in the Spark namespace (hence the "s"). In this chapter we'll look at the bulk of the other common components.

The predefined Flex components are often lumped into two types: *controls* and *containers*. Controls are visual interface elements: the user will see them and even interact with some of them. Containers aren't necessarily seen (some will be) and are used to hold, organize, and determine the display of controls, even other containers. In HTML terms, tags like **DIV**, **P**, and **SPAN** act as containers; **INPUT**, **IMG**, and others are controls. In Flash Builder, the Components view has sorted the various components in folders; the Controls and Layout groups hold the controls and containers, respectively.

When one component is placed within another, you have a parent-child relationship. **Figure 2.10** shows a sample interface with many nested components. The inner, contained elements are the children (or, in technical terms, the *nodes*) of the parent. The type of parent element, and some of its properties, will impact the look and behavior of its immediate children. The **Application** tag is the first parent, or root tag, for the entire document. To get a sense of the entire family tree for an application, you can use the Outline view in Flash Builder (**Figure 2.11**).

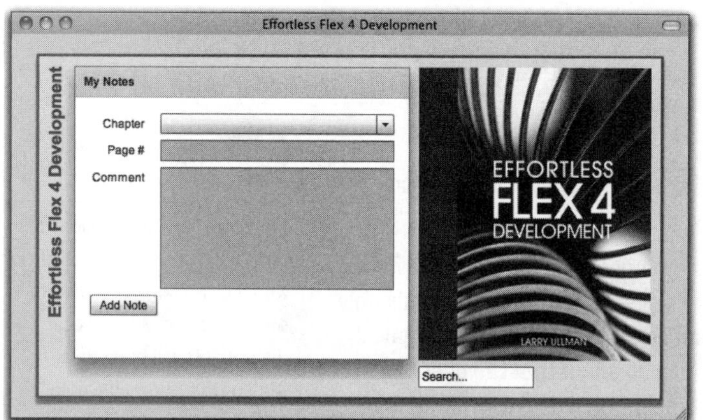

Figure 2.10

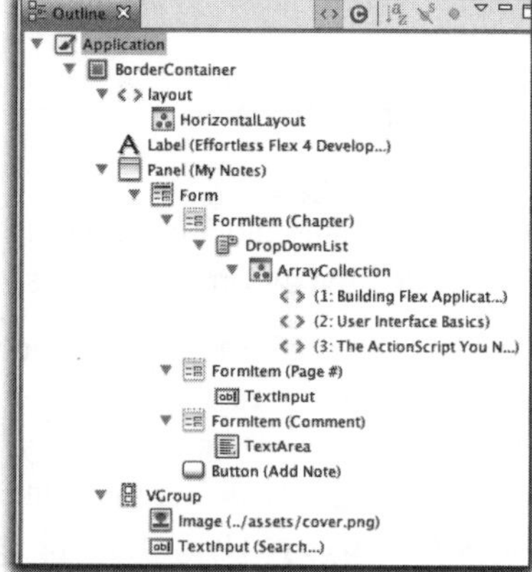

Figure 2.11

CUSTOMIZING THE APPLICATION

note

At the end of this chapter, I will recommend you create a specific application. For the other examples, you may want to create a new test project in which to practice.

Before getting into adding elements to an application, let's look at how you can customize the application itself. The **Application** tag has a number of properties that can be set, and I'll mention a quick handful of them here, starting with the size of the primary application window.

By default, a Flex application has no minimum height or width and no maximum possible size. If no dimensions are specified, the window will be 375 pixels wide by 500 pixels high when run in the standalone Flash Player and take up the entire browser window when run in a Web browser through the Flash Player plug-in. To change any of this, add the appropriate properties to the **Application** tag:

- The **width** and **height** properties establish the window's initial dimensions.
- The **minWidth** and **minHeight** properties prevent the user from resizing the window smaller than you would want.
- The **maxWidth** and **maxHeight** attributes prevent the user from resizing the window larger than you would want.

Be careful with the application's initial and minimum sizes, as not everyone will be viewing your application on a large screen.

So the following **Application** tag says that the window should start at 500 pixels square, be no more than 700 pixels square, and no less than 300 pixels square:

```
<s:Application xmlns:fx="http://ns.adobe.com/mxml/2009"
    xmlns:s="library://ns.adobe.com/flex/spark"
    xmlns:mx="library://ns.adobe.com/flex/mx"
    width="500" height="500"
    maxWidth="700" maxHeight="700"
    minWidth="300" minHeight="300">
```

An important change in Flex 4 is that **Application** does not automatically generate scrollbars (for when the content takes up more space than the sized window). Fortunately, it's quite easy to add scrollbars as needed, as I'll demonstrate later in the chapter.

Properties are always added to an element's opening tag.

The **pageTitle** property is of marginal usefulness, but you should be aware of it so as to understand its limitations. The **pageTitle** property is intended to be equivalent to the HTML **title** tag. If you add this property, you'll see the value in the browser bar after clicking Run in Flash Builder (see the top of Figure 2.10). Just know that what's really happening here is that Flash Builder is setting the actual HTML **title** tag value, using the application's **pageTitle** value. If the SWF file is embedded in a page with other content, or if you don't otherwise take special steps, the **pageTitle** won't be reflected in the browser.

Finally, there's the **backgroundColor** property. It uses standard HTML six-character hexadecimal notation to set the application's background color: **#ffffff** (white), **#cccccc** (gray), **#66aa00** (green), **#000000** (black), etc. The default background color is white and case doesn't matter (**#FFFFFF** is the same as **#ffffff**).

Chapter 13, "Improving the Appearance," goes through a number of other ways to more fully and professionally change the look of an application and its components.

There are other ways to customize and manipulate the **Application** tag itself, but they involve ActionScript and events, discussed in the next two chapters.

SIMPLE CONTROLS

This section discusses some of Flex's *simple controls*. This isn't an official label, just my way of grouping a bunch of components that are easy to use and that don't fall under the categories of form or layout controls (i.e., containers). I've subdivided this group into *text*, *media*, and *other*.

Many components have the same common properties:

- **id**, a unique identifier
- **enabled**, a Boolean value indicating whether or not the element is active (for example, clickable by a user)
- **visible**, a Boolean value indicating whether or not the element can be seen
- **toolTip**, text shown when the cursor is over the component (**Figure 2.12**)

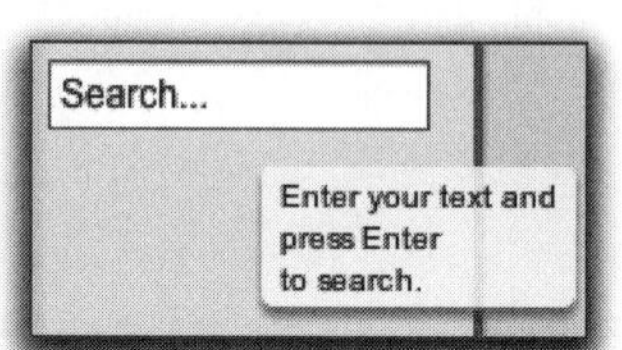

Figure 2.12

tip

The ***toolTip*** text can be placed over multiple lines (as in Figure 2.12) by adding this character sequence: ***
***

Of these, **id** is the most important property as it allows you to refer to a component. You would need to do so in order to find out what the user did with it (like enter text or select an option), to change its behavior, and so forth. But investigating and manipulating components require ActionScript, not yet covered. For this reason I won't be using **id** in this chapter but will rely upon it in future ones.

Along with these, there are a few attributes that affect the component's size and positioning:

- **x** and **y**, the coordinates for the element's upper-left corner
- **height** and **width**, the size of the component, in pixels
- **percentHeight** and **percentWidth**, the size of the component as a percentage of its parent

I'll get into size and positioning later in the chapter, but know now that the role that these last properties will play will depend upon the other components and attributes involved. For example, say you place a **Label** component within a **Panel** component, the latter being one type of container:

```
<s:Panel title="Some Panel">
    <s:Label text="Hello, World" x="18" y="47" />
</s:Panel>
```

The x- and y- coordinates of the **Label** will be relative to the content area of the **Panel**, meaning that 0, 0 is the upper-left corner of the ***Panel***'s body, not of the application.

Conversely, group containers are often used to control the layout of elements. Within a group, x- and y- coordinates of subelements have no meaning as the group controls the positioning (and not by using specific coordinates).

Text Controls

Unlike a Microsoft Word document or even an HTML page, you can't just enter text in an MXML file by putting your cursor somewhere and typing. All content in an MXML page must be placed within a component. If you want to add some text, you'll need to add one of the text controls.

The text controls have changed significantly in Flex 4. Using the new Spark components, Flex 4 text controls can take advantage of the Flash Text Engine (FTE) and Text Layout Framework (TLF), part of Flash Player 10 and Adobe AIR 1.5. Both allow you to easily lay out and manipulate text using advanced typography, text rotation, CSS styles, and more.

For displaying text, there are three controls: **Label**, **RichText**, and **RichEditableText**. **Label** is the simplest and most efficient of these. It can display multiple lines of text, but only in a single paragraph and using one format. This means that you can't have some of the text in bold and some of it in a larger font; two text blurbs formatted differently require two **Label**s. The content also cannot contain hyperlinks, use scrollbars, be selected by the user, or be edited by the user (i.e., the text will be non-interactive).

```
<s:Label text="Label in one format." textDecoration="underline"
fontSize="30"/>
```

RichText is like **Label** in that it can display multiple lines of text and is still non-interactive (i.e., not scrollable, selectable, or editable). But **RichText** does add support for multiple text formats within the same content. You'll see how to do that in a little bit.

```
<s:RichText text="RichText content." />
```

RichEditableText's content can be in multiple formats like **RichText**, but it can also be navigated using scrollbars, and can be both selected and edited by the user. There is a catch, though: The component does not automatically provide its own scrollbars. Without modifications, a user can click within a **RichEditableText** component and move up and down using the arrow keys, but you'll need to provide your own scrollbars if you want that to be visually apparent. Fortunately, that's not hard to do, as you'll see in just a couple of pages.

```
<s:RichEditableText text="RichEditableText content." />
```

tip

Because ***RichText*** and ***RichEditableText*** have the extra ability to richly format the text (compared with ***Label***s), they are less efficient and should only be used when you need the added capabilities.

Later in the chapter I'll discuss two components you'd use for taking user text input: **TextInput** and **TextArea**. If you want to create a text area where the user can edit **and** format text, you'll need to use the older Halo **RichTextEditor** control. This provides a basic, WYSIWYG-like editor. There is currently no equivalent in Spark.

```
<mx:RichTextEditor title="RichTextEditor" />
```

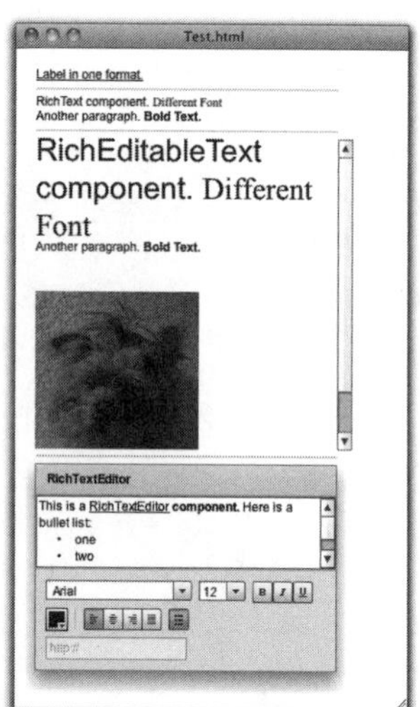

Figure 2.13

Figure 2.13 shows, from top, **Label**, **RichText**, **RichEditableText**, and **RichTextEditor** components in use.

You'll notice for each of the above that the **text** property is used to display the content. For each, some formatting can be applied to the entire content block using the component's properties. To apply multiple formats within the same block of text, you'll need to tap into the Text Layout Framework. The new Text Layout Framework supports a different way of laying out text. By using HTML-like tags, text, links, and images can be used in Flash content in a much more flexible and sophisticated manner. The supported tags are

- **a**
- **br**
- **div**
- **img**
- **p**
- **span**
- **tab**
- **tcy**

You probably haven't seen this last tag before: It's used to place text horizontally within a block of vertical text.

tip

The use of ***textFlow*** tags within ***RichText*** tags is really just an alternate way to assign a value to the ***RichText*** component's ***textFlow*** property.

There are many ways you can use these tags, plus whatever text, with a **RichText** or **RichEditableText** component. The preferred way is to place the content between the element's opening and closing tags, but inside both **textFlow** and **TextFlow** tags:

```
<s:RichText>
<s:textFlow>
<s:TextFlow>
   <s:div>
   <s:p>Some text.</s:p>
   </s:div>
</s:TextFlow>
</s:textFlow>
</s:RichText>
```

Content that uses the TLF has to be created as a **TextFlow** object, which is what's happening in the above. You can get away without using the **textFlow** and **TextFlow** tags, but then you'll force Flash to generate the **TextFlow** object for you, which is less efficient.

Note that you can only use these tags in **RichText** and **RichEditableText** components and that there are restrictions as to how they're used:

- **div**'s can only contain text, other **div**'s, and **p**'s.
- **p**'s can contain anything except **div**'s.
- **a**'s and **tcy**'s cannot contain **div**'s or **p**'s.
- **span**'s cannot contain any other tags.

Media Controls

Nice-looking user interfaces require more than just text: You'll normally want to integrate multimedia as well. To add images to an application, turn to the **Image** control. This component is part of the Halo set, meaning it's defined in the *mx* namespace.

You can add images to your application in one of two ways:

1. Embed them at compile time.
2. Import them at runtime.

Embedded images will be wrapped up in the compiled SWF file. This means that embedded media will be loaded immediately and is automatically distributed with the application (i.e., when you put the SWF file online, you don't need to remember to also upload your images). On the other hand, embedding images increases the size of the SWF file and adversely affects the load time of the application as a whole. You'll also need to recompile the application every time you change an image. You can embed GIF, JPEG, PNG, SVG, and SWF files.

Images imported at runtime have the opposite pros and cons as embedded ones. The distributed application will be smaller in size and will load more quickly. You can even change an image without recompiling (so long as it has the same name and is stored in the same location). However, the images will take a moment to appear and you'll need to ensure that the image file is always available to the application. You can import GIF, JPEG, PNG, and SWF files at runtime but not SVG.

tip

The ***Embed*** directive can take other parameters, like the asset's MIME type and whether to compress the image (for GIFs and PNGs). You'll occasionally see the code ***@Embed(source='/path/to/filename.ext')***, which specifically names the source parameter.

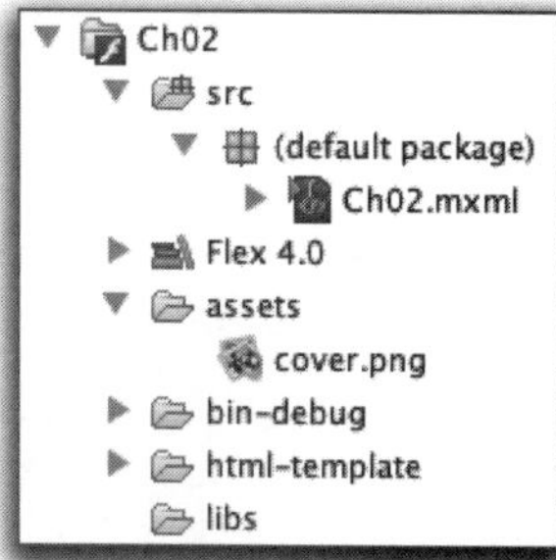

Figure 2.14

The **Image** tag's **source** property is used to identify the image file. To embed an image at compile time, use this syntax:

<mx:Image source="@Embed('*/path/to/filename.ext*')" />

To import the image at runtime, use

<mx:Image source="*/path/to/filename.ext*" />

In both cases, the */path/to/filename.ext* part needs to be replaced with the *actual path* to the content. This can be a relative or absolute value. A relative path is one that pinpoints the resource relative to the MXML file that references it. For example, if you take the project structure shown in **Figure 2.14** with the primary MXML file in the **src** directory and the media in the **assets** directory, then the relative path from the primary MXML file to **cover.png** is **../assets/cover.png.** This means "go up one level, then into the **assets** folder, and access cover.png there." Note that the MXML file in the **src** directory is found within *default package*, which isn't to be thought of as a folder, and that the **assets** directory is on the same level as **src**.

An absolute path is one that's always correct, regardless of the location of the file referencing it. Absolute paths might begin with the computer root (like *C:* on Windows or just / on Mac OS X, Linux, and Unix). This is the case with local assets: those on the same computer as the file referencing them.

You also have the option of using remote assets—those stored on a different computer than the file referencing them. You cannot use a relative path to reference a remote asset; you'd have to use an absolute path, which might begin with *http:*. However, there are security restrictions in doing so, as discussed in the sidebar.

LOCAL VS. REMOTE ASSETS

Another factor to consider when choosing between local assets and remote ones (which would have to be imported at runtime) is the restrictions placed on importing content into Flash applications. Flash applications can import content either locally (i.e., using the file system of the same computer it is running on) or remotely (over a network connection), but not both. And content imported remotely has security restrictions placed on it. Without taking extra steps, you cannot load network resources from a foreign domain. This is to say that the default Flash security model won't allow content on *www.example.com* to load content from *www.example.edu* without the proper pre-authorization. Later in the book I'll talk about the security restrictions in more detail, but for now I would recommend using local assets to keep things simple.

Whether you use local or remote assets, a relative or an absolute path, and embedded, compiled images or ones imported at runtime can seem like a complicated series of options. When you're just getting started, stick with embedded images, referenced using a relative path to the file on the same computer. Here's how I recommend you do it:

1. Create a new folder in your project directory called **assets**.

   In Flash Builder you do this by control-clicking the project in the Package Explorer view and selecting New > Folder, then following the prompts. If you're not using Flash Builder, use your operating system's interface to create a new folder in your project directory or your development tool, if that's an option.

2. Copy the image(s) you want to use to the **assets** directory.

3. In your MXML file, where you want to place the image, add an **Image** tag:

   <mx:Image source="" />

   Again, note that this is an *mx* component, not Spark.

4. For the source, use **@Embed('../assets/*imageName.ext*')**, inserting the actual image's name and extension accordingly.

   Because the default MXML file is in the **src** directory, you'll need to go up one level (the two periods), then into the **assets** directory to find the image. This is true for Flash Builder's default application structure; if you created your own project directory, you'll need to change the reference to make it accurate.

By default, Flex will automatically read and use the image's original dimensions to display it in the application. But you can forcibly resize the image by setting the **Image** component's **width** and **height** values.

tip

Multiple usages of the same image within an application will not increase the application's size or load time.

Another common media type you might use is video. The **VideoPlayer** component provides an easy way to drop Flash video into your application. It supports both FLV and F4V video types, and automatically creates the appropriate interface, including the ability to play and pause the video, adjust the volume, move back and forth within the video, and play it in fullscreen mode. As with the **Image** tag, **source** is the most important attribute. With videos, though, you're not going to embed video files, as they're quite large and a certain amount of delay in loading a video is expected by most users. So just provide the path to the video file:

<s:VideoPlayer source="../assets/somefile.flv" />

tip

Another type of media can be added to your application using the ***SWFLoader*** component. It's used to incorporate other Flash applications (i.e., other SWF files) within the current application.

As with **Image** components, the application will show the video using its actual size. But do note that unlike **Image**, **VideoPlayer** is a Spark component. There is an older Halo component called **VideoDisplay** that provides the same functionality but can also be used to tap into the user's camera, if required.

Other Controls

Most of the remaining controls I'm going to discuss in this chapter are found at the end of this chapter, in a section on forms. Without going into many details, I want to at least mention the existence of the following:

- **HSlider**
- **ProgressBar**
- **Spinner**
- **VSlider**

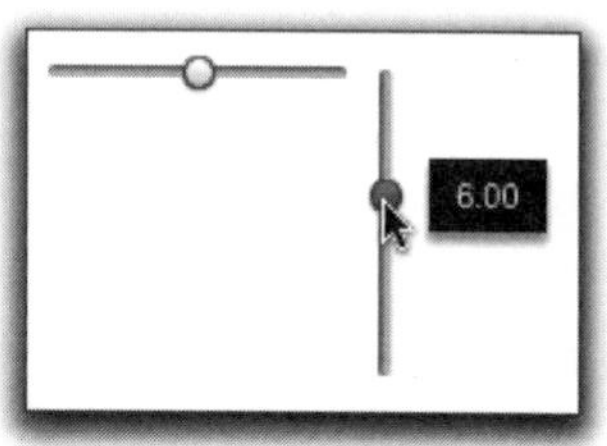

Figure 2.15

Using these requires knowledge of ActionScript and event handling, so there's no point in full demonstrations here. But know that the sliders create markers along a horizontal or vertical bar (**Figure 2.15**), the movement of which would be tied to a result, like the changing of a font size.

The **ProgressBar** is exactly that. And **Spinner** is a combination of up and down arrows that can be used for all sorts of purposes, from changing a value to navigating through content.

I do want to take a moment to discuss the **Scroller** component. Flex 4 components (i.e., Spark) don't automatically create scrollbars when they're needed. If you think they might be, for the application as a whole or for just an individual component, add **Scroller**. For example, to make a **RichEditableText** component scrollable, you would code

```
<s:Scroller>
    <s:RichEditableText width="200" height="100" />
</s:Scroller>
```

tip

You can add just a horizontal or a vertical scrollbar using the ***VScrollBar*** and ***HScrollBar*** controls.

The **Scroller** component creates both horizontal and vertical scrollbars when needed. If you add **width** and **height** properties to the opening **Scroller** tag, you can restrict the viewable area (called the *viewport*) to those dimensions. If you want to add scrollbars to an entire application, you would add them just inside of the **Application** tags.

To add visual divides to your application, invoke the **HRule** and **VRule** controls. Both are much more accommodating versions of the HTML **hr** tag (Figure 2.13 has small, gray horizontal rules between the components). Both components are defined in Halo. You can set the **height** and **width** properties to size the rule and **strokeColor** and **shadowColor** to color it. Here's a 300- by 5-pixel gray vertical rule with a black shadow:

```
<mx:VRule height="300" width="5" strokeColor="#cccccc"
shadowColor="#000000" />
```

Finally, there are the following buttons (**Figure 2.16**):

Figure 2.16

- **Button**
- **LinkButton**
- **ToggleButton**

Button and **ToggleButton** are very similar (in fact, in Halo, toggle buttons were created by just adding another property to **Button**). They have **label** attributes used to set the displayed text and automatically size themselves to fit the label. But **Button** will appear as depressed for as long as it's being clicked, whereas the **ToggleButton**'s state switches between depressed and not depressed (happy?) with each click. Figure 2.16 shows a **ToggleButton** in its depressed state. You'll tie both to some functionality using ActionScript, so that something actually happens when the button is clicked.

tip

By using skins, you can add icons to buttons. You'll see how in Chapter 13.

tip

For more on these, or on any Flex component, check out the Adobe documentation, Tour de Flex, or any number of resources available online.

A simple **Button**, like the one in Figure 2.16, is created using:

```
<s:Button label="Button"/>
```

LinkButton is a Halo component used to create a link that will open the associated URL in the user's Web browser. Using it requires a bit of event handling, to be discussed in Chapter 4.

CONTROLLING THE LAYOUT

When you use HTML to develop a Web page's layout, there are few guarantees that it'll look right for everyone who views the page. This is because of the vast number of browsers out there, each with its own quirks. Fortunately, when you lay out applications using Flex, your content will only run using the Flash Player or Adobe AIR, so the look you create will be much more reliable.

note

The layout options are a significant change in Flex 4, making use of new Spark components. Older Flex code uses Halo components for layout control.

Flex has a number of components dedicated to controlling how elements are positioned within the application. These are called *containers*, and they have significantly changed in Flex 4. In this section of the chapter, I'll walk through the fundamental containers and how they're used. As you'll see, you have lots of options for controlling the layout; practice and experimentation will help you figure out how to design interfaces in a way you like best.

Layout Classes

Before getting into the specific components that act as layout containers in Flex 4, I should talk about the four layout classes Flex has defined. They are

- **BasicLayout**
- **HorizontalLayout**
- **VerticalLayout**
- **TileLayout**

I say that these are "classes" because they are predefined behaviors, not individual elements. In fact, these classes can be used with many different components, as you'll see in this book.

BasicLayout uses absolute positioning, which is to say that every child is placed using x- and y- coordinates. This is easy to use and is also the default behavior for the application as a whole. A side effect of absolute positioning is that if you don't provide x- and y- coordinates for elements, they'll just all overlap each other. Also, absolute positioning can fare poorly when the user resizes the application window.

The other three classes use relative positioning, where the existence of component A affects the placement of component B. **HorizontalLayout** places elements in a single horizontal row. **VerticalLayout** places elements in a single vertical column. **TileLayout** creates a series of horizontal rows and vertical columns, like a table.

For **HorizontalLayout**, the height of the row will be based upon the tallest item within the row. For **VerticalLayout**, the width of the column will be based upon the widest item within it. For **TileLayout**, the height of every row will be based upon the tallest item in any row and the width of every column will be based upon the widest item in any column. In other words, every cell will be the same size. The **TileLayout** also has an **orientation** property that can be set to the values *columns* or *rows*. This setting dictates whether the component creates more rows or more columns when needed to display every child.

The syntax for using these classes is different than anything you've seen thus far. You'll use them like so:

```
<s:layout>
   <s:BasicLayout />
</s:layout>
```

In reality, the **layout** tag is actually acting as a property of the parent component, but by using this syntax, it makes layout indicators more overt. There are three things to note about using this syntax:

- The word *layout* is entirely lowercase.
- The children of the parent tag come after the closing **</s:layout>**, not before it.
- The layout will only affect the immediate children of the parent tag.

For this last item, imagine that you have an application that contains an image, a form, and some text:

```
<?xml version="1.0" encoding="utf-8"?>
<s:Application xmlns:fx="http://ns.adobe.com/mxml/2009"
   xmlns:s="library://ns.adobe.com/flex/spark"
   xmlns:mx="library://ns.adobe.com/flex/mx">
<s:layout>
   <s:HorizontalLayout />
</s:layout>
<mx:Image source="@Embed('../assets/image.png')" />
<mx:Form width="100%" height="100%">
<!-- FORM ELEMENTS -->
</mx:Form>
<s:Label text="Hello, World!" />
</s:Application>
```

The layout applied to the application as a whole will only affect those three elements. The formatting of the elements within the form will actually be dictated by the form container they reside in. So the application could use horizontal layout while the form uses vertical. You'll see an example of this at the end of the chapter.

Layout Containers

Moving on to the actual container components, there are two types. The first type has no *skin*, which is to say that in themselves the components are not visible, nor can they be made visible. These are

- **Group**
- **DataGroup**
- **HGroup**
- **VGroup**

tip

Later in the book you'll learn about a different way to control layout, using navigation components. Such components both organize content and provide an easy way to access it all.

The other type of containers either comes with a visual appearance or can be customized using skins:

- **SkinnableContainer**
- **SkinnableDataContainer**
- **Panel**

tip

Non-skinnable components cannot be aesthetically customized but will perform better in your applications.

Later in the chapter you'll use the **Panel** container, which creates an area with both a border and a heading. And, of course, you've been using one skinnable container all along: **Application**.

Each container type also has a default layout behavior. For example, **Application**, **Group**, and **SkinnableContainer** all default to **BasicLayout** (i.e., absolute positioning). **HGroup** uses **HorizontalLayout** and **VGroup**, **VerticalLayout**.

Besides affecting how child elements are positioned, containers can also align them. The **horizontalAlign** and **verticalAlign** properties adjust how children are aligned within the container. In **VerticalLayout** and **TileLayout** containers, you can set **horizontalAlign** to *left*, *right*, *center*, *justify*, or *contentJustify*. In **HorizontalLayout** and **TileLayout** containers, you can set **verticalAlign** to *top*, *bottom*, *middle*, *justify*, or *contentJustify*.

To affect the spacing, you can use the **paddingLeft**, **paddingRight**, **paddingTop**, and **paddingBottom** properties to increase the space around the entire container. To increase the spacing among the children within the container, use the **gap** property. The padding and the gap can be set for **HorizontalLayout** and **VerticalLayout** but not **TileLayout** or **BasicLayout**.

tip

If you use something a bit larger for the children of the test example, like a small image or text in a big font, you'll also be able to see the effect that resizing the window has on the layout.

To see for yourself how these changes affect the layout, just create a test application that places a few **Label**s (or whatever) within a **Group**:

```
<s:Group>
   <s:layout>
      <s:BasicLayout />
   </s:layout>
   <s:Label text="one" />
   <s:Label text="two" />
   <s:Label text="three" />
   <s:Label text="four" />
   <s:Label text="five" />
   <s:Label text="six" />
   <s:Label text="seven" />
</s:Group>
```

Run the application to see what happens. With **BasicLayout**, which uses absolute positioning, you'll see all of the **Label**s on top of each other. Then change only the layout, and repeat (**Figures 2.17**, **2.18**, and **2.19**).

Horizontal Layout
one two three four five six seven

Figure 2.17

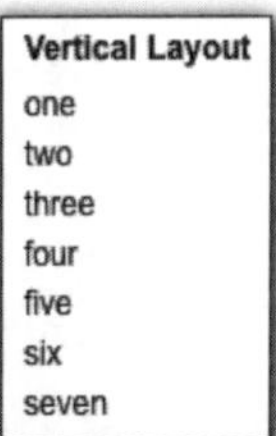

Figure 2.18

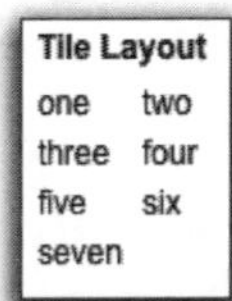

Figure 2.19

Early in the chapter I mentioned that the properties of a container also affect its children. This is true for layouts, of course, but even other properties such as **enabled** and **visible**. If a container has an **enabled** value of **false**, its children are dimmed and non-interactive. If a container has a **visible** value of **false**, its children are hidden, too.

Constraint-Based Layout

Another way you can affect the layout of an application is to use *constraint-based layout*. This only works for children falling under **BasicLayout** (i.e., absolute positioning) but doesn't involve specific x- and y-coordinates. Instead you provide pixel adjustments for a combination of properties:

- **baseline**
- **top**
- **bottom**
- **left**
- **right**
- **horizontalCenter**
- **verticalCenter**

For example, say you have the following:

```
<s:Panel>
    <s:RichText top="10" left="10" right="10" text="Spam Spam Spam" />
</s:Panel>
```

This code both sizes and positions the **RichText** component within the Panel. Specifically, the top of the **RichText** component will always be 10 pixels down from the top of the **Panel**; its left side will be 10 pixels in from the left side of the **Panel**; and its right side will be 10 pixels in from the right side of the **Panel**. If the panel is resized by the user, perhaps by resizing the browser window, the **RichText** will adjust accordingly.

As another example, this **Image** will always be both horizontally and vertically centered within the application as it's set to be 0 pixels off of the horizontal and vertical axes:

```
<mx:Image horizontalCenter="0" verticalCenter="0" />
```

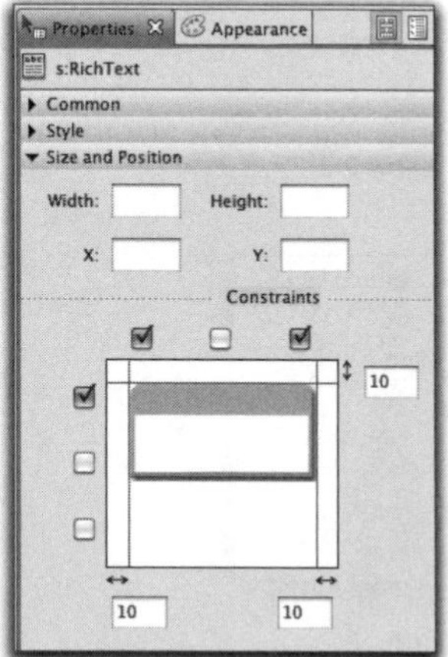

Figure 2.20

You may find it easiest to grasp constraints by visually setting them using the Constraints subsection of the Properties panel in Flash Builder (**Figure 2.20**).

RELATIVE SIZES

You can control the size of a component relative to its parent by expressing the child's **height** and/or **width** as a percentage. Such percentages will be with respect to the child's immediate parent, not the application as a whole. For example, in this code, the **VGroup** is set to be 90% of the application's width and also horizontally centered:

```
<s:Application xmlns:fx="http://ns.adobe.com/mxml/2009"
    xmlns:s="library://ns.adobe.com/flex/spark"
    xmlns:mx="library://ns.adobe.com/flex/mx">
    <s:VGroup width="90%" horizontalCenter="0">
```

CREATING FORMS

Forms are one of the most fundamental tools for user interfaces, as they create a way for the user to make choices and provide information. If you've ever designed an HTML form, you'll have no problems with them in Flex, although you'll come to find that Flex has

- A slew of additional elements that you'll wish HTML supported out of the box.
- A different client-server relationship that impacts how forms are handled.

Over the next couple of pages, I'll introduce several Flex components that will amaze you by their usefulness, and yet, simplicity, like **ColorPicker** and **DateChooser**. Elements like these can only be added to an HTML form using JavaScript.

More importantly, however, forms in a Flash application don't work the way they do in a Web browser. HTML is a stateless technology, meaning that each individual page is a separate entity with no relationship to any other. When a user submits an HTML form, the data contained therein gets passed to the page that handles the form. That page will use a server-side technology like PHP (my personal favorite) to store the data in a database, send it in an e-mail, etc.

The model is different in Flash applications because a Flash application isn't a static entity like a Web page. A Flash application is more like a desktop application in that it runs until it's stopped. While running, the Flash application responds to user events, like the filling out of a form. The application can still store the form data in a database, send it in an e-mail, and so forth, but it can do so behind the scenes, unbeknownst to the end user.

Before getting into some actual form code, let me also be clear in stating that the **Form** component in Flex is really just a container used to group and lay out form elements. In an HTML form, only elements within the **FORM** tags will have their data passed on to the handling page. Because Flash behaves differently, a form is an organizational structure that's not required but is still often worth using.

So you can start with a **Form** component, which is defined within the Halo namespace. A **Form** will automatically size itself based upon the dimensions of its children, or you can set it to a specific size. This form will use all of the space made available by the parent:

```
<mx:Form width="100%" height="100%">
```

Because **Form** is a container, you can use padding and constraints to adjust how it's positioned within its parent. You can also apply stylistic changes to the **Form** component that will affect its children. For example, here I'm changing the default font family and size for the form elements:

```
<mx:Form fontFamily="Verdana" fontSize="18">
```

(As you'll see, these values will end up affecting the labels of the form items.)

The **Form** component's **verticalGap** and **horizontalGap** properties adjust the spacing between form elements. The default values are 6 and 8 pixels, respectively.

And, not to belabor the point, note that Flex forms don't have the same **action** attribute that HTML forms do, as the form will not be submitted anywhere. Rather, event handlers take on that task, as you'll learn about in subsequent chapters.

Before getting into the specific form element types, it's conventional to place each form element within its own **FormItem** component. This component takes a **label** attribute that'll set some text next to the element itself. By using these **FormItem**s, your forms will have a consistent appearance and be easy to style using skins or CSS.

I've already mentioned that **TextInput** and **TextArea** components are used to take text input. Let's drop those into a form:

```
<mx:Form width="100%" height="100%">
    <mx:FormHeading label="Contact Us!"/>
    <mx:FormItem label="Name">
        <s:TextInput width="150"/>
    </mx:FormItem>
    <mx:FormItem label="Comments">
        <s:TextArea width="150" height="150"/>
    </mx:FormItem>
</mx:Form>
```

 **note**

Form, ***FormHeading***, and ***FormItem*** are all defined in Halo, so they use the mx namespace.

Figure 2.21

Figure 2.22

Figure 2.23

Each component is given an explicit width, so that they line up exactly. Also, I've added a **FormHeading** component to title the entire form. **Figure 2.21** shows how this form looks.

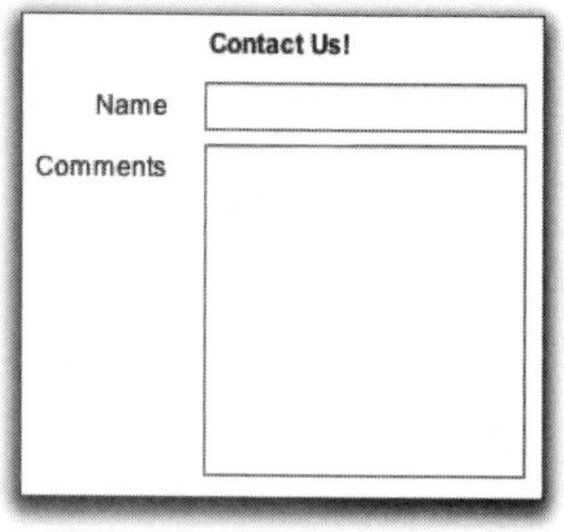

The **Form**, **FormHeading**, and **FormItem** components each have an **indicatorGap** property to adjust the amount of space between the label and the element. Each can also set the padding of the form, the form heading, and the individual form item, accordingly.

If multiple components are placed within one **FormItem**, by default they'll be placed vertically, one above the next. This makes sense if, for example, you're taking two inputs for a person's address. If you'd like the components to be organized horizontally, like one for the user's area code and another for the rest of the phone number, set the **FormItem**'s **direction** property to *horizontal* (**Figure 2.22**):

```
<mx:FormItem label="Phone" direction="horizontal">
    <s:TextInput text="(123)" width="45" paddingRight="5" />
    <s:TextInput text="456-7890" width="100"/>
</mx:FormItem>
```

The **FormItem** component also has a **required** attribute that takes a Boolean value. If true, a red asterisk will appear beside that item's label. While the **FormItem**'s **required** attribute indicates that the corresponding component is required, it actually does nothing to ensure that the component is used. Chapter 6, "Manipulating Data," addresses this issue.

As for the components used in forms, I've just mentioned and demonstrated **TextInput**, which takes a small amount of text, and **TextArea**, intended for much more text input. **TextArea** will also automatically create scrollbars as needed. Earlier in the chapter I discussed **RichEditableText**, which allows the user to enter text that can make use of the new Text Layout Framework. Now let's look at components that are equivalent to HTML elements you might know.

First, there's the **CheckBox**, which creates a...um...uh...checkable box (**Figure 2.23**):

```
<mx:FormItem label="Toppings" direction="horizontal">
    <s:CheckBox label="Ham" />
    <s:CheckBox label="Black Olives" />
    <s:CheckBox label="Extra Tomato" />
    <s:CheckBox label="Anchovies" />
</mx:FormItem>
```

One nice feature of the **CheckBox** is that the label itself is clickable, so that the user can select or deselect that option by clicking its name.

RadioButton is used within a **RadioButtonGroup** to create multiple options of which the user can only select one. The restriction exists when two or more **RadioButtons** have the same **RadioButtonGroup** name:

```
<mx:FormItem label="Gender" direction="horizontal">
    <s:RadioButton label="Male" groupName="gender"/>
    <s:RadioButton label="Female" groupName="gender"/>
</mx:FormItem>
```

If you're using Flash Builder, it has a nice little wizard for creating **RadioButtonGroups** (**Figure 2.24**). This wizard will also create a non-visual component of type **RadioButtonGroup**. As a non-visual element, it's defined within a **Declarations** section:

```
<fx:Declarations>
    <s:RadioButtonGroup id="gender"/>
</fx:Declarations>
```

Figure 2.24

Another common HTML form element is **SELECT**, which creates a drop-down menu of options. It's replicated in Flex via three different components: **ComboBox**, **DropDownList**, and **List**. Each has a slightly different look and behavior but the principles are the same.

In Part 2 of the book you'll learn a lot of ways to dynamically populate these controls, but for now I'll explain how to hard-code the options. To do so, place an **ArrayList** tag within the component and any number of **String** elements within **ArrayList**:

```
<mx:FormItem label="Size">
    <s:ComboBox>
        <s:ArrayList>
            <fx:String>Small</fx:String>
            <fx:String>Medium</fx:String>
            <fx:String>Large</fx:String>
            <fx:String>Extra Large</fx:String>
        </s:ArrayList>
    </s:ComboBox>
</mx:FormItem>
```

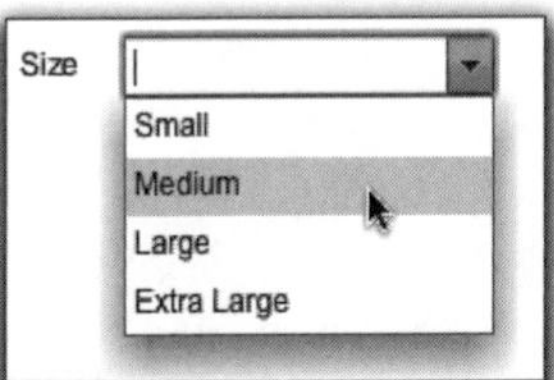

Figure 2.25

What this all means will make more sense in Part 2, but note that **ArrayList** is in the Spark namespace (the initial *s*), whereas **String** is part of the Flex Core namespace (*fx*). **Figure 2.25** shows the end result.

HTML forms also use submit buttons. That same functionality can be provided by the **Button** component, already discussed.

tip

The drop-down menu-like components, as well as heretofore-unmentioned components for displaying data, will be well covered in the second part of the book.

Finally, I want to mention four components that don't exist in standard HTML:

- **ColorPicker**
- **DateChooser**
- **DateField**
- **NumericStepper**

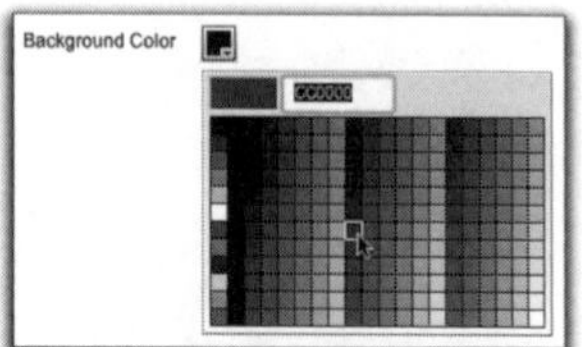

Figure 2.26

Figure 2.27

Figure 2.28

The first is used to create an interface in which the user can select a color (**Figure 2.26**). The second and third create interfaces for selecting dates (**DateField** also shows the selected date in a box, **Figure 2.27**). All three of these are defined in Halo. **NumericStepper**, new in Spark, creates up and down arrows for incrementing and decrementing a number (**Figure 2.28**). All of these can be thoroughly customized, from limiting the number of colors shown in **ColorPicker** to changing the step increment (say to 2 or 10) in **NumericStepper**.

PUTTING IT ALL TOGETHER

I've run through quite a bit of information in this chapter, while still trying to restrain myself from overdoing it with descriptions and properties for every single component. That information can easily be found within Flash Builder, online, and in tools like the Flex Component Explorer. My hope in this chapter was to give you a proper survey of the user interface landscape, pointing out the major landmarks and indicating the kinds of things you'll want to be aware of, and look for, as you go forward. But most of the examples were lacking context, so I thought I'd wrap up the chapter by putting it all together to discuss how I created the interface shown in Figure 2.10.

As Figure 2.11 shows in outline form, within the application itself, there's only one child, a **BorderContainer**. Within it, there are three components: a **Label**, a **Panel**, and a **VGroup**. The **Panel** contains the form. The **VGroup** contains the image and the search input. Here's how to code that interface:

1. Create a new Flex project using Flash Builder or your own development tools.
2. In the primary MXML file, begin with the XML declaration.

   ```
   <?xml version="1.0" encoding="utf-8"?>
   ```

   Of course, if you're using Flash Builder, this code, as well as some to follow, will automatically be created for you.

3. Next, add the opening **Application** tag.

```
<s:Application xmlns:fx="http://ns.adobe.com/mxml/2009"
    xmlns:s="library://ns.adobe.com/flex/spark"
    xmlns:mx="library://ns.adobe.com/flex/mx"
backgroundColor="#DDE7D3">
```

   The only alteration I made to the application itself is to provide a background color (a light green).

4. Add the **BorderContainer**.

```
<s:BorderContainer backgroundColor="#F5F1B0" dropShadowVisible=
"true" borderWeight="3" horizontalCenter="0" verticalCenter="0">
```

   The **BorderContainer** holds the interface itself. It has a different background color, a drop shadow, and a stronger border. By providing it with **horizontalCenter** and **verticalCenter** values of 0, the **BorderContainer** will always remain centered in the application (this is an example of constraint-based layout).

5. Set the layout for the **BorderContainer**.

```
<s:layout>
    <s:HorizontalLayout paddingLeft="10" paddingRight="10"
    paddingTop="10" paddingBottom="10" gap="10" />
</s:layout>
```

   The **BorderContainer**'s children will be laid out horizontally, from left to right. I've added padding all around, so that each child is placed 10 pixels on all sides within the **BorderContainer**. There's also a 10-pixel gap between children.

6. Add the **Label**.

```
<s:Label text="Effortless Flex 4 Development" fontSize="18"
fontWeight="bold" color="#293B95" rotation="270" />
```

   The **Label** displays the text *Effortless Flex 4 Development* in a size 18, bold font. The font has also been colored in blue. By setting the **rotation** property to 270, the text will run vertically from bottom to top.

7. Create the **Panel**.

```
<s:Panel title="My Notes" height="300">
```

   The **Panel** will hold the form. It has a title at the top.

8. Begin the **Form**.

```
<mx:Form width="100%" height="100%">
```

   The form will take up the entirety of the **Panel**'s body.

9. Add a **DropDownList** for selecting a chapter.

```
<mx:FormItem label="Chapter">
    <s:DropDownList width="250">
        <s:ArrayList>
            <fx:String>1: Building Flex Applications</fx:String>
            <fx:String>2: User Interface Basics</fx:String>
            <fx:String>3: The ActionScript You Need to Know
            </fx:String>
        </s:ArrayList>
    </s:DropDownList>
</mx:FormItem>
```

The **FormItem** labels the component to follow. I'm then using a **DropDownList**, providing it with the names of the first three chapters of this book. Each is placed within a Flex Core **String**, and all of them within an **ArrayList**.

10. Add a **TextInput** for the page number.

```
<mx:FormItem label="Page #">
  <s:TextInput width="250" contentBackgroundColor="#CCCCCC"/>
</mx:FormItem>
```

I've styled this slightly by changing the background color of the input itself.

11. Add a **TextArea** for the comment.

```
<mx:FormItem label="Comment" borderColor="#696969">
    <s:TextArea width="250" height="125" contentBackgroundColor=
    "#CCCCCC" />
</mx:FormItem>
```

The background color of this **TextArea** matches that of the **TextInput**.

12. Add a button for submitting the form.

```
<s:Button label="Add Note"/>
```

13. Complete the **Form** and **Panel**.

```
    </mx:Form>
</s:Panel>
```

14. Create a **VGroup**.

```
<s:VGroup>
```

All of the content to this point is laid out horizontally within the **BorderContainer**. I want the two elements in the last section of the

BorderContainer—the image and the search box—to be positioned one above the other. To accomplish this, I create a **VGroup** to contain them. The **VGroup** will arrange its children vertically.

15. Add an **Image**.

```
<mx:Image source="@Embed('../assets/cover.png')" />
```

I discuss the **Image** tag in some detail earlier in the chapter. The image itself is named *cover.png*, and is stored in the project's **assets** directory.

16. Add a search box.

```
<s:TextInput width="123" text="Search..." toolTip="Enter your text
and&#13;press Enter&#13;to search."/>
```

The **TextInput** makes use of the **toolTip** property to instruct the user (see Figure 2.12). The two uses of **
** create newlines (like pressing Enter) within the tip text.

17. Complete the **VGroup**, the **BorderContainer**, and the **Application**.

```
        </s:VGroup>
    </s:BorderContainer>
</s:Application>
```

18. Save and run the project.

ADOBE AIR-SPECIFIC CONTROLS

This book does not go into AIR development in great detail, although most of the book's content will apply there as well, including pretty much all of this chapter's information. There are several components that are specific to AIR applications that I want to quickly mention here.

To start, a handful of controls exist for working with the user's file system. The **FileSystemComboBox** allows the user to browse and select a location on his or her computer. The **FileSystemTree** component shows the contents of a directory as a navigable tree hierarchy and **FileSystemList** shows the contents of a directory as a scrollable list. The **FileSystemDataGrid** shows the contents of a directory in a table. These last three components also allow the user to select a file or directory from the display.

Next, there's the **HTML** control (i.e., **mx:HTML**) for displaying HTML content within an application. And **FlexNativeMenu** is used to create an operating system-appropriate application menu.

Flex has also defined two containers specific to AIR applications. The application's primary window is a **WindowedApplication**. Chapter 1, "Building Flex Applications," demonstrated this already. There's also the **Window** container, used for creating secondary windows.

3 ACTIONSCRIPT YOU NEED TO KNOW

In Chapter 1, "Building Flex Applications," I say that ActionScript provides the brains or logic in a Flex program. ActionScript is an object-oriented programming language used by Flash applications (whether developed using Flex, Flash Professional, or Flash Catalyst). Like JavaScript, ActionScript is derived from something called *ECMAScript*, although ActionScript does a few things differently.

In this chapter, I'll walk you through the ActionScript you need to know in order to develop real-world Flex applications today. Entire books are written on ActionScript, so I obviously can't go into all of the details of the language. But the chapter does cover the fundamentals and should be approachable even if you've never done any programming before. If you have programmed before, especially if you've worked with even a bit of JavaScript, this chapter should be a breeze. And within the chapter, you'll see a couple of really nice examples that tie MXML and ActionScript together to create interactive programs. What you learn here will be more than sufficient for the next several book chapters. In the third part of the book, though, I'll discuss a few more advanced uses of the language.

DATA BINDING

I want to start the chapter with something fun (if you don't mind associating "fun" with programming): *data binding*. Data binding is this cool little feature in Flex that's quite useful and yet very easy to grasp and implement. Data binding is where the value of a thing A is dynamically determined based upon another source. For example, a **Label**'s **text** property is normally hard-coded into the application (i.e., it's set when the program is compiled):

```
<s:Label text="Display this text." />
```

But you can set the text value on the fly, by *binding* it to something else. To use data binding for a property's value, place the name of the source between curly braces: ***{something}***. So the above **Label** might become

```
<s:Label text="{something}" />
```

Assuming that **something** has a value that's usable for the **Label**'s **text** property, Flex will do the rest. This last statement will mean more in time, but, as an example, the **text** property takes a simple string as its value, so you couldn't bind it to a list of strings or an image.

One easy way to get your "something" is to refer to other components. Just as a **Label** has a **text** property that dictates what text is displayed, **TextInput** has a **text** property that reflects what the user entered. By assigning the value of the **TextInput**'s **text** property to the **Label**'s **text** property, what's entered in the **TextInput** will automatically be reflected—as the user types—in the **Label**. Cool beans, right? But for this to work, we need a way to reference the **TextInput**. To do that, assign the **TextInput** a unique **id**:

As you begin using data binding and ActionScript, providing ***id*** values to components becomes more important. The values you use must be unique throughout the application.

```
<s:TextInput id="userName"/>
```

Now, bind the **TextInput**'s **text** value to the **Label**'s **text**:

```
<s:Label text="{userName.text}"/>
```

If you want to see this for yourself, place these two components in an MXML file, then save and run the application. As you enter text in the **TextInput**, you'll see it appear in the **Label** (**Figure 3.1**). Change the inputted text and the **Label** changes, too, like magic!

Figure 3.1

Over the course of this book you'll see many examples of data binding. Some will be simple like the above. Others will involve binding to more complex variable types. You can also use function calls when binding, or a combination of literal text and a source:

```
<s:Label text="Hello, {userName.text}!"/>
```

Flex even supports two-way binding, where two items are bound to each other. Say you want to compare how some text looks with two different formats. You can create two **RichEditableText** areas and have their content bound to each other.

Now, you may be wondering why I'm starting off a chapter on ActionScript with a section on data binding. That's because when you use the ***{something}*** syntax for a value, that invokes ActionScript. By comparison, values assigned to properties without the curly brackets are treated literally (**Figure 3.2**):

Figure 3.2

```
<s:Label text="userName.text"/>
```

If you ran any of the above code for yourself, not only does that mean you've now done a bit of ActionScript programming (in a way), it also means you've touched upon Object-Oriented Programming (OOP). I'll explain...

USING THE BINDING COMPONENT

Most things in Flex can be accomplished using either MXML or ActionScript. For example, you can also create bindings using the **fx:Binding** component. As this is a non-visual element, it gets placed within a **Declarations** section of your code. Use its **source** and **destination** properties to associate two items together. For the **TextInput-Label** example, the corresponding MXML would be:

```
<fx:Declarations>
<fx:Binding source="username.text" destination="userNameLabel.text" />
</fx:Declarations>
<s:TextInput id="userName"/>
<s:Label id="userNameLabel"/>
```

You should note two things with this format. First, you do not use the curly brackets around the values. Second, both components need an ID value.

OOP FUNDAMENTALS

ActionScript, like JavaScript, Ruby, Java, and many others, is an *object-oriented programming* language. Object-oriented programming can seem quite daunting, especially if you haven't programmed before. However, one thing I like to stress about OOP is that you can reasonably practice it without fully grasping it, just as you can own a house without knowing how to build one. This is true with OOP in general, and the fact is, with the Flex framework, most of the hard OOP work has been done for you; you can just reap the rewards.

The alternative to OOP is *procedural programming*, which focuses on steps: Do this, then this, then this. Object-Oriented Programming focuses on the pieces involved. As an example, say you want to design a video game where you control virtual people. The people have friends, do activities, go places, and so forth. Two objects the game would need are right there: people and places. Looking at the first, you would then think about what information needs to be known about a person: name, age, hair color, profession, etc. And you'd need to identify the things a person does: eats, sleeps, works, walks, talks to a friend, and so forth. With an understanding of what a person object should be (what information it contains and what it can do), you then define a *class*. A class is simply a template for creating something. So the **Person** class establishes the information and actions involved with virtual people. An *object*, then, is a variable in an application that represents a specific instance of a class: this virtual person, as opposed to another one.

Within an object, information is stored in variables, called *properties* or *attributes* within the object context. The actions an object can perform are represented by functions, which are called *methods* when defined within a class.

So perhaps the variable **miniMe** would be an object of **Person** type that represents the virtual me in the game. The application in which **miniMe** exists would then know how to retrieve the **miniMe**'s name or job by referring to the appropriate property (i.e., the object variable that stores that data). The game could also move **miniMe** around by calling the **walk( )** method or feed **miniMe** by invoking the **eat( )** method. All of that can easily be done for every **Person** object as the entire functionality is wrapped up in the **Person** definition. That's the premise behind OOP: Design a blueprint for a thing, then create objects of that type for the application to manipulate.

Learning the syntax for creating classes in ActionScript is simple, but mastering proper OOP design skills and implementation takes time, just as learning to build a house takes a long time. This is especially true when you start getting into inheritance (see the sidebar). However, ActionScript and Flex have already defined a solid foundation of classes for you—you just need to know how to use them. For example, ActionScript defines a **Date** class. If you create an object of **Date** type named **today**, that object can be used to tell you the current day, month, year, day of the week, hour, minute, second, and even milliseconds. Very little new code on your part has a huge payoff.

OOP in ActionScript (and in most languages, but not PHP) uses *dot syntax* to reference an object's properties and methods. Use the object variable's name, followed by a period, followed by the property or method (methods have parentheses after their names): ***objName.propertyName*** and ***objName.methodName( )***. With a **Date** object, you can get the current year by either referencing the property,

tip

The ***Date*** object differs from many in that you can retrieve values by either directly citing the property or by calling an associated method.

today.fullYear

or by calling a method:

today.getFullYear( )

Hopefully this syntax looks familiar to you, as I just used it in the section on data binding with **userName.text**. *In fact, every component in MXML is actually a defined ActionScript class.* Therefore, the uses of those components in your applications are objects (instances of classes) and the component properties and methods are object properties and methods. Say you create this **Label** in MXML:

```
<s:Label id="someLabel" text="Hello, OOP!" />
```

What you're really doing is creating an instance of the **Label** ActionScript class. The MXML **id** and **text** attributes are just ways of assigning values to the **id** and **text** attributes defined in the class.

tip

OOP syntax supports (depending upon the language) chaining multiple "dots" together, as in **someObj.someProperty.someThing.someFunction( )**.

In this chapter, in which I cover the basics of programming with ActionScript, you're going to learn the syntax and techniques you need. What you'll also need is knowledge of what properties and methods exist for a given object. You can find a detailed listing of ActionScript's classes and MXML components, and all of their properties and methods, using the Adobe Help system that comes with Flash Builder or by looking online (start with *http://help.adobe.com/en_US/Flex/4.0/UsingSDK/index.html* and *http://help.adobe.com/en_US/FlashPlatform/reference/actionscript/3/*). Knowing how to proceed when you program using Flex is going to greatly depend upon using these and other resources to investigate the available objects.

AN INTRODUCTION TO INHERITANCE

Inheritance is a key concept in object-oriented programming, providing real advantages that procedural programming can't match. OOP is all about creating blueprints, called classes, for something, then creating instances of those classes, called objects. Inheritance takes this idea further, basing some blueprints on other blueprints. By doing so, you can use the thought and effort that went into developing the primary class, but tweak the definition to your needs.

For example, cats, dogs, horses, and other animals can all be pets. As pets, they have a lot in common: They have names, they eat, they sleep, they speak (make a sound), and so forth. Instead of defining separate **Cat**, **Dog**, and other classes, an application might start with a generic **Pet** class that defines the key, common elements to all of these. The **Cat**, **Dog**, and other classes would first be defined as an extension of **Pet**, which is to say they inherit their behaviors from that other class. If the **Pet** class has a **name** property and **Cat** extends **Pet**, then **Cat** has a **name** property, too. If the **Pet** class has an **eat( )** method and **Dog** extends **Pet**, then **Dog** has an **eat( )** method, too. In this scenario, **Pet** is a parent or superclass and **Cat** and **Dog** are children or subclasses.

But these animals differ from each other as well: Cats meow, dogs fetch things, horses can be ridden. To address these differences, subclasses can define their own properties and methods, like **Dog** might have a **fetch( )** function. And subclasses can even alter the functionality created in the parent class. This is called *overriding* a method: where the child class defines alternate functionality for a method defined in the parent.

MXML has an elaborate hierarchy, which I try to avoid talking about too much in this book (because it can be confusing), but is readily apparent in the official documentation. For example, the Spark **Label** class is actually an extension of the **TextBase** class, which is an extension of **UIComponent**, which is an extension of... In terms of this chapter, what you need to understand about inheritance is that some aspects of an object—its properties and/or its methods—won't be defined within its class, but rather inherited from a superclass. The official documentation distinguishes between inherited and original properties and methods as well.

ACTIONSCRIPT AND MXML

There are a couple of ways to write ActionScript in a Flex application. You've already seen one option: putting it within the properties of components. This is quite common when handling events, discussed in the next chapter (and just slightly later on in this one). But this approach is best for short pieces of ActionScript, like a single instruction. When you have larger blocks of code to add to an MXML file, you can place it within **Script** tags:

```
<fx:Script>
<![CDATA[
// ActionScript goes here!
]]>
</fx:Script>
```

Note that **Script** is defined within the Flex Core components namespace, *fx*. This namespace isn't used in the first two chapters, although Flash Builder adds **fx:Declarations** tags to the default MXML file.

note

The ***Script*** tags must be a direct child of ***Application*** (or ***WindowedApplication*** for AIR development). Do not place them within other components.

Also, you should surround your code with the **<![CDATA[** and **]]>** tags. Because the MXML file is XML, many characters commonly found within ActionScript will be invalid when the XML interpreter looks at the page. By wrapping the ActionScript within those tags, the ActionScript code will be ignored by the XML interpreter.

A second way to add ActionScript to a Flex application is to store it in a separate text file. There are two primary benefits to going this route. First, it makes it easier to navigate and develop your application, with content in multiple files, saving you from searching through increasingly large and complex MXML documents for any particular code. The second benefit is that once you've separated some ActionScript into another file, you can easily reuse it in other projects. Although it's considered to be a best practice to write your ActionScript in a separate file, most of the examples in this book will not do so, for the sake of simplicity.

tip

The more complex the application, the more files it should contain. Strive for clear separation of logic and presentation. Part 3 of the book will cover more techniques for doing so.

A separate ActionScript file can then be included by, or imported into, the MXML document. From a functional standpoint, *including* an ActionScript file has the same effect as if the code were inserted directly into the MXML. *Importing* an ActionScript file is different, but before talking about that, let's look at what happens behind the scenes.

The Compilation Process

ActionScript is an object-oriented programming language, as already stated. This means that everything is defined within classes, and then objects are created as needed, based upon those class definitions. What's not obvious, though, is that MXML itself is written in ActionScript. When you go to use, say, a **TextInput**, you're actually creating an object of **TextInput** type, based upon the **TextInput** class definition that comes with the Flex framework. But the Flex OOP paradigm doesn't stop there...

When you compile an application, the compiler takes the default MXML file and turns that into an ActionScript class definition as well. The ***ProjectName*.mxml** file becomes a ***ProjectName*** class, and the application itself is an instance of that class.

It's good to have an understanding of this process as it impacts what you can do where. ActionScript placed within, or included through, the **Script** tags becomes part of the default class created from the MXML file. Variables defined within those tags become properties of the MXML class; functions defined there become the MXML class's methods. For this reason, there are limits as to what kinds of programming you can do within the **Script** tags. Most of the code will be placed within function definitions, although there are a few exceptions you'll see, like declaring variables. Most importantly, you *cannot* define a class in code within or *included* by **Script** tags because you cannot define a class within a class (and the MXML file becomes a class). Conversely, you *must* define a class for code that's going to be *imported* into an application.

Including ActionScript

Here's how you go about including a separate ActionScript document:

1. Create a new, plain-text file in your text editor or IDE.

   If you create this using Flash Builder, you'll want to create a new ActionScript File, not a new ActionScript Class (**Figure 3.3**).

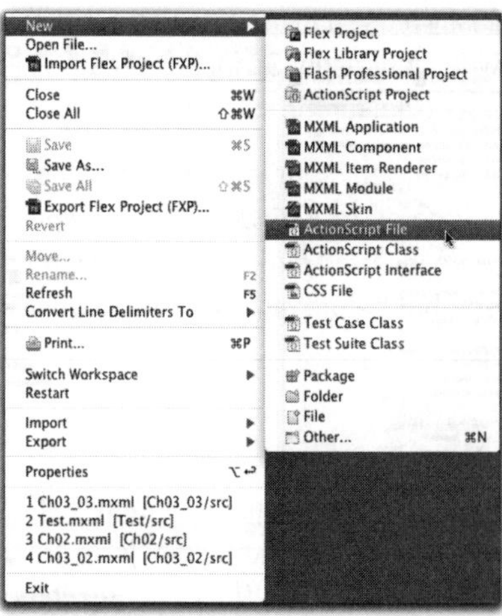

Figure 3.3

2. Add your ActionScript code.

   You just write your code within the file. Do not use **Script** tags! And do not define any classes.

3. Save the file as **something.as**.

   The name should be meaningful, but it's very important that you do not use the same name for the ActionScript file (minus the extension) that you have for the project itself. If you do so, you'll see an error when you go to compile the application.

   You'll also want to put the ActionScript file within an appropriate directory, such as **scripts** or **actionscript** or **as**. Different developers do different things, but you'd likely create the ActionScript directory within your project's **src** folder.

4. In your MXML file, add a **Script** tag:

   <fx:Script />

   Instead of using separate opening and closing tags, you can just close the opening tag, as no code will be entered here.

5. Add a **source** property to the tag, referencing the ActionScript file already created:

   <fx:Script source="*path/to/filename*.as" />

   You include an ActionScript file by using it as the **source** value in the opening **Script** tag. You'll need to change the *path/to/filename.as* to match your project's structure and names. For example, if you have the organization portrayed in **Figure 3.4**, the code to include **something.as** from **Test.mxml** would be:

   <fx:Script source="scripts/something.as" />

   This would also work:

   <fx:Script source="../scripts/something.as" />

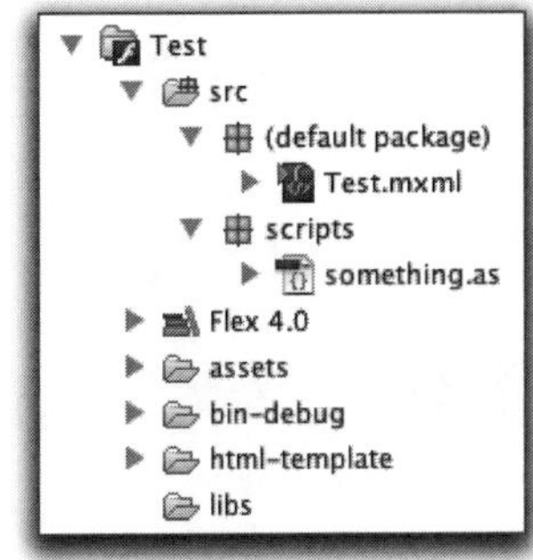

Figure 3.4

That's all there is to including an ActionScript file. If you have multiple ActionScript files to include, you'd use multiple **Script** tags. If you want to include an ActionScript file and place some ActionScript within the MXML document, you'll also need multiple **Script** tags. You cannot use a **Script** tag to both include an external file and to write code.

Importing ActionScript

Importing ActionScript into an MXML file has different rules than including it. Whereas an included file cannot define a class, an imported one *must* define a class. I'm not going to get into hard-core OOP here, but the syntax for creating a class is simple:

```
public class ClassName {
    // Class definition.
}
```

The word public in the class definition has big implications as to how the class can be used. In time, I'll explain what this means, but for now just use public there.

It's conventional to use an initial capital letter for the class's name, and CamelCase from there on out: *ClassName*, not *className* or *class Name*. Class names are normally restricted to just letters, although that's not a formal limitation.

The ActionScript file's name must match the name of the class, with an **.as** extension: **ClassName.as**. But there's more to know...

The classes you define are normally organized within *packages*. You can think of packages as a collection of one or more similar classes. For example, the Flex framework contains the **spark.components** package, with the following classes (among others): **Application**, **Button**, **Group**, **Label**, and **RichEditableText**. Hopefully, those all look familiar to you by now.

To put a class within a package, use

```
package packageName {
    public class ClassName {
        // Class definition.
    }
}
```

tip

Each class in a package must have a unique name.

Each package name identifies a specific collection, and multiple classes are likely to be part of the same collection. The reverse-domain syntax is recommended for identifying packages. For example, my company's name is DMC Insights, so I might use *com.dmcinsights.gaming* as the package for part of my theoretical online game (applications can use multiple packages, too). Two of the classes in that game would be defined, in separate files, like so:

```
package com.dmcinsights.gaming {
    public class Person {
        // Class definition.
    }
}
```

and

```
package com.dmcinsights.gaming {
    public class Place {
        // Class definition.
    }
}
```

Once you've created your ActionScript files, they must also be organized properly (if they use packages). If the package name is *com.example.something*, you would store those class definition files—**Person.as** and **Place.as** for the above—in **/src/com/example/something**, where the initial slash is the application root directory.

If you're using Flash Builder, the File > New > ActionScript Class selection prompts you for the class and package information (**Figure 3.5**). It will create the necessary file and directories.

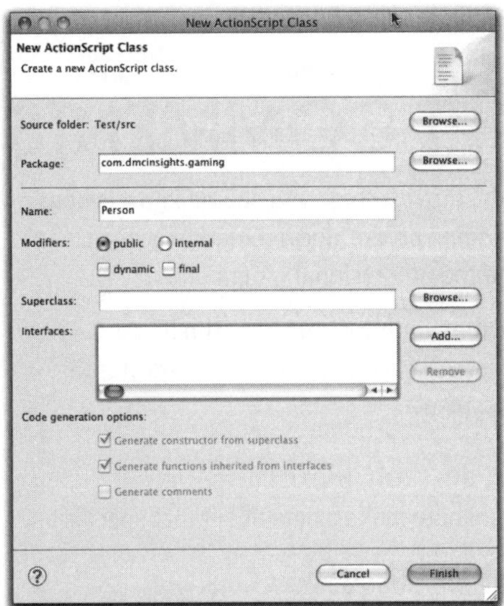

Figure 3.5

To import the ActionScript class files, so that you can create objects of those class types, you use the **import** command and the package and class names *within* the **Script** tags:

```
<fx:Script>
<![CDATA[
import packageName.ClassName;
]]>
</fx:Script>
```

Using the gaming examples, I could import both files this way:

```
<fx:Script>
<![CDATA[
import com.dmcinsights.gaming.Person;
import com.dmcinsights.gaming.Place;
]]>
</fx:Script>
```

Or I could use the wildcard (an asterisk) to include every class defined in a package:

```
<fx:Script>
<![CDATA[
import com.dmcinsights.gaming.*;
]]>
</fx:Script>
```

Now the application has those class definitions available, and can create new objects of those types.

tip

The Flex compiler is pretty smart about imported code. If you import an ActionScript class but don't actually use it, the class will not be incorporated into the compiled SWF file.

ACTIONSCRIPT COMMENTS

Before getting into some actual code, the last thing you should know is how to add comments to your work. Providing proper documentation is one clear difference between the amateur and the professional programmer.

ActionScript supports two syntaxes for creating comments. The first is a single-line comment, created using two slashes. Anything after those two slashes, until the end of the line, will be a comment:

```
// This is a comment.
```

This syntax is also used after a statement to make a note about that specific line:

```
var totalCost:Number; // For storing the order total.
```

(In the next section of the chapter you'll see what the non-comment part of that code means.)

You can create multi-line comments using **/*** to begin the comment and ***/** to end it:

```
/* This comment
can go over
multiple lines. */
```

Multi-line comments are also a useful debugging tool, as I'll explain towards the end of the chapter.

SIMPLE DATA TYPES

Programming is really all about manipulating data. This could include taking it from the user, retrieving it from a database or text file; validating the data; converting it; storing it; etc. How you manipulate data will depend, in part, on the type of data involved. ActionScript has these simple data types:

- **String**, anything quoted
- **Number**, any numeric value
- **int**, integers (whole numbers)
- **uint**, non-negative integers (called "unsigned")
- **Boolean**, *true* or *false* (both words are unquoted)

These are all *scalar* types, which means they only ever store a single value. Note the case of each, with **String**, **Number**, **Boolean** being capitalized while **int** and **uint** are all in lowercase. You'll have to use the exact same case when you reference these types.

A program uses variables to temporarily store data. In ActionScript, you create variables by first *declaring* them with the keyword **var**. The syntax for that is ***access*** **var** ***variableName:type*****;**

Looking at the italicized bits in order, *access* is a somewhat complicated OOP concept. Classes, variables, and functions can all be designated as *public*, *protected*, or *private* (and, technically, *Internal*, which is ActionScript's default value). Each term designates the item's *access control*, which is to say what can be done with the class, variable, or function. Without an understanding of the more sophisticated concepts of inheritance and scope, access control has little meaning. And that's really fine at this point in your ActionScript training. For now, just use **private** for the access control and you'll be fine. In Chapter 10, "Creating Custom Code," you'll learn more about these terms.

The variable's name can consist of letters, numbers, underscores, and the dollar sign but cannot begin with a number. Variable names are case-sensitive in ActionScript, meaning that **userName** and **username** are two different, and confusing, entities.

The variable's type will come from the above list, or be one of the more complex data types I discuss later in the chapter.

 tip

ActionScript allows you to omit a specific variable type when you create it by using * instead of the actual type. Using a specific type is always best, however.

TYPECASTING

Because a variable can only be assigned a value that matches its type, you'll sometimes need to apply *typecasting* to convert values. For example, the following will create an error:

```
var x:Number;
var y:String = '22';
x = y;
```

Since the value assigned to **y** is quoted, it's a string and cannot be directly assigned to **x**. To convert the value from the string '22' to the number 22, use a **Number** object as an agent:

```
var x:Number;
var y:String = '22';
x = Number(y);
```

Here, then, are declarations for three variables of different types:

```
private var me:String;
private var quantity:uint;
private var canPlay:Boolean;
```

tip

There's an argument to be made that for best performance, you should use ***int*** for whole numbers, not ***uint***, even if the variable cannot be negative. I still use ***uint*** in this book to be precise.

Simple variables are assigned values using the equals sign (which is the assignment operator), followed by the value. The value being assigned must match the type the variable is declared to be. You could not assign a number to a string or vice versa. Assuming these variables have been declared as above, here they are assigned values:

```
me = 'Larry Ullman';
quantity = 14;
canPlay = true;
```

If you want, you can declare a variable and set its value (i.e., *initialize* it) in one step:

private var *variableName*:*type* = *value*;
private var me:String = 'Larry Ullman';
private var quantity:uint = 14;
private var canPlay:Boolean = false;

There's a lot you can do with a variable, as you'll see throughout the chapter. Much of the power will come from the object-oriented nature of the language. Whereas in PHP, a string is just a string, in ActionScript, a string is an object, with pre-defined capabilities. For a string in particular, the **length** property reflects the number of characters in the string and the **substring()** method can be used to pull out parts of the string. To find out more about what an object can do, check out the ActionScript documentation. For example, the language reference for the **String** data type can be found at *http://help.adobe.com/en_US/FlashPlatform/reference/actionscript/3/String.html*. On that page, you will see that the **length** property stores an integer representing the number of characters in the string and that the **toUpperCase()** method returns the string in all uppercase letters.

Making Variables Bindable

There's one more thing you should know when it comes to declaring variables: how to make them *bindable*. In the first section of this chapter I discuss data binding, where the value of a property is based upon some other thing. In those examples, a component's **text** property was derived from another component. But you can tie components to variables as well. To do so, ActionScript needs to be informed of your intent to use the variable in this way. That's done by prefacing the variable's declaration with **[Bindable]**:

```
[Bindable]
private var cost:Number;
```

Now **cost** can be used as a bindable object, as in

```
<mx:FormItem label="Cost">
    <s:TextInput text="{cost}"/>
</mx:FormItem>
```

You can initialize the variable and see for yourself how this works. **Figure 3.6** shows the result of running the following code:

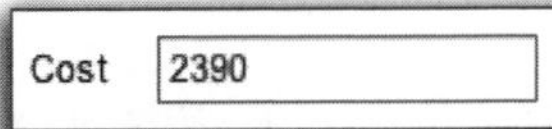

Figure 3.6

```
<?xml version="1.0" encoding="utf-8"?>
<s:Application xmlns:fx="http://ns.adobe.com/mxml/2009"
    xmlns:s="library://ns.adobe.com/flex/spark"
    xmlns:mx="library://ns.adobe.com/flex/mx">
    <fx:Script>
        <![CDATA[
            [Bindable]
            private var cost:Number = 2390.00;
        ]]>
    </fx:Script>
```

code continues on next page

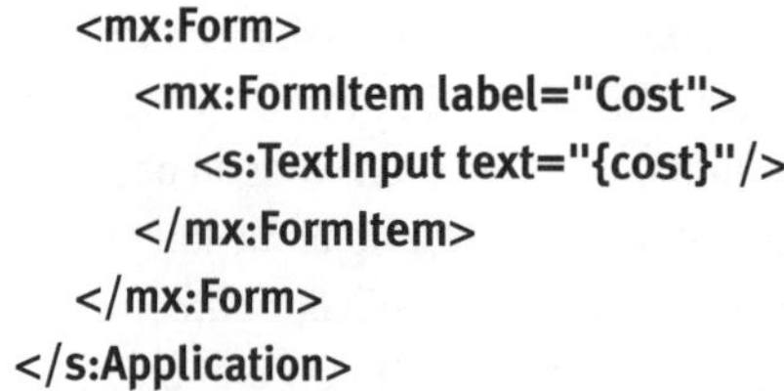

```
    <mx:Form>
        <mx:FormItem label="Cost">
            <s:TextInput text="{cost}"/>
        </mx:FormItem>
    </mx:Form>
</s:Application>
```

If the value of **cost** changes during the execution of the program, the **TextInput** would be quickly updated automatically.

tip

The ***[Bindable]*** code is an example of a metadata tag: information used to describe other data.

Note that for every variable you want to bind, you have to preface it with **[Bindable]**:

```
[Bindable]
private var cost:Number;
[Bindable]
private var quantity:uint;
```

Constants

Whereas a variable stores data that can be changed by the application, a constant stores data that cannot be changed. Constants can be of the same simple types as variables, but there are four differences in the syntax for creating them:

tip

Constants can also have a defined access control; use ***private*** until you know you're in a situation where you'd want to do otherwise.

- Instead of using the **var** keyword, use **const**.
- A constant's name is written in all uppercase, conventionally using underscores to separate words.
- Constants *must* be assigned a value when they are declared.
- Constants cannot be marked as bindable.

This last fact makes sense if you think about it, as the purpose of binding one thing to another is to reflect any changes that occur. As a constant cannot change, there's no point in binding to it.

tip

Constants can be used to represent any simple data type, not just numbers, but they are commonly used in place of numbers.

With all of that in mind, here's the complete syntax:

```
private const TAX_RATE:Number = .0575;
```

Constants are normally used in place of "magic numbers": Applications will make use of significant numbers, like the value of Pi, or the ratios used to convert one unit to another (like inches to centimeters). Using the numbers themselves can be confusing when you look at the code. And, if the number ever needs to be changed, it can be tedious going through lots of code to find and replace each occurrence. Conversely, if you use a constant, you'll have a textual description of the value instead, and a single change will update the entire program.

Operators

Table 3.1 lists the bulk of the operators available in ActionScript.

Table 3.1 ActionScript Operators

Operator	Use	Type
+	addition	arithmetic
-	subtraction	arithmetic
*	multiplication	arithmetic
/	division	arithmetic
%	modulus	arithmetic
++	increment	arithmetic
--	decrement	arithmetic
&&	and	logical
||	or	logical
!	not	logical
==	equals	comparison
!=	not equals	comparison
===	identical	comparison
!==	not identical	comparison
<	less than	comparison
>	greater than	comparison
<=	less than or equal to	comparison
>=	greater than or equal to	comparison

The arithmetic operators are used in mathematical calculations:

```
private var quantity:uint = 5;
private var price:Number = 19.95;
private const PAYMENTS:uint = 12;
private var monthlyPayment:Number = (quantity * price) / PAYMENTS;
```

A common programmer error involves mistakenly using the assignment operator (a single equals sign) in place of the equality comparison operator (two equals signs), or vice versa.

Modulus, in case you're not familiar with it, returns the remainder of a division.

Table 3.2 Operator Precedence

Operators
[] () new
x++ x--
++x --x !
* / %
+ -
< > <= >=
== != === !==
&&
||
= += -= *= /=

You'll notice in the above code that I used parentheses to make sure that the arithmetic was performed as intended. Conversely, you could memorize the precedence order of the operators and rely upon that. **Table 3.2** lists operators from highest to lowest precedence, with many operators having the same level of precedence. For example, multiplication takes precedence over addition, but addition and subtraction have the same precedence. (I've included a few operators that you haven't seen yet, but will, in this chapter.)

There are also two incremental operators that are very important: **++** and **--**. The former increases the value of a number by 1; the latter decreases the value of a number by 1. Both can be used in a prefix (**++x**) and a postfix (**x++**) form, the difference being in precedence.

The logical operators and (**&&**), or (**||**), and not (**!**) are often used to create conditionals, as you'll see later in the chapter. The same goes for the many comparison operators.

There's one more operator to highlight not listed above. The concatenation operator (a plus sign) is used to join strings together, appending one to the end of the next:

```
private var firstName:String = 'Larry';
private var lastName:String = 'Ullman';
private var fullName:String = firstName + ' ' + lastName;
```

CREATING FUNCTIONS

tip

Functions defined inside of classes are formally called methods. In this section, I'm going to mostly use the term function, because: A) the ***function*** keyword is used, and, B) it's not obvious that these functions are being defined within a class.

The code to this point in the chapter has been necessarily out of context to a degree. As I explain earlier in the chapter, all of the code you write will end up inside of a class. Even if you just write code within the **Script** tags, or a file included by a **Script** tag, that code goes within the primary application class that the compiler generates. And in classes, aside from a few exceptions (like declaring variables), all of the action has to occur inside of a function. But creating functions is really rather simple.

The syntax for creating a function is

```
access function functionName(parameters):type {
    // Function statements.
}
```

From its lack of italics, you can see that only one word is set in stone: **function**. Looking at the others, in order, I've already discussed access in the section on variables. This is going to be one of three values—**public**, **protected**, and **private**, but I recommend you just use **private** until further notice.

The function's name can consist of letters, numbers, and the underscore. Conventionally, only letters are used, starting with a lowercase letter, and CamelCase breaks up the words: *functionName*, not *FunctionName* or *functionname*.

The parameters are completely optional but, if present, allow you to provide information to a function when the function is called. For example, the **String** class's **toUpperCase()** method, which returns the string in capital letters, does not take any arguments:

```
private var quiet:String = 'hello';
private var loud:String = quiet.toUpperCase(); // HELLO
```

On the other hand, the **String** class's **replace()** method takes two arguments—the character(s) to find in the string and the character(s) to replace the found sequence with:

```
private var greeting:String = 'hello';
private var gelatin:String = greeting.replace('h', 'J'); // Jello
```

To define a function so that it takes arguments, you declare variables by name and type (but without the **var** keyword) within those parentheses:

```
private function greetSomeone(userName:String, greeting:String):Type {
    // Do whatever.
}
```

The function would then be called like so:

```
greetSomeone('Zoe', 'Good morning');
greetSomeone('Sam', 'Good day');
```

Arguments can be given default values by assigning them to the variables in the function definition:

```
public function greetSomeone(userName:String, greeting:String =
'Hello'):Type {
    // Do whatever.
}
```

This version of the function can be called in two different ways:

```
greetSomeone('Sam');
greetSomeone('Zoe', 'Good day');
```

In the first case, since no second argument was provided, the default greeting of *Hello* will be used. In the second use, the default greeting will be overridden with *Good day*.

Finally, there's the function's *type*. Just as variables can be defined as a certain type using the *:type* syntax, functions are defined as *returning* a certain type of value. If the function does not return any value, its type is **void**:

```
private function doNothing( ):void {
}
```

For a function to return a value, use the **return** keyword. The returned value can be a literal or, more likely, the value of a variable. This function takes one or two string arguments, and returns them concatenated together:

```
private function greetSomeone(userName:String, greeting:String =
'Hello'):String {
    return greeting + ' ' + userName;
}
```

LOOKING AHEAD: THE CLICK EVENT

As I just stated, most of your ActionScript code must be placed within a function definition. This means that you cannot call a function directly within your **Script** tags like so:

```
<fx:Script>
    <![CDATA[
    private function whatever( ):void {
        // Do whatever.
    }
    whatever( ); // Won't work!
    ]]>
</fx:Script>
```

So in order to provide you with a way to see something actually happen in your Flex applications, I'm going to skip ahead to content otherwise covered in the next chapter.

tip

You do not use the curly brackets around the function call as you do with data binding. The value associated with events is assumed to be ActionScript.

Chapter 4, "Event Management," discusses events and event handling in detail, but I'd like you to meet *click*, one of many events that can occur in Flash. Many MXML controls recognize the **click** event. As the programmer, it's up to you to decide what, if anything, should happen when the user clicks a particular control. One possibility is for a function to be called at such a time. To make that connection, assign the function call as the value for the control's **click** property:

```
<s:Button click="someFunction( )" label="Click Me!" />
```

With that in place, when the user clicks the **Button**, the **someFunction()** function will be called, executing whatever statements are therein.

With just this little bit of information, and what you already know from the rest of the chapter, let's create a cost calculator, like one you might have in an e-commerce application (**Figure 3.7**).

1. Create a new Flex project.
2. In your MXML file, create a form:

```
<mx:Form x="50" y="50">
    <mx:FormHeading label="Widget Cost Calculator" fontSize="18"/>
</mx:Form>
```

   This is the start of the form, with a heading.

3. Within the form, add a **Label** to show the price:

```
<mx:FormItem label="Price">
    <s:Label text="{PRICE}"/>
</mx:FormItem>
```

   The price will be hard-coded into the application (you generally don't want end users being able to change how much they pay for something!). Its value will come from a constant named **PRICE**. That will be defined in a **Script** block in a few steps.

4. Add a **NumericStepper** for the quantity:

```
<mx:FormItem label="Quantity">
    <s:NumericStepper id="quantity" minimum="1"/>
</mx:FormItem>
```

   The **NumericStepper** control provides a small text box and some arrows for the user to select a whole number value (any non-negative integer). It's perfect for situations like this. Note that the control is given an **id** value of *quantity*.

5. Add a **TextInput** for the tax rate:

```
<mx:FormItem label="Tax Rate %">
    <s:TextInput id="taxRate" width="30"/>
</mx:FormItem>
```

   To make things a bit more interesting, the form takes the applicable tax rate as a percent. The control's **id** value is *taxRate*.

6. Create a button that will call a function:

```
<s:Button label="Calculate Total" click="calculateTotal()"/>
```

   When this button is clicked, the **calculateTotal()** function will be called. That function does all the work.

tip

If you download the source code from the corresponding Web site (*www.dmcinsights.com/flex4*), you'll find this code in the **Ch03/Ch03_01** folder.

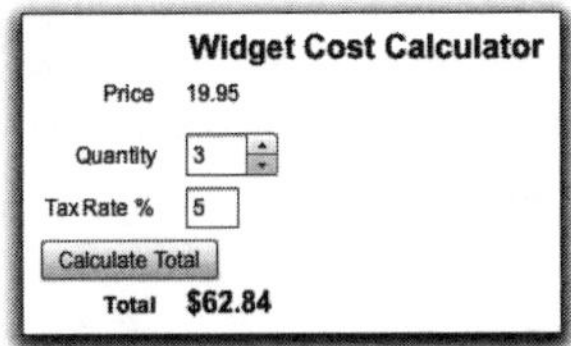

Figure 3.7

7. Create a **Label** to display the total:

```
<mx:FormItem label="Total" fontWeight="bold">
  <s:Label id="displayTotal" fontWeight="bold" fontSize="16"/>
</mx:FormItem>
```

The **Label** starts with no initial text value, but is given an **id** of *displayTotal*.

note

It's important that the ***id*** values assigned to MXML components are unique and are not the same as any variables used within the ActionScript code.

8. Create a pair of **Script** tags:

```
<fx:Script>
  <![CDATA[
  ]]>
</fx:Script>
```

It actually doesn't matter where in the MXML file you write these, so long as **Script** is a direct descendent (i.e., child) of the **Application** tag. My inclination is to write it just after the opening **Application** tag.

9. Define a constant that stores the price:

```
private const PRICE:Number = 19.95;
```

The constant is a private number named **PRICE**, set to a value of 19.95. This constant will be used both in the form (see Step 3) and in the **calculateTotal( )** function.

10. Begin defining the **calculateTotal( )** function:

```
private function calculateTotal( ):void {
```

This function will be called whenever the **Button** is clicked. It's a private function that returns nothing (hence, the **void**).

11. Begin the calculations:

```
var total:Number = PRICE * quantity.value;
total += ( (Number(taxRate.text)/100) * total );
```

To start, a new variable is defined that will only exist within this function (because it's only declared within it). This variable is first assigned a value of the price (represented by the constant) times the value of the **quantity NumericStepper**.

note

Variables declared within functions do not need access control modifiers (***public***, ***protected***, or ***private***) as the variables only exist within the function.

Next, some fancy math takes place in order to factor in the tax rate. This value will be entered by the user in the **taxRate TextInput**. It should be a percentage, like 5 or 6.75. To determine what the total is with the tax, you add to the total (the **+=** is the addition-assignment operator) the tax rate divided by 100 times the current total. So if ten widgets are being purchased with a 5% tax rate, the total of the price times the quantity is 199.5. The tax rate divided by 100 is .05. That number—.05—times the total—199.5—equals 9.975. This is added to the total, so that after these two lines, the **total** variable would equal 209.475.

One catch here is that the **TextInput** value will be a string, not a number. To convert it to a usable number, **taxRate.text** is typecasted using syntax outlined in an earlier sidebar. This wasn't necessary with the **quantity NumericStepper**, as that value is a number already.

12. Format the number:

    total = Math.round(total * 100)/100;

    To address the possibility of more than two decimal places in the number (as in 209.475), I multiply the total times 100 (to get 20947.5), then call the **Math** class's **round()** method to round it off to the nearest integer (20948). Then I divide this by 100 to get my decimals back (209.48).

tip

In Chapter 6, "Manipulating Data," you'll learn a better way to format numbers, but this method will work for now. It does not guarantee two decimal places, though.

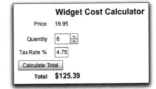

13. Assign the total to the **displayTotal Label**:

    displayTotal.text = '$' + String(total);

    Finally, the **text** property of the **displayTotal Label** will be assigned a value of a dollar sign plus the calculated total. As that total is a number, it should be typecasted to a string to be used as the **text** value.

14. Complete the function:

    }

15. Save and run the project (**Figure 3.8**).

    Now do a little dance, for you are a full-fledged Flex developer, with a mastery of MXML and ActionScript! Okay, maybe not a *mastery*, but you've got a good couple of steps down already.

Widget Cost Calculator
Price 19.95
Quantity 6
Tax Rate % 4.75
Calculate Total
Total $125.39

Figure 3.8

CONTROL STRUCTURES

Like any programming language, ActionScript has the standard control structures: conditionals and loops. I'll address loops separately later in the chapter and focus on conditionals here. The most basic conditional looks like this:

```
if (condition) {
    // Do whatever.
}
```

The condition can be any statement or combination of statements that can be evaluated as either true or false. This normally involves some combination of the logical and comparison operators already listed, or perhaps some object methods. For example:

```
if (showResults == true) {
    // Show the results.
}
```

or

```
if (password.length < 6) {
    // Password is too short!
}
```

The **if** conditional can take an optional **else** clause. The statements in the **else** clause will be executed if the primary condition is false:

```
if (condition) {
    // Do this.
} else {
    // Do this instead.
}
```

Here is an example:

```
if ( (age > 12) && (age < 20) ) {
    teenager = true;
} else {
    teenager = false;
}
```

By adding **else if** clauses (note: **else if** is written as two separate words), you can have multiple conditions:

```
if (condition) {
    // Do this.
} else if (another condition) {
    // Do this instead.
} else if (yet another condition) {
    // How about this?
}
```

If the first condition is evaluated as true, the following statement(s) will be executed. Otherwise the next condition is checked. The process is repeated until the end of the construct. If an **else** clause exists, and it must always come last (if present), that will take effect if no condition is found to be true.

Say you wanted to vary the price of something based upon how many are being ordered (represented by the **quantity** variable):

```
if (quantity >= 10) {
    price = 15.00
} else if (quantity >= 5) {
    price = 17.00
```

```
} else if (quantity >= 2) {
    price = 19.00
} else {
    price = 20.00
}
```

If **quantity** is 20, then the first condition is true. If it's 7, then the first is false but the second is true. If **quantity** is 1, then the three conditions are false and the **else** applies.

Syntactically, the opening and closing curly braces are only required if more than one statement is the result of an **if**, **else if**, or **else**. You *can* get away with

```
if (condition)
    // Do this one thing.
```

However, I would highly recommend always using the curly braces. I believe that by doing so, you'll make your code more legible and minimize the potential for bugs.

A prolonged **if-else if-else** conditional can be written as a **switch** instead. That syntax is

```
switch (thing) {
    case valueA:
        // Do whatever.
        break;
    case valueB:
        // Do this instead.
        break;
    default:
        // How about this?
        break;
}
```

A **switch** is most often used to compare a simple variable against multiple possible values. Those values would be quoted if strings, and unquoted if numeric. In a **switch**, when a match is made, the subsequent statements are executed, up until the **break**. For this reason, you must use **break**s. The **default** case acts like an **else** clause. Similarly, it is optional but must come last if present.

The following two constructs are functionally equivalent:

```
switch (gender) {
    case 'M':
        // Male
        break;
    case 'F':
        // Female
        break;
    default:
        // Nothing selected
        break;
}
```

and

```
if (gender == 'M') {
    // Male
} else if (gender == 'F') {
    // Female
} else {
    // Nothing selected
}
```

Whether you use a **switch** is largely personal preference, but it's most often used in place of an extended **if-else if** conditional with lots of **else if** clauses.

SPECIAL VALUES

ActionScript has a number of special keywords you'll come across, especially in conditionals. I'm thinking of **void**, **undefined**, **null**, and **NaN**. You've already seen **void**: It's used to indicate that a function does not return a value, but **void** generally represents nothingness. Perhaps confusingly, **undefined** is the value of **void**. In reality, **void** is just another simple data type, but the only value it can ever have is **undefined**.

A **String** variable, as well as more complex data types you haven't yet seen, that haven't been assigned values have a value of **null**, which is to say no known value. If a **Number** variable does not have a numeric value, its value will be **NaN** instead, short for *not a number*. This will be true if it hasn't yet been assigned a value or some process attempts to assign a non-numeric value to it.

In short, **void**, **undefined**, **null**, and **NaN** are all ways of saying nothing, but each is used in its own particular way. In a conditional, you might see things like

```
if (firstName != null) {...
```

or

```
if (someNum == NaN) {...
```

To test if a number is not a number, you can also use the **isNaN( )** method:

```
if (isNaN(someNum)) {...
```

ARRAYS

Arrays are a powerful mainstay of any programming language. Unlike strings and numbers, which represent only a single value, arrays can store lists of values, even of different types. Because an array contains multiple values (or *elements*), they use a different syntax to add and retrieve any individual value. Whereas a variable like **fullName** might represent a single string, the array variable **team** might represent a dozen strings at once (i.e., the names of the people on the team).

An array can be created by making a new object of type **Array**:

```
private var someArray:Array = new Array( );
```

This is a standard OOP construct for creating an object. The variable name is **someArray** and it's an object of type **Array**. It is created as a new, empty array by using the **Array** class as its model.

tip

You can create a new, empty string using ***var someString: String = new String( )***, although it's just not commonly done.

With an existing array variable, you can add elements to the array by "pushing" them onto the list:

```
someArray.push(value);
```

The values can be strings, in which case they'd be quoted, numbers, or even other arrays (creating a multidimensional array). The **push( )** method adds the new values to the end of the array. You can add new values to the front of the list, bumping the others back, by calling the **unshift( )** method:

```
someArray.unshift(value);
```

To remove an item from an array, use **pop( )** to remove the value found at the end of the list and **shift( )** to remove the item found at the beginning. Here's a quick example of this, with the array's contents indicated in the comments:

```
private var numbers:Array = new Array( ); // null
numbers.push(1); // 1
numbers.push(2); // 1, 2
numbers.unshift(3); // 3, 1, 2
numbers.pop( ); // 3, 1
numbers.shift( ); // 1
```

To create an array and populate it at once, you can use this syntax:

```
private var someArray:Array = new [value1, value2, ...];
```

The use of square brackets is shorthand for **Array**. Again, the values would be quoted if strings, not quoted if numeric:

```
private var someArray:Array = new [1, 2, 3];
```

To access individual values within an array, you use its *index* or *key*. Each value stored in an array has a key-value association: Reference the key and you get the associated value.

Arrays can be indexed using numbers or strings. A numerically indexed array has its first element (or value) at 0. If you populate an array without establishing the keys, ActionScript will automatically number the elements for you:

```
private var groceries:Array = new Array( );
groceries.push('apples');
groceries.push('kiwi');
```

At this point, the **groceries** array contains two elements. To reference a specific element, follow the array's name with the key between square brackets: **groceries[0]** is *apples*.

You can also name the key for a new element when it's added by again using the square brackets:

```
groceries[2] = 'passion fruit';
```

Using this syntax for adding elements, you can use strings as the keys, too:

```
private var meals:Array = new Array( );
meals['breakfast'] = 'Waffles';
meals['lunch'] = 'Grilled Cheese Sandwiches';
```

To later retrieve an individual element, use the same key:

```
lunchLabel.text = meals['lunch'];
```

When an array uses strings for its indexes, it's called an *associative array*. In such cases, it's important to know that the stored values are not in any meaningful order. The only meaning is in the key-value associations.

Whether the keys of an array are numbers or strings, all indexes must be unique. Attempting to add an element using an existing key just replaces the value stored there:

```
groceries[0] = 'bananas'; // Replaces 'apples'
meals['breakfast'] = 'Pancakes'; // Replaces 'Waffles'
```

An interesting trick with associative arrays in ActionScript is that you can also create them as generic **Object** types and then use dot syntax to create individual elements or retrieve their values:

```
private var thisBook:Object = new Object( );
thisBook.title = 'Effortless Flex 4 Development';
thisBook.writer = 'Larry Ullman';
private var citation:String = thisBook.title + ' by ' + thisBook.writer;
```

You can simplify the creation of an **Object** even further using this syntax:

```
private var thisBook:Object = {title:'Effortless Flex 4 Development',
writer:'Larry Ullman'};
```

You'll notice in that syntax that the keys are not quoted, even though they are strings.

To put this information to use, along with the conditionals, let's look at a little demo application for identifying different meal options (**Figure 3.9**). I won't walk you through creating it in detail, but I'll explain the important bits.

1. Create a new project in Flash Builder or your alternative text editor or IDE.

   I'll leave it up to you to create the initial XML declaration, the Application element, and the other basic stuff.

2. Create a simple form.

```
<mx:Form x="50" y="50">
    <mx:FormHeading label="Meal Options"/>
    <mx:FormItem label="Meal">
        <s:DropDownList id="meal">
            <s:ArrayList>
                <fx:String>Breakfast</fx:String>
                <fx:String>Lunch</fx:String>
                <fx:String>Dinner</fx:String>
            </s:ArrayList>
        </s:DropDownList>
    </mx:FormItem>
    <mx:FormItem label="Option">
        <s:TextInput id="option"/>
    </mx:FormItem>
    <s:Button label="Add" click="addMealOption()"/>
    <s:Label id="labelCounter" text="There are currently 0 items
    stored." />
</mx:Form>
```

   The **DropDownList** displays three meal options: *Breakfast*, *Lunch*, and *Dinner* (see the previous chapter for an explanation of this component and **ArrayList**). Its **id** value is *meal*. Then there's a **TextInput** with an **id** value of *option*. The **Button**, when clicked, calls the **addMealOption()** function. And the **labelCounter Label** will be used to display the number of items currently stored. It starts off with an initial display of 0 items stored.

tip

If you download the source code from the corresponding Web site (*www.dmcinsights.com/flex4*), you'll find this code in the **Ch03/Ch03_02** folder.

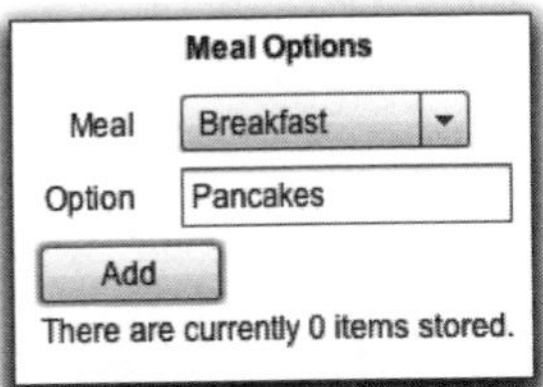

Figure 3.9

tip

In the second part of the book, dealing with data, you'll learn how to use arrays to populate combination boxes and other components.

3. Within a **Script** block, create three variables.

```
private var breakfast:Array = new Array( );
private var lunch:Array = new Array( );
private var dinner:Array = new Array( );
```

The magic happens in the ActionScript, of course. Three arrays are first declared, one for each meal.

4. Start defining the **addMealOption( )** function.

```
private function addMealOption( ):void {
    if (option.text.length > 3) {
```

The first thing the function does is confirm that something was entered into the **TextInput**. My assumption is that any meal option must be more than three characters in length, but you could just check for a non-null value, if you wanted.

5. Create a **switch** conditional.

```
switch (meal.selectedItem) {
    case 'Breakfast':
        breakfast.push(option.text);
        break;
    case 'Lunch':
        lunch.push(option.text);
        break;
    case 'Dinner':
        dinner.push(option.text);
        break;
} // End of switch.
```

A **switch** is used to determine onto which array the new option should be pushed. The value being added to the array is found in **option.text** (i.e., what the user entered into the **TextInput**).

tip

There are many ways you could improve upon this application to make it more professional, but for now rejoice in what you already have the knowledge to do.

6. Update the **Label** to reflect the current count.

```
labelCounter.text = 'There are currently ' + String(breakfast.length +
lunch.length + dinner.length) + ' items stored.';
```

To do this, concatenation is involved, plus some arithmetic, references to each array's **length** property, and that value is typecasted to a string.

7. Complete the **if** conditional and the function.

```
    } // End of IF.
} // End of function.
```

8. Save, run, and test the completed application.

   And that's it. If you enter all this into a new Flex project (or just download the code from the book's corresponding Web site), you can try the application for yourself (**Figure 3.10**).

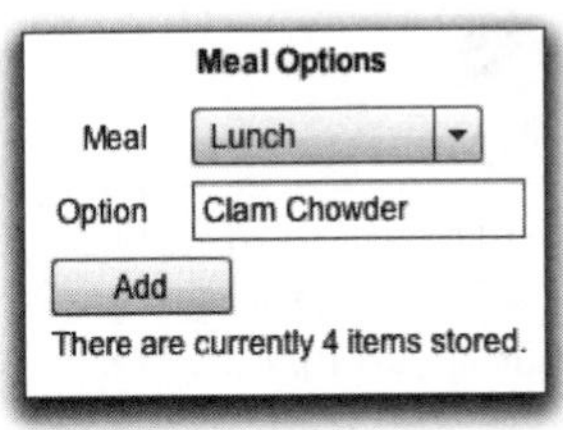

Figure 3.10

Arrays go hand-in-hand with another control structure: loops. Let's look at those next.

LOOPS

Loops are used in programming to perform the same sequence of actions repeatedly. ActionScript supports the two most common loop constructs: **for** and **while**.

for Loops

The **for** loop is generally used to execute a task a known number of times. Its syntax is:

```
for (before statement; condition; after statement) {
    // Do whatever.
}
```

The first time the loop is encountered, the *before* statement is executed. Normally this is used to initialize a counter variable: **var x:uint = 1**. Next, the *condition* is checked. If true, then the statements within the loop will be executed. After those statements are executed, the third statement is run. This is normally used to increment a counter—**x++**—or to otherwise do something that will eventually make the condition false. **Figure 3.11** shows the flow of a **for** loop.

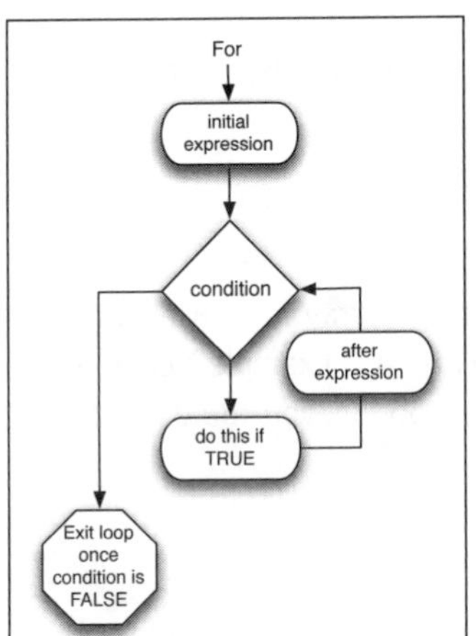

Figure 3.11

tip

It's conventional to use a single-letter variable name for loop counters, like i, j, k, x, y, or z.

note

Because indexed arrays start with a value of 0, you want the condition to be less than the array's length, not less than or equal to.

As a simple example, this first loop counts from 1 to 10, the second from 0 to 100 by 10's:

```
for (var x:uint = 1; x <= 10; x++) {
    // Do whatever.
}
for (var x:uint = 0; x <= 100; x += 10) {
    // Do whatever.
}
```

The **for** loop can also be used to access every element in an indexed array. As indexed arrays begin at 0, you would set the counter to 0. Then you'd want to execute the loop once for every element in the array. That value can be found by referencing the array's **length** property. Within the loop, the index can be used to access a specific array value. Finally, after doing whatever with that value, the index should be incremented:

```
for (var x:uint = 0; x < someArray.length; x++) {
    // Use someArray[x].
}
```

There are two variations on the **for** loop that are also used with arrays. With an associative array, where the keys are strings, a variation on the **for** loop—**for...in**—can be used to retrieve the individual values:

```
for (var k:String in someArray) {
    // Do something with someArray[k].
}
```

With each iteration of the loop, the next key in the array is assigned to the variable **k**. With that information, you can access the value stored at that index by using **someArray[k]**.

If you don't actually need the key and just want the values, use **for each**:

```
for each (var v:String in someArray) {
    // Do something with v.
}
```

In that code, the variable **v** is being assigned a single array value with each iteration. For example, if you wanted to update the code example a couple of pages back so that it displayed every stored meal option, you could iterate through the arrays:

```
for each (var v:String in breakfast) {
    // Use v.
}
```

while Loops

A **while** loop is used to execute something an unknown number of times (i.e., so long as a condition is true). Whereas it's easy to count to a certain number, or know how many values can be found in an array, some operations aren't known up front, like how many records will be returned by a database query or how many values will be in a server response. For these situations, use a **while** loop. It has a much simpler syntax than **for**:

```
while (condition) {
    // Do whatever.
}
```

So long as the condition is true, the statements inside of the **while** loop will be executed. You'll need to make sure that the conditional statement, or something within the **while** loop, will eventually make the condition false. Otherwise you'll end up with an infinite loop.

The **do...while** loop is a variation that will always be executed at least once, as its condition is evaluated at the end of the construct:

```
do {
    // Do whatever.
} while (condition);
```

MANIPULATING COMPONENTS

Throughout this chapter I've discussed using ActionScript to interact with MXML components in simple ways: Click this component and this function is called, update the text of a component to some new value, etc. But you can do far, far more than that with your ActionScript. Most of a component's properties can be altered using ActionScript, meaning that you can do such things as

- Show and hide components by changing their **visible** status
- Move components by changing their **x** and **y** values
- Enable or disable form elements
- Dynamically set the values for lists and menus
- Replace a movie file with another one

and much, much more.

To do these things you just need to have a unique **id** for the components being manipulated and then assign new values to their properties as desired. For example, this next bit of code defines a **Button** that calls a function every time it's clicked. The function moves the **Button** down the application window and to the right, 10 pixels at a time.

```
<fx:Script>
    <![CDATA[
    private function moveMe():void {
        mover.x += 10;
        mover.y += 10;
    }
    ]]>
</fx:Script>
<s:Button x="0" y="0" id="mover" click="moveMe()" label="Move Me!"
/>
```

But you can take this same premise further by using ActionScript to add, or remove, components from the application. To do so, start by importing the appropriate class or package. To create a **Label** on the fly, you'd first import **spark.components.Label**:

```
import spark.components.Label;
```

Or you could just import the whole package:

```
import spark.components.*;
```

Next, create a new object of that type:

```
public function makeLabel():void {
    var myLabel:Label = new Label();
```

Now, assign the values you want to the properties:

```
myLabel.text = 'This is a new label.';
myLabel.x = 20;
myLabel.y = 20;
```

Finally, call the **addElement()** method, *on the parent object,* to add the new component to the application. If you wanted to add the **Label** to a **Panel** that has an **id** of *myPanel*, you'd write

```
myPanel.addElement(myLabel);
```

The item will be added as the last child of the parent. You can specify where the child is added using the **addElementAt()** method. It takes two arguments:

the new object being added and the indexed position, starting at 0, where it should be placed. This line adds the **Label** as the third element in the **Panel**:

```
myPanel.addElementAt(myLabel, 2);
```

You can remove components from an application by calling the **removeElement( )** method on the parent of the component, providing it with the **id** of the element to be dropped:

```
myPanel.removeElement('newLabel');
```

Or you can use **removeElementAt( )** to remove a component by its index. This removes the first child of **myGroup**:

```
myGroup.removeElementAt(0);
```

Or, for dramatic effect, remove every child component using **removeAllElements( )**.

One thing to note is that these methods are all for use on Spark components. Older Halo components use **addChild( )**, **addChildAt( )**, **removeChild( )**, **removeChildAt( )**, and **removeAllChildren( )**. Which functions you use depends upon the *parent* object. Adding a Spark **Label** to a Halo **Form** requires the Halo methods.

Figure 3.12 shows a somewhat trivial use of this information, and a loop. Here's how you can replicate it:

Figure 3.12

tip

If you download the source code from the corresponding Web site (*www.dmcinsights.com/flex4*), you'll find this code in the **Ch03/Ch03_03** folder.

1. Create a new project in Flash Builder or your alternative text editor or IDE.

   Again, I'll leave it up to you to create the initial XML declaration, the Application element, and the other basic stuff.

2. In the MXML file, create a **NumericStepper** and a **Button.**

   ```
   <s:HGroup paddingLeft="15" paddingTop="15">
      <s:Label text="Number of images to add: " />
      <s:NumericStepper id="numImages" minimum="1" />
      <s:Button label="Add Image(s)" click="makeImages( )" />
   </s:HGroup>
   ```

   The **NumericStepper** allows the user to select how many images to add. Its minimum value is 1. The **Button** calls the **makeImages( )** function, which will do the actual work. I've also added a **Label**, to provide some text, and wrapped it all in an **HGroup** to affect the layout.

3. Add a **Group**.

   ```
   <s:Group id="imageGroup">
      <s:layout>
         <s:TileLayout />
      </s:layout>
   </s:Group>
   ```

The **Group** has an **id** of *imageGroup*. This is where the new images will be placed. It uses **TileLayout** so that images are presented in a grid.

4. Within a **Script** block, import the **mx.controls.Image** class, which defines the **Image** component.

   ```
   import mx.controls.Image;
   ```

   Because the ActionScript is going to dynamically create **Image** components, it needs to import this definition first.

5. Begin defining the **makeImages( )** function.

   ```
   public function makeImages( ):void {
       for (var x:uint = 1; x <= numImages.value; x++) {
   ```

   The loop will go from 1 to whatever number the user entered in the **NumericStepper** (whose **id** is *numImages*).

6. Within the loop, create a new **Image** object.

   ```
   var newImage:Image = new Image( );
   newImage.source = '../assets/trixie.jpg';
   ```

   First, the new **Image** is created as a new variable. Then its **source** property is assigned a relative path to the image I want to use:

note

The image's ***source*** property does not use the ***@Embed*** directive because the image is being added at runtime, not when the application is compiled.

7. Finally, add the new component to the group.

   ```
   imageGroup.addElement(newImage);
   ```

8. Complete the **makeImages( )** function.

   ```
   }
   ```

9. Save, run, and test the completed application.

Figures 3.13 and 3.14 show the result after adding one image, then four more.

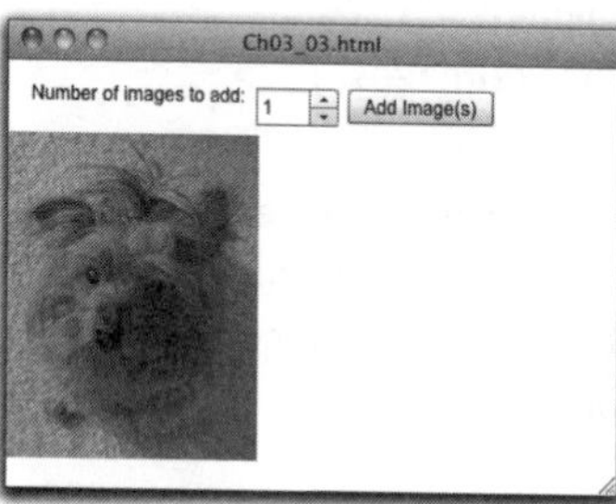

Figure 3.13

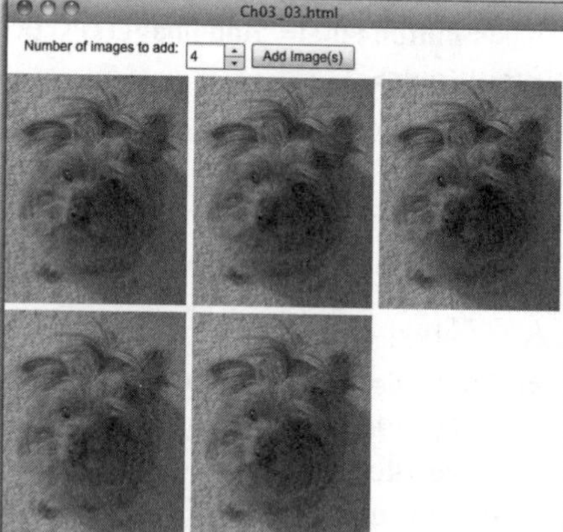

Figure 3.14

DEBUGGING TECHNIQUES

Adding ActionScript to your Flex programs results in a more powerful and interesting application, but it greatly expands the possible causes of bugs and errors. Debugging any programming language is a skill only mastered in time (and by pulling out a lot of hair), but there are a few tips I can provide up front.

For starters, learn how to use the Flash Debug perspective in Flash Builder or Eclipse, if you're using those tools. Unfortunately, this topic is too large to cover here (and much I would say wouldn't make sense at this juncture), but the Flash Debug perspective presents a workbench oriented towards debugging applications (**Figure 3.15**).

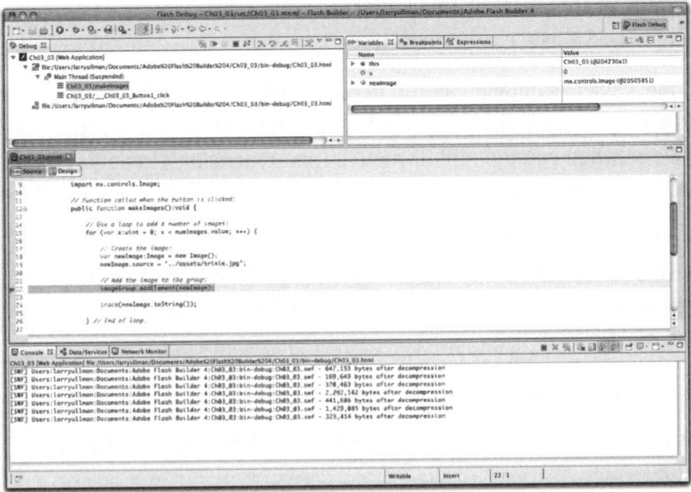

Figure 3.15

Design-related views, like Package Explorer and Components, are hidden, with Debug, Variables, Breakpoints, and Expressions being made visible (the also-useful Console view appears in both perspectives). To make use of some of these, you'll need to select the Run > Debug *ProjectName* option instead of the standard Run. You'll also want to make sure you're using a debug version of the Flash Player to take advantage of some of these views. Note that after starting an application in debug mode, you'll need to click the red square in the Debug panel to exit debug mode.

tip

For more information on the Flash Debug perspective, use the Adobe Help or search the Web.

One useful debugging technique involves breakpoints. In Flash Builder, if you double-click on a line number (the actual number itself), a little blue circle will appear to the left of the number (you can also use the Run menu to add and remove breakpoints). When the application runs, it will stop once the execution gets to that line. If you look at the Variables panel (see Figure 3.15), you can inspect the values of variables at that point in the application's execution. This is a great way to confirm what information the application is dealing with.

With a debug version of the Flash Player, you can have an application communicate with you using **trace( )**. This function takes a simple string as an argument and writes that string to the console. The console is found at the bottom of the workbench in Flash Builder (see Figure 3.15) or is the command-line interface for your operating system when compiling Flex applications that way. With ActionScript it's quite common for your program to do nothing (apparently) when it should do something. To see what's going on behind the scenes, leave yourself messages like:

```
trace('In the something( ) function');
trace('The value of someVar is ' + someVar);
trace('Trying to add a new component.');
```

Make your messages as detailed as you need to help you solve the problem. Sometimes just finding out that a function is not being called, that a conditional is not true when you thought it would be, or what value a variable has is all you need to solve the problem.

If you don't like the command-line **trace( )**, you can have messages appear in an alert window where the application is running (i.e., within the browser, a standalone Flash Player, or an AIR application). First you'll need to import **mx.controls.Alert**:

```
import mx.controls.Alert;
```

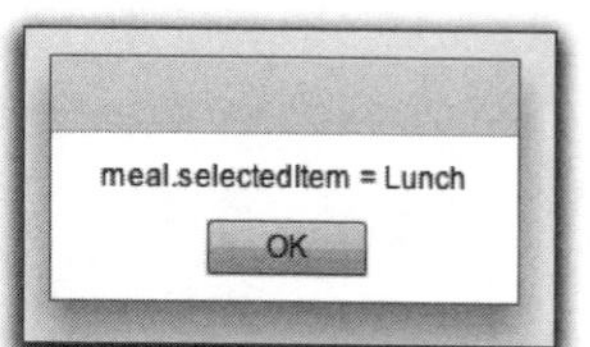

Figure 3.16

Then call **Alert.show( )**, providing it with whatever string should be displayed (**Figure 3.16**):

```
Alert.show('meal.selectedItem = ' + meal.selectedItem);
```

The **trace( )** and alert techniques require that any variables being used as part of the message are strings. If they're not, you can typecast them to strings:

```
Alert.show('someNum = ' + String(someNum));
```

Many objects have a **toString( )** method that serves the same purpose, or otherwise reveals something useful about the object. Or you can use the **mx.utils.ObjectUtil.toString( )** method. It examines an object and returns information about that object as a string:

```
import mx.utils.ObjectUtil;
trace(ObjectUtil.toString(someObj));
```

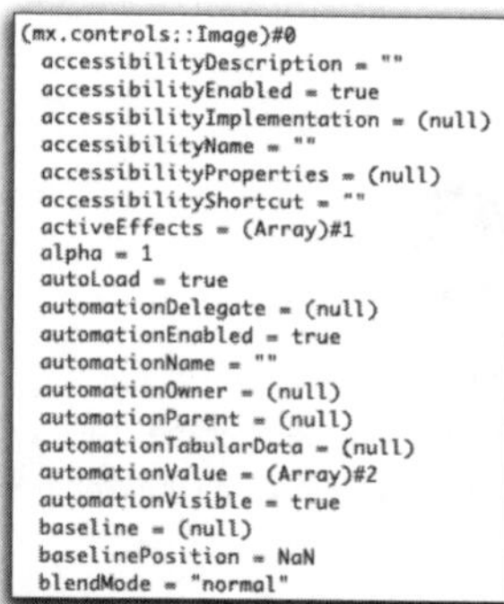

```
(mx.controls::Image)#0
  accessibilityDescription = ""
  accessibilityEnabled = true
  accessibilityImplementation = (null)
  accessibilityName = ""
  accessibilityProperties = (null)
  accessibilityShortcut = ""
  activeEffects = (Array)#1
  alpha = 1
  autoLoad = true
  automationDelegate = (null)
  automationEnabled = true
  automationName = ""
  automationOwner = (null)
  automationParent = (null)
  automationTabularData = (null)
  automationValue = (Array)#2
  automationVisible = true
  baseline = (null)
  baselinePosition = NaN
  blendMode = "normal"
```

Figure 3.17

Figure 3.17 shows just some of the output when examining the **newImage** object used in the previous code example.

Another way to learn about an object is to use *object introspection*. The workhorse involved is the **describeType( )** method, defined within the **flash.utils** package. This method returns information as XML, but that can easily be translated into text:

```
import flash.utils.*;
var info:String = describeType(someObj).toString( );
```

Figure 3.18 shows just some of the output when examining the same **newImage** object using **describeType( )**.

```
<type name="mx.controls::Image" base="mx.controls::SWFLoader" isDynamic="false"
  <extendsClass type="mx.controls::SWFLoader"/>
  <extendsClass type="mx.core::UIComponent"/>
  <extendsClass type="mx.core::FlexSprite"/>
  <extendsClass type="flash.display::Sprite"/>
  <extendsClass type="flash.display::DisplayObjectContainer"/>
  <extendsClass type="flash.display::InteractiveObject"/>
  <extendsClass type="flash.display::DisplayObject"/>
  <extendsClass type="flash.events::EventDispatcher"/>
  <extendsClass type="Object"/>
  <implementsInterface type="mx.core::IChildList"/>
  <implementsInterface type="mx.controls.listClasses::IDropInListItemRenderer"/>
  <implementsInterface type="mx.managers::ILayoutManagerClient"/>
  <implementsInterface type="mx.core::IDeferredInstantiationUIComponent"/>
  <implementsInterface type="mx.core::IUIComponent"/>
  <implementsInterface type="mx.core::ILayoutElement"/>
  <implementsInterface type="mx.styles::IAdvancedStyleClient"/>
  <implementsInterface type="mx.styles::IStyleClient"/>
  <implementsInterface type="mx.styles::ISimpleStyleClient"/>
  <implementsInterface type="mx.core::IFlexDisplayObject"/>
  <implementsInterface type="mx.core::IInvalidating"/>
```

Figure 3.18

Finally, another way to help solve problems in ActionScript is to remove code until the application works as you would expect it to (without that code), and then gradually add back in code until it breaks again. By doing so, you can narrow down the cause of the problem. You could actually cut all the code, then paste it back in, but a better solution is to use multi-line comments to disable sections. When doing so, you just need to make sure you don't break the syntax. For example, this is fine:

```
private function blah( ):void {
/*
   Not going to be executed now!
*/
} // End of function.
```

But this will create a syntax error as the function won't be properly closed:

```
private function blah( ):void {
/*
   Not going to be executed now!
} // End of function.
*/
```

4 EVENT MANAGEMENT

If you've been reading this book sequentially, you should already have a pretty sound sense of the Flex landscape. The first chapter shows how to create applications. The second introduces the basic elements of a user interface. And the third teaches the fundamentals of ActionScript programming. But in order for applications to be truly a user experience (which is to say, *interactive*), you need to know how to manage events. A lot of what applications do is watch for, and respond to, events.

You can develop Flash content using Flash Professional, the old standard, or Flash Builder (previously known as Flex Builder). Flash Professional tends to start with animation that runs over a timeline. Conversely, Flex development is event-driven: The application is told to respond to things that happen. This take may be different than what you've done before, but it's really easy to adopt. If anything, the biggest hurdle will be making the most of what's possible.

Flex uses an event system that's quite close to the Document Object Model (DOM) Level 3 Event Specification present in Web browsers (to varying degrees). What this means is that if you've done a wee bit of JavaScript programming, much of the syntax and theory in this book will be familiar. And even if you haven't, you may be pleasantly surprised to see how obvious much of this information is. For example, can you guess what event represents the cursor going over an element? Yes, *mouseOver*.

The chapter begins with several pages discussing the premise of event management and what pieces are involved. Then you'll learn how to handle events by placing ActionScript code within MXML components. The third section of the chapter walks through using functions to handle events (the functions are called *event handlers* in such circumstances). After that, I discuss the types of events in a bit more detail. The chapter concludes with an alternate way to manage events in an application.

FUNDAMENTAL CONCEPTS

Event-driven development can be summed up as follows: When *this event* occurs with *this thing,* take *these actions*. Just a few examples are

- Fetch some data from a server after the application loads.
- Change the choices in one drop-down menu after the user makes a selection in another (e.g., one drop-down represents car makes, the other car models).
- Reveal a block of information when the user moves the cursor over an image.
- Make new application options available once a network connection is detected.
- Store user-supplied data in a database after the user clicks a button.
- Move some other components around after one is removed.
- Update the contents of a **DataGrid** (a table-like component, introduced in the next chapter) as new information becomes available.

The events are already predefined for you within the framework. Events fall under two categories: system events and user events. System events are not caused by user actions. Specific types include the application being fully loaded (i.e., ready to run), components being created, responses being received (like from a network connection), and so forth. User events are the direct result of a user action: moving the cursor, typing in a text input, selecting from a drop-down menu, checking a check box, clicking a button, and more.

The things involved are the application's elements: its controls, containers, even the root application itself. The actions to be taken are defined by you, and represent the greatest range of possible options. This is where you would decide to update a drop-down menu, show a block of information, and so forth.

Once you've identified the event you want to watch for and the element it should be associated with, there are two ways of telling the application what actions to take when that event occurs. You can place your instructions inline or in a function. Chapter 3, "ActionScript You Need to Know," demonstrates both. The following button gets moved to the right ten pixels every time it is clicked:

```
<s:Button id="myButton" x="20" y="20" click="myButton.x += 10"
label="Click Me!" />
```

The inline ActionScript, used as the value for the *click* property, does the work.

Chapter 3 also has examples of the *click* event calling a user-defined function:

```
<fx:Script>
<![CDATA[
private function moveMe( ):void {
    myButton.x += 10;
}
]]>
</fx:Script>
<s:Button id="myButton" x="20" y="20" click="moveMe( );" label="Click
Me!" />
```

Again, this is all there really is to event-driven programming: Tell the application that when *this event* occurs with *this thing*, take *these actions*. Establishing this connection in your application results in *event handlers*, also called *event listeners*.

Before moving on, there are two more things to understand about events in Flash and Flex. First, the events themselves are going to occur whether you address them or not. Say you have a **VGroup** that has not been instructed to respond to a mouseover event:

```
<s:VGroup>
</s:VGroup>
```

When the user moves the cursor over this **VGroup**, the mouseover event still occurs, but nothing happens as a response.

It's also important to know that Flex events are *asynchronous*, which means that they don't have to wait for each other, or their responses. In other words, multiple events and multiple event reactions can, and often will, take place simultaneously. For example, while a user may be moving the cursor over a component, the application itself may also be handling the data sent back from a server request.

The Event Object

ActionScript is an object-oriented language, which means that most everything you work with in Flex, from components to strings, is an object. This includes events, as well. ActionScript has a generic **Event** class that defines much of the functionality needed to work with events. From this root class, there are many children that inherit from **Event**; each child being a more specific type of event. Every time an event occurs within a Flash application, some type of object from the **Event** lineage is created.

The **Event** family of objects, like any other, has properties and methods for you to use. Here are the three key properties:

- **type**
- **target**
- **currentTarget**

The **Event**'s **type** property reflects what kind of event just happened. This may be click, initialize, mouseover, change, etc. The actual values will be represented by constants like **MouseEvent.CLICK**.

The **target** property of **Event** is an object reference to the component that generated the event. If you click a **CheckBox** with an **id** of *someCheckBox*, the **target** of that click event will be **someCheckBox**. This means that by referencing the **Event**'s **target** property, you can get to the properties and methods of that target object. This will mean more later in the chapter.

tip

You can investigate the properties and values of an event, like any other variable, using Flash Builder's Debug perspective, specifically the Variables window. See the end of Chapter 3 for an introduction to this.

The **currentTarget** property—as well as two others, **bubbles** and **eventPhase**—comes into play when dealing with the flow of events, to be covered next.

More specific event types add new properties and methods. For example, the **MouseEvent** object has an **altKey** property that returns a Boolean value indicating if the ALT key was pressed when the mouse event took place. When you go to handle events, you have the option of working with the generic **Event** object or a specific event object. You'll see this later in the chapter.

You'll want to familiarize yourself with the ActionScript documentation for the various events. Start by looking up the **flash.events.Event** class in either the standalone Adobe Help application or online (*http://help.adobe.com/en_US/FlashPlatform//reference/actionscript/3/flash/events/Event.html*, **Figure 4.1** on the next page). Near the top of the page are links you can click to go directly to listings of the class's properties, methods, and constants. The top of the page also shows every class that is derived from **Event** (i.e., subclasses). You can click any subclass name to see the documentation for that class.

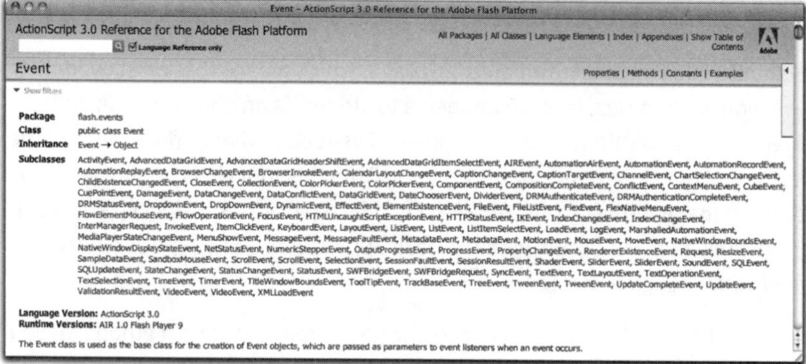

Figure 4.1

The second thing you'll often want to do within the ActionScript documentation is view the events that can be triggered by any given component. If you load the reference for a component, like **Label** in **Figure 4.2**, you'll see an *Events* link near the top of the page after *Properties* and *Methods*. Clicking that link takes you to the full listing of events that the component supports. There are several dozen possible events just for the **Label** component, and all that component does is display a bit of text!

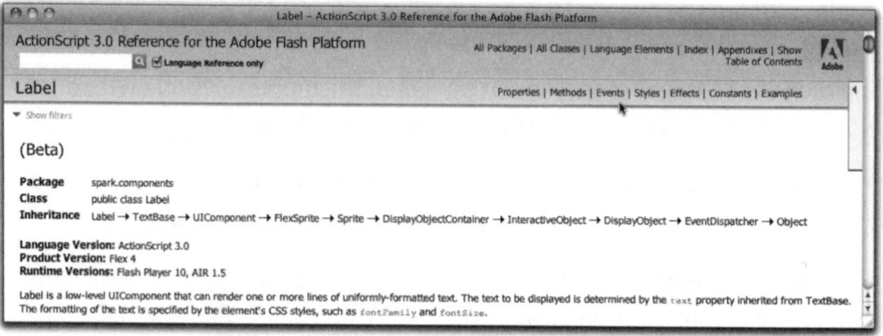

Figure 4.2

Obviously, considering the limitations of a book, I cannot go through uses of every possible event for every possible component (and you wouldn't want that anyway), which is why you'll need to familiarize yourself with navigating the ActionScript documentation. If you're using Flash Builder, you'll see that it provides code hinting for common and available events, too. Events in Flash Builder are represented by a lightning bolt (**Figure 4.3**).

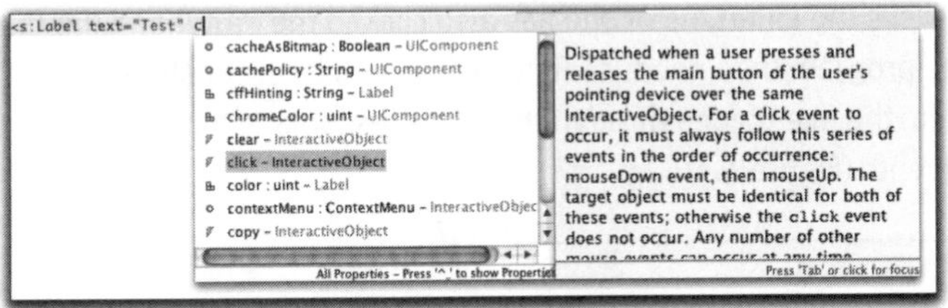

Figure 4.3

Later in the book I'll cover movement-related events (for dragging and dropping), and those having to do with effects. There are also many events specific to AIR application development. These include objects of type **AIREvent**, **FileEvent**, **SQLEvent**, among others. Any property, constant, or method only available in AIR applications are marked with the AIR icon (as in the **Label**'s **contextMenu** event in **Figure 4.4**).

Label - ActionScript 3.0 Reference for the Adobe Flash Platform

Events

Click for more information on events

▾ Hide Inherited Events

Event	Summary	Defined By
activate	[broadcast event] Dispatched when the Flash Player or AIR application gains operating system focus and becomes active.	EventDispatcher
add	Dispatched when the component is added to a container as a content child by using the addChild(), addChildAt(), addElement(), or addElementAt() method.	UIComponent
added	Dispatched when a display object is added to the display list.	DisplayObject
addedToStage	Dispatched when a display object is added to the on stage display list, either directly or through the addition of a sub tree in which the display object is contained.	DisplayObject
clear	Dispatched when the user selects 'Clear' (or 'Delete') from the text context menu.	InteractiveObject
click	Dispatched when a user presses and releases the main button of the user's pointing device over the same InteractiveObject.	InteractiveObject
contextMenu	Dispatched when a user gesture triggers the context menu associated with this interactive object in an AIR application.	InteractiveObject
copy	Dispatched when the user activates the platform specific accelerator key combination for a copy operation or selects 'Copy' from the text context menu.	InteractiveObject

Figure 4.4

Event Flow

The final thing to know about events, before getting into some actual programming, is how events are *propagated* in an application, which is to say how events move about. It's not as simple as just clicking a **Button** creates a click event: That does happen, but so does much more.

To start, let's say there's a **Label** within a **Panel** that's a direct child of the **Application**:

```
<s:Application xmlns:fx="http://ns.adobe.com/mxml/2009"
xmlns:s="library://ns.adobe.com/flex/spark"
    xmlns:mx="library://ns.adobe.com/flex/mx" minWidth="955">
    <s:Panel>
        <s:Label id="myLabel" text="Click Me!" click="doThis();"/>
    </s:Panel>
</s:Application>
```

tip

Event management goes hand-in-hand with creating good user interfaces. Unless you're purposefully creating Easter eggs, you'll need to ensure that what the user can do is successfully communicated. For example, clicking a button is a logical action, but clicking a bit of text, like a ***Label***, is not.

When the user clicks the **Label**, he or she has also clicked the **Panel** and the **Application**. The program then needs to figure out how that event should be handled. To do so, the event goes through three phases looking for event-handler assignments (**Figure 4.5**):

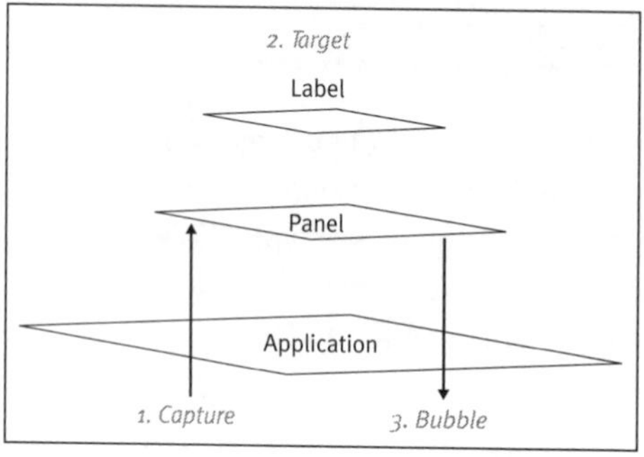

Figure 4.5

1. Capture
2. Target
3. Bubble

In the capture phase the program will start looking for event handlers from the outside (or top) parent to the innermost one. The capture phase stops at the parent of the object that triggered the event. So in my example, the capture phase starts at the **Application** and ends at the **Panel**. If either component has an associated event handler, it will be triggered during this phase (and, consequently, before the **Label**'s event handler).

By default, the capture phase is disabled as it's not commonly used and it can take its toll on the application's performance. But you can define event handlers to watch the capture phase when needed. You might do so to handle an event in a parent component, then prevent it from being handled within a child. Towards the end of the chapter I'll discuss this less common approach to event management.

The second phase, target, is the most important phase. Here the actual subject of the event (i.e., the component that triggered it) is checked for an event handler. This is where most event handling takes place.

Finally, the bubble phase is like capture in reverse, working back through the structure, from the target component's parent on up. There are a couple of reasons you may add handlers to parent components that will catch events during the bubble phase:

- To execute additional actions, besides those triggered by the target phase.

- To execute the same actions when an event is triggered by any of a component's children.

For example, if you have a form with multiple components, you may want to validate an individual component when that component's value changes, and also do something with the entire body of form data at the same time.

The event object's **eventPhase** property stores a number, also represented by a constant, that reflects the current stage (**Table 4.1**).

Table 4.1 Event Phase Values and Constants

Value	Constant
1	**EventPhase.CAPTURING_PHASE**
2	**EventPhase.AT_TARGET**
3	**EventPhase.BUBBLING_PHASE**

Do note that just as not every component can trigger every event type, not all events participate in all three phases. The event object's **bubbles** property returns a Boolean indicating if the event participates in the bubbling phase, in particular.

As already mentioned, the event object's **target** property refers to the component that triggered the event. This value will not change over the course of the event flow. In the example I'm discussing, the target would always be the **Label** object (assuming that was what the user clicked).

The event object also has a **currentTarget** property that reflects the object currently being examined for an event handler. This value will change repeatedly over the course of the event flow. In the **Label-Panel-Application** example, the **currentTarget** would go from **Application** to **Panel** (in the capture phase) to **Label** (in target) to **Panel** to **Application** (in the bubble phase). I'll demonstrate a utility program in this chapter that may help you understand the phases and targets.

INLINE EVENT HANDLING

The first, most direct, way you can handle events is *inline*. To do so, you assign some ActionScript code to the corresponding event property of a component. For example:

```
<s:Label id="myLabel"/>
<s:TextInput id="myText" change="myLabel.text=myText.text"/>
```

Every time the **TextInput** is changed, the **Label**'s **text** property will be assigned the value of the **TextInput**'s text property. This is functionally equivalent to data binding the two components together:

```
<s:Label id="myLabel" text="{myText.text}"/>
<s:TextInput id="myText" />
```

In fact, data binding is just a simple and direct way to place an event handler on a variable (or object property in this example). When that variable's value changes, an event is triggered. The event handler itself updates the component that is bound to that variable.

You should note Flex assumes that the values assigned to *event properties*, like **change**, will be ActionScript, so the curly braces are not necessary. Using ActionScript for the values of *non-event properties*, like **text**, does require the curly braces.

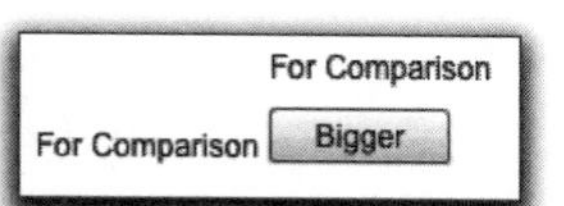

Figure 4.6

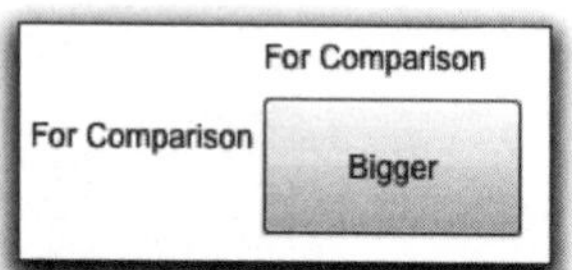

Figure 4.7

Inline event handling can be applied across components, as in the **Label-Text Input** example, or on a component to itself. An earlier example had a **Button**'s horizontal location moved 10 pixels each time it is clicked. This next **Button** will be made 10 pixels taller with each click:

```
<s:Button label="Bigger" id="myButton" click="myButton.height += 10" />
```

If you wanted to increase the **Button**'s height *and* width by 10 with each click, you can add a second ActionScript command after a semicolon (**Figures 4.6 and 4.7**):

```
<s:Button label="Bigger" id="myButton" click="myButton.height += 10;
myButton.width += 10" />
```

While you *can* put multiple commands inline, assigning more than one command to a component property can get ugly pretty quick. Also, you'll find there are limits to what you can do inline. Say you had a check box that, if checked, showed an image; if unchecked, the image should be hidden. Accomplishing that requires more complex logic, best put into a function.

FUNCTIONS AS EVENT HANDLERS

Functions often provide a better way to handle events. Some examples of functions as event handlers are used in Chapter 3. Having a function be called when an event occurs is easy:

- Define the function in a **Script** block.

- Assign the function call as the value of whatever event property in the MXML component.

This approach does a better job of separating your presentation from your logic, allows you to handle events in a more sophisticated manner, and will also let you use the same function to handle all sorts of events on all sorts of components.

tip

The same component can have multiple associated events. A ***Panel*** may watch for mouseover, mouseout, and even click events. Each event needs to be assigned a listener separately, although they can all be assigned the same event handler, when appropriate.

Creating Simple Event Handlers

If you want to create an application that only displays an image if a box is checked (**Figures 4.8** and **4.9**), you can start by defining the components:

```
<s:CheckBox id="showImageCheckBox" label="Show Image?"
change="showHideImage( )" />
<mx:Image id="myImage" source="@Embed('assets/trixie.jpg')"
visible="false" />
```

Figure 4.8

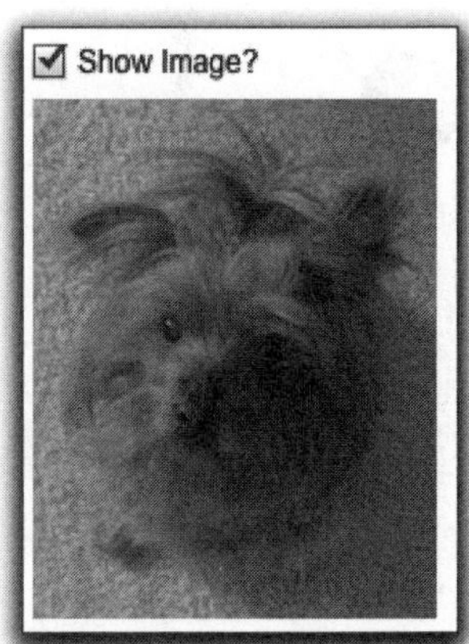

Figure 4.9

The check box has an **id** value of *showImageCheckBox* and, when changed, calls the **showHideImage( )** function. You'll notice that I'm referencing the *change* event here, because I want the function to be called whenever the check box's status changes, whether that means the user just checked or unchecked it.

The image has an **id** of *myImage* and its **source** property will embed the image file at compilation, using a relative path to the image. The image itself is initially invisible (its **visible** property is *false*), meaning it's part of the application but not seen. (In fact, it could even affect the layout while invisible).

Within the **Script** tags, the **showHideImage( )** needs to be defined:

```
private function showHideImage( ):void {
    // Actually functionality.
}
```

The function takes no arguments and returns no values. Within the function, the image's visibility should toggle depending upon whether the check box is selected or not. A simple conditional takes care of that:

```
if (showImageCheckBox.selected == true) {
    myImage.visible = true;
} else {
    myImage.visible = false;
}
```

And that's all there is to it: Check the box and the image appears, uncheck it and the image disappears.

Sending Values to Event Handlers

Event-handling functions can also be written so that they take arguments, just like any function. The value then needs to be passed when the function is called. To do so, you would write that into the component. Here are two **RadioButtons**, each of which calls the same function but sends a different Boolean value to it:

```
<s:RadioButton label="show" click="showHideImage(true);" />
<s:RadioButton label="hide" click="showHideImage(false);" />
```

And here is that function definition:

```
private function showHideImage(visible:Boolean):void {
    myImage.visible = visible;
}
```

The function takes one parameter, of type **Boolean**. Inside the function, the image's **visible** property is assigned the value passed to the function.

Sending Events to Functions

tip

Flash Builder can automatically define the shell of event handlers for you. You'll see this option appear via code completion in Source mode and by clicking the icon of a lightning bolt with a plus sign in the Properties panel of Design mode.

It's probably not obvious why, offhand, but the most likely value you'll want to send to an event-handling function would be an event object. To do so, just define the function call so that it sends along the event variable:

```
<s:Button text="Click Here!" click="myEventHandler(event);" />
```

Then you write the function so that it takes an argument of type **Event**:

```
private function myEventHandler(event:Event):void {
    // Actual functionality.
}
```

By convention, the parameter is named **event** or just **e**.

Within the function, you can make use of the event object's properties and methods. This includes **type**, **currentTarget**, **eventPhase**, and so forth. Most importantly, you can access the object that triggered the event by referencing **event.target**. Any of the target object's available properties and methods are then accessible using **event.target.*whatever***. For example, here's another way of writing the **moveMe( )** function (for moving a component):

```
private function moveMe(event:Event):void {
    event.target.x += 10;
}
```

Instead of hard-coding the component's **id** value in the function, you can refer to the **id** value of **event.target**, where **target** represents the object that triggered the event. There may be no apparent benefit to this approach, but now that same function can be used on any number of components without a knowledge of what those components are (so long as they have an **x** property):

```
<s:Button id="myButton" x="20" y="20" click="moveMe(event);"
label="Click Me!" />
<s:Label id="myLabel" x="20" y="120" click="moveMe(event);"
text="Click Me!" />
<mx:Image id="myImage" x="20" y="220" click="moveMe(event);"
source="@Embed('assets/image.png')" />
```

Taking this a step further, you could call the same function when any member of the group is clicked:

```
<s:Group click="moveMe(event);">
<s:Button id="myButton" x="20" y="20" label="Click Me!" />
<s:Label id="myLabel" x="20" y="50" text="Click Me!" />
<mx:Image id="myImage" x="20" y="70" source="@Embed('assets/
image.png')" />
</s:Group>
```

Now the same function call applies to the click event in all four objects (clicking anywhere in the group, but not one of the children moves the entire group over ten pixels). **Figure 4.10** shows the application as it originally displays; **Figure 4.11** shows it after multiple clicks.

tip

If you wanted an event handler to take different actions depending upon the type of component involved, refer to the ***target***'s ***className*** property: ***event.target.className***. You can write a conditional that checks if that property equals ***Button***, ***Label***, etc.

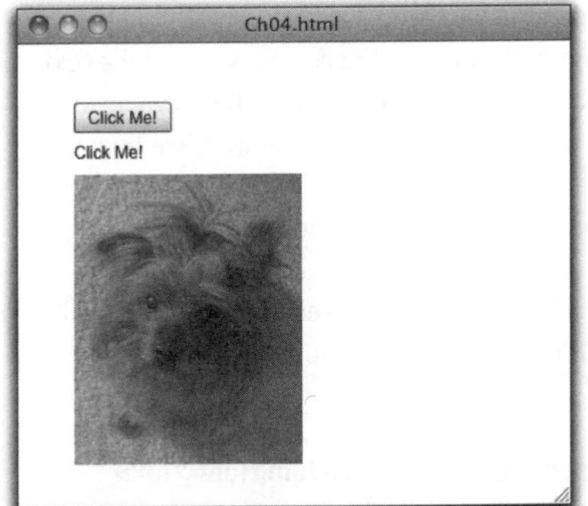

Figure 4.10

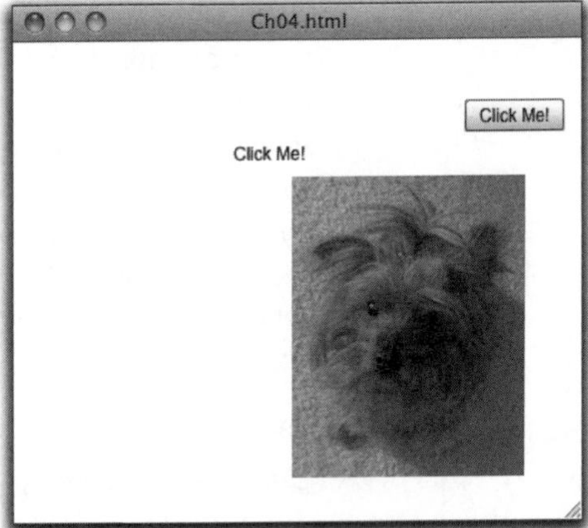

Figure 4.11

Before going further, let's take this information and create a utility for reporting upon what events were triggered by what components. Doing so will better demonstrate the event flow.

1. Create a new Flex project for the Web.

2. In the **Application** tag, associate the **reportOnEvent()** function with any click:

```
<s:Application xmlns:fx="http://ns.adobe.com/mxml/2009"
    xmlns:s="library://ns.adobe.com/flex/spark"
    xmlns:mx="library://ns.adobe.com/flex/mx"
    click="reportOnEvent(event)">
```

By assigning this event handler in the **Application** tag, the **reportOnEvent()** function will be called when the user clicks anywhere in the application. The function is passed an event object.

tip

If you download the source code from the corresponding Web site (*www.dmcinsights.com/flex4*), you'll find this code in the **Ch04/Ch04_01** folder.

3. Within a **Script** block, define the function:

```
<fx:Script>
<![CDATA[
private function reportOnEvent(event:Event):void {
    results.text += "Target: " + event.target.id + "\ncurrentTarget: " +
    event.currentTarget.id + "\nPhase: " + event.eventPhase +
    "\n----------\n";
}
]]>
</fx:Script>
```

The function expects one argument of type **Event**. Within the function, the **text** property of the **results** component will be updated. This will be a **RichText** component, added in the next step. Each call of this function will concatenate several strings and values to the current value of the **text** property. Those strings are: *Target:*, followed by a space; the **id** value of **target**; a newline (**\n**, which will space the output over multiple lines), *currentTarget:*, followed by a space; the **id** value of the **currentTarget** property; another newline, followed by *Phase:* and a space; the **eventPhase**, which will be the number 1, 2, or 3; and a newline, followed by several dashes, and another newline. If you're at all confused about how this will look, take a peek at the next three figures in the book.

4. Define the components:

```
<s:VGroup id="myVGroup" paddingLeft="10" paddingTop="10">
    <s:Label id="myLabel" text="Click on Me!" />
    <s:Panel title="Results">
        <s:RichText id="results" />
    </s:Panel>
</s:VGroup>
```

To best demonstrate what's going on, I want to add a couple of components, so I started with a **Label** inside of a **VGroup**. To display the results, I added a **RichText** component within a **Panel**, also in the **VGroup**. **Figure 4.12** shows the application when first loaded.

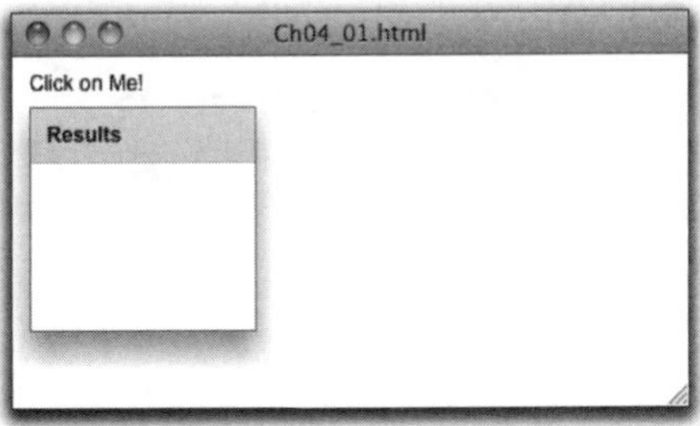

Figure 4.12

5. Save, compile, and run the application.
6. Click the various components, and not any components at all, to see the results (**Figure 4.13**).

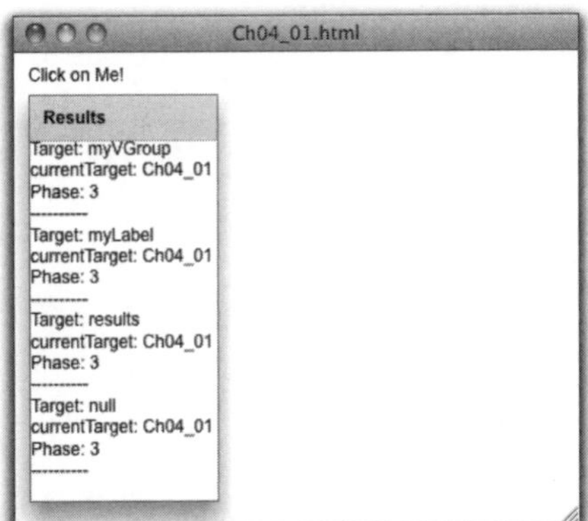

Figure 4.13

The figure shows the results after clicking the **VGroup** first (I clicked to the left of the **Panel**), clicking the **Label** next, the body of the **Panel** (i.e., the **RichText** component) after that, and, finally, outside of any component. You'll note that the **target** for each is the item clicked, except when I clicked outside of any component, in which case the **target** was null. The **currentTarget** is the application (*Ch04_01*) and the phase is 3, bubble, for every click. This is because the only event handler was assigned to the application itself. Let's see what happens when the components get their own event handlers.

7. Add click event handlers to the **VGroup**, **Label**, and **RichText** components:

```
<s:VGroup id="myVGroup" paddingLeft="10" paddingTop="10"
click="reportOnEvent(event)">
    <s:Label id="myLabel" text="Click on Me!"
click="reportOnEvent(event)" />
    <s:Panel title="Results">
        <s:RichText id="results" click="reportOnEvent(event)" />
    </s:Panel>
</s:VGroup>
```

   Each component now also calls the **reportOnEvent( )** function when a click event occurs.

8. Save, compile, and run the application.

9. Click the various components, and not any components, to see the results (**Figure 4.14**).

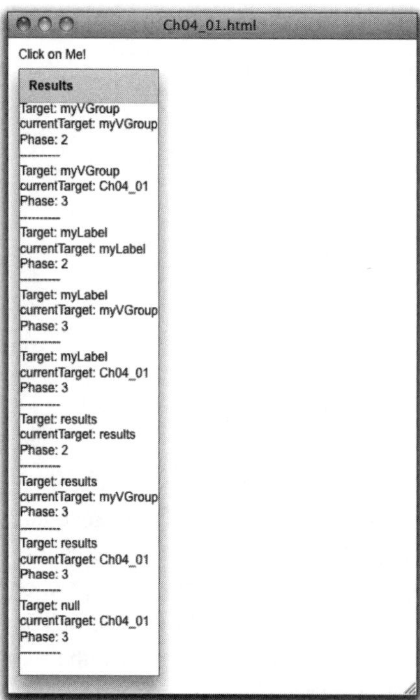

Figure 4.14

The figure shows the results after clicking the components in the same order as in Step 6: **VGroup**, **Label**, **RichText**, nothing. Now when you click a component, the first event triggered has matching **target** and **currentTarget** values, and occur in the second phase (target). Secondarily, after each target phase, one or more bubble phase events are triggered, depending upon how nested the target is. For example, clicking the **VGroup** creates one target phase event (when the **VGroup**'s event handler is triggered) and one bubble phase event (when the **Application**'s event handler is triggered). In this latter event, the **target** remains the **VGroup** but the **currentTarget** becomes the application (*Ch04_01*).

You may also notice that no capture phase events are taking place (event phase 1). This is because capture phase event handling is disabled by default. Later in the chapter I'll show you how to change that.

Using Specific Events

As mentioned earlier, it's often best to use specific event object types in your functions rather than the generic **Event**. Doing so requires no change in how the function call is defined:

```
<s:Button text="Click Here!" click="myEventHandler(event)" />
```

But you do need to change the expected parameter type in the handling function:

```
private function myEventHandler(event:EventType):void {
    // Actual functionality.
}
```

The *EventType* value needs to be one of the defined types in ActionScript: **MouseEvent**, **KeyboardEvent**, **DateChooserEvent**, **ToolTipEvent**, etc. Here's how the **moveMe()** function would be written to take a **MouseEvent** object:

```
private function moveMe(event:MouseEvent):void {
    event.target.x += 10;
}
```

By specifying the event type, you can take advantage of that event's extended abilities. For example, **MouseEvent** has **stageX** and **stageY** properties that reflect where, on the application's stage, the mouse was clicked. You could use that to move an image to the user-designated location:

tip

It is possible for a function to take a generic ***Event*** parameter and then typecast that object to a more specific type, but there are fewer justifications for doing so.

```
private function moveImage(event:MouseEvent):void {
    myImage.x = event.stageX;
    myImage.y = event.stageY;
}
```

With this particular event handler, it would have to be associated with the application, or a container, and you'd have to reference the image directly by its **id**, as it wouldn't be the **target** of the event (because you wouldn't be clicking the image).

Before getting any further, understand that in order for the application to have access to that event type definition, you may need to import the corresponding class or package. Many events, like **MouseEvent** and **KeyboardEvent** are part of the **flash.events** package, which does not need to be manually imported. Some other events, like **ToolTipEvent** and **DropDownEvent** are defined within **mx.events** and **spark.events** respectively. If you want to use one of these other event types in a function, you'll need to import the class first:

```
import spark.events.*;
import mx.events.*;
```

The ActionScript documentation shows the package each class is defined in.

Using specific types of event objects in your code will

- Provide additional functionality through added properties and methods
- Result in tighter, less bug-prone code
- Perform better

  You'll see examples of this in action over the course of the rest of the chapter.

SYSTEM EVENTS

The past several pages have looked at how you handle events, but let's look at some of the specific events in more detail. As previously mentioned, there are two categories of events: system and user-generated. System events are not triggered by user behavior but rather by application occurrences. There are three events that are triggered by every component as they are created, in the following order:

- **preInitialize**
- **initialize**
- **creationComplete**

A **preInitialize** event is triggered when a component has just been created (because it has to exist in order to have events) but none of its children have been generated. The **initialize** event is triggered when a component has been created as have its immediate children, but the component hasn't been fully sized and drawn. In other words, the component has been fully realized save for being visually manifested. When this event is triggered, you can tweak some of the component's properties, like those used to size the component, if need be. The **creationComplete** event occurs when a component has been created, as well as all of its direct descendents. Further, the component has been sized and fully drawn in the application.

Similar to how the event flow works, components are *initialized* from the outside in but *created* from the inside out. So if you have two **Button**s within a **VGroup** within the **Application**, the **Application** will be initialized, then the **VGroup**, then the **Button**s. Conversely, the **Button**s will be created (completely) first, then the **VGroup**, then the **Application** (**Figure 4.15**).

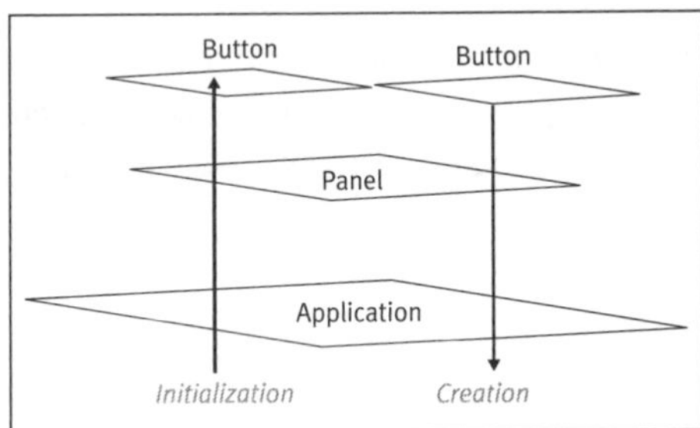

Figure 4.15

The application itself has a variation on **creationComplete**: **application Complete**. This event is triggered when every component in the application has been triggered. This event is frequently used, as programs will take this cue as the time to perform any kind of setup code:

```
<?xml version="1.0" encoding="utf-8"?>
<s:Application xmlns:fx="http://ns.adobe.com/mxml/2009"
   xmlns:s="library://ns.adobe.com/flex/spark"
   xmlns:mx="library://ns.adobe.com/flex/mx"
   applicationComplete="init()">
   <fx:Script>
   <![CDATA[
   private function init():void {
      // Do whatever.
   }
   ]]>
   </fx:Script>
```

Typically, a function named **init()**—short for *initialize*, but that may be a bit confusing here—is called when the application is ready to run. It might set the values of variables, populate data-driven components, start network requests, etc.

tip

Another system event is ***show***, which is when a component switches from being invisible to being visible.

USER EVENTS

Already in this chapter and in Chapter 3, I've made frequent references to two user events: *click* and *change*. The former is a mouse event, occurring when the user clicks a component. The later is a general event type, and is triggered when the user changes something, like what's entered in a text box or selected in a drop-down menu. Let's look at user-generated events in more detail.

Keyboard and Mouse Events

Many of the user events are driven by keyboard and mouse activities (and "mouse" does include the range of cursor inputs, like trackpads, trackballs, and tablets). Here's a list of the most common keyboard and mouse-related events:

- **click**
- **doubleClick**
- **focusIn**
- **focusOut**
- **keyDown**
- **keyUp**
- **mouseDown**
- **mouseOut**
- **mouseOver**
- **mouseUp**
- **mouseWheel**
- **move**
- **rollOut**
- **rollover**
- **toolTipShow**
- **toolTipHide**

Each should be rather obvious. For some user actions several events come into play: pressing a key can trigger both **keyDown** and **keyUp**; clicking a component can entail **mouseOver**, **mouseDown**, **mouseUp**, **mouseOut**, and **click**.

As an example, let's create an application that when you mouseover a word, it displays the Spanish version of that word (**Figure 4.16**). The application will need to respond to two events: **mouseOver**, to show the Spanish word, and **mouseOut**, to show no word (**Figure 4.17**).

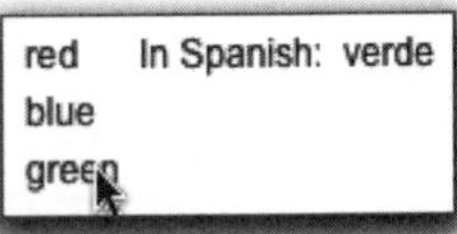

Figure 4.16

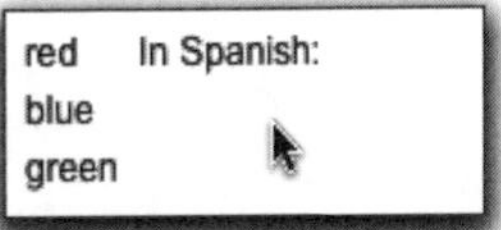

Figure 4.17

1. Create a new Flex project for the Web.
2. Within a **Script** block, define a function:

```
<fx:Script>
<![CDATA[
private function updateSpanish(spanishWord:String = ''):void {
    spanishWordLabel.text = spanishWord;
}
]]>
</fx:Script>
```

   The function expects one argument of type **String**. It has a default value of an empty string, making that argument optional. Within the function, the **text** property of the **spanishWordLabel** component will be assigned the received value.

3. Create an **HGroup** that contains a **VGroup** and two **Label**s:

```
<s:HGroup x="10" y="10">
    <s:VGroup mouseOut="updateSpanish()">
    </s:VGroup>
    <s:Label text="In Spanish: " /><s:Label id="spanishWordLabel" />
</s:HGroup>
```

   The **HGroup** is used to lay the elements out horizontally. Within it, there's a **VGroup**, which will contain the list of words, and two **Label**s. The first **Label** is a, um, label, for the second, which will actually display the Spanish version of the word. It's the only component that needs an **id** value.

   The **VGroup** has an event handler tied to the **mouseOut** event. When that event occurs on the **VGroup** or on any children of the **VGroup** (thanks to event bubbling), the **updateSpanish()** function will be called. Since the function is called without passing along any values, the function will assign an empty string to the text property of the **spanishWordLabel** Label.

4. Within the **VGroup**, add three **Label**s:

```
<s:Label text="red" mouseOver="updateSpanish('rojo')" />
<s:Label text="blue" mouseOver="updateSpanish('azul')" />
<s:Label text="green" mouseOver="updateSpanish('verde')" />
```

tip

If you download the source code from the corresponding Web site (*www.dmcinsights.com/flex4*), you'll find this code in the **Ch04/Ch04_02** folder.

The three **Label**s differ in two ways: Each has a different text value and each sends a different string to the **updateSpanish( )** function, called when the cursor moves over the **Label**.

5. Save, compile, and run the application.

Keyboard and Mouse Event Objects

When you have keyboard and mouse events, you have the option of the event handler receiving a **KeyboardEvent** or **MouseEvent** object. Along with the properties inherited from the **Event** class, both keyboard and mouse objects have each of the following:

- **altKey**
- **ctrlKey**
- **shiftKey**

Each returns a Boolean value indicating if the key in question was also pressed down when the click, or other key press, occurred. For example, if you want to program your application so that Shift+clicking a component has a different effect, the event handler might be written like so:

```
private function handleClick(event:MouseEvent):void {
    if (event.shiftKey == true) {
        // Do this.
    } else {
        // Do this instead.
    }
}
```

As said earlier, mouse events also have **stageX** and **stageY** properties that store where, on the application, the click occurred, in pixels.

Keyboard events have their own **charCode** and **keyCode** properties. The latter is a numeric representation of which key on the keyboard was pressed. The former is a numeric representation of which character in the user's character set was pressed. In some cases, as with the capital letters, these numbers will be the same. For example, if you wanted to take some action when the user pressed Control+E (actually, the lowercase letter e, whose character code is 101), you could write the function like so:

```
private function handleKeys(event:KeyboardEvent):void {
    if ( (event.ctrlKey == true) && (event.charCode == 101) ) {
        // Do this.
    }
}
```

You can find the symbolic equivalents of the codes at *www.signar.se/blog/as-3-charcodes/*, among other places.

With keyboard-related events, you most likely want to set the handler on the entire application. For example, if pressing Control+T should do something, the whole program has to watch for that. That being said, be forewarned that if you're using the modifier keys and overriding default browser behavior, the results may not be expected. For example, you could assign the combination of Command+W (on Mac) or Control+W (on Windows) to have meaning within your Flash application. However, these are already used by the browser to close the window. In all likelihood, when the user presses that combination, the window will close and the Flash application will never get the chance to respond to the input.

Other User-Driven Events

There are a number of common events not specific to the keyboard or mouse:

- **copy**
- **cut**
- **paste**
- **select**
- **selectAll**
- **open**
- **close**
- **change**

These are all defined within the generic **Event** class, and therefore inherited by the other specific classes. The editing events—cut, copy, paste, and select all—are triggered when the user takes those actions, allowing the application to respond if need be. The open and close events apply to things like drop-down menus and combo boxes. And change has been demonstrated many times over by now.

There are four other specific event classes worth mentioning:

- **ColorPickerEvent**
- **DateChooserEvent**
- **DropDownEvent**

tip

In Chapter 10, "Creating Custom Code," you'll learn how to create your own event types.

A **ColorPickerEvent** object is created when the user makes a selection within a **ColorPicker** component. A **DateChooserEvent** object is created when the user makes a selection within a **DateChooser** component. And **DropDownEvent** (an update in Spark from **DropdownEvent** in Halo) applies to drop-down menus. All of these objects are manufactured when the component experiences a **change** event.

MANAGING EVENT HANDLERS WITH ACTIONSCRIPT

You can make the event-component-event handler connection in two ways. The first has been the focus thus far; create the association within the component's MXML:

```
<s:Label id="myLabel" x="20" y="120" click="moveMe(event)"
text="Click Me!" />
```

The alternative is to use ActionScript to make the association. Although the MXML approach is easy to understand, there are some good reasons to go the ActionScript route.

First of all, there are some occasions where you cannot identify event handlers in MXML. This would be the case if you were using ActionScript classes that aren't defined in MXML, or when you create objects on the fly.

Second, by using ActionScript, you can add *and remove* event handlers as needed. For example, you might have part of an application wherein the user selects one of three images by clicking it. Once the image has been selected, you could remove the event handlers from all of the images, so that the selection could not be changed.

A third benefit of using ActionScript in this way is that it further separates the application's behavior from its markup (i.e., its visual elements). In Web development, this concept is called *unobtrusive scripting* (there are other benefits to this approach in Web development that don't apply to Flash).

To add an event handler to a component using ActionScript, call the **addEventListener()** method on the component. The method's first argument is the event to watch for, the second is the function to call when that event occurs:

```
someObject.addEventListener(EVENT_TYPE, someFunction);
```

You'll note by the capitalization that the event type is to be identified using a predefined constant. You'll find these constants listed under Public Constants in the ActionScript documentation; here are several examples:

You can use a string to indicate the event type: *'click'*, *'change'*, *etc., but you're less likely to have bugs and problems if you use the constants.*

- **Event.CHANGE**
- **KeyboardEvent.KEY_DOWN**
- **KeyboardEvent.KEY_UP**
- **MouseEvent.CLICK**
- **MouseEvent.DOUBLE_CLICK**
- **MouseEvent.MOUSE_DOWN**
- **MouseEvent.MOUSE_MOVE**
- **MouseEvent.MOUSE_OUT**
- **MouseEvent.MOUSE_OVER**
- **MouseEvent.MOUSE_UP**
- **MouseEvent.MOUSE_WHEEL**
- **MouseEvent.ROLL_OUT**
- **MouseEvent.ROLL_OVER**

The function to be called is the name of the function, without quotes, and without the parentheses (because it's a function *reference*, not a function *call*).

With this in mind, here is how you would replicate the previous bit of MXML, which associates the **move( )** function with the click event on the **myLabel Label**, using ActionScript:

```
myLabel.addEventListener(MouseEvent.CLICK, moveMe);
```

It's up to you to decide when it's appropriate to add event listeners, but you cannot do so before the component has been initialized. For that reason, you may want to establish the event handlers in an **init( )** function after the entire application has been created:

```
<s:Application xmlns:fx="http://ns.adobe.com/mxml/2009"
    xmlns:s="library://ns.adobe.com/flex/spark"
    xmlns:mx="library://ns.adobe.com/flex/mx"
    applicationComplete="init()">
    <fx:Script>
    <![CDATA[
```

code continues on the next page

```
private function init():void {
    myLabel.addEventListener(MouseEvent.CLICK, moveMe);
    // Add other event listeners.
}
]]>
</fx:Script>
```

Apply **addEventListener()** multiple times to an object to add multiple event handlers:

```
someObj.addEventListener(MouseEvent.MOUSE_DOWN, doThis1);
someObj.addEventListener(MouseEvent.MOUSE_UP, doThis2);
```

Or the same function can be used for the same event on different components:

```
someObj1.addEventListener(MouseEvent.DOUBLE_CLICK, doThis);
someObj2.addEventListener(MouseEvent.DOUBLE_CLICK, doThis);
```

When you add event listeners in this manner, the event object will automatically be passed to the handling function. You need to write the function to accept that parameter. You can write it to accept either the generic **Event** or the specific event type, as appropriate:

```
private function moveMe(event:Event):void {
}
private function moveMe(event:MouseEvent):void {
}
```

Watching for Phases

The **addEventListener()** method has two required arguments but three more optional ones. I want to look at the first of these. The next parameter is **useCapture**, which takes a Boolean value. If set to **true**, the listener will watch for events during the capture phase. If **false**, which is the default for most components, the listener will only watch for events during the target and bubble phases.

```
someObj.addEventListener(MouseEvent.CLICK, doThis, true);
```

This means that if you want to have a listener watch for events under all phases, you'll need to call **addEventListener()** twice—once with a **false** value for **useCapture** (the default) and once with a **true** value:

```
someObj.addEventListener(MouseEvent.CLICK, doThis);
someObj.addEventListener(MouseEvent.CLICK, doThis, true);
```

Let's use this knowledge to recreate the event-reporting utility created earlier in the chapter.

1. Create a new Flex project for the Web.

2. In the **Application** tag, associate the **init()** function with the complete creation of the application:

```
<s:Application xmlns:fx="http://ns.adobe.com/mxml/2009"
   xmlns:s="library://ns.adobe.com/flex/spark"
   xmlns:mx="library://ns.adobe.com/flex/mx"
   creationComplete="init()">
```

   All of the event handlers are going to be assigned using ActionScript, which means that a function needs to be called once every component has been created.

3. Within a **Script** block, define the **init()** function:

```
<fx:Script>
<![CDATA[
private function init():void {
   this.addEventListener(MouseEvent.CLICK, reportOnEvent);
   this.addEventListener(MouseEvent.CLICK, reportOnEvent, true);
   myVGroup.addEventListener(MouseEvent.CLICK, reportOnEvent);
   myVGroup.addEventListener(MouseEvent.CLICK, reportOnEvent, true);
   myLabel.addEventListener(MouseEvent.CLICK, reportOnEvent);
   myLabel.addEventListener(MouseEvent.CLICK, reportOnEvent, true);
   results.addEventListener(MouseEvent.CLICK, reportOnEvent);
   results.addEventListener(MouseEvent.CLICK, reportOnEvent, true);
}
]]>
</fx:Script>
```

   This function is called after the application has been created. Its job is to add event handlers to the application, **VGroup**, **Label**, and **RichText** components, just like in the earlier version of this program. For each element, **addEvent Listener()** is being called twice: once with no value for **useCapture** (meaning it'll be **false**) and once with a **true** value. For every case, the **reportOnEvent()** function is being associated with the mouse click.

   Note that the **Application** tag cannot be given an **id** value, but the special keyword **this** refers to the **Application**.

4. Still within the **Script** block, define the **reportOnEvent()** function:

```
private function reportOnEvent(event:Event):void {
   results.text += "Target: " + event.target.id + "\ncurrentTarget: "
+ event.currentTarget.id + "\nPhase: " + event.eventPhase +
"\n----------\n";
}
```

   The function is defined exactly as it was before.

tip

If you download the source code from the corresponding Web site (*www.dmcinsights.com/flex4*), you'll find this code in the **Ch04/Ch04_03** folder.

tip

In OOP, the keyword ***this*** refers to the current object. In a Flex application, the current object is the application itself.

5. Define the components:

```
<s:VGroup id="myVGroup" paddingLeft="10" paddingTop="10">
    <s:Label id="myLabel" text="Click on Me!" />
    <s:Panel title="Results">
        <s:RichText id="results" />
    </s:Panel>
</s:VGroup>
```

   These components are defined exactly as they were before, using the same **id** values, but they no longer have event listeners defined within the MXML.

6. Save, compile, and run the application.

7. Click the various components, and not any components at all, to see the results (**Figure 4.18**).

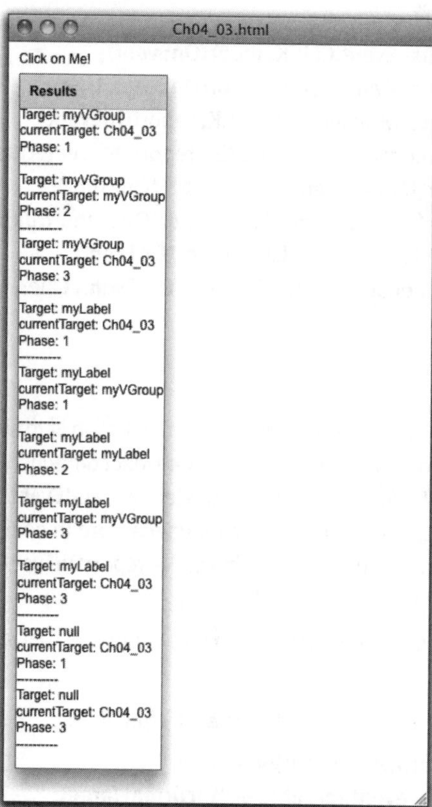

Figure 4.18

The figure shows the results after clicking the **VGroup** first (I clicked to the left of the **Panel**), the **Label** next, and, finally, outside of any component.

The **target** value for each is what you would expect. But now you have at least one capture-phase event (phase 1) for each click. And in the capture phase, just as in the bubble phase, the **currentTarget** value differs from the actual **target**.

EVENT PRIORITIES

The fourth argument to **addEventListener()** is for assigning priorities to event handlers. If two events are triggered at the same time, like if you have click event handlers on both a **Button** and the **Panel** it's in, the listener with the higher priority will be called first. The value can be any integer, positive or negative, with the default value being 0.

Removing Event Handlers

To remove an event handler from an object, apply the **removeEventHandler()** method, passing it the same two values as were used to add the event handler (three values if the **addEventListener()** method):

```
someObj.removeEventListener(MouseEvent.CLICK, doThis);
someObj.removeEventListener(MouseEvent.CLICK, doThis, true);
```

tip

The ***hasEventListener()*** method returns a Boolean value indicating if the object has the indicated event listener. It takes the event type as its only argument.

To demonstrate how you might dynamically add and remove event handlers on the fly, this next application will either show, or not show, the answer to a series of (easy) math questions based upon whether a box is checked. If the box is checked, then event handlers are added so that when the user moves the cursor over a question, the answer is revealed (**Figure 4.19**). If the box is unchecked, the event handlers are removed so that moving the cursor over a question has no effect (**Figure 4.20**).

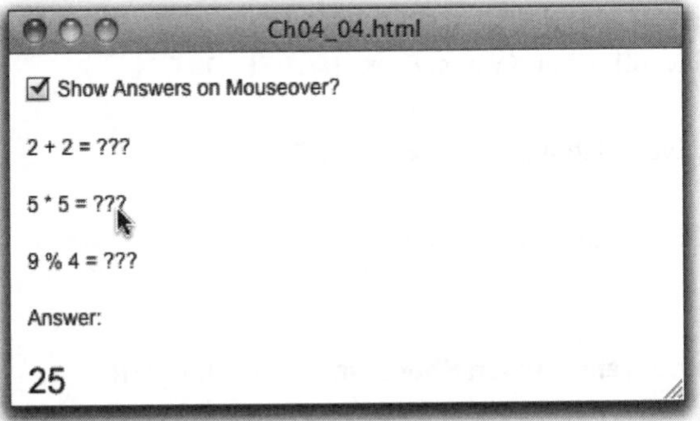

Figure 4.19

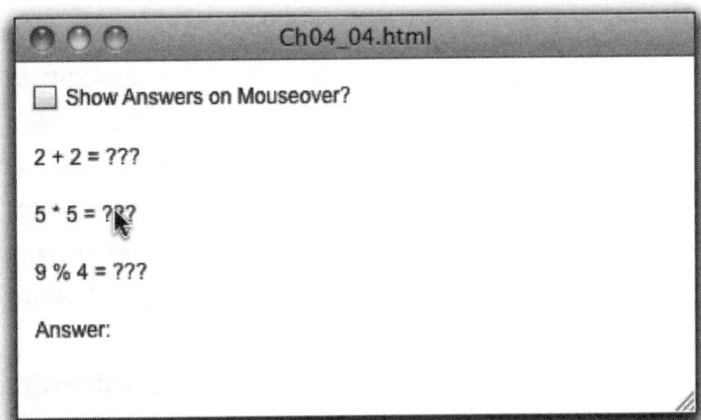

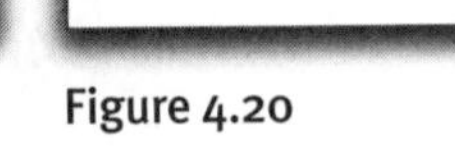

Figure 4.20

 tip

If you download the source code from the corresponding Web site (*www.dmcinsights.com/flex4*), you'll find this code in the **Ch04/ Ch04_04** folder.

1. Create a new Flex project for the Web.
2. Define the components:

```
<s:VGroup x="10" y="10" gap="20">
    <s:CheckBox id="showAnswers" change="addRemoveHandlers();"
    label="Show Answers on Mouseover?" />
    <s:Label id="question1" text="2 + 2 = ???" />
    <s:Label id="question2" text="5 * 5 = ???" />
    <s:Label id="question3" text="9 % 4 = ??? " />
    <s:Label text="Answer: " />
    <s:Label id="answerLabel" fontSize="20" />
</s:VGroup>
```

   This application has a handful of components, placed within a vertical group. Only one of these components—the check box—has an MXML-assigned event listener. When the check box is changed, the **addRemove Handlers()** function will be called.

   Each **Label** is given a unique **id** so that its answer can be displayed. The answer itself will be shown in the **answerLabel** component.

3. Within a **Script** block, define the **addRemoveHandlers()** function:

```
<fx:Script>
<![CDATA[
private function addRemoveHandlers():void {
    if (showAnswers.selected == true) {
        question1.addEventListener(MouseEvent.MOUSE_OVER,
        showAnswer);
        question2.addEventListener(MouseEvent.MOUSE_OVER,
        showAnswer);
        question3.addEventListener(MouseEvent.MOUSE_OVER,
        showAnswer);
        question1.addEventListener(MouseEvent.MOUSE_OUT,
        clearAnswer);
        question2.addEventListener(MouseEvent.MOUSE_OUT,
        clearAnswer);
        question3.addEventListener(MouseEvent.MOUSE_OUT,
        clearAnswer);
    } else {
        question1.removeEventListener(MouseEvent.MOUSE_OVER,
        showAnswer);
```

```
        question2.removeEventListener(MouseEvent.MOUSE_OVER,
        showAnswer);
        question3.removeEventListener(MouseEvent.MOUSE_OVER,
        showAnswer);
        question1.removeEventListener(MouseEvent.MOUSE_OUT,
        clearAnswer);
        question2.removeEventListener(MouseEvent.MOUSE_OUT,
        clearAnswer);
        question3.removeEventListener(MouseEvent.MOUSE_OUT,
        clearAnswer);
    }
}
]]>
</fx:Script>
```

The function takes no arguments. Within the function, an **if-else** conditional either adds or removes event listeners based upon the **selected** property of the check box. If the box is selected, then two event listeners are added to each of the three components. If the box is not selected, then those same two event listeners are removed from each component.

The first event listener watches for a mouseover, at which point the **showAnswer()** function will be called. The second event listener watches for a mouseout event, at which point the **clearAnswer()** function will be called. This function removes the previously displayed answer.

tip

Through much more complicated code, you could streamline this process, but for demonstration purposes I'm going with a bit more code in the hopes that the process is clearer.

4. Also within the **Script** block, define the **showAnswer()** function:

```
private function showAnswer(event:MouseEvent):void {
    var answer:String = '';
    switch (event.target.id) {
        case 'question1':
            answer = '4';
            break;
        case 'question2':
            answer = '25';
            break;
        case 'question3':
            answer = '1';
            break;
    }
    answerLabel.text = answer;
}
```

note

Even though the answers are all numbers, I create them as strings as they'll be assigned to a property that expects a string.

The goal of this function is to display an answer in **Label** by assigning a value to that component's **text** property. To determine what the right answer is, the function looks at the **event.target.id** property within a **switch**.

5. Still within the **Script** block, define the **clearAnswer( )** function:

```
private function clearAnswer(event:MouseEvent):void {
    answerLabel.text = '';
}
```

All this function does is assign an empty string to the **text** property of the **Label**. Even though it doesn't use the event object, the function will still receive one, as is always the case when using **addEventListener( )**.

6. Save, compile, and run the application.

CONTROLLING EVENTS

There's a lot more you can do with events than what I demonstrate in this chapter, although certainly this chapter's material covers the information you'd use the majority of the time. In Flash you can prevent event responses from taking place by calling the **preventDefault( )** method of an event object. This doesn't stop the event from happening, just stops whatever default behavior is associated with that event. To stop an event itself, you'd call the event object's **stopPropagation( )** or **stopImmediate Propagation( )** methods.

On the other side of the coin, you can dispatch events manually, if you need. You can even create your own event types, which you might do in conjunction with a custom component you've created.

PART TWO
DATA AND COMMUNICATIONS

5 DISPLAYING DATA

This second part of the book focuses on a single, but critical, aspect of Rich Internet Applications: data. Three later chapters discuss the client-server relationship, and demonstrate how to transmit data between the two, but first you should have an understanding of how to display data just using Flex. The book has already presented many examples of displaying data, but those all used simple formats, such as strings and numbers. Here it's time to get into displaying more complex kinds of data. Towards that end, the chapter first introduces some new data types, and how you can create those in both ActionScript and MXML. Next, you'll see the ways you can associate created data with MXML components.

The rest of the chapter introduces and demonstrates several data-driven controls. These components are the real workhorses of Flex and will be essential to your Rich Internet Applications. The following chapter will expand upon the information in this one by talking about, among other things, the many ways you can customize the components introduced here. As with earlier chapters, this one doesn't attempt to address every feature of every component, but rather focuses on the information you'll need most of the time.

REPRESENTING DATA

There are a number of ways to make data available to an application. Later chapters will use network communications towards this end, but here I want to briefly show how you can use ActionScript or MXML—in the current program—as a data source. Chapter 3, "ActionScript You Need to Know," uses bound variables as representative data, but those examples are simple scalar variables: strings and numbers. For the more complex, data-driven MXML components, you'll want to use more complex data types. For example, the **DropDownList** is capable of displaying a series of values and the **DataGrid** can portray an entire table (**Figure 5.1**). In neither case will a simple string suffice.

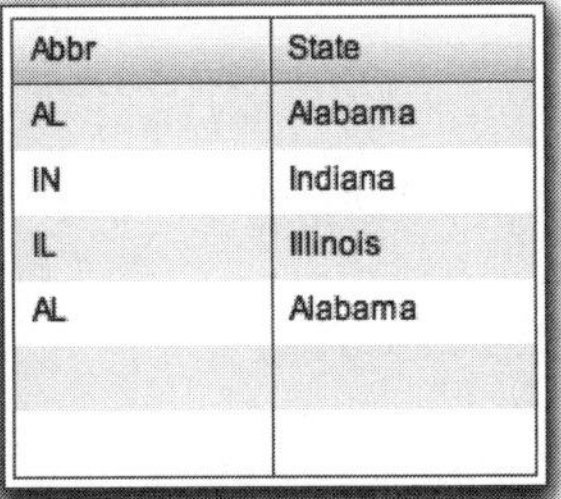

Abbr	State
AL	Alabama
IN	Indiana
IL	Illinois
AL	Alabama

Figure 5.1

The more complex data types I've already discussed in this book are arrays and objects: Both are capable of storing more than a single value at a time. You may think that these would be excellent candidates to use with data-driven components, but they actually aren't. Arrays and objects in ActionScript lack some of the features required by the data-driven controls, such as the ability to be sorted and filtered. More importantly, arrays and objects do not trigger events when they are altered, meaning they are not bindable. What you'll actually want to use are the Flex *collections*, such as **ArrayList**, **ArrayCollection**, and **XMLListCollection**. Collections take common structures, like arrays and XML, and add these necessary features. Let's look at creating collections in ActionScript and MXML.

tip

In order for something to be used as the source for data binding, it must trigger events when its value changes. This is why you can use, say, an ***ArrayCollection*** as a bound source but not an array.

In ActionScript

As part of Chapter 3's introduction to ActionScript, there's a section on creating arrays by making a new variable of type **Array**:

```
private var someArray:Array = new Array( );
```

Or you can use the array notation shortcut:

```
private var someArray:Array = [1, 2, 3];
```

Arrays, while great, don't support data binding in every Flex 4 component, meaning that you can't always directly identify an array as the data source. What you can reliably use instead are **ArrayList** and **ArrayCollection** variables.

CREATING ARRAYLIST AND ARRAYCOLLECTION VARIABLES

The **ArrayList** class is defined in **mx.collections**, so that must be imported first:

```
import mx.collections.ArrayList;
```

The **ArrayList** class is basically an array plus the necessary extra functionality to bind the data to something else.

After importing the definition, you can then create an **ArrayList** by providing it with an existing array:

```
private var someArrayList:ArrayList = new ArrayList(someArray):
```

If you don't have a formally defined array to use, you can again use the array notation as a shortcut for creating one:

```
private var colorsList:ArrayList = new ArrayList(['red','blue','green']);
```

The **ArrayList** collection type will suffice for many situations, especially when creating drop-down menus. If you'll need to sort, filter, and navigate through the list of items, you'll want to move up to the more sophisticated **ArrayCollection** type. It's created just like an **ArrayList**:

```
import mx.collections.ArrayCollection;
private var someAC:ArrayCollection = new ArrayCollection(someArray);
```

or

```
private var colorsAC:ArrayCollection = new ArrayCollection(['red', 'blue',
'green']);
```

tip

For more on the properties and methods in ***ArrayList*** or ***ArrayCollection***, see the Adobe documentation.

With both **ArrayList** and **ArrayCollection**, instead of using **push( )** and **pop( )** to add elements to the existing variable (as you would an array), you can use **addItem( )**, **addItemAt( )**, **getItemAt( )**, **removeItemAt( )**, **setItemAt( )**, and so forth. For example, to add another color to the list, you would use

```
colorsList.addItem('yellow');
colorsAC.addItem('yellow');
```

To change an item, you would use

```
colorsList.setItemAt('navy', 1);
colorsAC.setItemAt('navy', 1);
```

tip

If you want to see how many items are in an ***ArrayList*** or ***ArrayCollection***, refer to the object's ***length*** property.

The above replaces *blue* (the second item in each collection, indexed at 1) with *navy*. An example towards the end of the chapter will demonstrate adding and removing **ArrayCollection** items on the fly.

Whether creating an **ArrayList** or an **ArrayCollection**, the previous examples were just based upon arrays of simple strings and numbers. When representing more complex data sets, you'll often want to use arrays of objects. In ActionScript you can create a new, generic object by creating a variable and adding property-value pairs:

```
private var me:Object = new Object( );
me.name = 'Larry';
me.age = 37;
```

You can also use shortcut notation to create an object:

```
private var me:Object = {name:'Larry', age:37};
```

The curly brackets represent the object as a whole. Within that, properties are written first, unquoted, followed by a colon, followed by the value for that property. Each property-value pair is separated by a comma.

Taking this one step further, you can create an array of objects:

```
private var people:Array = [{name:'Larry', age:37}, {name:'Jessica', age:35},
{name:'Zoe', age:3}, {name:'Sam', age:3}];
```

Now **people** is a variable of type **Array** that has four elements, each of which is an object. And, looking further, **people[0].name** equals *Larry* and **people[2].age** equals 3.

To turn this into an **ArrayCollection**, you would just do the following:

```
private var peopleAC:ArrayCollection = new ArrayCollection(people);
```

This may all seem unnecessarily complicated to you, but an array of objects (or, more precisely, an **ArrayCollection** of objects) will be one of the most common data constructs used in MXML components. The other will be **XML**.

CREATING XML, XMLLIST, AND XMLLISTCOLLECTION VARIABLES

Chapter 7, "Common Data Formats," goes into the XML specification in greater detail, as well as how to manipulate XML in ActionScript, but I want to highlight some of the basic concepts here so that you can begin creating and using XML in your applications. XML starts with a *root element*, like **Application** in the primary Flex MXML file. XML contains only one root element, and all of the information must be stored within that. One of the hard things for those new to XML to grasp is that you're the one making up all of the tags. Unlike MXML, which defines the allowed tags, *you* decide what to name elements. Conventionally, elements are named using "CamelCase" and letters only: *firstName*, *lastName*, etc.

For an example, if you want to represent a series of colors as XML, you might start with a **colors** root element:

```
<colors></colors>
```

Next, within that root tag, you may have an element for each individual color:

```
<colors>
   <color>red</color>
   <color>blue</color>
   <color>green</color>
</colors>
```

tip

Frequently, XML will use the plural form of a word—colors or employees—*for its root tag and multiple, singular forms of the same word*—color or employee—*for the individual records within. This is not required, though.*

The values for the elements go within the tags. You can add *attributes* (also called *properties*) to the opening tag in order to provide additional information:

```
<states>
    <state abbr="AL">Alabama</state>
    <state abbr="AK">Alaska</state>
    <state abbr="AR">Arkansas</state>
</states>
```

It's not always clear whether information should be placed as an element's value or as an attribute, but neither option has an adverse impact on the usability of the data. The following three representations of the same data are all equivalent and equally usable:

```
<state abbr="AL">Alabama</state>
```

and

```
<state abbr="AL" name="Alabama" />
```

and

```
<state>
    <abbr>AL</abbr>
    <name>Alabama</name>
</state>
```

tip

If an element does not contain data (i.e., it only has attributes), no closing tag is used; instead, the opening tag ends with a slash.

To create XML in ActionScript, you declare a variable of type **XML** and assign it XML data:

```
private var colorsXML:XML = <colors>
    <color>red</color>
    <color>blue</color>
    <color>green</color>
</colors>;
```

note

XML and ***XMLList*** are known data types in ActionScript. No class definition must be imported in order to use them.

You should note that you're not using quotes to make the assignation, as that would create a string that contains XML (which is a different thing than literal XML).

ActionScript also has an **XMLList** data type, which just stores a series of XML values. This next variable will contain three pieces of XML, one for each **color** child element of **colorsXML**:

```
private var colorsXMLList:XMLList = colorsXML.colors;
```

The **colorsXMLList** variable now stores the following:

- **<color>red</color>**
- **<color>blue</color>**
- **<color>green</color>**

Unfortunately, as with arrays, you cannot use an **XML** or **XMLList** ActionScript variable as a data source. So, just as you can turn an array into an **ArrayList** or an **ArrayCollection**, you can turn an **XMLList** into an **XMLListCollection**:

```
private var colorsXLC:XMLListCollection = new XMLListCollection(colorsXM
LList);
```

But you'll need to import the **XMLListCollection** definition first:

```
import mx.collections.XMLListCollection;
```

So that's how you can create three different types of collections—**ArrayList**, **ArrayCollection**, and **XMLListCollection**—directly in ActionScript. Let's now look at how these can also be created in MXML.

In MXML

As with most things in Flex, where you can accomplish a task using either ActionScript or MXML, you can represent data in ActionScript as variables or in MXML as components. Instead of creating visual components, like a **Label**, you can use MXML to create non-visual components, such as an **Array**, **String**, **XML**, or **XMLList**.

The first thing to know is that all non-visual MXML components get placed within the **fx:Declarations** tags (this is new in Flex 4):

```
<fx:Declarations>
</fx:Declarations>
```

tip

You can also define data components within data-driven components; doing so explicitly ties the two together. You'll see this in just a couple of pages.

Within the **Declarations** section you can create data components as you would any other component:

```
<fx:String>Hello, World!</fx:String>
```

All of the data components are defined in the *fx* namespace. The value of the data component will be placed between the opening and closing tags, but, unlike in ActionScript, need not be quoted (as with the above string).

To make the data usable by other components, you'll likely want to add an **id** property:

```
<fx:Number id="price">19.95</fx:Number>
```

You've now seen how to create a string and a number in MXML. The available data components include

- **Array**
- **Boolean**
- **Date**
- **int**
- **Number**
- **String**
- **uint**

Both int and uint are in all lowercase letters.

With the exception of **Array** and **Date**, all of these components only have **id** properties. **Array** also has a **length** property, used to identify the number of elements in the array. **Date** has several properties used to give the date its value:

```
<fx:Date id="today" date="1" fullYear="2010" month="0" />
```

The **date** property is the day of the month, **fullYear** is the year as four digits, and **month** is a numeric representation of the month, with January starting at 0. You can also specify hours, minutes, seconds, and more.

CREATING ARRAYS ET AL.

It's rare that you'd have the need to create a **Boolean** or **String** in MXML within **fx:Declarations** tags. However, you might do so as part of creating an array:

```
<fx:Array id="item">
    <fx:Number id="price">19.95</fx:Number>
    <fx:String id="name">Wonder Widget</fx:String>
    <fx:Boolean id="inStock">true</fx:Boolean>
</fx:Array>
```

As already mentioned, arrays are more limited in their usability, so perhaps you'd want to make an **ArrayList** in MXML instead:

```
<s:ArrayList id="beatles">
    <fx:Array>
        <fx:String>John</fx:String>
        <fx:String>Paul</fx:String>
        <fx:String>George</fx:String>
        <fx:String>Ringo</fx:String>
    </fx:Array>
</s:ArrayList>
```

Three things to note here: First, unlike the other data types, **ArrayList**, **Array Collection**, and **XMLListCollection** are all defined in the Spark namespace. Second, even though **ArrayList** is defined in the Spark namespace, not *fx*, it's still used within the declaration section as it's a non-visual component. Third, when using **ArrayList**, **ArrayCollection**, and **XMLListCollection** in MXML, you don't need to import the class definition as you would in ActionScript (as the namespace declarations in the **Application** tag make the definitions available).

tip

An ***Array*** is the default data provided to the ***ArrayList*** and ***ArrayCollection*** components in MXML. Because of this, the ***Array*** component is implied and you can omit those tags when creating the ***ArrayList*** or ***ArrayCollection***.

If you'd rather use an **ArrayCollection**, for the extra sorting and filtering functionalities, you can use that component instead. This next example defines an **ArrayCollection** of objects:

```
<s:ArrayCollection id="people">
    <fx:Object name="Lary" age="37"/>
    <fx:Object name="Jessica" age="35"/>
    <fx:Object name="Zoe" age="3"/>
    <fx:Object name="Sam" age="3"/>
</s:ArrayCollection>
```

CREATING XML ET AL.

If you'd rather work with XML instead of an **ArrayCollection**, you can use the **XML** and **XMLList** components. One obvious difference between these is that XML has a single root element, whereas **XMLList** has no root element.

Here's an **XML** component:

```
<fx:XML id="beatles"><beatles>
    <beatle>John</beatle>
    <beatle>Paul</beatle>
    <beatle>George</beatle>
    <beatle>Ringo</beatle>
</beatles></fx:XML>
```

And here's an **XMLList**:

```
<fx:XMLList id="peopleXMLList">
<person>
    <name>Larry</name>
    <age>37</age>
</person>
<person>
    <name>Jessica</name>
    <age>35</age>
</person>
```

code continues on next page

```
<person>
    <name>Zoe</name>
    <age>3</age>
</person>
<person>
    <name>Sam</name>
    <age>3</age>
</person>
</fx:XMLList>
```

Unlike **XML** and **XMLList** variables created in ActionScript, the **XML** and **XMLList** data components in MXML *are bindable* and therefore can be used as the source for a data-driven component. Still, you can also create an **XMListCollection** out of an **XMLList**:

```
<s:XMLListCollection id="peopleXLC">
<fx:XMLList id="peopleXMLList">
<person>
    <name>Larry</name>
    <age>37</age>
</person>
<person>
    <name>Jessica</name>
    <age>35</age>
</person>
<person>
    <name>Zoe</name>
    <age>3</age>
</person>
<person>
    <name>Sam</name>
    <age>3</age>
</person>
</fx:XMLList>
</s:XMLListCollection>
```

If you just want to create an XML tree-like structure, without creating meaningful element names, you can just use generic elements, like **node**:

tip

The fx namespace also defines a ***Model*** component, which can be used similarly to ***XML***.

```
<fx:XML id="data">
<node label="Something">
    <node>Value</node>
    <node>Another Value</node>
</node>
```

```
<node label="Something Else">
  <node>Value</node>
  <node>Another Value</node>
</node>
</fx:XML>
```

USING LOCAL DATA FILES

All of the examples in the chapter thus far have relied upon data defined, either in ActionScript or in MXML, within the same file as the rest of the application. As your programs become more complex, it only makes sense to separate your data from your programming logic. Over the rest of the book, much of the data involved will be derived from an external source, namely a call to a server resource. But I want to quickly demonstrate here how you can use data stored outside of the primary MXML file that does not require a call to a server.

tip

Chapter 3 discusses how to include external ActionScript files. Using those, you can define data sets as ActionScript variables that are then included by programs as needed.

The **XML** component has a **source** property that I haven't yet discussed. Just like the **source** property of the **Script** tag (see Chapter 3), the **XML source** property can identify the file that contains the XML data, rather than defining it inline:

```
<fx:XML source="/path/to/file.xml" />
```

The ***/path/to/file*.xml** must be correct, from the perspective of the MXML file that contains the XML tag. For example, if you have the project structure represented by **Figure 5.2**, then the proper code would be

```
<fx:XML id="statesXML" source="../assets/states.xml" />
```

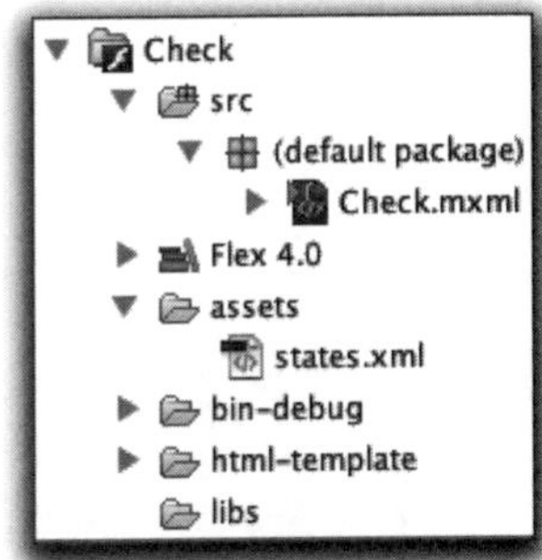

Figure 5.2

The XML file must contain valid XML, with a single root node. Also, XML files always begin with an XML declaration line, just like your application's primary MXML file. Here, then, is how you could store the list of US states in an XML file:

```
<?xml version="1.0" encoding="utf-8"?>
<states>
  <state abbr="AL">Alabama</state>
  <state abbr="AK">Alaska</state>
  <state abbr="AR">Arkansas</state>
</states>
```

tip

Content within the external XML file (that will be included during the compilation process) can include data binding references to objects found elsewhere in the application.

When using this approach, the XML file will be compiled into the finished application. This means that you do not need to distribute the XML file with the compiled Flash application, but it also means that you must recompile and redistribute the SWF file every time that the XML data changes.

PROVIDING DATA TO COMPONENTS

Once you have a defined data set, you can identify it as the source for a data-driven MXML component. As always, there are a couple of ways of doing so. One route is to indicate, in the component, the data source. To do that, use data binding to associate the data set with the component's **dataProvider** property. All of the data-driven components have this property and it's used to indicate where the component's data should come from. Here is an example with a **DropDownList**:

```
<s:DropDownList id="beatle" dataProvider="{beatles}" />
```

note

When using server-provided data, the process will often go in reverse: First you'll associate a data source with a component, then that data source will be populated via a server call.

As with any data binding declared within MXML, you need to wrap the data source within curly brackets. Also, when you do this, it's important to remember that not all data types can be bound (**Table 5.1**).

Table 5.1 Bindable Complex Data Types

Type	Bindable
Array	No
Object	Yes
ArrayList	Yes
ArrayCollection	Yes
XMLListCollection	Yes
XML	Only when defined in MXML
XMLList	Only when defined in MXML

tip

Halo components (those in the mx namespace) do not require collections as the data source but will, behind-the-scenes, wrap non-collections within collections. It's still best to explicitly use collections, however.

Alternatively, you can assign a value to a component's **dataProvider** property using ActionScript:

```
private var beatle:DropDownList = new DropDownList( );
beatle.dataProvider = beatles;
```

Because this is ActionScript, you assign the actual data object to the **data Provider** property, without using quotes or curly brackets.

A third way to associate data with a component is to define the data in MXML within the component itself:

```
<s:DropDownList id="beatles">
    <s:ArrayList>
        <fx:String>John</fx:String>
        <fx:String>Paul</fx:String>
        <fx:String>George</fx:String>
        <fx:String>Ringo</fx:String>
    </s:ArrayList>
</s:DropDownList>
```

tip

As mentioned earlier in the chapter, the ***Array*** component is implied within ***ArrayList*** and ***ArrayCollection***, so I'll be omitting it from future examples.

For any component, the data placed between its opening and closing tags will be used as the value for that component's default property. For **DropDownList** and other data-driven components, the default property is **dataProvider**. The above is equivalent to the following more explicit (and verbose) code:

```
<s:DropDownList id="beatles">
    <s:dataProvider>
        <s:ArrayList>
            <fx:Array>
                <fx:String>John</fx:String>
                <fx:String>Paul</fx:String>
                <fx:String>George</fx:String>
                <fx:String>Ringo</fx:String>
            </fx:Array>
        </s:ArrayList>
    </s:dataProvider>
</s:DropDownList>
```

There is one more property, along with **dataProvider**, that you should be aware of: **labelField**. This property identifies which value, from a complex data set, is to be used as the visible text (**Figure 5.3**):

```
<s:DropDownList id="person" labelField="name">
    <s:ArrayList id="people">
        <fx:Object name="Lary" age="37"/>
        <fx:Object name="Jessica" age="35"/>
        <fx:Object name="Zoe" age="3"/>
        <fx:Object name="Sam" age="3"/>
    </s:ArrayList>
</s:DropDownList>
```

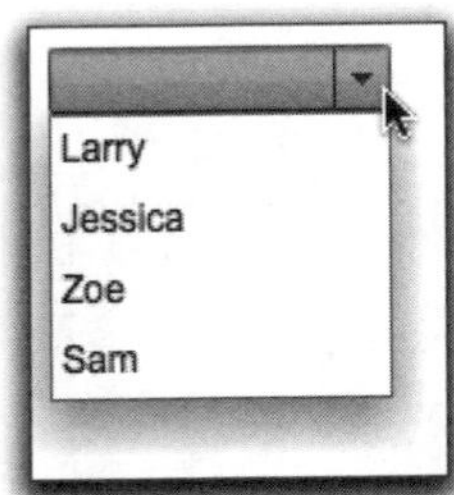

Figure 5.3

An alternative is to use the **label** identifier in your data set. When present, the component will automatically use those values for the visible text. This next **DropDownList** will look the same as that in Figure 5.3:

tip

If a data source object has a ***label*** property, that will automatically be used for the data component's ***labelField*** value.

```
<s:DropDownList id="person">
    <s:ArrayList id="people">
        <fx:Object label="Lary" age="37"/>
        <fx:Object label="Jessica" age="35"/>
        <fx:Object label="Zoe" age="3"/>
        <fx:Object label="Sam" age="3"/>
    </s:ArrayList>
</s:DropDownList>
```

Quite frequently, when you're defining your own data objects and they only have two properties, one will be **label** and the other **data**:

tip

In Chapter 6, "Manipulating Data," you'll learn about the ***labelFunction*** property. It's used to identify the function to call whose return value would be used for the visible text.

```
<s:ArrayList id="states">
    <fx:Object data="AL" label="Alabama"/>
    <fx:Object data="AK" label="Alaska"/>
    <fx:Object data="AR" label="Arkansas"/>
</s:ArrayList>
```

COMBOBOX AND DROPDOWNLIST COMPONENTS

Flex has two components that behave like **SELECT** menus in HTML: the **ComboBox** and the **DropDownList**, both defined in Spark. Both allow the user to select one or more elements from a menu of options.

From a programming perspective, how you use both components is the same. As suggested just a couple of pages ago, you can either provide a data set within the component itself (**Figure 5.4**),

Figure 5.4

```
<s:ComboBox>
    <s:ArrayList>
        <fx:String>American Express</fx:String>
        <fx:String>Mastercard</fx:String>
        <fx:String>Visa</fx:String>
    </s:ArrayList>
</s:ComboBox>
```

or you can use the component's **dataProvider** property:

```
<s:DropDownList id="beatle" dataProvider="{beatles}" />
```

Both components have a **requireSelection** property that, when set to true, will initialize the component with the first item selected so that it's impossible for an item not to be selected. This property's default value is false.

You can also pre-select any item by providing the item's index number to the **selectedIndex** property (**Figure 5.5**):

```
<s:DropDownList id="beatle" dataProvider="{beatles}"
selectedIndex="2" />
```

Figure 5.5

tip

As with arrays, indexing in MXML data components begins at 0.

Events

The **ComboBox** and **DropDownList** components respond to many events, the most commonly used being **change**, **open**, and **close**:

```
<s:DropDownList dataProvider="{beatles}"
change="beatleSelected(event)" />
```

The **change** event will be indicative of a user selection; **open** is triggered when the actual component is clicked (to open it); **close** is triggered when the component is closed, which can happen when the user clicks it again or makes a selection.

Within the event-handling function, you'll want to refer to the component's **selectedItem** or **selectedIndex** property:

```
private function beatleSelected(event:Event):void {
    var favorite:String = event.target.selectedItem;
}
```

You could also explicitly reference the component itself, if you'd rather:

```
var favorite:String = beatle.selectedItem;
```

tip

Referring to components by their ***id***s in an event handler is most obvious, but referring to them via the event object makes the event handler more universal.

If the **DropDownList** or **ComboBox** is populated using strings, the **selectedItem** value will also be a string and **selectedIndex** will be an integer, starting at 0 for the first selected item. If the **DropDownList** or **ComboBox** is populated using objects, you can use knowledge of the object to get the information you need. For example, consider the following MXML:

```
<s:DropDownList id="person" change="personSelected(event)"
labelField="name">
    <s:ArrayList id="people">
        <fx:Object name="Larry" age="37"/>
```

code continues on next page

```
        <fx:Object name="Jessica" age="35"/>
        <fx:Object name="Zoe" age="3"/>
        <fx:Object name="Sam" age="3"/>
    </s:ArrayList>
</s:DropDownList>
<s:Label id="response" />
```

When an item is selected in the **DropDownList**, a **change** event is triggered, calling the **personSelected( )** function. That function receives an event object; in it, the **event.target.selectedItem** property refers to one of the objects in the **ArrayList**. Thus, the handling function can be defined as

```
private function personSelected(event:IndexChangeEvent):void {
    response.text = event.target.selectedItem.name + ' is ' + event.target.
    selectedItem.age + ' years old.';
}
```

Figures 5.6 and 5.7 show the result.

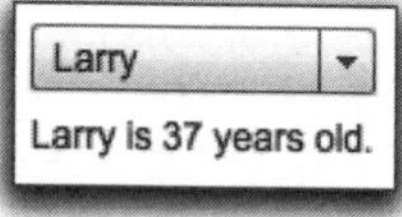

Figure 5.6

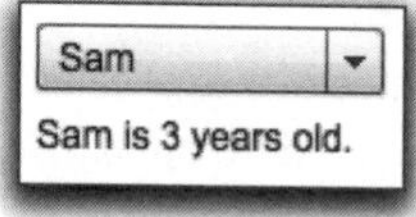

Figure 5.7

tip

If you don't want users to be able to add new values, use ***DropDownList***. If you use ***ComboBox***, then you should add code acknowledging what the user types. See the Flex 4 documentation for specifics.

As you can see in that function, the **DropDownList** triggers an **IndexChangeEvent**, defined in **spark.events**. You can import that definition if you want to catch this specific event type (as opposed to a generic **Event**):

```
import spark.events.IndexChangeEvent;
```

tip

If a ***DropDownList*** has a ***selectedIndex*** value, or if its ***requireSelection*** property is true, then the prompt will not be immediately shown; instead, the automatically selected item will appear in the prompt's place.

The **ComboBox** triggers the same event as well. Both components also trigger **spark.events.DropDownEvent** events when the component is opened and closed.

Although the two components have much in common, there are two distinctions to note. First, the **ComboBox** allows for the user to type within it, whereas a **DropDownList** does not. By typing within the **ComboBox**'s text area, the user can search through the existing values or enter a new one.

Second, **DropDownList** has a **prompt** property that dictates what the menu shows prior to any selection (**Figure 5.8**):

Figure 5.8

```
<s:DropDownList dataProvider="{beatles}" change="beatleSelected(event)"
prompt="Pick your favorite Beatle:" width="200" />
```

An Example

To demonstrate using the **ComboBox** and **DropDownList** components, let's create a pseudo e-commerce calculator, where the user can select a product and a quantity, and the application will display the total cost (**Figure 5.9**).

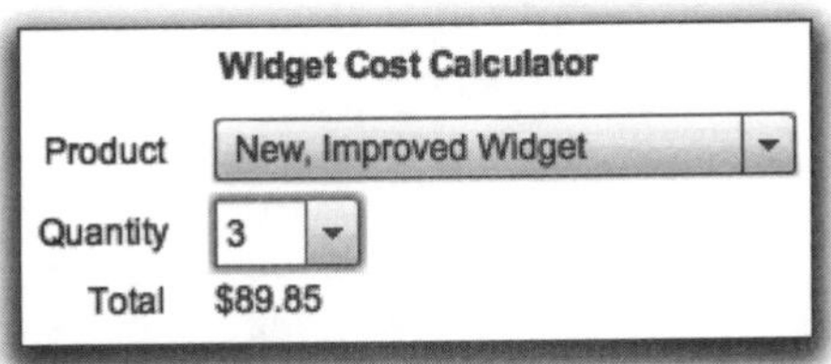

Figure 5.9

If you download the source code from the book's corresponding Web site (*www.dmcinsights.com/flex4*), you'll find this example in the **Ch05/Ch05_01** folder.

1. Create a new Web project in Flash Builder or your alternative development environment.

2. Add **Form** and **FormHeading** components to the application:

```
<mx:Form>
    <mx:FormHeading label="Widget Cost Calculator"/>
</mx:Form>
```

3. Add, within the form, a **DropDownList** for the products:

```
<mx:FormItem label="Product">
    <s:DropDownList id="product" change="updateTotal()"
    prompt="Choose One:" width="200">
        <s:ArrayList>
            <fx:Object price="19.95" label="Standard Widget" />
            <fx:Object price="29.95" label="New, Improved Widget" />
            <fx:Object price="49.95" label="Deluxe Widget" />
            <fx:Object price="99.95" label="Super Deluxe Widget" />
            <fx:Object price="199.95" label="Overpriced Widget" />
        </s:ArrayList>
    </s:DropDownList>
</mx:FormItem>
```

The **DropDownList** has an **id** value of *product*, a **prompt** of *Choose One:*, a **width** of 200, and, when a **change** event occurs, the **updateTotal()** function will be called. The component will be populated using an **ArrayList** of objects, defined inline. Each object has two properties: **price** and **label**. The label values will automatically be used for the displayed text.

4. Next, add a **ComboBox** for the quantity:

```
<mx:FormItem label="Quantity">
    <s:ComboBox id="quantity" change="updateTotal()" width="50">
        <s:ArrayList>
            <fx:uint>1</fx:uint>
            <fx:uint>2</fx:uint>
            <fx:uint>3</fx:uint>
            <fx:uint>4</fx:uint>
            <fx:uint>5</fx:uint>
        </s:ArrayList>
    </s:ComboBox>
</mx:FormItem>
```

   A **ComboBox** is a good choice for entering the quantity because it allows the user to both select from the given choices or enter his or her own value. It's populated using an **ArrayList** of unsigned integers. (If you've been paying close attention and reading this book sequentially, you'll realize that **NumericStepper** is a more logical component to use here, but I want to demonstrate **ComboBox**).

5. Add a **Label** for displaying the calculated result:

```
<mx:FormItem label="Total">
    <s:Label id="result" />
</mx:FormItem>
```

   The **Label** starts off blank, and will be assigned text in the event-handling function.

6. Within a **Script** block, begin defining the **updateTotal()** function:

```
<fx:Script>
<![CDATA[
private function updateTotal():void {
```

   This function takes no arguments and returns no values. You'll notice that the function is not written to take an event object, as the **change** events do not send the function an event object when they are triggered. If you did want to write the function to take an event object, you'd need to import the proper definition in the **Script** block, too.

7. Within the function, check that both **SELECT**-like components have valid values:

```
if ( (product.selectedIndex >= 0) && (quantity.selectedItem > 0) ) {
```

This function will be called when a **change** event is triggered by either the **DropDownList** or the **ComboBox**. This means that the first time the user selects a product, it'll be called, before any quantity has been chosen (or, if he or she enters a quantity before selecting a product). This conditional prevents calculations from being made until both elements have been properly used.

For the **DropDownList**, the conditional checks that the **selectedIndex** is greater than or equal to 0. If the user has not selected anything, then **selectedIndex** will be -1. If the user selects anything else, this part of the condition will be true.

The conditional for the **ComboBox** checks the selected value, which is **selectedItem**, making sure that it's greater than 0. This condition will be true once the user has selected or entered a positive number. If the user hasn't selected anything, or has entered "dog" as the quantity (which he or she could do), this part of the condition will be false.

8. Update the **Label**:

```
result.text = '$' + (product.selectedItem.price * quantity.selectedItem);
```

The displayed text in the **Label** will be a dollar sign followed by the calculation. The calculation uses the quantity component's **selectedItem** value and the corresponding **price** property from the item selected in the product component.

tip

In the next chapter you'll learn some techniques for validating user input and formatting output.

9. Complete the conditional, the function, and the **Script** block:

```
        }
}
]]>
</fx:Script>
```

10. Save, run, and test the completed application (**Figure 5.10**).

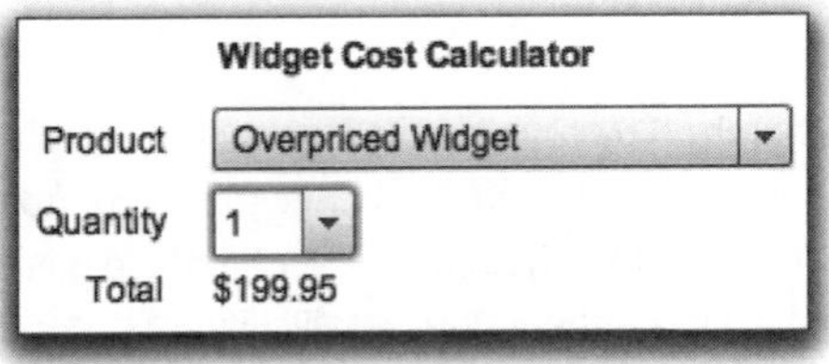

Figure 5.10

THE LIST COMPONENT

tip

Chapter 11, "Improving the User Experience," demonstrates a few more data-driven components used to add navigation to an application.

The **SELECT**-like components are fine for presenting a one-dimensional set of options. In other words, each element in the component displays only a single value. When you want to display two-dimensional values, like within a table, you'll need to turn to Flex's *list* components, primarily **List**, **Tree**, and **DataGrid**. These are referred to as "list" components, because they are all derived from the **ListBase** class. Let's start by looking at **List** itself.

List Basics

The **List** component initially seems a lot like **ComboBox** and **DropDownList,** as it creates a vertical list of options. But, it can display multiple options at one time (like an HTML **SELECT** menu with **size** property greater than 1), and how items are displayed can be much more elaborate.

To understand **List**, it helps to start things off simply by treating a **List** like a **DropDownList**:

note

A ***List*** will have a default size big enough to display every element without scrolling, if possible (i.e., if that doesn't make the ***List*** larger than its container).

```
<s:List id="cardType">
    <s:ArrayList>
        <fx:String>American Express</fx:String>
        <fx:String>Mastercard</fx:String>
        <fx:String>Visa</fx:String>
    </s:ArrayList>
</s:List>
```

If you were to run this code, the only noticeable difference is that the **List** will show all three items simultaneously, without the user having to open the component.

Figure 5.11

To further customize the **List**, add **height** and **width** properties to size its outer dimensions. If the **List** box is too small to display all the elements, the **List** will automatically create horizontal and vertical scrollbars as needed (**Figure 5.11**). While you can size the **ComboBox** and **DropDownList** components, neither makes use of scrollbars.

A **List** component can also be customized by changing its layout; it doesn't have to be a vertical list, it can be horizontal or even tiled. To change the layout from its default of vertical, use the layout classes that Chapter 2, "User Interface Basics," details. Here's how you would make a **List** appear horizontally (**Figure 5.12**):

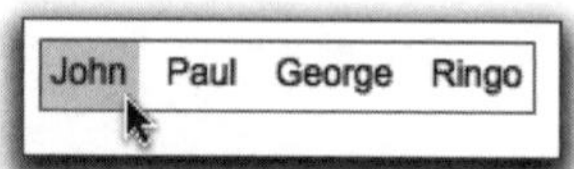

Figure 5.12

```
<s:List id="beatle" dataProvider="{beatles}">
    <s:layout>
        <s:HorizontalLayout />
    </s:layout>
</s:List>
```

If you were providing data within the MXML, just define that after you establish the layout:

```
<s:List id="beatle" dataProvider="{beatles}">
    <s:layout>
        <s:HorizontalLayout />
    </s:layout>
    <s:dataProvider>
        <s:ArrayList>
            <fx:String>John</fx:String>
            <fx:String>Paul</fx:String>
            <fx:String>George</fx:String>
            <fx:String>Ringo</fx:String>
        </s:ArrayList>
    </s:dataProvider>
</s:List>
```

Note that you cannot use **BasicLayout,** as a **List** does not support absolute positioning (for the children of the **List**).

tip

Flex 4's ***List*** component replaces Flex 3's ***List***, ***HorizontalList***, and ***TileList***.

You can easily customize the look of a **List** by assigning hexadecimal colors to the following properties:

- **borderColor**
- **contentBackgroundColor**
- **rollOverColor**
- **selectionColor**

There's also the **alternatingItemColors** property, which takes an array of hexadecimal values. The items in the **List** will be given alternating background colors from that array of values. **Figure 5.13** shows the following **List**:

```
<s:List dataProvider="{states}" borderVisible="false"
    alternatingItemColors="['#333333', '#CCCCCC']"
    rollOverColor="#567E3A"
    selectionColor="#EE0000">
</s:List>
```

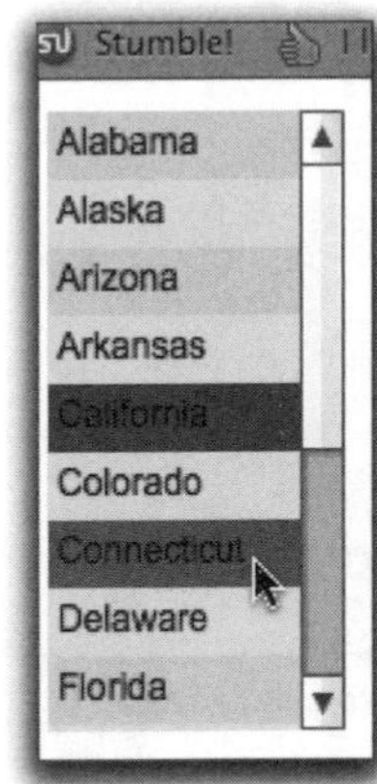

Figure 5.13

In the next chapter I'll go into customizing the **List** in greater detail, using *item renderers*, but for now I'll move on to the **List**-related events.

List Events

The **List** component supports many events: **change**, **click**, **doubleClick**, **item Click**, and so forth. The last three, as you would expect, are triggered when the user clicks or double-clicks a specific item in the list, and are all mouse events. The **change** event is triggered whenever the user selects a new item from the list. It creates an event of type **IndexChangeEvent**.

If you're watching for **change** events, you can, within the event handler, access the currently selected item by referencing **event.target.selectedItem**, which returns the displayed string, or **event.target.selectedIndex**, which returns the indexed number, starting at 0, of the item. (And, of course, you can always just refer to ***componentId*.selectedItem** and ***componentId*.selectedIndex**, if you'd rather.)

If you're watching for a mouse-click event, you'll want to use **event.currentTarget** instead of **event.target**. That's because the **target**, especially of a mouse event, may not be what you think it should be. If you click an item in a **List**, the actual target may be a **Label** (which displays the text) or something else, once you begin using item renderers. For this reason, it's best to use **currentTarget** to reference the **List** as a whole when handling clicks.

With this in mind, here are two ways of replicating what was accomplished using a **DropDownList** earlier in the chapter (and as demonstrated in Figures 5.6 and 5.7). In this first approach, the **change** event is tied to the **target** (because the **List** will change):

```
<s:List id="person" dataProvider="{people}" labelField="name" change=
"personSelected(event)" />
private function personSelected(event:IndexChangeEvent):void {
    response.text = event.target.selectedItem.name + ' is ' +
    event.target.selectedItem.age + ' years old.';
}
```

In this second approach, the **click** event is tied to the **currentTarget** (because the **List** may not be the target of a click but will be the **currentTarget** during the event bubbling phase):

tip

For more on ***target***, ***current-Target***, and event phases, see Chapter 4, "Event Management."

```
<s:List id="person" dataProvider="{people}" labelField="name" click=
"personSelected2(event)" />
protected function personSelected2(event:MouseEvent):void {
    response.text = event.currentTarget.selectedItem.name + ' is ' +
    event.currentTarget.selectedItem.age + ' years old.';
}
```

The **List** component has an **allowMultipleSelection** property which, when set to true, lets the user select multiple items. In such cases, you'd want to refer to **selectedIndicies** and **selectedItems** to fetch all the chosen members. Each returns an array, which you could loop through to access the individual selections.

The **List**'s **requireSelection** property, when set to true, will initialize the **List** with the first item selected so that the user will have to select at least one item. Its default value is false.

tip

List is an important component to familiarize yourself with, so the next chapter will have more examples of its use.

note

Tree components do not automatically update to reflect changes in the underlying data source.

THE CARET CONCEPT

The **List** component, among others, has a special *caret index*, which is different than the selected index. It's not obvious, but a user can move around within a **List** without actually selecting items. To do so, he or she will need to hold down the Control key on Windows or the Command key on Mac OS X, then use the arrow keys. When the user does this, he or she triggers **caretChange** events and the item that currently has focus will be outlined instead of highlighted. The **caretIndex** property of the component will reflect the item with focus. The caret's use is a bit esoteric, so I won't demonstrate it here, but you may run across it in other sources.

The Tree Component

The **Tree** component, defined in Halo, is used to represent a hierarchical data set, providing an interface for the user to drill down through the hierarchy in order to select an atomic element (**Figure 5.14**). You'll most often use it with elaborate data constructs such as XML. (There's also a tree component for AIR applications that provides a way to navigate through the file system; see the sidebar.)

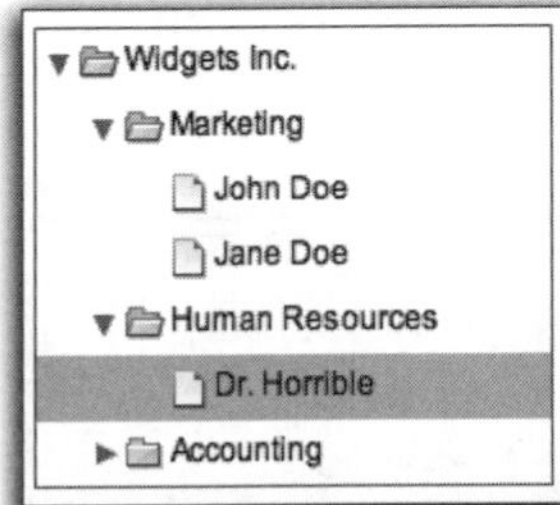

Figure 5.14

As you might hopefully expect by now, you can provide data to a **Tree** by using the **dataProvider** property or just inline MXML:

```
<mx:Tree dataProvider="{myFamilyXML}" labelField="@name"
width="200" />
```

When using XML as the data source for a **Tree**, you should use the **labelField** property to identify what in the data source should be used for the label. If you don't, the visual result will be a bit of a mess (**Figure 5.15**). Often, you can use a specific attribute, such as **name**, for this purpose. To specify an attribute, just use the ***@attributeName*** syntax. For example, this next bit of XML represents a simple MXML document, with a root **Application** tag that has three children.

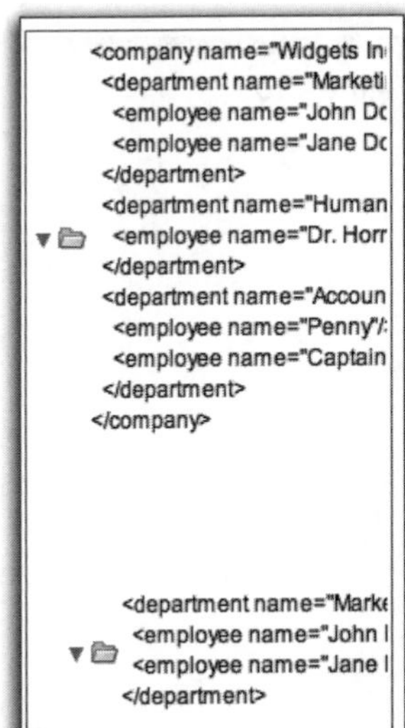

Figure 5.15

The XML data source is being defined inline and has generic element names. But its **tag** attributes, referred to using **@tag**, will be used as the labels in the **Tree**.

```
<mx:Tree labelField="@tag">
  <mx:dataProvider>
    <fx:XML><node tag="Application">
      <node tag="Script" />
      <node tag="Declarations" />
      <node tag="Tree">
        <node tag="XML" />
      </node>
    </node></fx:XML>
  </mx:dataProvider>
</mx:Tree>
```

In the next chapter, you'll learn how to use the **labelFunction** property and a formatting function to customize the **Tree**'s labels.

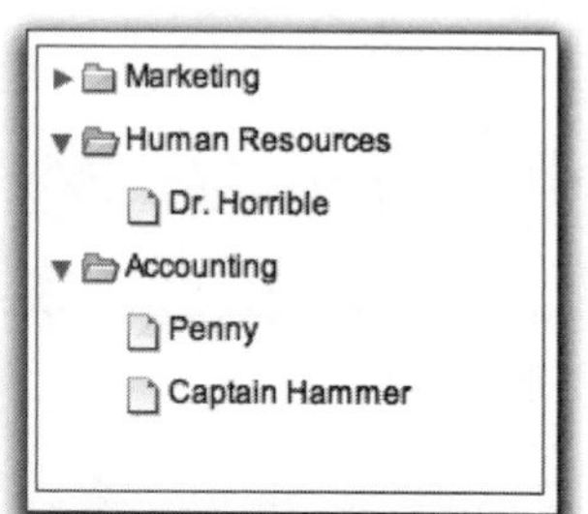

Figure 5.16

Another important property is **showRoot**. When set to false (true is the default), the **Tree** will not show the root element. You would want to do this when the root element is just a container, or otherwise meaningless. If there are multiple child elements, the **Tree** would then start with multiple top-level items (**Figure 5.16**).

Stylistically, you can impact the look of the tree by assigning hexadecimal colors to the following properties:

- **alternatingItemColors**
- **backgroundDefaultColor**
- **rollOverColor**
- **selectionColor**
- **textRollOverColor**
- **textSelectedColor**

You can also customize the icons in use, if you want.

Tree Events

The **Tree** triggers many of the same events that the other components discussed in this chapter do. First, of course, is **change**, for when the user selects a new item (a **change** event is not necessarily triggered when the user opens a new node). The **change** event creates an object of **ListEvent** type:

```
<mx:Tree id="someTree" dataProvider="{someData}" labelField="@attr"
change="handleTree(event)"/>
private function handleTree(event:ListEvent):void {
    // Use event.currentTarget.selectedItem.
}
```

The ***ComboBox***, ***DropDown-List***, and ***List*** components all generate ***IndexChangeEvents*** on change events; ***Tree***, defined in Halo, not Spark, generates a ***ListEvent*** type.

As with the other components, the **selectedItem** attribute will reflect the currently selected object of the data source. If using XML as the data provider, then **event.currentTarget.selectedItem**, or in the above, **someTree.selected Item**, will be XML, too.

A user can work the arrow keys to navigate through a **Tree**, triggering **change** events along the way. Or, more likely, use the mouse, which can also trigger **click**, **doubleClick**, and **itemClick** events. This last one is actually a **ListEvent**, not a **MouseEvent**, unlike the other two. The **Tree** has a few of its own events: **itemOpen**, **itemOpening**, and **itemClose**, defined in **mx.events.TreeEvent**. You can use these to take actions while the user is navigating the data hierarchy.

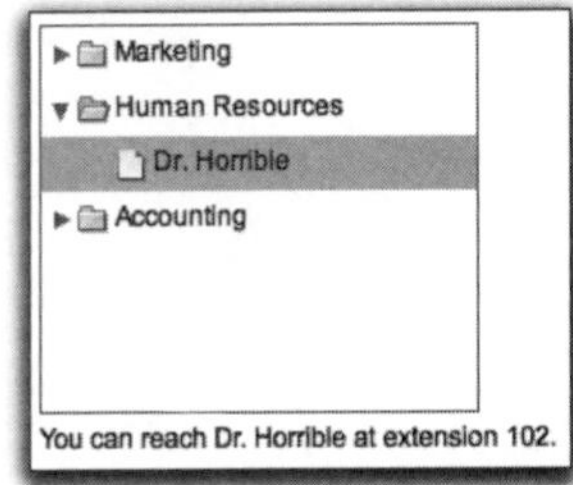

Figure 5.17

An Example

To demonstrate a use of a **Tree**, let's create a phone tree (mmm...pun). The **Tree** will let the user navigate through a company directory. When the user clicks an employee name, that person's phone extension will be displayed below the tree (**Figure 5.17**).

If you download the source code from the book's corresponding Web site (*www.dmcinsights.com/flex4*), you'll find this example in the **Ch05/Ch05_02** folder.

1. Create a new Web project in Flash Builder or your alternative development environment.

2. Within the **Declarations** section, create a new **XML** component:

```
<fx:Declarations>
    <fx:XML id="company"><company name="Widgets Inc.">
<department name="Marketing">
    <employee name="John Doe" ext="234" />
    <employee name="Jane Doe" ext="233" />
</department>
```

code continues on next page

```
<department name="Human Resources">
   <employee name="Dr. Horrible" ext="102" />
</department>
<department name="Accounting">
   <employee name="Penny" ext="345" />
   <employee name="Captain Hammer" ext="353" />
</department>
</company></fx:XML>
</fx:Declarations>
```

This XML component will be used as the data source for the tree. The root element is **company**. Within it are the departments and within each department are the employees. All of the data is stored in attributes: **name** and **ext**. Only employees have the phone extension properties, though.

3. Create a **Tree**:

```
<mx:Tree id="phoneTree" dataProvider="{company}" labelField=
"@name" change="handlePhoneTree(event);" width="200" />
```

The **Tree** has an **id** value of *phoneTree*, uses the **company** XML as the **dataProvider**, uses the **name** attribute for its labels, and calls the **handlePhoneTree()** function when a change occurs. I've also expanded its default width.

If you want, you can also set the **showRoot** property to false, so that the top-level listings will be the departments (see Figure 5.16).

4. Next, add a **Label** for the results:

```
<s:Label id="result" />
```

The **Label** starts off blank, and will be assigned text in the event handling function.

5. Within a **Script** block, import the **ListEvent** definition:

```
<fx:Script>
<![CDATA[
import mx.events.ListEvent;
]]>
</fx:Script>
```

The event-handling function will receive a **ListEvent** object whenever the **Tree**'s selected item changes. Therefore, the **ListEvent** definition must be imported here.

6. Also within the **Script** block, begin defining the **handlePhoneTree()** function:

```
private function handlePhoneTree(event:ListEvent):void {
```

This function takes one argument, an event, and returns no values.

7. Within the function, check that the currently selected item is an employee:

   if (event.currentTarget.selectedItem.name( ).localName == 'employee') {

   Only the **employee** nodes of the XML data have phone extensions, so the **Label** should only be updated when those nodes are selected. There are many ways you can check for that condition. Remember that **event.currentTarget.selectedItem** will be a bit of XML. To XML, I can apply the **name( )** method, which returns the name of the XML element in its **localName** property. Here I'm checking if the name equals *employee*.

   An alternative condition would be to check for the presence of the **ext** property:

   if (event.currentTarget.selectedItem.@ext != undefined)

8. Update the **Label**:

   result.text = "You can reach " + event.currentTarget.selectedItem.@name + ' at extension ' + event.currentTarget.selectedItem.@ext + '.';

   The displayed text in the **Label** will be some literal text plus the values of the XML's **name** and **ext** attributes.

9. Complete the conditional and the function:

   ```
     }
   }
   ```

10. Save, run, and test the completed application.

AIR DATA-DRIVEN COMPONENTS

When developing applications to run on the desktop through the Adobe AIR runtime, there are several more data-driven components you can use:

- **FileSystemComboBox**
- **FileSystemDataGrid**
- **FileSystemHistoryButton**
- **FileSystemList**
- **FileSystemTree**

All of these look to the user's file system (or, more commonly, a part of the file system) as the data source. For more information on any of them, see the official documentation.

THE DATAGRID COMPONENT

One of the most important data-driven components is the **DataGrid**, defined in the *mx* namespace. Unlike any other component, a **DataGrid** can display an entire table of information (see Figure 5.1). **DataGrid**s are highly customizable, making it possible for the user to

- Sort the table by clicking column headings
- Rearrange the order of columns
- Select multiple rows at once
- Edit records inline

As with many things in Flex, something this complicated is surprisingly easy to use, especially compared with the lengths one would have to go to in order to replicate the same functionality using HTML, CSS, and JavaScript.

tip

Generally speaking, an ***Array Collection*** will be the most common data source for ***DataGrid***s.

At a bare minimum, you create a **DataGrid** component by identifying the **dataProvider**:

```
<mx:DataGrid dataProvider="{statesAC}" />
```

tip

In Flash Builder, you can graphically customize a ***DataGrid***'s columns by clicking the Configure Columns button in the Properties panel.

Depending upon how the data source is defined, Flex may automatically generate corresponding columns and display all of the records accordingly. Still, it's pretty much always best to be explicit about the columns you want to use, and what the data source for each column should be. To do that, add **DataGrid Column** components within **columns** tags:

```
<mx:DataGrid dataProvider="{statesAC}">
    <mx:columns>
        <mx:DataGridColumn headerText="Abbreviation"
dataField="abbr"/>
        <mx:DataGridColumn headerText="State" dataField="state"/>
    </mx:columns>
</mx:DataGrid>
```

note

DataGridColumn has a ***labelFunction*** property that can be assigned a function whose return value will be used for that column's display. The next chapter will demonstrate this.

The columns will be created in the **DataGrid**, from left to right, in the order they are listed. The two most important properties in **DataGridColumn** are **headerText** and **dataField**. The former creates the label at the top of the column, which would otherwise be pulled from the data source. The second property identifies which part of each row of data should be used for that particular column.

When you explicitly identify the columns in a **DataGrid**, you can also:

- Control their order
- Customize the formatting of the displayed data
- Choose not to display certain data

You can further customize each individual column by setting the **DataGrid Column** properties like **width** and **minWidth**, **backgroundColor**, **paddingLeft**, **paddingRight**, **textAlign**, or any of the numerous font-related properties (as always, see the documentation for all the gory details). Still, you may find it best to customize the aesthetics of the **DataGrid** as a whole, rather than each individual column (more on this soon).

You can impact how the user interacts with an individual column by adjusting the following Boolean properties: **resizable**, **sortable**, and **editable**. If a column's **editable** property is true, *and the **DataGrid's editable** property is true*, the user can edit the data within the **DataGrid** itself. You'll see an example of this in just a few pages.

Unlike tables in HTML, the ***DataGrid*** component is not to be used to control the layout of an application. Arguably, this was never the intent of HTML tables, either.

Returning to the **DataGrid** component itself, there are stylistic properties, each of which takes a hexadecimal color value, or, in the case of **headerColors**, an array of color values:

- **headerColors**
- **horizontalGridLineColor**
- **rollOverColor**
- **selectionColor**
- **verticalLineGridColor**

The **horizontalGridLines** and **verticalGridLines** properties take Boolean values, indicating if those should be visible.

When it comes to sizing the **DataGrid**, you can use its **height** and **width** properties to size the entire component. The **minColumnWidth** value ensures that each column will be at least a certain width, which may result in horizontal scrollbars being automatically added.

Four properties take Boolean values and dictate what the user can and cannot do with the **DataGrid**: **draggableColumns**, **editable**, **resizableColumns**, and **sortableColumns**. By default, a user can move columns around (i.e., drag them from one spot to another), resize columns, and sort the data by clicking column headings. If you want to deny any of these options, set the corresponding property to false. Conversely, the **editable** property is false by default, but if you want the user to be able to edit the data inline, you can set this to true. You can further control the editing by setting **editable** to be true in the **DataGrid** but false in columns that should not be editable (**Figure 5.18**):

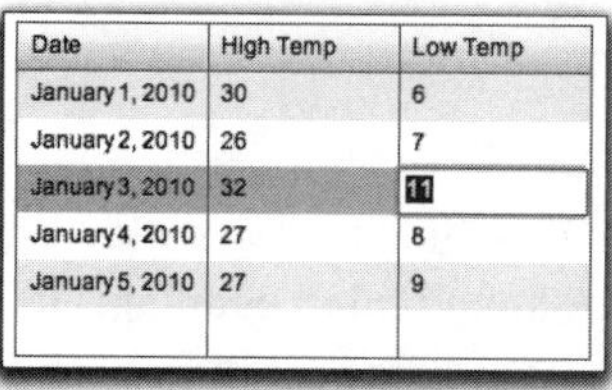

Date	High Temp	Low Temp
January 1, 2010	30	6
January 2, 2010	26	7
January 3, 2010	32	11
January 4, 2010	27	8
January 5, 2010	27	9

Figure 5.18

```
<mx:DataGrid dataProvider="{weatherInfo}" editable="true">
    <mx:columns>
        <mx:DataGridColumn headerText="Date" dataField="date"
        editable="false"/>
        <mx:DataGridColumn headerText="High Temp" dataField=
        "highTemp" editable="true"/>
        <mx:DataGridColumn headerText="Low Temp" dataField="lowTemp"
        editable="true"/>
    </mx:columns>
</mx:DataGrid>
```

tip

Since setting the ***DataGrid***'s ***editable*** property to true automatically makes every column editable, you don't have to set ***editable*** to true on the specific columns. I think it's best to still include them, however, so as to be explicit about the intent.

DataGrid Events

The **DataGrid** and **DataGridColumn** components trigger a number of events, the two most important being **click** and **change**. When the user clicks any item in a **DataGrid**, he or she will select the entire row of data. Doing so will trigger a **click MouseEvent** and a **change ListEvent**. In this regard, **DataGrid** behaves just like **List**, **DropDownList**, and **ComboBox**. There are other mouse events as well, such as **itemClick**, **itemDoubleClick**, and **itemRollOver**.

note

The ***change*** event is triggered when the user selects a new row. It does not reflect the changing of some of the ***DataGrid***'s data.

The **selectedItem** property of the component returns the currently selected row. You can also use the **rowIndex** and **columnIndex** properties to narrow down the focus a bit. Like most things in Flex, both begin indexing at 0.

Updating Data in a DataGrid

As I said, the **DataGrid** can be set so that the user can edit its records. To do so, you'll need to start by setting the **DataGrid**'s **editable** property to true. By setting the entire **DataGrid** to editable, every column will therefore be editable. If you don't want any particular columns to be editable, set their respective **editable** properties to false.

When a **DataGrid** is editable, the user just needs to click any singular piece of data to edit it (you may want to include instructions indicating such). By default, the user will be editing the value using a simple **TextInput** (it may not be apparent that the editor is, in fact, a **TextInput**). You can identify a custom editor, however, which I'll discuss in the next chapter.

As I said, the **DataGrid** is already defined so that it can do lots of things without any effort on your part. This is so true that you don't even need to add any programming to handle the user's editing of the data. After the user clicks a field and edits the data therein, the changes will automatically be reflected in the underlying data source, if possible (e.g., if the data came from a remote server call, the server data would not automatically be updated).

tip

If you download the source code from the book's corresponding Web site (*www.dmcinsights.com/flex4*), you'll find this example in the **Ch05/Ch05_03** folder.

As an example of this, let's create an application for managing employees (**Figure 5.19**). A **DataGrid** will display the list of current employees and allow the user to edit that information inline. A new employee can be added by filling out the form, then clicking a button; a current employee can be removed by selecting him or her in the **DataGrid** and clicking a different button.

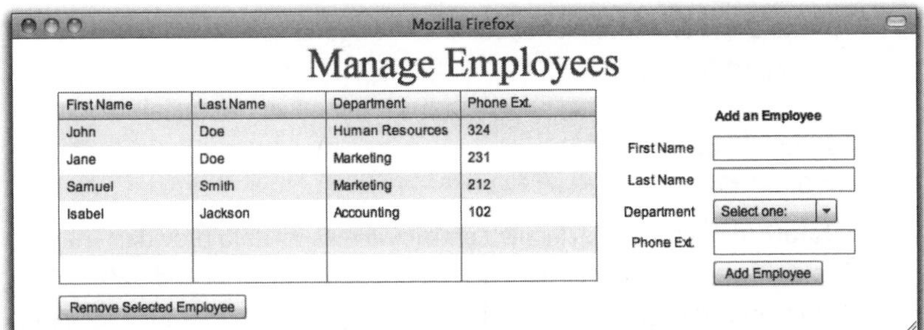

Figure 5.19

1. Create a new Web project in Flash Builder or your alternative development environment.

2. Create a **Label** for a title:

```
<s:Label text="Manage Employees" horizontalCenter="0" top="10"
fontSize="36" fontFamily="Times New Roman" color="#362EDE"/>
```

   The **Label** is centered horizontally, 10 pixels down. I've stylized the font a bit, too.

3. Add an **HGroup**:

```
<s:HGroup width="90%" height="80%" verticalCenter="20"
horizontalCenter="0">
</s:HGroup>
```

   To display the interface as two parts, I'll use an **HGroup**. The **DataGrid** will go on the left side and the form on the right. The **HGroup** takes up most of the available area and is horizontally centered, and vertically centered 20 pixels down.

4. Within the **HGroup**, add a **VGroup**:

```
<s:VGroup width="50%" gap="10">
</s:VGroup>
```

So that the button for removing an employee displays below the **DataGrid** (and not horizontally to the right), the **DataGrid** and button will go within a **VGroup**.

5. Create the **DataGrid**:

```
<mx:DataGrid width="100%" id="employeesDG" dataProvider=
"{employees}" editable="true">
   <mx:columns>
      <mx:DataGridColumn headerText="First Name" dataField=
      "firstName"/>
      <mx:DataGridColumn headerText="Last Name" dataField=
      "lastName"/>
      <mx:DataGridColumn headerText="Department" dataField=
      "department"/>
      <mx:DataGridColumn headerText="Phone Ext." dataField="ext"/>
   </mx:columns>
</mx:DataGrid>
```

The **DataGrid** uses an object called **employees** as its data provider. The grid contains four columns, with each column's **headerText** and **dataField** explicitly indicated. The component's **editable** property is set to true so that any column can be edited inline.

6. Add a button for removing employees:

```
<s:Button label="Remove Selected Employee" click=
"removeEmployee()" id="removeEmployeeButton"/>
```

This button, when clicked, will call the **removeEmployee()** function, sending along no arguments.

7. Add a **Form**:

```
<mx:Form width="50%">
   <mx:FormHeading label="Add an Employee"/>
</mx:Form>
```

8. Within the form, add inputs for the employee's first and last names:

```
<mx:FormItem label="First Name">
   <s:TextInput id="employeeFirstName"/>
</mx:FormItem>
<mx:FormItem label="Last Name">
   <s:TextInput id="employeeLastName"/>
</mx:FormItem>
```

This part is really straightforward, just be certain to create unique, meaningful **id**s.

9. Within the form, add a **DropDownList** for the employee's department:

```
<mx:FormItem label="Department">
  <s:DropDownList id="employeeDepartment" prompt="Select one:">
      <s:ArrayList>
          <fx:String>Accounting</fx:String>
          <fx:String>Human Resources</fx:String>
          <fx:String>Marketing</fx:String>
          <fx:String>Sales</fx:String>
      </s:ArrayList>
  </s:DropDownList>
</mx:FormItem>
```

To add a new employee, his or her department will be chosen from a list of four possibilities. To create that list, an **ArrayList** component is defined within the **DropDownList**.

10. Complete the form by adding an input for the phone extension, and a button:

```
<mx:FormItem label="Phone Ext.">
      <s:TextInput id="employeePhoneExt"/>
</mx:FormItem>
<mx:FormItem>
      <s:Button label="Add Employee" id="addEmployeeButton"
click="addEmployee()"/>
</mx:FormItem>
```

The button, when clicked, will call the **addEmployee()** function.

11. Within a **Script** block, create an **ArrayCollection**:

```
<fx:Script>
<![CDATA[
import mx.collections.ArrayCollection;
[Bindable]
private var employees:ArrayCollection = new ArrayCollection([{firstName:
'John', lastName:'Doe', ext:324, department:'Human Resources'},
{firstName:'Jane', lastName:'Doe', ext:231, department:'Marketing'},
{firstName:'Samuel', lastName:'Smith', ext:212, department:'Marketing'},
{firstName:'Isabel', lastName:'Jackson', ext:102,
department:'Accounting'}]);
]]>
</fx:Script>
```

This **ArrayCollection**, named **employees**, will be the main data set used by the application. To create it, the **ArrayCollection** definition must be imported first. Then the variable is declared and initialized with four starter employees. The variable must be declared as bindable in order to be properly used by the **DataGrid**.

The data provided to the **ArrayCollection** is an array of four objects. Each object has **firstName**, **lastName**, **ext**, and **department** properties. The syntax can be a bit hairy, so you can create the array (or the objects) separately, then create the **ArrayCollection**, if you prefer.

12. Within the **Script** block, define the **removeEmployee( )** function:

```
private function removeEmployee( ):void {
    if (employeesDG.selectedIndex >= 0) {
        employees.removeItemAt(employeesDG.selectedIndex);
    }
}
```

This function is called when the user clicks the Remove Selected Employee button. The function's job is to remove the selected employee from the data source, which is the **employees ArrayCollection**. To do that, you can call the collection's **removeItemAt( )** method, providing it with the index of the item to remove. To get that number, refer to the **DataGrid**'s **selectedIndex** property.

As a precaution, the removal will only be attempted if the **selectedIndex** is greater than or equal to 0, which will be the case when any row in the **DataGrid** has been selected. Since the **DataGrid**'s **allowMultipleSelections** property has not been set to true, only a single row at a time can be selected.

Because the **employees** variable is bound as the data provider to the **DataGrid**, removing an item from **employees** will automatically be reflected in the **DataGrid**.

13. Still within the **Script** block, define the **addEmployee( )** function:

```
private function addEmployee( ):void {
    employees.addItem({firstName:employeeFirstName.text,
    lastName:employeeLastName.text, ext:employeePhoneExt.text,
    department:employeeDepartment.selectedItem});
}
```

This function is called when the Add Employee button is clicked. This function's role is to add another element (i.e., object) to the **employees** collection. To do so, the collection's **addItem( )** method is called, providing it with the value, which in this case is an object.

The object has the same properties as the other objects in the collection. Its values are found by referring to the appropriate properties of the form elements: **text** for the **TextInputs** and **selectedItem** for the **DropDownList**.

Again, because the **employees** variable is bound as the data provider to the **DataGrid**, adding an item to **employees** will automatically be reflected in the **DataGrid**.

note

Because the form data is not validated, incomplete employee records can be added. You'll learn techniques in the next chapter for preventing this.

14. Save, run, and test the completed application.

    Figure 5.20 shows the result after removing one employee, adding another, and editing a third within the **DataGrid**.

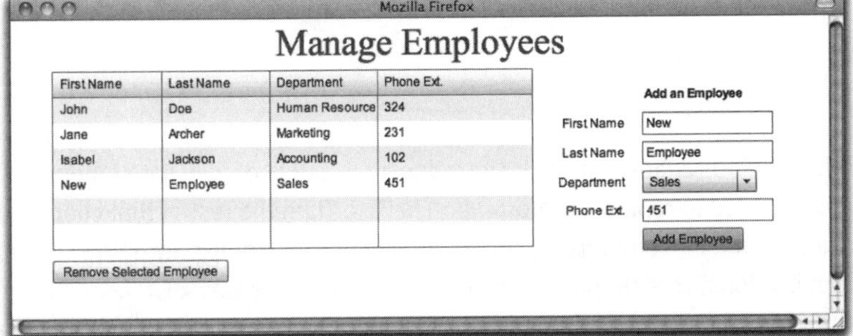

Figure 5.20

THE ADVANCEDDATAGRID

The **AdvancedDataGrid** component was added in Flex 3 (and is still defined in the Halo namespace) to provide oft-requested functionality. The **AdvancedDataGrid** takes a standard **DataGrid** and adds the ability to

- Sort using multiple columns (e.g., by last name, then first name)
- Further customize the look of rows and columns
- Display hierarchical or grouped data
- Aggregate data
- Create column groupings
- Select multiple cells (as well as multiple rows)

There are also extended item-rendering capabilities, which will mean more in the next chapter.

Because the **AdvancedDataGrid** is most useful for complex data sets and requires a hefty amount of code, I've chosen to omit discussion of the **AdvancedDataGrid** in any detail. Should the day come that you feel the **DataGrid** is no longer sufficient, check Adobe's documentation, or examples in Tour de Flex and other resources, for specifics on the **AdvancedDataGrid**.

6 MANIPULATING DATA

The previous chapter starts by introducing a couple of new data types that can be used to represent information in Flex. Then the rest of that chapter goes through the most important components you'll use to display data in Flash applications. This chapter builds on that one in many ways. First, you'll learn how to customize how data is displayed in those components by using *label functions* and *item renderers*. You'll also be introduced to one more data-driven component, the **DataGroup**, which uses item renderers exclusively. The chapter concludes with Flex's built-in formatters and validators, both of which provide quick and easy ways to work with common data elements.

USING LABEL FUNCTIONS

Chapter 5, "Displaying Data," which discusses many of the Flex data-driven components, often uses the **labelField** property. This property identifies the element, from the data source, that's to be used as the visible label. But if you would like to customize the displayed label in any way, including by applying a Flex formatter, you can go with the **labelFunction** property instead. This property gets assigned the name of a function to call, whose returned value will be used as the displayed label.

ComboBox, DropDownMenu, List, and Tree Label Functions

To use the **labelFunction** property with a **ComboBox**, **DropDownMenu**, **List**, or **Tree** component, assign it the name of the function that's to be called for generating the visual labels:

```
<s:List id="someList" dateProvider="{someDataSource}" labelFunction=
"someFunction">
```

You then define the function in ActionScript. You would need to write it so that it takes one argument, of generic type **Object**, and returns a string:

```
private function someFunction(item:Object):String {
}
```

The function will be called once for each item to be displayed in the component. Within the function, knowledge of the source object is used to change the displayed value. For example, in the previous chapter, I created and displayed a list of people. When a person was selected, his or her age was displayed in a **Label** (**Figure 6.1**).

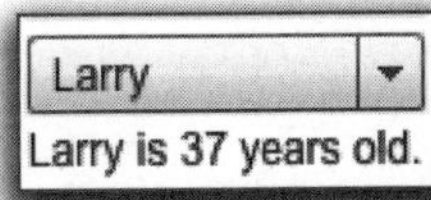

Figure 6.1

Here's how I could modify that **DropDownList** so that it displays each person's name and age (**Figure 6.2**):

Figure 6.2

```
<s:DropDownList id="person" labelFunction="formatPerson">
    <s:ArrayList id="people">
        <fx:Object name="Larry" age="37"/>
        <fx:Object name="Jessica" age="35"/>
        <fx:Object name="Zoe" age="3"/>
        <fx:Object name="Sam" age="3"/>
    </s:ArrayList>
</s:DropDownList>
```

The function would look like this:

```
private function formatPerson(item:Object):String {
    return item.name + ' (' + item.age + ')';
}
```

As another example, you might want to adjust the label used in a **Tree** based upon the type of element currently being displayed. If you have the following XML

```
<fx:Declarations>
    <fx:XML id="company"><company name="Widgets Inc.">
```

code continues on next page

```
<department name="Marketing">
    <employee name="John Doe" ext="234" />
    <employee name="Jane Doe" ext="233" />
</department>
<department name="Human Resources">
    <employee name="Dr. Horrible" ext="102" />
</department>
<department name="Accounting">
    <employee name="Penny" ext="345" />
    <employee name="Captain Hammer" ext="353" />
</department>
</company></fx:XML>
</fx:Declarations>
```

that XML could be used by the following **Tree** (without a label function):

```
<mx:Tree id="phoneTree" dataProvider="{company}" />
```

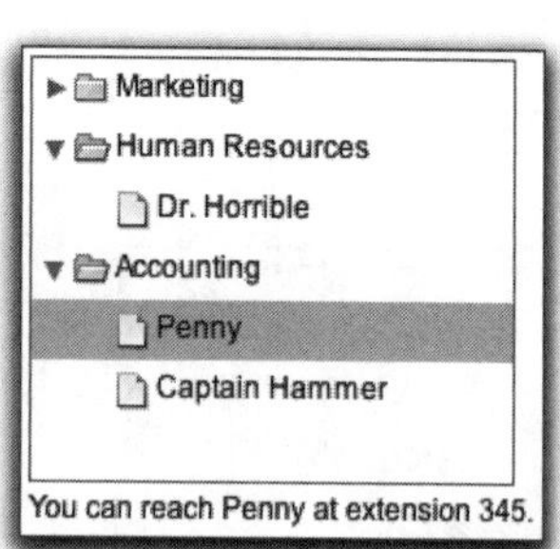

Figure 6.3

In the previous chapter, such a tree just displayed each name and, when the user selected an employee, the employee's extension appeared in a **Label** below the **Tree** (Figure 6.3).

Another way of accomplishing the goal of displaying each employee's extension would be to use label function with the **Tree**. The label function might be defined so that it adds the phone extension to employee labels and the word *Department* to non-employee elements. Here's how you would do that:

1. Create a new function within the ActionScript block:

   ```
   <fx:Script>
   <![CDATA[
   private function formatTreeLabel(item:Object):String {
   }
   ]]>
   </fx:Script>
   ```

   The function needs to be defined so that it takes one argument, of type **Object**, and returns a **String**.

2. Typecast the incoming data as **XML**:

   ```
   var node:XML = XML(item);
   ```

   This is an extra precaution you can take with XML data. This line converts the received generic **Object** (which is an object that contains XML) into a formal **XML** object.

3. Check if the XML's tag equals *employee*:

```
if (node.name( ).localName == 'employee') {
    return node.@name + ' (' + node.@ext + ')';
```

The **name( ).localName** property will return the name of the current element. If that's *employee*, then the function returns the employee's name and phone extension.

4. Check if the XML's tag equals *department*:

```
} else if (node.name( ).localName == 'department') {
  return node.@name + ' Department';
```

This is a variation on the conditional in Step 3. For department nodes, the department's name plus the word *Department* are returned.

5. If a *name* attribute exists, return it:

```
} else if (node.@name != undefined) {
  return node.@name;
```

With the above XML data, this clause will apply when showing the root node, which is an element of type *company*. Generally, though, this clause will come into play for any element that's not *employee* or *department* but that does have a *name* attribute.

tip

When using label functions, make sure they're written to properly handle whatever data may be displayed by the component.

6. Otherwise, return nothing:

```
} else {
  return '';
}
```

This **else** clause wouldn't apply with the above XML data, but is an extra precaution.

7. Complete the function:

```
}
```

8. Save, run, and test the completed application (**Figure 6.4**).

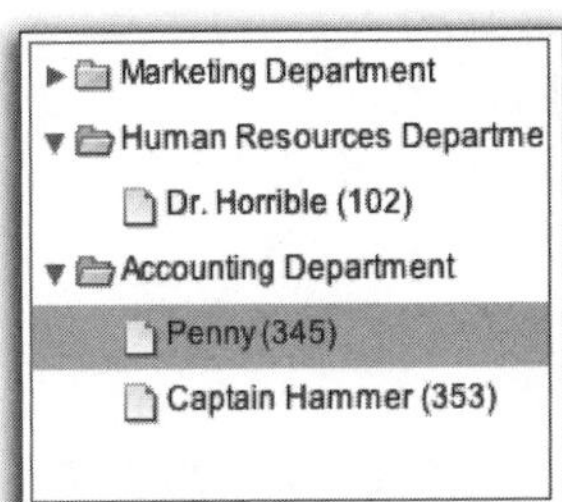

Figure 6.4

DataGrid and DataGridColumn Label Functions

In the previous examples, I've used label functions with **DropDownList** and **Tree** components (it's used the same for the **List** and **ComboBox**, too). The **DataGrid** and **DataGridColumn** components also have a **labelFunction** property, but the function in these two cases is defined and applied differently. If assigned to the **DataGrid** component, the same label function will be called for every column of every row of displayed data. If assigned to just a **DataGrid Column**, only the values displayed in that column of every row will be determined using the function.

The associated function is written differently than those for **List**, **ComboBox**, **DropDownList**, and **Tree**. Instead of taking one argument, the function will take two:

tip

The names ***item*** and ***column*** are commonly used as the arguments for label functions, but this is not required.

```
private function someFunction(item:Object, column:DataGridColumn):String {
}
```

The function still returns a string, and its first argument is still a generic **Object**, representing the data to be displayed; the added second argument is of type **DataGridColumn**. You can use the second argument to flexibly adjust how the function responds.

For example, say you have the following **ArrayCollection** of information:

```
[Bindable]
private var checkbook:ArrayCollection = new ArrayCollection([{entry:'Rent',
amount:-900}, {entry:'Groceries', amount:-150.67}, {entry:'Salary',
amount:1845.23}, {entry:'Interest', amount:3.87}]);
```

entry	amount
Rent	($900.00)
Groceries	($150.67)
Salary	$1,845.23
Interest	$3.87

Figure 6.5

Now say you wanted to display this information in a **DataGrid**, and wanted to wrap negative numbers in parentheses, accounting style (**Figure 6.5**).

As that formatting will only apply to a single column in the **DataGrid**, you could have that column use the **formatNumbers( )** function:

```
<mx:DataGrid dataProvider="{checkbook}">
    <mx:columns>
        <mx:DataGridColumn dataField="entry" />
        <mx:DataGridColumn dataField="amount" labelFunction=
        "formatNumbers" />
    </mx:columns>
</mx:DataGrid>
```

And the function would just need to be defined like so:

```
private function formatNumbers(item:Object, column:DataGridColumn):String {
    return currencyFormatter.format(item.amount);
}
```

The desired output is achieved thanks to the following formatter (which you'll learn about in detail at the end of the chapter):

```
<mx:CurrencyFormatter id="currencyFormatter" useNegativeSign="false"
precision="2" />
```

This is a perfectly good use of a label function in a **DataGrid**. However, in that function, the second argument—the **DataGridColumn**—was never used because you already knew exactly which column would be formatted. So what if you wanted to apply this same approach to a larger set of values, such as in the following:

```
private var monthlyCheckbook:ArrayCollection = new
ArrayCollection([{entry:'Rent', January:-900, February:-900, March:0},
{entry:'Groceries', January:-150.67, February:-123.40, March:-144.89},
{entry:'Salary', January:1845.23, February:1849.50, March:1845.23},
{entry:'Interest', January:3.87, February:2.17, March:0}]);
```

In this case, the **DataGrid** would call the function for every column:

```
<mx:DataGrid dataProvider="{monthlyCheckbook}" labelFunction=
"formatNumbers">
    <mx:columns>
        <mx:DataGridColumn dataField="entry" headerText="Entry" />
        <mx:DataGridColumn dataField="January" />
        <mx:DataGridColumn dataField="February" />
        <mx:DataGridColumn dataField="March" />
    </mx:columns>
</mx:DataGrid>
```

The function would then need to be defined in such a way that it formatted and returned the appropriate value for each column. It would also need to recognize that the first column—which is a string description of a line item—does not get the currency formatting treatment. Here's how that function would be defined:

```
private function formatNumbers(item:Object,
column:DataGridColumn):String {
    if (column.dataField == 'entry') {
        return item[column.dataField];
    } else {
        return currencyFormatter.format(item[column.dataField]);
    }
}
```

As **column** represents the current **DataGridColumn**, you can refer to its properties, such as **dataField,** within the function. This value corresponds to what's been set in the MXML. So the first time this function will be called will be for the first column in the first row. At that point, **column.dataField** will be equal to *entry*, so the function should just return the item's entry value for the first row. To do that, you can treat item as an array and return **item.entry**, **item[entry]**, or, as above, **item[column.dataField]**.

If it's not the first column, then the same formatting of the numbers (as in the earlier label function) should occur. To do that, the actual value is referenced via **item[column.dataField]**. Unlike the previous **return** statement, you could not return **item.January** or **item[January]** here, as that would not always be the column currently under examination. **Figure 6.6** shows the end result.

Entry	January	February	March
Rent	($900.00)	($900.00)	$0.00
Groceries	($150.67)	($123.40)	($144.89)
Salary	$1,845.23	$1,849.50	$1,845.23
Interest	$3.87	$2.17	$0.00

Figure 6.6

ITEM RENDERERS

Many of the data-driven components, including **List**, **ComboBox**, **DropDownList**, **Tree**, **DataGrid**, and **AdvancedDataGrid**, can use *item renderers* to control how data is displayed. Whereas a **labelFunction** can customize the displayed information, an item renderer acts more like a template, and allows you to display more than just a string.

Item renderers can be written in ActionScript or MXML, but I'll use MXML here to make the discussion most approachable. For the example, I'm going to (egotistically) list a few of the books I've written. To start, I've got the following **ArrayList** of information about the books:

```
private var myBooks:ArrayList = new ArrayList([
{title: 'PHP 6 and MySQL 5 for Dynamic Web Sites', year: 2008, image:
'../assets/php6mysql5.png'},
{title: 'Adobe AIR with Ajax', year: 2008, image: '../assets/air.png'},
{title: 'Ruby', year: 2009, image: '../assets/ruby.png'}
]);
```

I can easily display each title in a **List** like so (**Figure 6.7**):

```
<s:List dataProvider="{myBooks}" labelField="title" />
```

PHP 6 and MySQL 5 for Dynamic Web Sites
Adobe AIR with Ajax
Ruby

Figure 6.7

If I want to display the title and publication year, I could make use of a label function:

```
<s:List dataProvider="{myBooks}" labelFunction="formatListLabel" />
private function formatListLabel(item:Object):String {
    return item.title + ' (' + item.year + ')';
}
```

But if I wanted to also display the image, I can't do that using a label function, as such functions only return strings. The alternative is to use an item renderer. An item renderer allows me to specify the components and formatting to use to display an individual item. This is how I might want each item to be displayed using components:

```
<s:HGroup gap="5">
    <mx:Image source="image" />
    <s:Label text="title" fontSize="16" />
    <s:Label text="(year)" fontSize="12" />
</s:HGroup>
```

That combination of components, wrapped within an **HGroup**, will give me the layout shown in **Figure 6.8**. Certainly you could do more to make this look fancy, but this is already so much more elaborate than what can be accomplished using a label function.

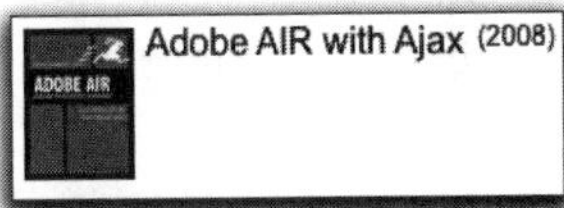

Figure 6.8

In those components, the *image*, *title*, and *year* values need to come from the individual item being displayed. Within item renderers, the currently rendered item will automatically be available through an object named **data**. So the item renderer template can actually be defined as

```
<s:HGroup gap="5">
    <mx:Image source="{data.image}" />
    <s:Label text="{data.title}" fontSize="16" />
    <s:Label text="({data.year})" fontSize="12" />
</s:HGroup>
```

There are three places you can define this renderer so that it's usable by a component: in an external file, in the **Declarations** section, and inline. I'll demonstrate each separately. Note that over the next several pages, I'll create an item renderer to be used with a **List** component. After those demonstrations, I'll briefly discuss how item renderers to be used by other components will differ.

 **tip**

Defining item renderers using ActionScript is much more sophisticated, requiring more knowledge of object-oriented programming, and is beyond the scope of this book.

External Item Renderers

Here are the steps you would take to define an item renderer in an external file:

tip

If you're using Flash Builder, you can choose File > New > MXML Item Renderer to start the wizard that will help you create the renderer in an external file.

1. Create a new, MXML file.
2. Add the XML declaration:
   ```
   <?xml version="1.0" encoding="utf-8"?>
   ```
   All XML documents should begin with this.
3. Create an opening **ItemRenderer** tag:
   ```
   <s:ItemRenderer xmlns:fx="http://ns.adobe.com/mxml/2009"
           xmlns:s="library://ns.adobe.com/flex/spark"
           xmlns:mx="library://ns.adobe.com/flex/mx">
   ```
   The **ItemRenderer** component is defined in Spark. In its opening tag, you should declare the namespaces, just as you do in the primary MXML file's **Application** tag. This is necessary so that this file can reference components such as **Image** and **Label,** defined in the Halo and Spark namespaces.
4. Define the item renderer:
   ```
   <s:HGroup gap="5" paddingTop="15">
     <mx:Image source="../assets/{data.image}" />
     <s:Label text="{data.title}" fontSize="16" />
     <s:Label text="({data.year})" fontSize="12" />
   </s:HGroup>
   ```
   This code is exactly as you've already seen it, save for the addition of the **paddingTop** property. As the renderer will be used by multiple, subsequent items, I want to create a gap between each, accomplished using **paddingTop** (you could also use **paddingBottom**). Conversely, the **HGroup**'s **gap** property creates a five-pixel gap among the children of the **HGroup**: the **Image**, **Label**, and **Label**.
5. Close the **ItemRenderer** tag:
   ```
   </s:ItemRenderer>
   ```
6. Save the file in your project's directory.

   I would recommend using the backwards domain naming scheme, first introduced in Chapter 3, "ActionScript You Need to Know." My company's name is DMC Insights, so I would create, within the *src* folder, a *com* folder. Within that I would create a *dmcinsights* folder. Within that folder, I would save this file as *BookListRenderer.mxml* (**Figure 6.9**).

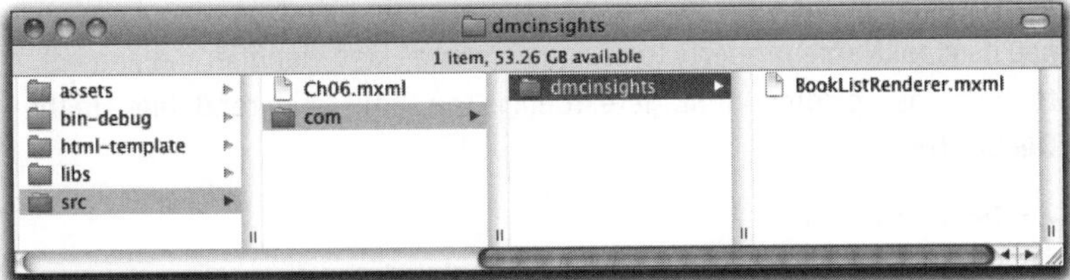

Figure 6.9

Alternatives would be to store the file in *src/components/renderers* or *src/views/renderers*. It's really a matter of personal preference how you organize these files; just choose a route that makes sense to you.

tip

In Chapter 10, "Creating Custom Code," you'll learn how to create custom components, which is very similar to creating item renderers.

To use the item renderer, add **itemRenderer="*path/to/renderer*"** to the **List** tag in the primary MXML file. Assuming the renderer is stored in *src/com/dmcinsights/BookListRenderer.mxml*, you would use

```
<s:List dataProvider="{myBooks}" itemRenderer="com.dmcinsights.BookListRenderer">
```

Note that you just use the basename of the file as the name of the renderer, without the *.mxml* extension. **Figure 6.10** shows the same **List** as in Figure 6.7, now using the item renderer.

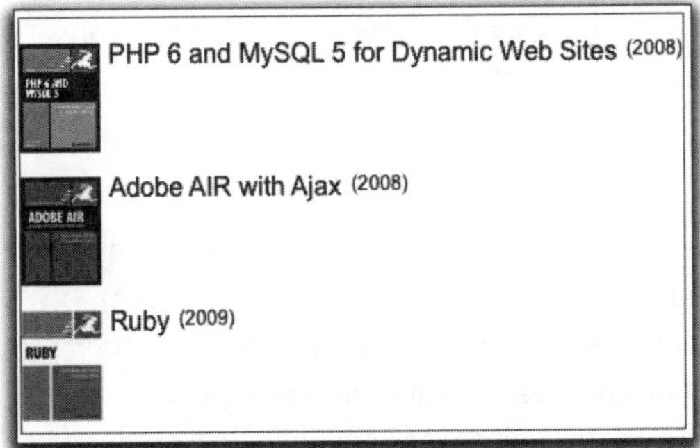

Figure 6.10

Declared Item Renderers

If you'd rather not separate out your renderer definition from the application that uses it, you can define a renderer in the primary MXML file. As the renderer is a non-visual component (on its own, that is; it's used by a visual component), you would create it within the **Declarations** section. To do so, you still make use of the **ItemRenderer** tags, but you don't need to include the namespace declarations, as the file already has those. But **ItemRenderer** element must be wrapped within a **Component** element, defined in the *fx* namespace. This element is used to define your own components. You use its **className** property to assign a unique class identifier (i.e., *name*) to the made-up component. Here, then, is the same renderer defined in the **Declarations** section:

```
<fx:Declarations>
<fx:Component className="BookListRenderer">
   <s:ItemRenderer>
      <s:HGroup gap="5" paddingTop="15">
         <mx:Image source="{data.image}" />
         <s:Label text="{data.title}" fontSize="16" />
         <s:Label text="({data.year})" fontSize="12" />
      </s:HGroup>
   </s:ItemRenderer>
</fx:Component>
</fx:Declarations>
```

You'll note that the renderer still uses the **data** object to reference individual values.

To use this renderer in a component, identify it with the **itemRenderer** property:

```
<s:List dataProvider="{myBooks}" itemRenderer="BookListRenderer">
```

In this case, as the renderer is defined within the same application file, you don't need to provide any reference to it such as *com.dmcinsights*.

Inline Renderers

The third way to define renderers is inline. Just as you can declare a data source within a component, you can also declare a renderer within a component. When you do so, you don't use the **itemRenderer** property in the opening tag. Instead, use opening and closing **itemRenderer** tags within the component, where the definition will take place. As with defining a renderer in the **Declarations**, you don't need to include the namespace declarations, but you do need to wrap the renderer within **Component**. Here's the same **List**:

tip

You can define item renderers inline within ***DataGridColumns***, too.

```
<s:List dataProvider="{myBooks}">
   <s:itemRenderer>
      <fx:Component>
         <s:ItemRenderer>
            <s:HGroup gap="5" paddingTop="15">
               <mx:Image source="{data.image}" />
               <s:Label text="{data.title}" fontSize="16" />
```

```
                <s:Label text="({data.year})" fontSize="12" />
            </s:HGroup>
        </s:ItemRenderer>
    </fx:Component>
  </s:itemRenderer>
</s:List>
```

Drop-In Item Renderers

Another way you can work with item renderers is by using so-called *drop-in* renderers, which is to say using another Flex component as the renderer. For example, a **DataGridColumn** uses a **Label** as its renderer by default. **Figure 6.11** shows how my list of books would be displayed in a **DataGrid** without any customization of the renderers.

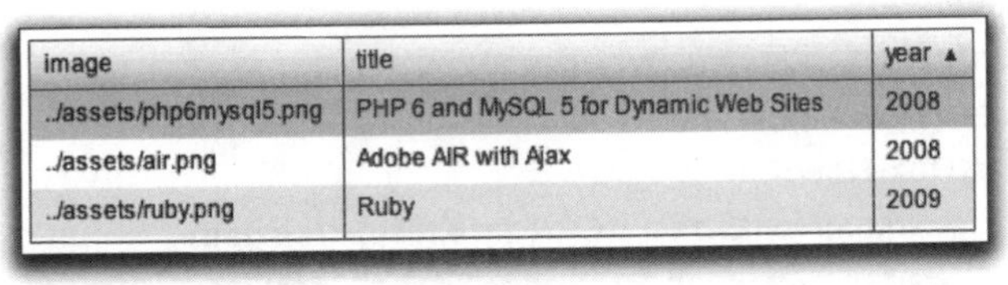

image	title	year ▲
../assets/php6mysql5.png	PHP 6 and MySQL 5 for Dynamic Web Sites	2008
../assets/air.png	Adobe AIR with Ajax	2008
../assets/ruby.png	Ruby	2009

Figure 6.11

Logically, instead of showing the name of the image, I would want to show the image itself. To simply accomplish this, just tell the **DataGridColumn** to use an **Image** component as its renderer (**Figure 6.12**):

```
<mx:DataGrid dataProvider="{myBooks}" rowHeight="50">
  <mx:columns>
    <mx:DataGridColumn dataField="image" itemRenderer=
    "mx.controls.Image" />
    <mx:DataGridColumn dataField="title" />
    <mx:DataGridColumn dataField="year" />
  </mx:columns>
</mx:DataGrid>
```

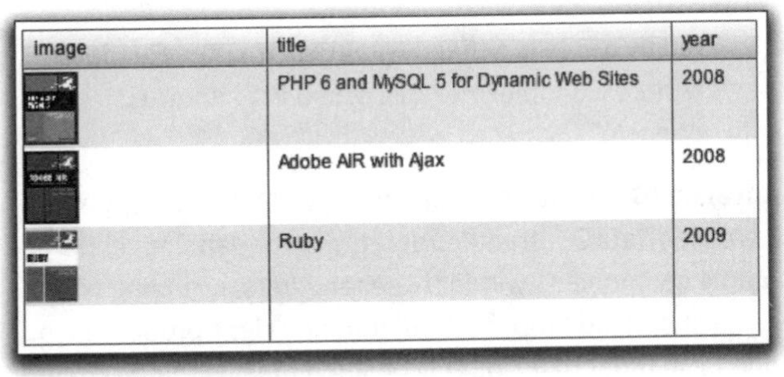

image	title	year
	PHP 6 and MySQL 5 for Dynamic Web Sites	2008
	Adobe AIR with Ajax	2008
	Ruby	2009

Figure 6.12

Comparing Component Renderers

Except for the preceding example of a drop-in renderer used by a **DataGrid Column**, the item renderers created in this section were all used by a **List** component. In every case, the renderer was defined within **s:ItemRenderer** tags. When creating renderers for a **ComboBox** or a **DropDownList**, you would still want to use the **ItemRenderer** tags. However, the **ComboBox** and **Drop DownList** components can only display a single line of text for each element, so you're pretty much restricted to using the **Label** and **RichText** components in the renderers. But you can still do more using, say, **RichText** in a renderer than you can just using a label function. Note the following example (**Figure 6.13**):

tip

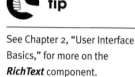

See Chapter 2, "User Interface Basics," for more on the ***RichText*** component.

```
<s:DropDownList dataProvider="{myBooks}" width="400">
  <s:itemRenderer>
    <fx:Component>
      <s:ItemRenderer>
        <s:RichText>
          <s:textFlow>
            <s:TextFlow>
              <s:span fontSize="16">{data.title}</s:span>
              <s:tab/><s:span fontStyle="italic" fontSize=
              "12">{data.year}</s:span>
            </s:TextFlow>
          </s:textFlow>
        </s:RichText>
      </s:ItemRenderer>
    </fx:Component>
  </s:itemRenderer>
</s:DropDownList>
```

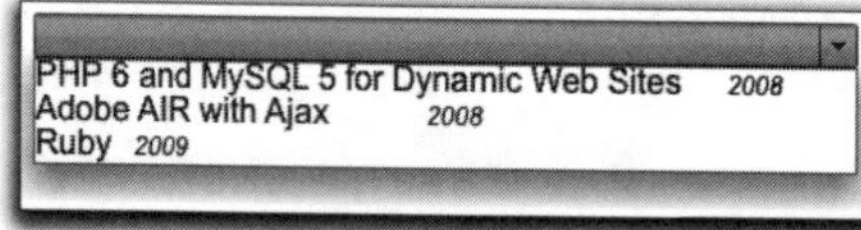

Figure 6.13

An item renderer to be used by a **Tree** is defined within **MXTreeItemRenderer** tags. It makes use of *view states*, a topic to be discussed in Chapter 11, "Improving the User Experience."

tip

Item renderers applied to a ***DataGrid*** or ***AdvancedDataGrid*** as a whole will also apply to the column headings.

The **DataGrid** and **AdvancedDataGrid** components have **MXDataGridItem Renderer** and **MXAdvancedDataGridItemRenderer** tags for defining renderers. You can use multiple components within these renderers, including non-text ones. However, you should add **top**, **bottom**, **left**, and **right** properties to the renderer components in order to absolutely position them within each cell.

CHANGING THE EDITOR

In the previous section on item renderers, I mention how you can use existing Flex components as an item renderer, such as an **Image** in place of a **Label** (this is called a *drop-in* renderer). In very much the same way, you can customize how data is *edited* within components that allow inline editing, such as the **DataGrid**.

When you set a **DataGrid**'s **editable** property to true, the user can alter the displayed data by clicking any cell. When he or she does so, the cell will turn into a **TextInput** (**Figure 6.14**).

First Name	Last Name	Department	Phone Ext.
John	Doe	Human Resources	324
Jane	Doe	Marketing	231
Samuel	Smith	Marketing	212
Isabel	Jackson	Accounting	102

Figure 6.14

To change the item editor, assign a component to the column's **itemEditor** property. For example, if you have editable data that should be a positive integer, editing this as a **NumericStepper** would make more sense. Here's how that **DataGridColumn** would be defined (**Figure 6.15**):

```
<mx:DataGridColumn dataField="qty" itemEditor="mx.controls.
NumericStepper" editorDataField="value" />
```

You'll notice there that you must use the full name for the component: *mx.controls.NumericStepper*, not just *NumericStepper*.

By default, the **DataGridColumn** will base its edited value upon the **text** property of the editor. This makes sense for the default **TextInput**, but a **NumericStepper** doesn't have a **text** property, so the above code assigns *value* to the **editorDataField** property. In other words, the edited value will come from the **value** property of the editor (the **NumericStepper**).

If you want to tweak the use of the editor component, you can just create the editor within the column's **itemEditor** property tags:

```
<mx:DataGridColumn dataField="qty" editorDataField="value">
    <mx:itemEditor>
        <fx:Component>
            <mx:NumericStepper minimum="0" stepSize="1" />
        </fx:Component>
    </mx:itemEditor>
</mx:DataGridColumn>
```

note

Changing editors apply to ***DataGrid***, ***AdvancedDataGrid***, ***List***, and ***Tree*** components. For the sake of simplicity, I'm just using ***DataGrid***s in this section.

tip

If you use, say, a ***Numeric Stepper*** as an item renderer, it will also be available as the item editor.

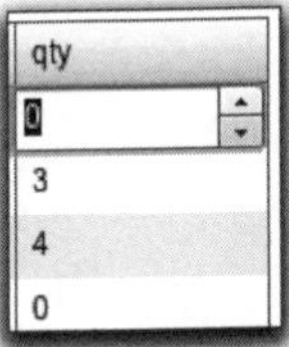

Figure 6.15

tip

The ***DateChooser*** and ***Color Picker*** components would also make good choices as drop-in editors as both provide functionality far beyond a ***TextInput***.

 **tip**

The ***DataGroup*** is, generally speaking, a new and improved version of the older Flex 3 Repeater component. The ***Repeater*** still exists in Flex, but I don't discuss it in this book.

 **tip**

Flex 4 also defines a ***Skinnable-DataContainer***, which is a more customizable ***DataGroup***. You'll see it in Chapter 13, "Improving the Appearance."

As you might imagine, you don't have to use just predefined Flex components as editors—you can create your own custom ones. This is a more advanced topic, requiring more knowledge of object-oriented programming, so I'll return to it in Chapter 10.

THE DATAGROUP COMPONENT

There is one more data-driven component I want to discuss, the **DataGroup**. This component wasn't addressed in Chapter 5 because it requires item renderers. But the **DataGroup** is easy to use because it's really just a bare-bones **List**. I say "bare-bones" because the **DataGroup** lacks default item renderers and scrollbars, so without customization a **DataGroup** won't do anything. On the other hand, it performs well because it has no additional overhead, and you can implement just the features you require. A **DataGroup** can be used like a **List**, to merely display information, but a **DataGroup** can also display visual components, which is to say it can take MXML as all or part of its data source.

Creating a DataGroup

The minimal syntax for creating a **DataGroup** is

```
<s:DataGroup dataProvider="{someData}" itemRenderer="someRenderer" />
```

The **itemRenderer** property needs to be assigned an actual item renderer. There are two already defined: **spark.skins.spark.DefaultItemRenderer** and **spark.skins.spark.ComplexItemRenderer**. The former renders simple text; the latter renders visual controls. You can see an example of rendering MXML in the Adobe documentation and tutorials.

You'll often use a **DataGroup** with a custom item renderer you've created using the steps already outlined. The renderer could be defined in an external MXML file, in the **Declarations** section, or even inline. This **DataGroup** will look similar to the earlier **List**, but without an outline or scrollbars (**Figure 6.16**):

```
<s:DataGroup dataProvider="{myBooks}">
    <s:itemRenderer>
        <fx:Component>
            <s:ItemRenderer>
                <s:HGroup gap="5" paddingTop="15">
                    <mx:Image source="{data.image}" />
                    <s:Label text="{data.title}" fontSize="16" />
```

```
            <s:Label text="({data.year})" fontSize="12" />
        </s:HGroup>
    </s:ItemRenderer>
  </fx:Component>
 </s:itemRenderer>
</s:DataGroup>
```

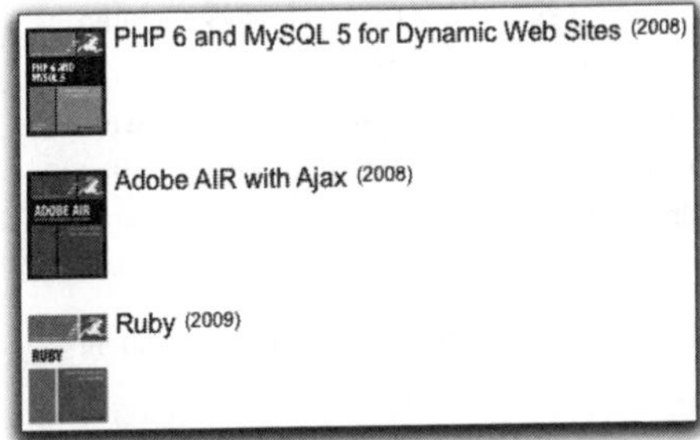

Figure 6.16

note

Multiple components defined within an item renderer must be defined within a container, such as ***HGroup***.

As with the earlier item renderer examples, the renderer makes use of the **data** object to access each item to be displayed.

tip

The ***DataGroup*** also allows you to create your own, custom layout, in lieu of using the predefined ones.

Controlling the Layout

The **DataGroup**, like a **List**, has a **layout** property that can be used to display the **DataGroup** in different ways. Note that the default layout is **BasicLayout**, which is absolute positioning. This means that each item being displayed will be placed on top of the previous one, unless special measures are taken. In order to create the layout shown in Figure 6.16, I had to apply the **VerticalLayout**:

tip

You can add scrollbars to a ***Data Group*** by wrapping it within the ***Scrollers*** element. See Chapter 2 for more on this component.

```
<s:DataGroup dataProvider="{myBooks}">
  <s:layout>
    <s:VerticalLayout />
  </s:layout>
  <s:itemRenderer>
    <fx:Component>
      <s:ItemRenderer>
        <s:HGroup gap="5" paddingTop="15">
          <mx:Image source="{data.image}" />
          <s:Label text="{data.title}" fontSize="16" />
          <s:Label text="({data.year})" fontSize="12" />
        </s:HGroup>
      </s:ItemRenderer>
    </fx:Component>
  </s:itemRenderer>
</s:DataGroup>
```

USING VIRTUALIZATION

The **DataGroup** component supports *virtualization*, which is an internal system for improving an application's performance when dealing with large data sets. If you were to display, using a **DataGroup**, several hundred items, the amount of memory required, as well as how long it would take to draw every item on the screen, would be problematic. Further, it would not make sense for all of those to be actually generated, as there's no way the user can see them all at once. In such cases, you can enact *virtualization*, wherein only the visible elements will be created at first. Then, when the user scrolls or takes whatever action to view more elements, the **DataGroup** will reuse the existing renderers to display the now-visible items, rather than creating new renderers for each one.

To enable virtualization, set the **useVirtualLayout** property of the layout type element to true:

```
<s:DataGroup dataProvider="{someData}" itemRenderer="someRenderer">
    <s:layout>
        <s:VerticalLayout useVirtualLayout="true" />
```

This feature is only available when using **VerticalLayout**, **HorizontalLayout**, or **TileLayout** (i.e., not with **BasicLayout**).

You can also provide the **DataGroup** with a typical object that represents the basic data it'll display. By doing so, you can help size the items appropriately.

FORMATTING DATA

Quite commonly an application will need to format some of the data it displays, be it an item's price, a specific date, or what-have-you. For this reason, Flex has five predefined formatting tools that you can use in your applications:

 **tip**

The formatting components are defined in the Halo namespace, specifically ***mx.formatters***.

- **CurrencyFormatter**
- **DateFormatter**
- **NumberFormatter**
- **PhoneFormatter**
- **ZipCodeFormatter**

I'll begin the chapter by explaining how to create, customize, and apply these formatters to your code.

Creating Formatters

To use a formatter, you must first create an instance of it. As formatters are non-visual elements, they are created within a **Declarations** section. You'll also want to give each formatter a unique **id** value:

```
<fx:Declarations>
    <mx:ZipCodeFormatter id="zipFormatter" />
</fx:Declarations>
```

That's the bare minimum for creating a formatter and sometimes that alone will be all you need to do in an application. Still, each formatter has its own unique properties that you can tweak to alter the formatting.

For example, the **NumberFormatter** has these properties: **decimalSeparator From, decimalSeparatorTo, precision, rounding, thousandsSeparatorFrom, thousandsSeparatorTo, useNegativeSign**, and **useThousandsSeparator**. The **decimalSeparatorFrom, decimalSeparatorTo, thousandsSeparatorFrom**, and **thousandsSeparatorTo** properties establish the character to use to indicate decimals and thousands, both in the original data (the "from") and the output (the "to").

By default, no precision is set, meaning that all decimals will be displayed. You can assign to the **precision** property the number of digits to show after the decimal point. The **rounding** property can be assigned the values *none*, *up*, *down*, *nearest*; the default is *none*. The **useNegativeSign** and **useThousands Separator** properties take Boolean values dictating if those should be present, when appropriate.

With all this in mind, this next component will format numbers as 12345, rounded down to the next integer:

```
<mx:NumberFormatter id="integerFormatter" precision="0" rounding=
"down" useThousandsSeparator="false" />
```

The **CurrencyFormatter** is just **NumberFormatter** plus the addition of properties for setting and aligning the currency symbol. The **alignSymbol** property places the currency symbol on the left or right side of the number. The **currencySymbol** property changes the symbol itself. The defaults are to format numbers using the standard Canadian-American approach: $12,456.78. If you wanted currency formatted as Euros, with decimals and commas switched, and the Euro symbol on the right, you'd define the formatter as

```
<mx:CurrencyFormatter id="euroFormatter" alignSymbol="right"
currencySymbol="€" decimalSeparatorTo="," thousandsSeparatorTo="."
precision="2" />
```

The **PhoneFormatter** formats US and international phone numbers. Its most important property is **formatString**, which dictates how the entire number should be formatted. The assigned value uses a combination of #, to represent each digit, and literal characters. The default formatting is (###) ###-####.

The **ZipCodeFormatter** formats US and Canadian zip codes. For the United States, the zip code can be either five or nine digits long (called 5+4); Canadian zip codes contain six numbers. Again, the **formatString** property is most important; it can have one of five possible values:

- #####-####
- ##### ####
- ##### (the default)
- ###-###
- ### ###

The first three formats are for U.S. zip codes; the last two for Canadian.

The **DateFormatter** just has a **formatString** property to set. You assign to it a string indicating the desired format. The string should be composed of the meaningful characters listed in **Table 6.1**, plus any other literal characters you want, such as spaces, commas, slashes, and hyphens.

Table 6.1 DateFormatter Formatting Characters

Characters	Meaning	Example(s)
YY	Two-digit Year	10
YYYY	Four-digit Year	2010
M	Month as one or two digits	1, 12
MM	Two-digit month	01, 12
MMM	Month as three characters	Jan, Dec
MMMM	Full month name	January
D	Day as one or two digits	1, 31
DD	Day as two digits	01, 31
E	Day of the week as one digit	0 (Sunday)
EE	Day of the week as two digits	00 (Sunday)

Table 6.1 DateFormatter Formatting Characters *(continued)*

Characters	Meaning	Example(s)
EEE	Day of the week as three characters	Sun
EEEE	Full day of the week name	Sunday
A	AM/PM	AM
J	Hour in 24-hour format as one or two digits	0, 23
JJ	Hour in 24-hour format as two digits	00, 23
H	Hour in 24-hour format as one digit or two digits, starting at 1	1, 24
K	Hour in 12-hour format, starting at 0	0, 11
L	Hour in 12-hour format, starting at 1	1, 12
N	Minute as one or two digits	1, 59
NN	Minute as two digits	01, 59
S	Seconds as one or two digits	1, 59
SS	Seconds as two digits	01, 59

So the following **DateFormatter** will output the date as *January 1, 2010*:

```
<mx:DateFormatter id="longDate" formatString="MMMM D, YYYY" />
```

This next one will output the date and time as *01/01/10 18:36*:

```
<mx:DateFormatter id="shortDate" formatString="MM/DD/YY JJ:NN" />
```

Applying Formatters

Formatters can be applied to any data source, from user input to server responses. All of the defined formatters are derived from the **Formatter** class, so they each use the **format( )** method to perform the actual formatting. This method takes an object as its lone argument and returns a string. For example, the four number-based formatters—currency, number, phone, and zip code—can take just a number or a string (i.e., a number plus some other characters, like $12,345 or 123-456). The **DateFormatter** can take a string or a **Date** object.

tip

Behind the scenes, a ***Date Formatter*** will cast a supplied string as a new ***Date*** object, which is what it needs to work with.

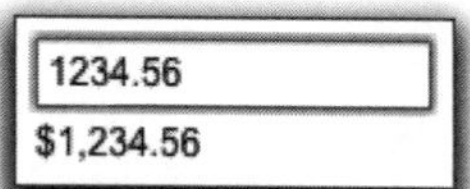

Figure 6.17

One way to apply a formatter is directly within your MXML components (**Figure 6.17**):

```
<fx:Declarations>
    <mx:CurrencyFormatter id="dollars" />
</fx:Declarations>
<s:TextInput id="cost" />
<s:Label text="{dollars.format(cost.text)}" />
```

You can also invoke the formatters from within ActionScript. As an example, in Chapter 5, I created a basic e-commerce calculator using a **DropDownList** and a **ComboBox**. Within a function, the results of multiplying the two selected values together were then assigned to a **Label**:

```
private function updateTotal( ):void {
    if ( (product.selectedIndex >= 0) && (quantity.selectedItem > 0) ) {
    result.text = '$' + (product.selectedItem.price * quantity.
    selectedItem);
    }
}
```

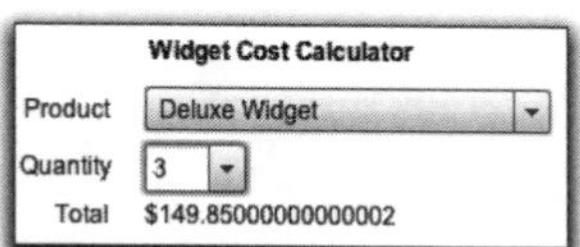

Figure 6.18

As written, the result could contain any number of decimals, from 0 on up, which isn't appropriate (**Figure 6.18**).

A solution is to apply a **CurrencyFormatter** in this situation. Start by defining that formatter in the **Declarations**:

```
<mx:CurrencyFormatter id="dollars" precision="2" />
```

Then the function would be changed to assign to **result.text** the string returned by the formatter:

```
result.text = dollars.format(product.selectedItem.price * quantity.
selectedItem);
```

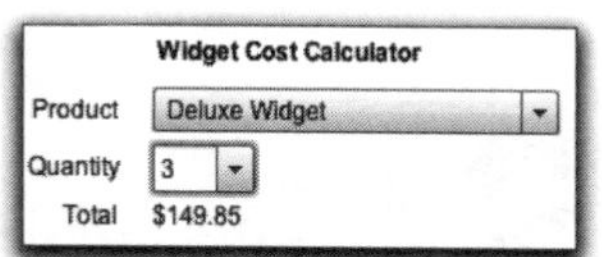

Figure 6.19

The dollar sign no longer needs to be concatenated onto the text, as it will be provided by the formatter. Now, if the calculated total is anything from 12904 to 4.09923785, it will be displayed appropriately (**Figure 6.19**).

But what if, for some reason, the value of **product.selectedItem.price * quantity.selectedItem** is not a usable number? It's important to know that all of the formatters will return an empty string should the input not be usable. You can test that the formatting worked by checking for an empty string:

```
var formattedString:String = dollars.format(product.selectedItem.price *
quantity.selectedItem);
if (formattedString == '') {
    result.text = 'Error!';
```

```
} else {
    result.text = formattedString;
}
```

The **error** property of the formatter can also be used to check for a problem. If one occurred, it'll have a value of either *Invalid value*, meaning that the input wasn't appropriate, or *Invalid format*, meaning that the formatting settings don't make sense. At the end of this chapter, you'll learn how to use validators in Flex to make sure the input is appropriate before attempting to format it, store it in a database, send it to a server, or whatever.

CREATING FORMATTERS IN ACTIONSCRIPT

As with pretty much every component, formatters can be created in MXML or in ActionScript. To do so, you start by importing the formatting definitions:

```
import mx.formatters.*;
```

Then you create an object of the appropriate type:

```
var longdate:DateFormatter = new DateFormatter( );
```

Then assign the properties to the object:

```
longDate.formatString = 'MMMM D, YYYY';
```

This sets the stage for the formatting. When appropriate, invoke the object's **format( )** method:

```
longDate.format(someDateInput);
```

One benefit of creating formatters entirely within ActionScript is that you may be processing the data, like that from a server response, using ActionScript anyway. You can also add flexibility by changing the formatting type or format string on the fly. Finally, using ActionScript, you can ensure that formatters only exist when needed, unlike the MXML-defined ones, which will exist for the life of the application.

VALIDATING DATA

Data validation is crucial for the integrity of your application. Whether the data is coming from a user or a server, ensuring that data is of the type and format required is one of the hallmarks of professional applications. Thankfully, the ease of data validation in Flex is one of the framework's strong suits. Flex has predefined nearly a dozen validators that are easy to apply, and you can even create your own as needed. A validator is simply a prescribed set of rules; you can then check any data you have against those rules to see if the data passes.

INDICATING REQUIRED ITEMS

As a good rule of user interface, you should indicate to the end user when an input is required. When using a **Form**, setting a **FormItem**'s **required** property to true adds a red asterisk to the component, indicating that it is required. This is a visual clue to the user, but is a separate matter than actually validating that the component was properly used.

note

I'll start by discussing validators using just MXML, then cover the parallel usage in ActionScript.

Validator Fundamentals

Flex has defined, within the Halo namespace, the following validators:

- **CreditCardValidator**
- **CurrencyValidator**
- **DateValidator**
- **EmailValidator**
- **NumberValidator**
- **PhoneNumberValidator**
- **RegExpValidator**
- **SocialSecurityValidator**
- **StringValidator**
- **ZipCodeValidator**

Each name is a clear indicator of what the validator does.

To use a validator, you have to start by creating a validator object. As this is a non-visual component, you define it within a **Declarations** block:

tip

You'll want to create a separate validator for each control that you'll be validating.

```
<fx:Declarations>
    <mx:EmailValidator id="myEmailValidator" />
</fx:Declarations>
```

All of the validators are derived from the same parent **Validator** class and all have the following same properties:

- **id**
- **source**
- **property**
- **required**
- **trigger**
- **triggerEvent**

The **id** property identifies the validator and must be unique, of course. The **source** property needs to be bound to the component that will be validated. To do that, you place the **id** value of the component being validated within curly braces, just as if you were using data binding: **{someComponent}**. The **property** property takes a string that names which property of the component being validated has the value that should be checked. For example, the following **EmailValidator** tests the **text** property of the **emailAddress** (**TextInput**) component:

```
<mx:EmailValidator id="myEmailValidator" source="{emailAddress}"
property="text" />
```

Whereas the following **NumberValidator** checks the **selectedValue** property of the **ComboBox**:

```
<mx:NumberValidator id="myNumberValidator" source="{myComboBox}"
property="selectedValue" />
```

The **required** property controls whether or not some value is necessary. The default value is true, but you could set it to false in situations where, say, the phone number is not required but, if present, must pass the **PhoneNumber Validator** rules:

```
<mx:PhoneNumberValidator id="myPhoneValidator" source="{phone}"
property="text" required="false" />
```

The **trigger** and **triggerEvent** properties are used to determine when the validation is actually performed. The **trigger** property identifies the component that will trigger the validation; the **triggerEvent** property indicates which event, caused by the trigger component, starts the validation. The default **triggerEvent** is **valueCommit**. When, exactly, a value is committed depends upon the component involved. It could be when a **TextInput** loses focus or when a user has selected an option from a **List**, **DropDownList**, or **ComboBox**. The **source** component is the trigger, by default. So, without any customization, validation occurs when the validated component's value is committed.

tip

You can also use constants for trigger values, such as ***MouseEvent.CLICK***, but you must use the curly brackets to bind these to the MXML.

Alternatively, you could have all of the validation routines take effect when something happens to a third-party component, like when a submit button is clicked:

```
<mx:EmailValidator id="myEmailValidator" source="{emailAddress}"
property="text" trigger="{submitButton}" triggerEvent="click" />
<mx:PhoneNumberValidator id="myPhoneValidator" source="{phone}"
property="text" required="false" trigger="{submitButton}"
triggerEvent="click" />
```

note

Depending upon the component type, its ***change*** event may not be triggered until that component loses focus (i.e., the user presses Tab, Enter, or Return, or clicks elsewhere).

Notice that the trigger value must be bound, so you place the **id** of the object within curly brackets.

You'll see an example of mass validation in just a few pages, but first, let's look at the individual validators in more detail.

Validators in More Detail

The validators, like the formatters, are predefined in very usable ways. When a component fails the validation test, by default it'll be outlined in red and display an error message near it when the user mouses over the component. The validators all have predefined error messages, depending upon the type of error (**Figure 6.20**).

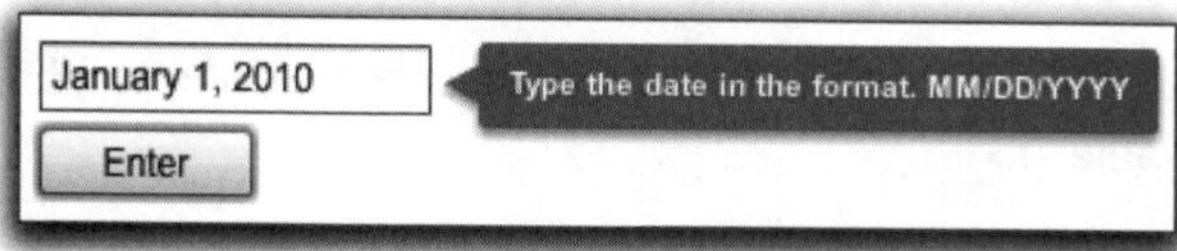

Figure 6.20

Most of the validators are customizable as to the errors they report. For example, the **DateValidator** (Figure 6.21):

```
<mx:DateValidator source="{someDate}" property="text"
   wrongLengthError="Please enter the date as" />
```

Figure 6.21

tip

The expected input format is automatically appended to some error messages as in Figure 6.21.

tip

To provide multiple allowed formatting characters, assign them all to ***allowedFormatChars*** as one string.

Some validators, such as the **PhoneNumberValidator** and the **SocialSecurity Validator** also have **allowedFormatChars** properties where you can indicate what characters are allowed, such as parentheses, dashes, spaces, periods, and plus signs:

```
<mx:SocialSecurityValidator source="{ssn}" property="text"
allowedFormatChars="-" />
```

The **StringValidator** has **minLength** and **maxLength** properties, to validate how many characters are entered (like for a password). You can also set its **tooShortError** and **tooLongError** properties to customize the response.

```
<mx:StringValidator source="{password}" property="text"
maxLength="20" minLength="6" />
```

The **NumberValidator** similarly has **minValue** and **maxValue** properties, plus **precision** (the number of decimal points required), **allowNegative** (which takes a Boolean value), and **domain**. This last property can be assigned the values *real* or *int*, thereby allowing any real number or just integers.

```
<mx:NumberValidator source="{price}" property="text"
allowNegative="false" domain="real" minValue="0.01" precision="2" />
```

note

Client-side validation is a convenience to the user; its presence does not negate the need for server-side validation, too.

The **CurrencyValidator** also has **allowNegative**, **minValue**, **maxValue**, and **precision**, plus **decimalSeparator**, **thousandsSeparator**, **currencySymbol**, and **alignSymbol**. This validator will allow currency values formatted with or without the currency symbol and thousands separators. But you can also dictate that, should the currency symbol, the thousands separators, and the decimal indicator be present, they be of specific types. For example, the default configuration works for United States and Canadian currency, among others:

tip

If you have multiple validators applied to the same component, they'll be executed in order just until a validation rule is broken. Not every validator will necessarily be tested.

```
<mx:CurrencyValidator source="{price}" property="text" />
```

Whereas this configuration will allow for values to be entered in Euros with European notation:

```
<mx:CurrencyValidator source="{price}" property="text"
alignSymbol="any" currencySymbol="€" decimalSeparatorTo=","
thousandsSeparatorTo="." precision="2" />
```

The **ZipCodeValidator** has just the **domain** property to set. It should be assigned a value of *US Only*, *US or Canada*, or *Canada Only*, to indicate which kind of zip code is allowed.

```
<mx:ZipCodeValidator source="{zip}" property="text" domain="US or
Canada" />
```

The DateValidator

The **DateValidator** and **CreditCardValidator** are slightly more elaborate in that they each can validate multiple components at once. The **DateValidator** can be applied to one component that represents an entire date (as shown above), or multiple that, when combined, represent a date. To do that, you indicate the source and property for the day, month, and year:

```
<mx:DateValidator id="myDateValidator"
daySource="{dayInput}" dayProperty="text"
monthSource="{monthInput}" monthProperty="text"
yearSource="{yearInput}" yearProperty="text"
trigger="{submit}" triggerEvent="click" />
```

When using multiple sources for a validator, you'll need to name a third party, like a button, as the trigger. Still, Flex, brilliant as it is, will add error messages to the individual problematic components as warranted (**Figure 6.22**).

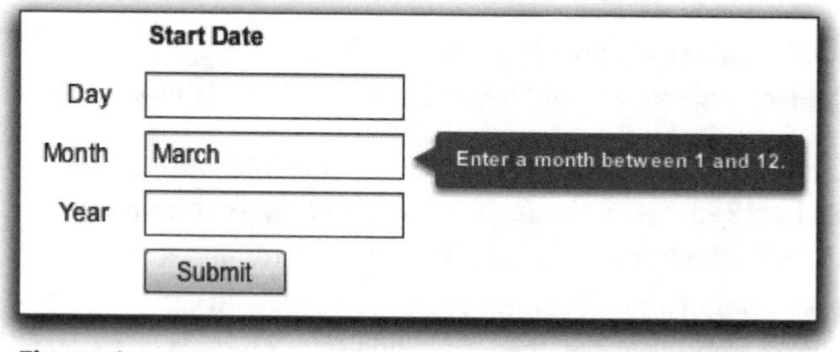

Figure 6.22

With any validator, but especially when validating multiple inputs at once, like with a date, you can use the **listener** property to name a different component that should display an error message (**Figure 6.23**):

```
<mx:DateValidator daySource="{dayInput}" dayProperty="text"
monthSource="{monthInput}" monthProperty="text"
yearSource="{yearInput}" yearProperty="text" trigger="{submit}"
triggerEvent="click" listener="{fh}"/>
<mx:FormHeading id="fh" label="Start Date"/>
    <mx:FormItem label="Date" direction="horizontal">
    <s:TextInput id="monthInput"/><s:Label text="/" />
    <s:TextInput id="dayInput"/><s:Label text="/" />
    <s:TextInput id="yearInput"/></mx:FormItem>
```

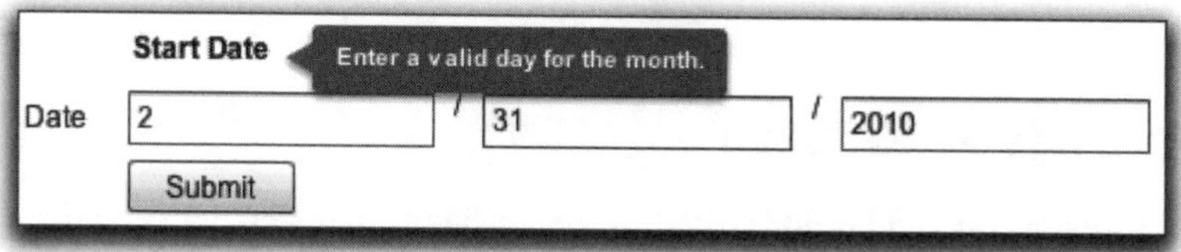

Figure 6.23

As you can see in Figure 6.23, both the problematic component (the second **TextInput**) and the *Start Date* **FormHeading** indicate the error that occurred, thanks to the **listener** property.

note

When using a single source for a date, the submitted text must match the ***inputFormat*** property. By default, this is mm/dd/yyyy.

The CreditCardValidator

The **CreditCardValidator** needs two components: one for the credit card number and another for the credit card type. Normally the number would be a **TextInput** and the type a **DropDownList**:

```
<s:DropDownList id="ccType">
    <s:ArrayList>
        <fx:String>American Express</fx:String>
        <fx:String>Diners Club</fx:String>
        <fx:String>Discover</fx:String>
        <fx:String>Mastercard</fx:String>
        <fx:String>Visa</fx:String>
    </s:ArrayList>
</s:DropDownList>
<s:TextInput id="ccNumber" />
```

You then indicate to the validator which component represents the number and which the type:

```
<mx:CreditCardValidator id="myCCValidator"
    cardTypeSource="{ccType}"
    cardTypeProperty="selectedValue"
    cardNumberSource="{ccNumber}"
    cardNumberProperty="text"/>
```

tip

The ***DropDownList*** reflects all of the card types that can be validated using ***CreditCardValidator***.

The **CreditCardValidator** will take the two pieces of information and validate the card's type, number of digits (between 13 and 16, depending upon the type), first digit, and Luhn mod10 compliance. This last bit is an algorithm used to see if a credit card number matches the proper pattern.

THE REGEXPVALIDATOR

The **RegExpValidator** is, on the one hand, just another predefined validator, but on the other hand, it's a tremendously powerful tool. This validator makes use of Perl-Compatible Regular Expressions (PCRE) to validate data against a pattern. The pattern gets assigned to the **expression** property. Pattern modifiers, such as a case-insensitive comparison, can be assigned to the **flags** property. What you really need to know about the **RegExpValidator** is the following: If you already know how to write and use regular expressions, take comfort in knowing that you can easily validate against regular expressions in Flex; if you don't know how to write and use regular expressions, ignore this validator until you do know, because Perl-Compatible Regular Expressions are not for the faint of heart.

Creating Validators in ActionScript

The previous bit of text shows how to create and apply validators using MXML, but, as with most things, you can do the same thing entirely within ActionScript. As with adding and removing event handlers in ActionScript, this route gives you finer control over the process.

The ActionScript process is a bit backwards compared to the MXML route. Instead of creating validator objects and then indicating what should trigger them, you'd create an event handler that, when called, creates the validator object and performs the validation. If you have a form with a submit button, you'd likely want to perform the validation when that button is clicked, so you'd start by adding a click event handler to that button in MXML:

```
<s:Button label="Button" click="checkForm(event)"/>
```

The rest of the functionality would take place within a **Script** block. To start, you will need to import the appropriate class definitions:

```
<mx:Script>
<![CDATA[
import mx.validators.*;
```

You'll also need to import the **mx.events.ValidationResultEvent** class, for reasons that will be explained shortly:

```
import mx.events.ValidationResultEvent;
```

Now you can start defining the **checkForm( )** function, which will be called when the user clicks the submit button:

```
private function checkForm(event:MouseEvent):void {
}
```

Within the function, you'd create and tweak the validators. To do so, you just generate variables as you would objects of any type:

```
var myEmailValidator:EmailValidator = new EmailValidator( );
var myPhoneValidator:PhoneNumberValidator = new
PhoneNumberValidator( );
```

Then you can set the properties of the objects using the dot syntax:

```
myEmailValidator.source = emailAddress;
myEmailValidator.property = 'text';
myPhoneValidator.source = phone;
myPhoneValidator.property = 'text';
myPhoneValidator.required = false;
```

There are a couple of things to pay attention to here. First, the **source** property takes an object as its value, so you'd assign to it an unquoted **id** value for the component being validated. Similarly, the **required** property takes a Boolean value, so *false* is not quoted either. On the other hand, the **property** property takes a string. Finally, you don't establish the **trigger** and **triggerEvent** properties here as the triggering has already been accounted for thanks to the event handler.

Once you've created and configured your validators, you can apply them in two ways. The first is to call the **validate( )** method on an individual validator. This method returns an object of type **ValidationResultEvent**:

```
var emailResult:ValidationResultEvent = myEmailValidator.validate( );
```

You can then use a conditional that checks the result's **type** property against two possibilities:

```
if (emailResult.type == ValidationResultEvent.VALID) {
    // Whohoo!
} else {
    // Oh no!
}
```

The **ValidationResultEvent.VALID** constant represents the state where the validation routine passed; **ValidationResultEvent.INVALID** is the alternative. Do note that the invocation of the **validate( )** method will also automatically add error reporting to the visual interface, so your conditional would not need to address that.

Rather than validate an individual component at a time, you can test all your validators by calling the **Validator** class's **validateAll( )** method. This is a *static method*, meaning it's called through the class name, not through any individual object:

```
var validationResult:Array = Validator.validateAll(validators);
```

The **validateAll( )** method takes as an argument an array of validators to check. The easiest way to do that is to use array notation and the names of the validator objects:

```
var vResult:Array = Validator.validateAll([myEmailValidator,
myPhoneValidator]);
```

The **validateAll( )** method returns an array of **ValidationResultEvent** objects for each *failed* validation routine. If you test three validators and two of them fail, the result variable will contain two elements. Therefore, if the length of the

The ***mx.events.Validation ResultEvent*** class has to be imported in order to create an object of type ***Validation ResultEvent***.

In order to call ***Validator. validateAll( )***, the application must have access to the ***Validator*** class definition. So you must either specifically import ***mx.validators.Validator*** or import the entire validators package using ***mx.validators.****.

By using ActionScript to create a validator, you can easily apply the same validator to multiple components.

result array variable equals 0, that means it's an empty array, indicating that no validations failed. Let's put this into practice using an example.

An Example

tip

If you download the source code from the book's corresponding Web site (*www.dmcinsights.com/flex4/*), you'll find this example in the *Ch06* folder.

To create a real-world example of using validators, I want to take the Employees Management application from Chapter 5 and add validation to the form. The existing application has the following: a **DataGrid** for displaying employees, and for editing them inline; a button to delete an employee selected in the **DataGrid**; and a form for adding new employees (**Figure 6.24**). I'll add one validator for each form element, and then invoke each when the *Add Employee* button is clicked.

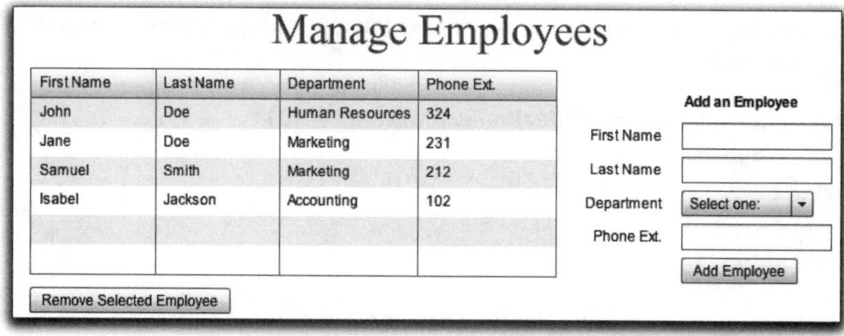

Figure 6.24

1. Open the Employees Management application in Flash Builder or your alternative text editor or IDE.

   If you downloaded this from the book's corresponding Web site, it'll have a project name of *Ch05_03*.

2. Within the **Declarations** section, create validators for the first and last names:

```
<fx:Declarations>
    <mx:StringValidator id="firstNameValidator" source=
    "{employeeFirstName}" property="text" maxLength="20"
    tooLongError="Please enter a valid first name." tooShortError=
    "Please enter a valid first name." />
    <mx:StringValidator id="lastNameValidator" source=
    "{employeeLastName}" property="text" maxLength="40"
    tooLongError="Please enter a valid last name." tooShortError=
    "Please enter a valid last name." />
```

   Names are a bit tricky to validate, even if you were to use regular expressions (see the sidebar "The RegExpValidator," on page 195). What constitutes a valid name, in terms of length, characters involved, and so forth, greatly differs from culture to culture. My solution is to just limit the maximum length to what I expect will be a reasonable restriction. The minimum for both will essentially be one character, as each will be required. I've also customized the error messages in both cases.

3. Create validators for the department and phone extension:

```
<mx:NumberValidator id="deptValidator" source=
"{employeeDepartment}" property="selectedIndex" minValue="0"
maxValue="3" lowerThanMinError="Please select a valid
department." exceedsMaxError="Please select a valid department." />
<mx:NumberValidator id="phoneValidator" source=
"{employeePhoneExt}" property="text" minValue="100"
maxValue="500" lowerThanMinError="The phone extension must be
between 100 and 500." exceedsMaxError="The phone extension must
be between 100 and 500." />
</fx:Declarations>
```

   For these two inputs, I'm using **NumberValidator** components. For the phone extension, this is logical, as a phone extension needs to be a number; in this case, hypothetically between 100 and 500.

   For the department, the **DropDownList** allows the user to select from one of four strings, so you could use a **StringValidator** to ensure that the **selectedItem** property of the **DropDownList** is within the appropriate **minLength** (of 5, for the *Sales* department) and **maxLength** (of 15, for *Human Resources*). However, what I've chosen to do is check that the **selectedIndex** property is between 0 and 3.

   Each validator has a custom error message, too.

4. Within the **Script** block, import the **Validator** definition:

```
import mx.validators.Validator;
```

   This will be required in order to use the **Validator.validateAll( )** method in the next step.

5. Within the **addEmployee( )** function, run all the validation routines:

```
private function addEmployee( ):void {
    var vr:Array = Validator.validateAll([firstNameValidator,
    lastNameValidator, deptValidator, phoneValidator]);
```

   The **addEmployee( )** function is called when the user clicks the *Add Employee* button. Previously, it just called the **employees.addItem( )** method to add the form data to the **employees** variable. Now it'll only do so after validating the data. Towards that end, first thing in the function, the **Validator.validateAll( )** method is called. It is passed an array of the four validators and the returned result is assigned to the **vr** variable.

6. If no errors occurred, add the new employee to the **ArrayCollection**:

```
if (vr.length == 0) {
    employees.addItem({firstName:employeeFirstName.text,
    lastName:employeeLastName.text, ext:employeePhoneExt.text,
    department:employeeDepartment.selectedItem});
```

The **vr** array will have a length of 0 only if all four validator routines passed. If so, then the **employees.addItem( )** method is called, as in the original application.

7. Disable every validator and clear the form inputs:

```
firstNameValidator.enabled = false;
lastNameValidator.enabled = false;
deptValidator.enabled = false;
phoneValidator.enabled = false;
employeeFirstName.text = '';
employeeLastName.text = '';
employeeDepartment.selectedIndex = -1;
employeePhoneExt.text = '';
```

As an added feature, I want to reset the form after successfully adding an employee (**Figure 6.25**). To do so, I can assign to every **TextInput** an empty string and assign to the **DropDownList**'s **selectedIndex** property the value -1, indicating no selection. However, if I were to do this straight away, all of the validation rules would immediately indicate errors. So my solution is to disable every validator by setting the **enabled** property to false, and then reset the form.

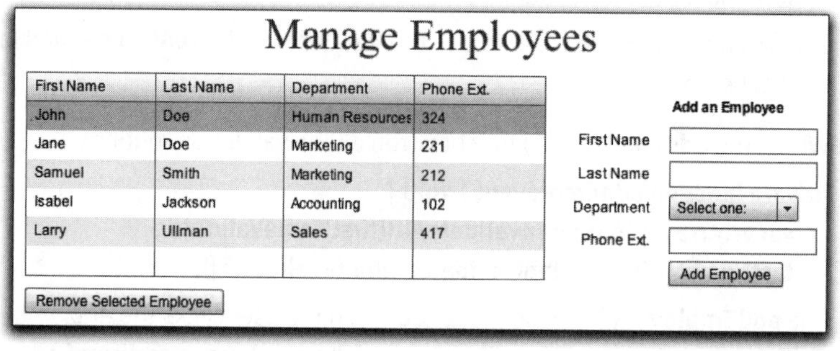

Figure 6.25

8. Re-enable the four validators:

```
firstNameValidator.enabled = true;
lastNameValidator.enabled = true;
deptValidator.enabled = true;
phoneValidator.enabled = true;
```

After resetting the form, the validators can be re-enabled.

9. Complete the **if** conditional and the function:

```
  }
}
```

10. Save, run, and test the completed application.

Figure 6.26 shows the result after attempting to add an invalid employee, something the previous version of the application would have allowed.

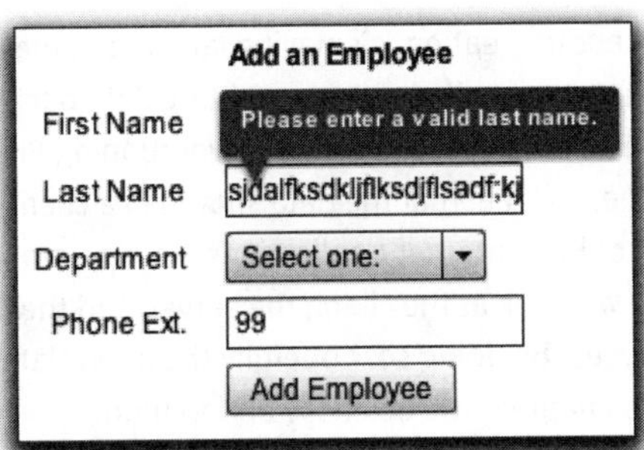

Figure 6.26

7 COMMON DATA FORMATS

The previous two chapters are all about creating, displaying, and manipulating data within Flex. The next two chapters are all about transmitting data back and forth between a Flash client (developed using Flex) and a server running PHP. These are all crucial chapters to me, as I feel that the data shared in a client-server relationship is at the heart of Rich Internet Applications. As a preamble to the next two chapters, this one will look at the client, the server, and the data being transferred as individual pieces. By doing so, hopefully the interrelation of these parts in the following two chapters will be easily understood.

The chapter begins with a quick discussion of the client-server relationship. After that, we'll look at the common data types you'll use in Flex applications: plain text, eXtensible Markup Language (XML), JavaScript Object Notation (JSON), and Action Message Format (AMF). To proceed through the next two chapters, you'll need to understand what information looks like in each of these formats, as well as the pros and cons of using any particular one.

After looking at the data formats on their own, I turn to how these data types are represented, created, manipulated, and transmitted using PHP. As Web-destined Flex applications do not have direct database access (AIR applications do), you'll need some server-side technology to provide data to the Flash client. For the server side of things, I'll be using PHP throughout this book.

Next, the chapter demonstrates how to work with these same four data types in ActionScript. The chapter concludes with a discussion of good debugging techniques, which should hopefully make the learning go more smoothly.

THE CLIENT-SERVER RELATIONSHIP

In this book, the client will always be a Flash application written using Flex, and running in the browser or on the desktop (using Adobe AIR). The server, for the most part, will be a Web host running PHP. To be absolutely clear, the same computer can act as both the client and the server. This will be the case if you're developing Flex applications with PHP on your own computer. This would also be the case when you have a Flash application hosted on your Web site that requests information from a PHP script also found on your own Web site.

tip

The Flash security model impacts the client-server relationship in ways that I'll discuss in the next chapter. For now, just know that you shouldn't run into problems if both the Flash application and the PHP script are in the same domain.

The client-server interaction has two primary paradigms. Most commonly, a client makes a request of a server without sending along any extra information. The server in return sends back a body of data (**Figure 7.1**). A standard request for a Web page is such a model (i.e., when you first load a URL in your browser or click a link).

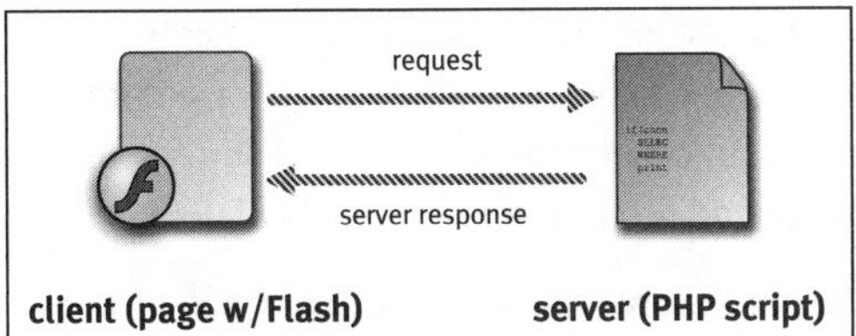

Figure 7.1

The second model has the client sending some data to the server as part of the request. That data would be used to affect the server's response (**Figure 7.2**). When you enter data into a Web form and click submit, that's what is happening.

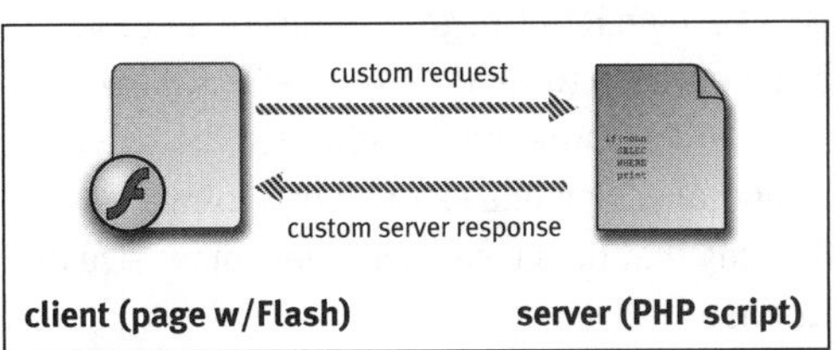

Figure 7.2

Regardless of the request type, the more critical aspect of the process is the response from the server; accordingly, that will really be the focus in the next 80 pages. For the most part, the data sent to the server by the client will just be *name=value* pairs, in plain text. It's really a no-brainer to create in the client, transmit, and handle in the server. You will see exactly how to do this in Flex, of course, and how to use that information in PHP, but it won't require pages and pages to explain that part of the process.

FOUR DATA FORMATS

There are four data formats that I'll discuss and use in this book: plain text, XML, JSON, and AMF. To start things off simply, I want to look at each on its own, out of context, so that you can better distinguish the data representation from the code being used to manipulate the data.

When evaluating the pros and cons of each format, there are four criteria to consider:

1. Ease of creation on the server
2. Ease of use on the client
3. Potential data complexity
4. Transmitted data size

For the first and second criteria, I'm thinking of how much code is required to generate data in a given format and to retrieve the data from that format. These considerations are tied together and are also reflective of the third criteria. (Implied in these is whether extra libraries are required as well.) Some data, like plain text, is easy to create and use but cannot convey that much information; conversely, JSON is harder to create and use but can convey lots of details.

A final matter is the size, in bytes, of the data itself. This is important, as the amount of data being transferred from the server to the client will have an impact on the application's performance and the server's scalability.

For example, if you want to send the word *Flex* from one computer to another, you're only sending four characters of data, which is probably also four bytes: not a big deal. But if you wanted, like in an HTML page, to indicate that the word Flex should be in bold, you'd now have to send *<strong>Flex</strong>*. By using HTML to mark up the text, you've more than quadrupled the amount of data being transferred while only conveying one extra bit of information (bold). As the number of people using that data increases, even minor size differences can have huge implications.

tip

To see real-world performance numbers on the various data formats, check out *www.jamesward.com/census/*.

You have to remember, however, that the data size is just one criteria; there is no benefit to data that is transmitted more quickly but isn't all that useful. As the developer, you'll need to select the appropriate data format for the situation, which is why it's necessary to be familiar with the options out there. Secondarily, if you're making use of third-party services, like Yahoo!, Amazon, and others, you likely won't have a choice as to what data format to use, and will just have to handle whatever that service returns.

Plain Text

Plain text is exactly as it sounds: characters without any formatting or markup. Examples are:

- 112.43
- true
- red,blue,green
- Franz Kafka was a 20th century writer...

It's just text: There's nothing to be evaluated or parsed or interpreted or anything. Plain text is universally readable and easily transmitted.

For the record, I'm making a distinction between plain text as a *data format* as opposed to a *file format*. XML, JSON, MXML, ActionScript, and lots of other languages are written in plain text files, whereas Microsoft Word documents, among many others, are binary files. The former are readable by many applications; the latter are stored in proprietary formats, and are only readable by a few programs.

As a data format, plain text contains no markup. For example, the HTML *<strong>Flex</strong>* contains tags that provide added meaning. Plain text data has none of this. The most elaborate meaning that might be conveyed in plain text would be commas or tabs used to break up individual values, and newlines to indicate individual lines of text. In other words, the most complex bit of plain text data will just be a list of comma-, tab-, or newline-separated values.

Plain text is the simplest data format to create and use. And when plain text is the media, the server only transmits the minimum amount of data, without any extra information. However, plain text can only be effective for representing the most basic information.

XML

XML has been around for years and is widely, widely used. In fact, MXML is derived from XML, as are HTML, Really Simple Syndication (RSS), and many other languages. XML is technically plain text, in terms of how it's created and stored, but it contains markup to provide additional details.

EXAMPLE XML

XML starts with a *root document element*, like **Application** in MXML. XML contains only one root document element, and all of the information must be stored within that. For an example, if you want to represent a catalog of artists as XML, you might start with an **artists** root element:

```
<artists></artists>
```

Next, within that root tag, you may have an element for each individual artist:

```
<artists>
   <artist></artist>
   <artist></artist>
   <artist></artist>
</artists>
```

Within the **artist** tag you'll want to represent all the information about a given artist: name, date of birth, works of art, etc. To make the data most usable, you wouldn't want to place this information just within the **artist** tag, but rather as atomically as possible, with each nugget in its own element:

```
<artist>
   <name>Georges Seurat</name>
   <birthDate>December 2, 1859</birthDate>
</artist>
```

Arguably, values like name and ***birthDate*** can be broken down more atomically. Such design decisions are up to you and will be influenced by how the data might be used.

To represent individual works of art, where multiple works would be associated with each artist, you would create a new **work** tag, one for each piece, but all within the **artist** record:

```
<artist>
   <name>Georges Seurat</name>
   <birthDate>December 2, 1859</birthDate>
   <work>
      <title>The Laborers</title>
      <year>1883</year>
   </work>
   <work>
      <title>The Models</title>
      <year>1888</year>
   </work>
</artist>
```

You can also add information using *attributes* (just like MXML components have attributes or properties). Again, what attributes you create where is really up to you:

```
<artist id="2490">
```

or

```
<work type="painting">
```

Of course, elements can have multiple attributes:

```
<work id="583782" type="painting">
```

In the end, a body of XML data is said to create a tree-like structure. You have the root element that contains one or more child elements (a child is also called a *node*). Each child can have its own children, and so on, until the data is fully represented.

XML SYNTAX RULES

You just saw an example of how XML is structured, but what are the exact syntactical rules? Chapter 1, "Building Flex Applications," discusses the basic XML rules with respect to MXML, but here they are again:

- XML is case-sensitive.
- Every attribute value must be quoted (and double-quotes are preferred).
- Every tag needs to be formally closed.
- Every tag needs to be properly nested.

With respect to closing tags, there are two options. The first is to create opening and closing tags, as in the example XML. This is normally done for any element that might contain values, including other elements. You can also close tags by concluding the opening tag with a slash before the closing angle bracket:

```
<tag />
```

tip

Whether you place a space before a closing slash or not is up to you.

You'll see this latter syntax in cases where the values are solely reflected in attributes:

```
<image source="somefile.png" />
```

As for nesting of tags, this only applies if you're using opening and closing tags. What is meant is that if you open element A, then open element B (so that element B is contained within—and is a child of—element A), you must then close B before closing A.

Because XML uses the angle brackets and quotation marks to create elements and attributes, you cannot use them within the values of elements or attributes, as in

```
<question answer="false">4 > 8</question>
```

In such cases, you'll need to use an *entity version* of any special character. **Table 7.1** lists the five entities to watch for in XML. Each begins with an ampersand and ends with a semicolon.

Table 7.1 XML Entities

Symbol	Entity Version
&	**&**
<	**<**
>	**>**
'	**'**
"	**"**

If you'd rather not use entities, you can use a **CDATA** block:

```
<question answer="false"><![CDATA[
4 > 8
]]></question>
```

Whether you use **CDATA** or entities will probably be determined by the amount of data being represented and the number of special characters found within that data.

Finally, in terms of XML syntax, know that XML stored or transmitted often includes the XML declaration, prior to the XML data itself:

```
<?xml version="1.0" encoding="utf-8"?>
```

This is the same code as found on the first line of MXML files. It indicates to the program reading the file that the file contains UTF8-encoded XML.

PROS AND CONS

XML is relatively easy to create, is extremely extensible ("extensible" is in the name, after all), and can convey lots of well-organized data. Thanks to something called *E4X*, XML is a snap to use in ActionScript, as you'll see later in the chapter.

On the other hand, XML syntax is demanding and, if it's not 100% right, like if you don't properly nest or close a tag, then the entire XML data will be unusable. This can be a common cause of problems when dynamically generating XML. Also, because of all the added tags, both opening and closing, XML involves transmitting extra data.

Still, all in all, XML is an excellent choice for most situations.

JSON

JavaScript Object Notation (JSON) is one of those acronyms that may sound obtuse but is really exactly what it means: In JSON, data is represented as a JavaScript object. Since JavaScript and ActionScript have the same lineage, JSON data is quite similar in syntax to an ActionScript object, too. A JavaScript (or ActionScript) object, at its root, is represented by curly braces: **{ }**. That is a valid, albeit empty, object.

JSON data objects have property-value pairs (properties just being variables found within an object). To add these to an object, use the ***property*: *value*** syntax, with each pair separated by a comma:

```
{
name: "Georges Seurat",
birthDate: "December 2, 1859"
}
```

The properties need not be quoted, but the values do unless they are numbers. Still, you'll commonly see all of the properties and values quoted:

```
{
"title": "House I",
"year": "1998"
}
```

If you have multiple objects to represent, you create an array of them, using the square brackets, separating each object by a comma:

```
[{
name: "Georges Seurat",
birthDate: "December 2, 1859"
},
{
name: "Roy Lichtenstein",
birthDate: "October 27, 1923"
}]
```

JSON is equally able to represent structured data easily, and with fewer characters than XML (because you're omitting the closing tags). But while you may think JSON's syntax is simpler than XML, the syntax can get hairy quickly. For example, this bit of XML,

```
<artist id="3955">
    <name>Roy Lichtenstein</name>
    <birthDate>October 27, 1923</birthDate>
    <work type="sculpture">
        <title>House I</title>
        <year>1998</year>
        <image source="3955_housei.png" />
    </work>
</artist>
```

would look like this in JSON:

```
{
  artist:{
    id:3955,
    name: "Roy Lichtenstein",
    birthdate: "October 27, 1923",
    work:{
      type: "sculpture",
      title: "House I",
      year:1998,
      image:{
        source: "3955_housei.png"
      }
    }
  }
}
```

Now imagine how the JSON would look when you start representing multiple artists and multiple works of art! And then, to be formal, wrap everything in double-quotes...

As with XML, make a slight mistake, like omitting a comma or curly bracket, and the data is useless. For this reason, you'll really want to use a special library in PHP to create the JSON data and a few extra steps are required to use the data in ActionScript. You don't have to transfer quite as much JSON data as you would with XML, but the efforts to encode and decode it minimize any comparable benefit.

While I'm inclined to choose XML over JSON (between the two), you might sometimes be in a situation where JSON is your only option.

AMF

Action Message Format (AMF) was created by Adobe specifically as a way to improve communications between a server and a Flash client. Unlike plain text, XML, and JSON, AMF uses a binary format, which means that it cannot be represented in a book like the others. More than a format for transmitting data, AMF provides a foundation for clients to directly communicate with servers. Instead of just calling a PHP script and seeing the results, AMF lets the client interact with PHP scripts, as appropriate. In this regard, the PHP script on the server is acting as an intelligent service, not as a single, standalone document.

Moreover, by using something called a *value object*, complex data types can be transmitted and used by both the client and server as if they were native to both ActionScript and PHP (this will mean more at the end of Chapter 9, "Using Complex Services").

Using AMF in PHP requires a special library and the use of object-oriented programming (OOP). But the OOP can be trivial and easy to implement, and the AMF response allows for complex data sets to be transmitted quite efficiently (much as a JPEG can represent an image using a fraction of the original bytes, AMF can create a more byte-efficient representation of data). And, when the AMF response returns to the Flash client, the result can be handled in ActionScript easily.

DATA FORMATS IN PHP

tip

For more information on using PHP with Flex, check out *www.flex.org/php*.

When it comes to these four data formats in PHP, there are two goals: *creating* the data and *transmitting* the data. Clearly these goals take place in that order, however, I'd like to start by looking at the transmission process first.

PHP is primarily a server-side language used to send HTML to the Web browser (what PHP can do has expanded greatly over the years, but that's still the heart of the language). To do so, PHP scripts echo or print combinations of literal text and HTML tags (and CSS and JavaScript). The following creates the word *Flex* in bold in the browser:

```
<?php
echo '<strong>Flex</strong>';
?>
```

Normally code like that would be used somewhere within a greater context, which is to say that a complete HTML page would include the opening **HTML** tag, the **HEAD** material, the **BODY**, and so forth. But when you're using Flash as the client, it's not going to display an entire HTML page, so you don't need to send all of that information from the server to the client. Therefore, you should omit the basic HTML stuff and just send, which is to say "print", the data needed by the end client. For a plain text example, where just a simple message is being returned by PHP, the entire PHP file may just be the following:

note

The server response generated by PHP should omit anything not required by the Flash client application.

```
<?php
// Connect to a database or do whatever.
echo 'This is the string message.';
?>
```

Of course, the contents of the exact message should be more dynamic than a hard-coded string, like something database-driven. But not that much can be well represented in plain text.

ASSUMPTIONS

In this book I'm going to assume you have basic familiarity with PHP or, if not that, you're comfortable looking at code and grasping what it does. Most of the examples will also make use of a MySQL database (*www.mysql.com*). It really doesn't matter what kind of database application you use—PHP supports all of the common ones, but MySQL is the most likely partner for PHP.

In all of my code, I'll be using the Improved MySQL extension functions (*www.php.net/mysqli*). These will work with PHP 5 and MySQL 4.1 or greater. If you're using earlier versions of either technology, you'll need to use the older MySQL functions instead (*www.php.net/mysql*). They have slightly different syntax, so check the PHP manual accordingly. The biggest difference between the two is the order of arguments when calling many of the functions. For example, to execute a query using the Improved MySQL functions, you would write

```
$r = mysqli_query($dbc, $q);
```

Where **$dbc** is the database connection, **$q** is the query, and **$r** is the returned result. Using the older MySQL functions, the syntax is

```
$r = mysql_query($q, $dbc);
```

Every PHP script that uses a MySQL database requires a database connection. In my example code, I'll use the following to establish one:

```
$dbc = @mysqli_connect(DB_HOST, DB_USER, DB_PASSWORD, DB_NAME);
```

One assumption I'll be making is that the four constants will be defined somewhere that the current script can access them. For example, maybe you've got a **mysql.inc.php** script that contains the following:

```
DEFINE ('DB_USER', 'username');
DEFINE ('DB_PASSWORD', 'password');
DEFINE ('DB_HOST', 'localhost');
DEFINE ('DB_NAME', 'flex_test');
```

That script could be stored in a more secure location, like inside of its own protected directory or outside of the Web directory (**Figure 7.3**). Every script that needs to connect to the database could then include the file:

```
require_once('/path/to/mysql.inc.php');
```

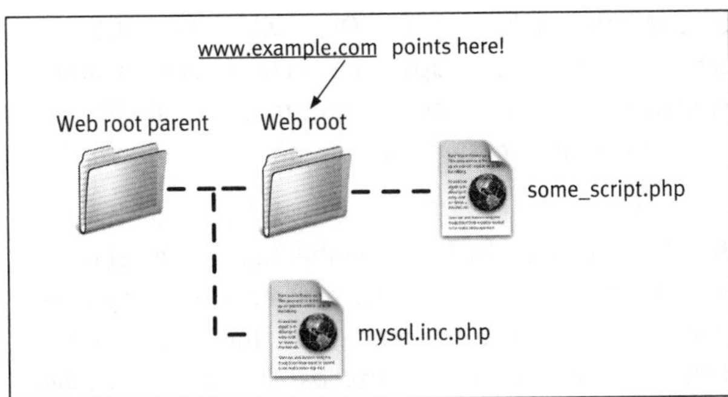

Figure 7.3

With the structure in Figure 7.3, *some_script.php* would contain:

```
require_once('../mysql.inc.php');
```

For the examples in the rest of this chapter, let's also assume that the *flex_test* database exists and has two tables defined, using the following SQL:

```
CREATE TABLE employees (
    id MEDIUMINT UNSIGNED NOT NULL AUTO_INCREMENT PRIMARY KEY,
    departmentId TINYINT UNSIGNED NOT NULL,
    firstName VARCHAR(20) NOT NULL,
    lastName VARCHAR(40) NOT NULL,
    email VARCHAR(60) NOT NULL,
    phoneExt SMALLINT UNSIGNED NULL,
    hireDate DATE NOT NULL,
    leaveDate DATE NULL,
    INDEX name (lastName, firstName),
    INDEX (departmentId) )
```

and

```
CREATE TABLE departments (
    id TINYINT UNSIGNED NOT NULL AUTO_INCREMENT PRIMARY KEY,
    name VARCHAR(40),
    UNIQUE KEY name (name) )
```

You'll also need to populate these tables using commands like

```
INSERT INTO departments VALUES (NULL, 'Human Resources'), (NULL,
'Marketing'), (NULL, 'Accounting');
INSERT INTO employees VALUES
    (NULL, 1, 'Liz', 'Lemon', 'll@example.com', 234, NOW(), NULL),
    (NULL, 3, 'Jack', 'Donaghy', 'jd@example.com', 130, NOW(), NULL),
    (NULL, 2, 'Pete', 'Hornberger', 'ph@example.com', 569, NOW(), NULL);
```

tip

All of the SQL commands for this, and the other chapters, can be downloaded from the corresponding Web site: *www.dmcinsights.com/flex4/*.

If you don't know how to create databases in MySQL, or what these SQL commands mean, I'd recommend you pick up a book on the subjects (Larry Ullman's *MySQL: Visual QuickStart Guide* comes highly recommended!) or turn to my support forum for assistance (*www.dmcinsights.com/phorum/*).

So those are my assumptions: You have PHP, you have MySQL, and you've created and populated the databases. Lastly, remember that PHP must be run through a Web server, meaning that every time you execute a PHP script, the address must begin with *http://*. If you're developing all of this on your own computer, then the URL will likely begin *http://localhost*. If you're using a live server, the URL will be *http://www.example.com*, replacing *www.example.com* with your actual hostname.

PLAIN TEXT

The first data format I've discussed—plain text—is the easiest to generate and send using PHP. Plain text is simply a string in PHP, which is any quoted combination of characters. Plain text is severely limited as to the complexity of the data it can represent, so it wouldn't likely be used to represent stored data. Instead, you might use plain text to return a quick message:

```
if (/* whatever condition was met */) {
    echo 'The record was updated.';
} else {
    echo 'The record could not be updated.';
}
```

And that's all there is to it. Just remember not to include HTML in a plain text response, as it won't be used in the handling ActionScript.

XML

Documents accessed over network connections, like PHP scripts, return headers that indicate all sorts of information about the following response. Among these headers is one identifying the *content-type*: what kind of information is to follow. For PHP scripts used as Web pages, the content-type is HTML or just plain text (**Figure 7.4** shows Firefox's information about a page response). The content-type does not need to be changed for plain text, JSON, or even AMF, but if the PHP script will be returning XML, the content-type header must be updated. To do so, call the **header( )** function at the top of the script, before anything else would be sent to the browser:

```
<?php
header("Content-Type: text/xml");
// Rest of PHP code.
```

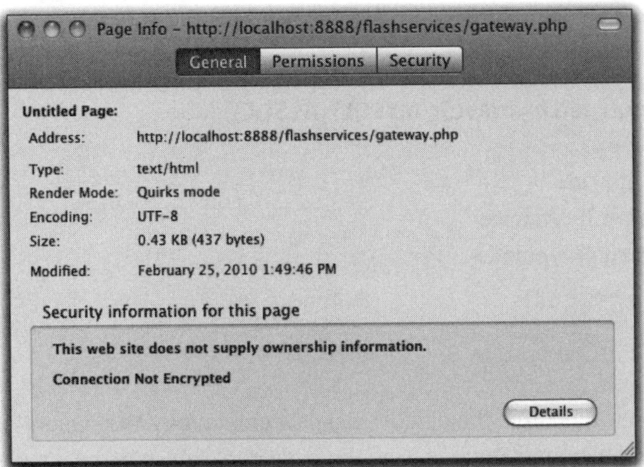

Figure 7.4

This line must be executed before anything, including even a space or a blank line, would be displayed. After it, you can generate and send the XML.

PHP does not have an XML data type, although you can use different internal and external libraries to work with XML. But I find these to be more necessary to parse existing XML in PHP; creating XML from scratch isn't that complex, particularly when you're working with something as straightforward as turning database records into XML.

After identifying the content-type, the PHP script would normally print the XML declaration, followed by the root document tag:

```
echo '<?xml version="1.0" encoding="utf-8" ?>
<employees>
';
```

tip

By placing the closing single quotation mark on its own line, the next XML tag to follow will appear on its own line in the output.

Now let's assume that the PHP script has established a connection to the database. The next thing to do is define and execute the query:

```
$q = "SELECT id, CONCAT(lastName, ', ', firstName) AS name, email FROM employees";
$r = mysqli_query($dbc, $q);
```

The query returns three pieces of information from the employees table: the employee id, the employee name concatenated as *lastName, firstName* and given the alias of just *name*, and the employee's e-mail address. **Figure 7.5** shows the result of running this query using phpMyAdmin.

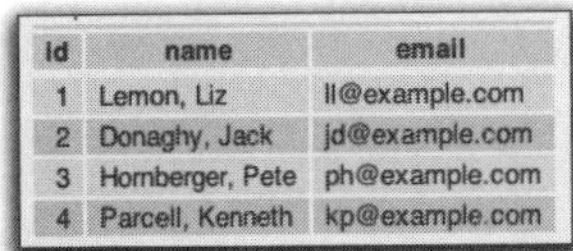

id	name	email
1	Lemon, Liz	ll@example.com
2	Donaghy, Jack	jd@example.com
3	Hornberger, Pete	ph@example.com
4	Parcell, Kenneth	kp@example.com

Figure 7.5

You could next check that some rows were returned, prior to fetching them:

```
if (mysqli_num_rows($r) > 0) {
```

Now, fetch the records using a **while** loop. Within the **while** loop, print the results as XML:

```
while ($row = mysqli_fetch_array($r, MYSQLI_ASSOC)) {
    echo "<employee>
<id>{$row['name']}</id>
<name>{$row['name']}</name>
<email>{$row['email']}</email>
</employee>
";
}
```

So for each record returned from the database, a new **employee** XML element is created, with child elements representing the individual values in the returned record.

You would then close the **if** conditional and print the closing root tag:

```
} // End of mysqli_num_rows() IF.
echo '</employees>';
```

You can see the generated XML code by loading the PHP script directly in a browser (**Figure 7.6**).

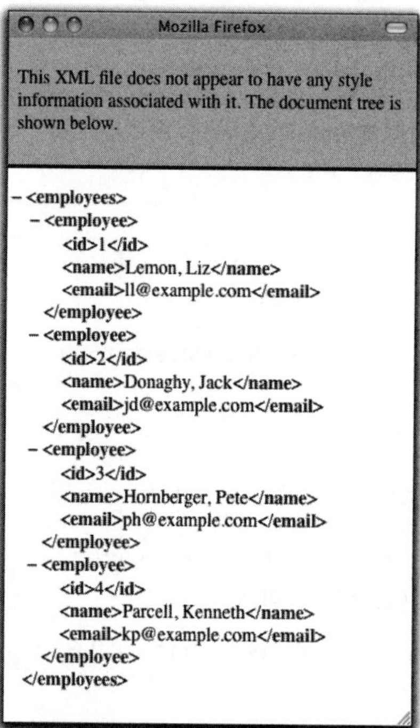

Figure 7.6

JSON

As with XML, there's not a built-in JSON date type in PHP. However, as of PHP 5.2, the JSON extension is part of the PHP core library, meaning you can generate JSON data with a single function call. The best approach is to create an array, most likely a multidimensional array, then send it through the **json_encode()** function.

To do so, you can start by establishing a connection to the database, then defining and executing the query. You don't need to alter the page's content-type or send anything else first (unlike with XML).

```
$q = "SELECT id, CONCAT(lastName, ', ', firstName) AS name, email FROM
employees";
$r = mysqli_query($dbc, $q);
```

The query returns three pieces of information from the employees table: the employee id; the employee name concatenated as *lastName, firstName* and given the alias of just *name*; and the employee e-mail address (see Figure 7.5).

At that point, I would create a new, empty array, to be populated shortly:

```
$employees = array();
```

You could next check that some rows were returned, prior to fetching them:

```
if (mysqli_num_rows($r) > 0) {
```

Now, fetch the records using a **while** loop. Within the **while** loop, add each record to the existing array. Here's a very direct way to do that:

```
while ($row = mysqli_fetch_array($r, MYSQLI_ASSOC)) {
    $employees[] = $row;
}
```

This one line works because, with each iteration of the loop, **$row** is an associative array. I'll explain in a bit more detail...

The **mysqli_fetch_array()** function returns one record at a time as an array. By default, the function returns each value in the record twice: once numerically indexed and once with a string as the index. Given the query above, which selects three values for each record, **mysqli_fetch_array()** would return this:

```
array(0 => 398, 1 => 'Jane Doe', 2 => 'jane.doe@example.edu', 'id' => 398,
'name' => 'Jane Doe', 'email' => 'jane.doe@example.edu')
```

The **mysqli_fetch_array()** takes an optional second argument, which is a constant: **MYSQLI_NUM**, **MYSQLI_ASSOC**, or **MYSQLI_BOTH**. The first constant tells the function to return the array using only the numeric indexes. The second tells the function to return the array using only the string indexes. In both cases, just the three elements would be in the array. The third constant generates the same result as the default behavior, with six elements in the example returned. The second argument to **mysqli_fetch_array()** is significant as it changes the particulars of the returned array. So by using **MYSQLI_ASSOC** in the above, I can just add the entire **$row** array to **$employees**.

If you prefer your code to be more obvious, you can explicitly make the array assignments:

```
while ($row = mysqli_fetch_array($r, MYSQLI_ASSOC)) {
    $employees[] = array('id' => $row['id'], 'name' => $row['name'],
    'email' => $row['email']);
}
```

The end result is the same either way (so long as you use **MYSQLI_ASSOC**). This second route is clearer and allows you to establish whatever indexes you want, though.

After the **while** loop, you now have the populated array. To turn that into JSON, provide it as the only argument to the **json_encode()** function. This function returns the result as JSON. As we want to send that result to whatever client is calling this PHP script, just echo out the function call:

```
echo json_encode($employees);
```

You can see the generated JSON code by loading the PHP script directly in a browser (**Figure 7.7**).

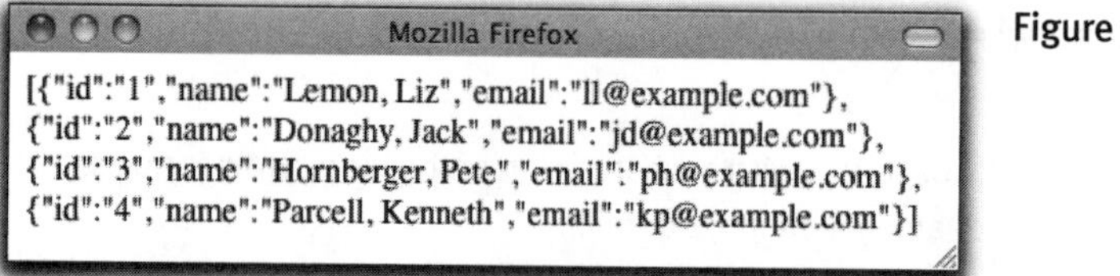

Figure 7.7

If you're not using a version of PHP with support for the JSON library, you'll need to include and use a third-party library. Zend JSON, part of the Zend Framework (*http://framework.zend.com*), is one possible option. (I'm not a particular fan of the Zend Framework in general, but the fact that you can use its individual components as needed makes it a good choice for such isolated needs.) To use any third-party library, you'll just need to make it available to your PHP scripts (i.e., put the library on the same server), include the required library file(s), and then call whatever function. So, to use Zend JSON, you'd only need to add one line and change another. First, include the library:

require_once('/*path*/*to*/Zend/Json.php');

Then call the library's encoding function instead of **json_encode( )**:

echo Zend_Json::encode($employees);

If Zend JSON isn't to your liking, you could use the PEAR library's Services_ JSON (*http://pear.php.net/package/Services_JSON*). Install and include the library, then use these two lines to output the JSON data:

$json = new Services_JSON( );
echo $json->encode($employees);

AMF

tip

In Chapter 9, I'll get into AMF and PHP in much more detail, including discussions of Flash Builder's Data/Services panel.

AMF is a special, binary format, which means that no type in PHP can represent it. In fact, using AMF to communicate between a Flash client and a PHP script is an entirely different process than having a PHP script return plain text, XML, or JSON. Instead of having the PHP script print out data, to use AMF the PHP script needs to define an OOP class. Within the class, a method returns values. An AMF call to a PHP script then creates an instance of the class (i.e., an object) and invokes one of its methods. The result of that method call is then returned to the client. This is an entirely different concept than the other examples, so I'll walk through an AMF example more explicitly.

To start, the PHP script will need access to an AMF library. The two most common library choices are AMFPHP (*www.amfphp.org*) and Zend AMF, part of the Zend Framework (*http://framework.zend.com*). These libraries will be used a bit differently than other PHP libraries: I'll explain the installation instructions for AMFPHP in these next steps, and Zend AMF will be used in Chapter 9.

1. Download the latest version of AMFPHP.
2. Expand the downloaded file.

   The download will be a ZIP file containing several folders and PHP scripts.
3. Create a new directory on your Web server named *flashservices*.

   It doesn't matter whether you're developing on your own computer or on a live server, just create a folder called *flashservices*, preferably in the root of the Web directory. In other words, the URL *http://hostname/flashservices* will work. This may be *http://localhost/flashservices* or *http://www.example.com/flashservices*.
4. Copy the entire contents of the expanded AMFPHP folder to this new *flashservices* directory.

5. Load *http://hostname/flashservices/gateway.php* in your browser.

   If the installation is okay, you'll see a message like that in **Figure 7.8**.

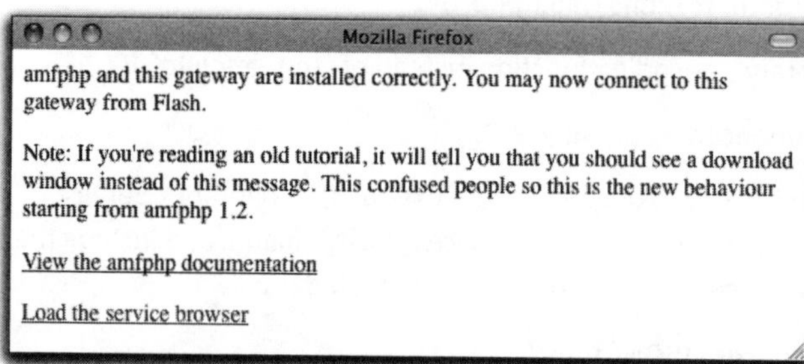

Figure 7.8

6. Click the link (in Figure 7.8) that takes you to the service browser.

   The actual URL will be *http://hostname/flashservices/browser/*. This is a wonderful utility for looking at existing PHP services, calling their methods to confirm their results, and more.

That's all you need to do to install AMFPHP. Next, you'll create a PHP script that will be stored in the *flashservices/services* folder.

note

Remove the *flashservices/services/amfphp* and *flash services/browser* folders from live, production servers. These folders are very useful for debugging purposes but too revealing from a security perspective.

More information about customizing and using AMFPHP can be found at the AMFPHP Web site. I'll also address a few things in a debugging section at the end of the chapter.

As I said, the PHP script used in an AMF communication is actually an OOP class, whose methods return data. Here is the shell of a basic PHP class:

```
class SomeClass {
    // Class properties (aka variables)
    // Class constants.
    // Special constructor method:
    public function __construct() {
    }
    // Other methods:
    public function doThis() {
    }
} // End of class.
```

As an example, let's create a **TestService** class:

1. Create a new PHP script in your text editor or IDE:

```
<?php
// This is a test service class.
// It communicates via AMF with a Flash client.
```

2. If appropriate, include the MySQL configuration script that defines the database access information:

   require_once('/*path*/*to*/mysql.inc.php');

   For security and maintenance reasons, it's best to place this sensitive information in another script.

3. Begin defining the class:

   class TestService {

   Classes are normally named using only letters, beginning with a capital letter, and using capital letters to break up words.

4. Create a private variable for the database connection:

   private $dbc;

   The database connection will be needed by multiple methods in the class, so I'm making it a class variable. It's marked as *private* as it shouldn't be accessible outside of the class.

5. Define the constructor:

```
public function __construct() {
    $this->dbc = @mysqli_connect(DB_HOST, DB_USER, DB_PASSWORD,
    DB_NAME);
}
```

   The constructor is a special method that's called when an object of this class type is created. This constructor creates the database connection and assigns it to the class **$dbc** variable, available through **$this->dbc**.

6. Define a function for retrieving every employee:

```
public function getEmployees() {
    $data = array();
    $q = "SELECT id, CONCAT(lastName, ', ', firstName) AS name, email
    FROM employees";
    $r = mysqli_query($this->dbc, $q);
    if (mysqli_num_rows($r) > 0) {
        while ($row = mysqli_fetch_array($r, MYSQLI_ASSOC)) {
            $data[] = $row;
        }
    }
    return $data;
}
```

All of this code is similar to that in the JSON example. First, an empty array is created. Then a query is defined and executed (using the database connection found in **$this->dbc**). Next, a conditional checks that some results were returned. If so, all of the results are retrieved using a loop, with each record added to the array within that loop. Finally, the array is returned by the function. That's all the function needs to do.

7. Create another function for retrieving every department:

```
public function getDepartments( ) {
  $data = array( );
  $q = "SELECT id, name FROM departments ORDER BY name";
  $r = mysqli_query($this->dbc, $q);
  if (mysqli_num_rows($r) > 0) {
     while ($row = mysqli_fetch_array($r, MYSQLI_ASSOC)) {
        $data[] = $row;
     }
  }
  return $data;
}
```

The structure of this function is exactly the same as that in Step 6; just the query differs.

tip

The class could have a _*destruct()* method, called when the object is destroyed. In ***TestService***, such a method would close the database connection.

8. Complete the class and the PHP script:

```
}
?>
```

9. Save the file as *TestService.php* in the *flashservices/services* directory.

10. Load *http://hostname/flashservices/browser* in your Web browser, if it is not already.

    One great feature of AMFPHP is that it comes with a browser that allows you to see and test your PHP services. It's an excellent debugging tool!

11. Click on *TestService* in the left-hand column.

12. Click on one of the methods listed and click *Call* to see the results (**Figures 7.9** and **7.10**).

That's one way you can communicate with a PHP script using AMF. Chapter 9 will have more examples of this, as it's a powerful way to transmit data from a server to a Flash client.

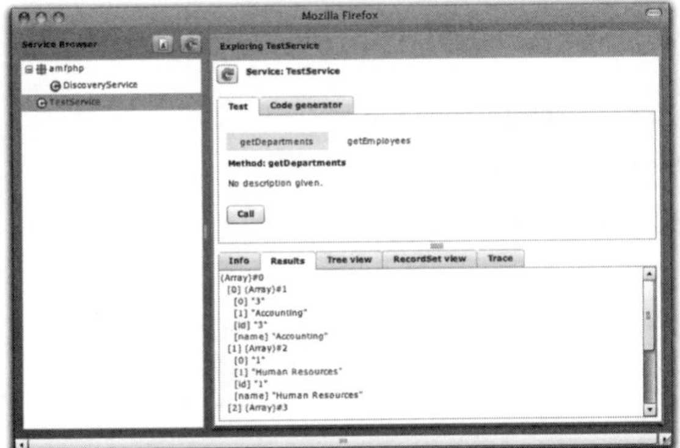

Figure 7.9

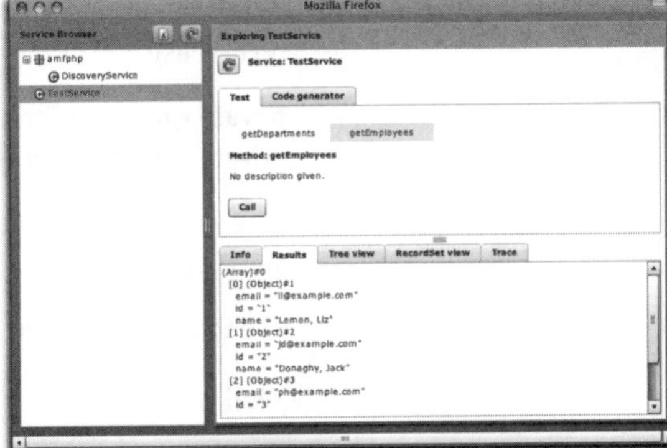

Figure 7.10

DATA TYPES IN ACTIONSCRIPT

Before looking at these four data formats in ActionScript, I want to talk about what will actually happen when this information is used in subsequent chapters.

In the client-server model, where the Flash application is the client, when the server responds, a predetermined ActionScript function will be called. That function will receive the server response as an event object, specifically of type **ResultEvent**:

```
private function handleServerResponse(event:ResultEvent):void {
        // Use event.
}
```

Within the function, the **event** object contains everything you need to know about the client-server interaction. Most importantly, the object's **result** property stores the actual result returned by the server, which is to say the data. So in examples throughout the rest of the book, you'll start with the data in **event.result** and use it as needed. As I'm purposely looking at the data out of context, I won't be using **event.result** in the next few pages (for the most part), so as not to muddle the basic ideas being covered.

Plain Text

Plain text, the simplest of the data formats, is represented in ActionScript as a string. Plain text can be assigned to a **String** object and manipulated using that object's methods. If the plain text contains a list of comma-separated values, for example, you could use the **String** class's **split( )** method to break up that list:

```
private var valuesString:String = 'blue,green,red';
private var valuesArray:Array = valuesString.split(',');
```

Now **valuesArray** contains three values—*blue*, *green*, and *red*, indexed at 0, 1, and 2, respectively.

And that's really about the most you'd do with plain text, so let's move on!

XML

ActionScript has native support for XML, thanks to a wonderful thing with a funny name: *ECMAScript for XML*, abbreviated E4X. Because of E4X, it is so simple to work with XML in ActionScript: The **XML** and **XMLList** classes provide all of the functionality you'll need. The **XML** class represents an entire body of XML data. To create an **XML** object in ActionScript, you would use the same declaration and assignment syntax as any other variable:

```
public var artistsXML:XML = <artists>
<artist id="2490">
        <name>Georges Seurat</name>
        <birthDate>December 2, 1859</birthDate>
        <work type="painting">
                <title>The Laborers</title>
                <year>1883</year>
                <image source="2490_laborers.png" />
        </work>
        <work type="painting">
                <title>The Models</title>
                <year>1888</year>
                <image source="2490_models.png" />
        </work>
</artist>
<artist id="3955">
        <name>Roy Lichtenstein</name>
        <birthDate>October 27, 1923</birthDate>
        <work type="sculpture">
                <title>House I</title>
                <year>1998</year>
                <image source="3955_housei.png" />
        </work>
</artist>
</artists>;
```

You'll note that no quotation marks are used to surround the XML (as quoted values are strings).

With that **artistsXML** object, you can use dot syntax to reference individual elements. For example, **artistsXML.artist** contains two subelements. You can also use array notation to go even further: **artistsXML.artist[0]** is the first artist element, making **artistsXML.artist[0].name** be a string with a value of *Georges Seurat*.

You can also find elements by referring to attributes using the @ character. This reference also has a value of *Georges Seurat*: **artistsXML.artist.(@id == 2490).name**. Reading backwards, it refers to the **name** child of the artist whose **id** attribute has a value of 2490.

Or you can look at element values to reference elements:

```
private var anArtistXML:XML = artistsXML.artist.(name == 'Georges Seurat');
```

To refer to the year that Lichtenstein's *House I* sculpture was created, you could use **artistsXML.artist.(name == 'Roy Lichtenstein').work.(title == 'House I').year**.

As you can see, XML can be navigated easily and in many different ways. However, you're not always going to want to grab individual elements like that; often you'll want to work with them all. One option for doing so is to create an **XMLList** object:

```
private var artistsList:XMLList = artistsXML.children();
```

Whereas an **XML** object represents one body of XML data, **XMLList** represents a collection of XML elements, like an array of XML values.

You can then use a **for each** loop to access the children:

```
for each (var artist:XML in artistsList) {
    // Use artist.name, artist.@id, artist.work[0], etc.
}
```

The **children()** method is just one of many defined in the **XML** class. There are methods for adding and removing elements, for searching for values, and much more (see the ActionScript documentation if you're curious). For debugging purposes, the **toString()** and **toXMLString()** methods will output the XML as a readable string (both methods do the same thing).

tip

A string that contains only XML can be converted to an XML object using type casting: ***private var someXML:XML = new XML(someString);***

tip

In these examples, I'm using object notation to retrieve the values of different elements, but you can assign values to the elements just as well.

JSON

JSON is an understood data type in JavaScript (because it's a JavaScript object), but it's not in ActionScript. In order for ActionScript to parse JSON, the application will first need to incorporate the ActionScript 3 Corelib library.

1. Download the library from *http://code.google.com/p/as3corelib/*.
2. Expand the downloaded ZIP file.
3. Copy the *src/com* directory to your Flex application's *src* directory.

   You really only need the *com/adobe/serialization* folder, but it's fine to copy it all over.
4. In your MXML's Script block, import the JSON class:

   import com.adobe.serialization.json.JSON;
5. Then, when appropriate, apply the **JSON.decode( )** method to the data to turn it into a usable format:

   var jsonData:Object = JSON.decode(data);

   The assumption is that **data** would be a variable storing the data in a string format, as if returned from a server call.

 tip

The ***JSON.encode( )*** method converts a string to the JSON format.

At this point you can use **jsonData** as an object. For example, if the JSON data contains the following two elements, then the ActionScript code would refer to **jsonData.name** and **jsonData.birthDate**:

```
{
"name": "Georges Seurat",
"birthDate": "December 2, 1859"
}
```

If the JSON data represents a multidimensional array, you can use a loop and object notation to access every value. Say you have the following:

```
[{
name: "Georges Seurat",
birthDate: "December 2, 1859"
},
{
name: "Roy Lichtenstein",
birthDate: "October 27, 1923"
}]
```

Then you could access individual objects using **jsonData[0].name** or **jsonData[1].birthDate** or loop through all the artists with

```
for each (var artist:Object in jsonData) {
    // Use artist.name and artist.birthDate;
}
```

AMF

As I mentioned, AMF communications transmit data in a binary form, so it can't be represented in text. But previewing what's to come, if you've used AMF to communicate with PHP, it's very easy to access the returned data. You'll just use object notation. For example, if a PHP script returns this array of two elements:

```
return array('title' => 'Effortless Flex 4 Development', 'publisher' =>
'Peachpit Press');
```

Then the ActionScript code would refer to **someObj.title** and **someObj.publisher**.

As already mentioned, and as you'll see in Chapter 9, **someObj** will really be **event.result**, meaning you'd use **event.result.title** and **event.result.publisher**.

If the PHP script returns a multidimensional array, you can use a loop and object notation to access every value. Say the PHP script does the following:

```
return array(
array('id' => 1, 'name' => 'Human Resources'),
array('id' => 2, 'name' => 'Marketing'),
array('id' => 3, 'name' => 'Accounting'),
array('id' => 4, 'name' => 'Research and Development')
);
```

The returned result will be assigned to an **event** variable, making **event.result** an array of four elements, with each value being another array. You can loop through that array like so:

```
for (var i:uint = 0; i < event.result.length; i++) {
    // Use event.result[i].id and event.result[i].name
}
```

Commonly, these complex data sets returned by a PHP script will just be displayed in an MXML data component, so you won't even need to specifically access them one element at a time in your ActionScript code.

DEBUGGING

When you begin adding client-server interactions to applications, the potential for problems increases exponentially and debugging becomes that much more difficult. But if you're systematic in your debugging approach, you can solve problems without too much headache. Client-server interactions are based upon two things:

- Proper data being returned by the server.
- The data being properly handled by the client.

Debugging, then, is largely a matter of confirming what data the server is sending out and what the client is doing with that data. When the data being sent is not correct, you'll need to debug your PHP script. When the data being received doesn't generate the proper end result, you'll need to debug your Flex application.

The best way to confirm what a PHP script is sending out is just to load it directly in a Web browser. This works for plain text, XML, and JSON. For the last two, I would also recommend that you take the generated output and use an online validation system to confirm that it's valid XML or JSON, accordingly. If you search online for "XML validator" or "JSON validator", you'll find the tools you need.

For AMF, the browser that comes with AMFPHP is perfect for confirming the results of executing specific methods in specific classes. Further, you can open the **gateway.php** script that comes with AMFPHP, and edit it for improved debugging. Specifically there are three lines to edit:

First, change the **PRODUCTION_SERVER** constant to *false*:

define("PRODUCTION_SERVER", false);

Obviously, you don't want to change this for a live server, so change it back to *true* when you take your application online for good.

Second, you can have AMFPHP log incoming and outgoing communications by providing two methods with paths to where you want the log files to go:

$gateway->logIncomingMessages('/*path*/*to*/logs/incoming/');
$gateway->logOutgoingMessages('/*path*/*to*/logs/outgoing/');

My recommendation is to create a **logs** directory, with **incoming** and **outgoing** directories therein. PHP will need to be able to write to both directories in order to create new files.

If your PHP scripts are not returning the proper data, you'll need to debug the script itself. Normally the problem is between PHP and the database. The best way to hunt down those issues is to do the following:

1. Call MySQL error reporting functions to display any database-reported errors.
2. Print out the query being run, for confirmation.
3. Execute the same query using another interface, like phpMyAdmin or the command-line MySQL client to see what the results are.

Another thing you may want to consider is to use some form of logging to record when PHP scripts are called, what data they receive, what data they return, and so forth (as AMFPHP is capable of doing). You can either write this information to a log file on the server, send it to yourself in an e-mail, or use something like FirePHP (*www.firephp.org*), which can output PHP messages to a Firebug console (*http://getfirebug.com/*) within the Firefox Web browser. If you are using Firefox, you can also install the FireAMF plugin (*http://code.google.com/p/fireamf/*) for added AMF-related debugging.

On a more advanced level, you can use a proxy sniffer such as Charles (*www.charlesproxy.com*), to watch the client-server interactions. This is more useful when data is being sent to the PHP script, and you want to confirm that the sent data is appropriate. If you're using Flash Builder, it has a wonderful Network Monitor built into it. That tool will let you examine, in detail, both sides of every client-server interaction. At the end of Chapter 8, "Using Simple Services," I discuss the Network Monitor in detail.

In terms of debugging the Flex application, start by using the Flash Debug Profile and running the application in debug mode. If you set a breakpoint (by double-clicking a line), you can view the application variable values at that point in the application's life (**Figure 7.11**). Also make good use of **trace()** to leave yourself notes as to what is and is not happening. And remember that most classes have **toString()** methods. You can call these on server responses to quickly see what's contained therein.

tip

As you'll see over the next couple of chapters, using the data wizards built into Flash Builder will help minimize bugs as well.

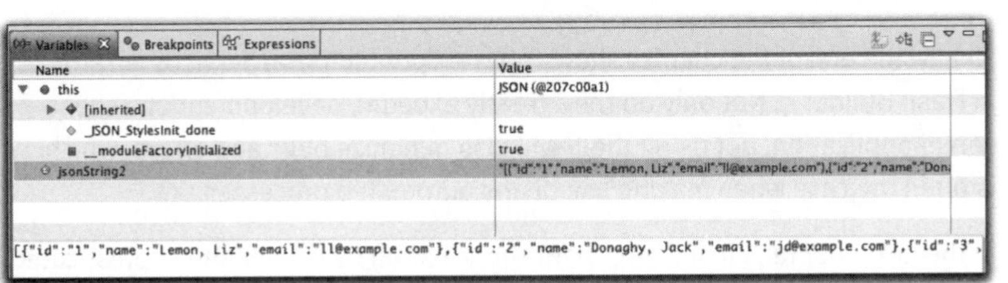

Figure 7.11

8 USING SIMPLE SERVICES

The previous three chapters deal with data in all its glory, from displaying data in Flex to rendering, formatting, and validating data, to the data involved in client-server interactions. In this chapter and the next you'll actually begin performing client-server communications. As mentioned several times over, I'll be using PHP as the server-side technology of choice. Not only is it my preferred technology, but increased support for PHP is a big feature of Flash Builder 4.

This chapter begins with some background information on the Flash Security model and how to set up a local environment (i.e., how to use your own computer as a server). The next section of the chapter walks through a couple of PHP scripts that will be used as the server interfaces for this chapter's examples.

After that, I introduce the three primary Flex components used to perform client-server interactions, and walk through one of these components—**HTTPService**—in much more detail. The interesting thing is that, due to features expanded upon in Flash Builder 4, you may rarely have the need to directly use this information. Still, the background knowledge is useful to have, and if you're not using Flash Builder 4, or are dealing with existing code, you'll appreciate the familiarity.

Finally, the end of the chapter shows off the updated Data/Services wizards in Flash Builder 4. Not only do they greatly expedite development of a client-server application, but using them will also minimize bugs and errors, which is often the case when making use of any automated processes.

In the next chapter, I'll build upon this information by using more sophisticated user-defined examples, as well as third-party services.

FLASH SECURITY MODEL

Before getting into some client-server interactions, you should have an understanding of the Flash Player security model. The Flash Player, for security purposes, creates a sandbox in which the Flash Player is allowed to do its thing. By restricting its actions within that sandbox, the Flash Player cannot be maliciously used to do bad things, such as muck around on the user's computer.

The Flash Player won't allow applications to access the user's computer, but Flash content running through Adobe AIR can access the file system.

One aspect of this sandbox is that, by default, a Flash program on one domain (a domain being *www.example.com*) cannot retrieve data from another domain (like *www.dmcinsights.com*). This is known as a *Same Origin Policy*, and is also a restriction present when using Ajax (i.e., don't think Flash is just being difficult). In order to overrule this default restriction, you'll need to create a *cross-domain policy file*.

A cross-domain policy file is an XML document with the name *crossdomain.xml*. Its root tag is **cross-domain-policy**, so it starts like so:

```
<?xml version="1.0"?>
<!DOCTYPE cross-domain-policy SYSTEM "http://www.macromedia.com/
xml/dtds/cross-domain-policy.dtd">
<cross-domain-policy>
</cross-domain-policy>
```

Within the root element, the domain's policy can be established. The tag to use is **allow-access-from**. Assign to its **domain** property the domain that should be allowed to connect. For example, say you develop a Flash application that's going to run from *www.example.com* that needs to make use of resources found on *www.example.info*. You would create, on *www.example.info*, a *crossdomain.xml* file that contains the following:

```
<cross-domain-policy>
    <allow-access-from domain="www.example.com" />
</cross-domain-policy>
```

If you wanted content on *www.example.info* to be available to both *www.example.com* and its subdomain *shop.example.com*, then the file would contain

```
<cross-domain-policy>
    <allow-access-from domain="www.example.com" />
    <allow-access-from domain="shop.example.com" />
</cross-domain-policy>
```

If you are running a site that provides services that should be available from any domain, the policy file would be defined as

```
<cross-domain-policy>
    <allow-access-from domain="*" />
</cross-domain-policy>
```

The asterisk is the wildcard, meaning that *any* domain is allowed to connect. This is essentially a disabling of any security restriction and should never be used on your own sites without other measures in place. For example, many public services require an authorization ID so that only registered applications can make use of the services.

tip

For the full particulars of the cross-domain policy file, see *www.Adobe.com/devnet/* or search online.

The **allow-access-from** tag has an optional **secure** attribute. If you set this to true, then a secure connection must be made from the Flash application to the server.

```
<cross-domain-policy>
    <allow-access-from domain="*" secure="true" />
</cross-domain-policy>
```

tip

As a security measure, you should create services, and the *crossdomain.xml* file, in a subdomain or subdirectory of your server, assuming your server needs to allow cross-domain requests at all.

The *crossdomain.xml* file is normally placed in the root directory (i.e., the folder that *www.example.com* points to). If the policy file is stored in a subdirectory, then it only applies to that subdirectory (and its subdirectories). To be absolutely clear, this isn't placed on the same computer as the Flash application itself: The Flash application already has access to its own domain.

PERFORMING CROSS-DOMAIN REQUESTS VIA PHP

You can circumvent the cross-domain request limitation using a PHP script. For example, if the Flash application is running from *www.example.com*, it can access a PHP script on that same domain. That PHP script can use the **fopen()** function or the curl library to read in a response from any domain, without restriction (assuming, of course, the domain doesn't have authentication requirements). The PHP script, having just read in the server response, could then output that response, just the same as if the data had come from the local database or file system instead.

All that being said, although you *can* circumvent Flash's cross-domain limitations via a local PHP script, it does not mean you *should*. Security precautions exist for a reason. If you have the need and justification for this approach, just be certain to validate and sanctify the incoming data, using both the PHP script and the Flash application, so as not to undermine the security of your application.

For the purposes of the rest of this book, I'll explain how to set up a server on your own computer. This way you can create, run, and debug your Flex applications locally. In this case you won't need to worry about cross-domain policy issues. Still, this is something to be aware of as you go forward and begin using services from other domains.

While discussing security, I want to reinforce the point that you must validate data being transmitted back and forth between the client and server. In particular, you want to validate user-supplied information in Flash, prior to sending it to the server, and validate that same data on the server, prior to using it in a database query or doing anything else potentially dangerous with it. You should also be cautious with server-provided data that will be used in a Flash application. You'll see plenty of examples in this chapter and the next for using data safely.

SETTING UP A LOCAL ENVIRONMENT

Once a Flash application has gone live, whether as a browser-based program or one destined for the desktop (thanks to Adobe AIR), you'll need a live PHP server to handle the back end of the client-server interactions. To be more explicit, you'll need to set up *www.example.com* so that it runs your PHP scripts, where *www.example.com* is your actual domain name. On the other hand, while just developing, testing, and debugging an application, before you make it live, there's a lot to be said for creating a local PHP environment. This means you'll want to install—on the same computer which you're using to write and test your Flex—a Web server running PHP and a database application. Generally, I prefer to go the *AMP* route—Apache, MySQL, and PHP, but you can use other Web servers and database applications, too.

tip

The third-party services that will be used in the next chapter may or may not be using PHP and MySQL. In reality, the server technology makes little difference to Flash.

There are several ways you can establish a local environment, starting with downloading, installing, and configuring the three pieces individually. I would highly recommend, however, that you consider an all-in-one package, such as XAMMP (*www.apachefriends.org*). It's available for Windows, and in beta versions for Mac OS X and Linux. If you want a more stable package for Mac OS X, try MAMP (*www.mamp.info*). Both XAMMP and MAMP are available in free versions, and are a snap to install and run.

In order to prepare your computer for developing Flex-PHP applications (and to try the examples to follow), take these next steps:

1. Download XAMPP, MAMP, or an alternate package.

   As I said, the first two are highly recommended, but other options exist. Just get one that works for your operating system, of course. The exact versions of PHP, MySQL, and Apache shouldn't matter with respect to this book's content, so long as you're using versions that support the Improved MySQL extensions, which I'll be using in my code. This means PHP 5 and up, MySQL 4.1 and up.

2. Install the package.

   I'm not going to waste pages explaining how to install these, so if you have any questions or problems, check out the package's corresponding documentation.

3. Start the application, if it does not start automatically.

   Any time you're testing a Flex application that connects to the local PHP server, you'll need to have the Web server application running. If not, you'll get an error in the browser when you go to run the Flash content.

4. Note the server's primary URL.

   You'll need to know the primary URL when you go to connect to PHP from within Flex. For some all-in-one packages, the primary URL will just be *http://localhost*. For others, such as MAMP, it'll include the port: *http://localhost:8888*.

   Most of these applications start with a splash page used to access some of the server information and configuration. The corresponding URL will likely be *http://localhost/something*, such as *http://localhost/xampp* or *http://localhost:8888/MAMP*. Note that you would not include the *something* part as the primary URL.

tip

You may be able to change the Web root directory if you'd like, using the application's preferences or configuration area.

5. Note the Web root directory.

   The Web root directory will be where Web files go. The defaults may be *C:\XAMPP\htdocs* or */Applications/MAMP/htdocs*.

   To understand the relationship between the Web root directory and the URL, if you place a *test.php* script in the Web root directory, then you can run the script by going to the main URL plus *test.php* (e.g., *C:\XAMPP\htdocs\test.php* is available at *http://localhost/test.php*).

tip

You can connect to a remote server from Flash content running on your computer, you'll just need to be online at the time. There may also be a greater time delay in the communications.

6. Create a new folder in the Web root directory.

   You can name this whatever you'd like, but for the sake of this chapter, *flex4ch08* makes sense. Now the URL you'll use in your Flex applications, for this chapter's examples, will begin *http://localhost/flex4ch08/* or *http://localhost:8888/flex4ch08/*.

7. Create and select a new database.

   Most all-in-one installers and hosted servers provide phpMyAdmin as a Web-based interface for managing databases. Through that, you should create a new database called *flex4_practice*.

8. Create two tables in the database.

Using phpMyAdmin, you should create two tables using this SQL:

```
CREATE TABLE departments (
    id TINYINT UNSIGNED NOT NULL AUTO_INCREMENT PRIMARY KEY,
    name VARCHAR(40),
    UNIQUE KEY name (name)
);
CREATE TABLE employees (
    id MEDIUMINT UNSIGNED NOT NULL AUTO_INCREMENT,
    departmentId TINYINT UNSIGNED NOT NULL,
    firstName VARCHAR(20) NOT NULL,
    lastName VARCHAR(40) NOT NULL,
    email VARCHAR(60) NOT NULL,
    phoneExt SMALLINT UNSIGNED NOT NULL,
    hireDate DATE NOT NULL,
    leaveDate DATE DEFAULT NULL,
    PRIMARY KEY (id),
    KEY name (lastName, firstName),
    KEY departmentId (departmentId)
);
```

These same tables were used in Chapter 7, "Common Data Formats," if you've already created them. You'll want to make sure you've created these tables in the database created in Step 7.

note

You can download the SQL, PHP, and Flex for this chapter from *www.DMCInsights.com/flex4/*.

9. Populate the two tables.

You'll need some sample data to get things going. You can use the downloadable SQL from the corresponding Web site or come up with your own sample data. Here are some of the commands I used:

```
INSERT INTO departments VALUES (1, 'Human Resources');
INSERT INTO departments VALUES (2, 'Marketing');
INSERT INTO departments VALUES (3, 'Accounting');
INSERT INTO departments VALUES (4, 'Research and Development');
INSERT INTO departments VALUES (5, 'Sales');
INSERT INTO employees VALUES (NULL, 1, 'Liz', 'Lemon', 'll@example.
com', 234, '1992-05-13', NULL);
INSERT INTO employees VALUES (NULL, 3, 'Jack', 'Donaghy', 'jd@
example.com', 130, '1999-02-24', NULL);
INSERT INTO employees VALUES (NULL, 2, 'Pete', 'Hornberger', 'ph@
example.com', 469, '1997-10-28', NULL);
INSERT INTO employees VALUES (NULL, 2, 'Kenneth', 'Parcell', 'kp@
example.com', 100, '2006-08-02', NULL);
```

tip

The semicolons in the SQL queries are used to indicate to MySQL the end of the command.

10. If you want, run some sample queries using phpMyAdmin to confirm their results.

When working with data, debugging applications is largely a matter of confirming what information you have at various steps. The source of the data will be this database, so querying the database directly first is a prudent move. Common queries that might be performed on this database include

```
SELECT * FROM departments;
SELECT * FROM employees;
SELECT * FROM employees WHERE departmentId=1;
SELECT employees.*, departments.name FROM employees,
departments WHERE employees.departmentId = departments.id;
```

In case you're not completely comfortable with SQL, the first two queries select every column of every row in the two tables. The third selects every column for only the employees in a specific department. The last query performs a join across the two tables, retrieving every column of every employee record, plus the matching department name (**Figure 8.1**).

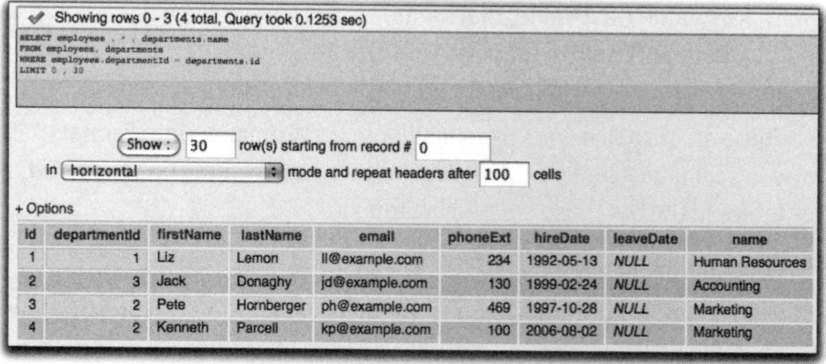

id	departmentId	firstName	lastName	email	phoneExt	hireDate	leaveDate	name
1	1	Liz	Lemon	ll@example.com	234	1992-05-13	NULL	Human Resources
2	3	Jack	Donaghy	jd@example.com	130	1999-02-24	NULL	Accounting
3	2	Pete	Hornberger	ph@example.com	469	1997-10-28	NULL	Marketing
4	2	Kenneth	Parcell	kp@example.com	100	2006-08-02	NULL	Marketing

Figure 8.1

CREATING THE PHP SCRIPTS

note

The PHP scripts can be found in the *Ch08/flex4ch08* folder, downloadable from *www.DMCInsights.com/flex4/*.

For the examples in this chapter, I want to create three PHP scripts: one for adding new employees, a second for retrieving all of the current employees, and a third that defines the MySQL connection information to be used by the first two. The first script should take a bunch of information (first name, last name, department, e-mail address, extension, and hire date), insert it into the database, and return a simple plain-text message indicating that the insert worked. The second PHP script will return lists of employees in XML format. I'll also build in some flexibility: If a department ID is passed along in the request, only employees in that department will be returned; otherwise every employee will be returned. I'll begin with the MySQL-specific script.

The MySQL Script

For both security and convenience it makes sense to define the values required to connect to a database in a separate script. By doing this, multiple scripts can easily use the same database access information and you can store that information in a more secure manner.

1. Begin a new PHP script in your text editor or IDE:

```
<?php
```

2. Create constants for each important value:

```
DEFINE ('DB_USER', '<username>');
DEFINE ('DB_PASSWORD', '<password>');
DEFINE ('DB_HOST', '<hostname>');
DEFINE ('DB_NAME', '<database_name>');
```

   You'll need to replace each instance of *<something>* with the appropriate value for your setup. For example, with MAMP without further customization, I can use *root* for the username and *root* for the password. When using a new installation of XAMPP, I can use *root* as the username, and an empty string as the password (i.e., no password). The database name should be that created and populated using the earlier steps. My recommendation was *flex4_practice*. The database host name will almost always be *localhost*.

3. Save the file as *mysql.inc.php*.

   I use the *.inc* extension to indicate that this file is to be included by others but also retain the *.php* extension so that it's treated as a PHP script. You may notice that I did not use a closing PHP tag. You can actually omit this. By doing so, you will avoid potential *headers already sent* error messages that can occur (in the file that includes this one) should this script have any extraneous spaces after the closing PHP tag.

   On a production server, I would store this file outside of the Web directory (i.e., not in *htdocs*). That's not an issue on a local, development server; just store the file somewhere that'll be easily referenced, such as *flex4ch08*.

Retrieving Employees

The next PHP script I'm going to develop will return all of the employees as XML. If the script receives a *departmentId* value in the URL, then it'll only return the employees in that department.

1. Begin a new PHP script:

```
<?php
```

2. Send the content-type header:

```
header('Content-Type: text/xml');
```

I explained in Chapter 7 that this line indicates that XML content is to follow. It's a good idea to use this when sending out XML data.

3. Begin the XML:

```
echo '<?xml version="1.0" encoding="utf-8" ?>
<employees>
';
```

The first line creates the XML declaration, which should always be present. The second creates the opening root tag.

4. Include the database information script:

```
require_once('mysql.inc.php');
```

This is the script that was just created. You'll need to change this line so that it's accurate, relative to the current script. If both are in your *flex4ch08* folder, then the above code will work.

5. Connect to the database:

```
$dbc = mysqli_connect(DB_HOST, DB_USER, DB_PASSWORD,
DB_NAME);
```

This line establishes a database connection, using the Improved MySQL functions. If your PHP installation does not support these functions, you'll need to use the older MySQL functions—**mysql_connect()** and **mysql_select_db()**—instead. See the PHP manual for the specifics.

6. If a connection was established, begin defining the query:

```
if ($dbc) {
    $q = 'SELECT employees.*, departments.name AS departmentName
    FROM employees, departments WHERE employees.departmentId =
    departments.id';
```

The conditional first checks that a connection to the database exists. Then I begin defining the query, assigning it to a variable named **$q**. The query selects every column from the **employees** table and the **name** column from departments. An alias is created for the department name. A join is used across the two tables, where the **departmentId** in **employees** equals **id** in **departments**.

7. Add another conditional to the query if a **departmentId** was passed to this script in the URL:

```
if (isset($_GET['departmentId']) && ( ((int)$_GET['departmentId']) > 0 )
){
    $q .= ' AND employees.departmentId = ' . (int) $_GET['departmentId'];
}
```

If a **departmentId** is passed to this script in the URL, it'll be available in the PHP code as **$_GET['departmentId']**. The first part of the conditional just checks that this variable has a value (i.e., that it exists). The second conditional typecasts the value to an integer, then checks that the result is greater than 0.

You cannot know that **$_GET['departmentId']** is a valid department ID without querying the database first, but these steps provide a reasonable amount of validation.

If the conditional is true, an extra condition is added to the query's **WHERE** clause: **AND employees.departmentId=*X***. The value of X will be **$_GET['departmentId']** typecast as an integer (the earlier typecasting only applied to that PHP conditional).

By typecasting numeric values, if someone attempts to hack this script by passing verybadcode as the value of ***$_GET['departmentId']***, that string will be typecast as the number 0.

8. Run the query and confirm that some rows were returned:

```
$r = mysqli_query($dbc, $q);
if (mysqli_num_rows($r) > 0) {
```

9. Fetch each row and print it as XML:

```
while ($row = mysqli_fetch_array($r, MYSQLI_ASSOC)) {
        echo "<employee>
    <id>{$row['id']}</id>
    <firstName>{$row['firstName']}</firstName>
    <lastName>{$row['lastName']}</lastName>
    <email>{$row['email']}</email>
    <phoneExt>{$row['phoneExt']}</phoneExt>
    <hireDate>{$row['hireDate']}</hireDate>
    <departmentName>{$row['departmentName']}</departmentName>
</employee>
";
} // End of WHILE loop.
```

Similar code to this was explained fully in Chapter 7. The **while** loop fetches one row at a time. Then each row is printed as an XML element called *employee*.

10. Complete the PHP page:

```
    } // End of mysqli_num_rows() IF.
} // End of $dbc IF.
// Complete the XML:
echo '</employees>';
?>
```

Make sure that you close the root **employees** element at the end.

11. Save the script in your Web directory as *getEmployees.php*.

You should save it in the *flex4ch08* folder created earlier.

12. If you want, test the PHP script by running it directly in your Web browser (**Figure 8.2**).

Figure 8.2

To test the **departmentId** conditional, append *?departmentId=X* to the URL.

Adding Employees

tip

In the next chapter you'll learn some approaches for validating the person using the Flash application.

This next PHP script I'm going to develop will add a new employee to the database. To do so, it'll require that lots of information be posted to this script. From a security standpoint, there are two concerns. The first, and most important, is that a malicious user can't do anything to reveal pertinent information about the server or the database. I'm specifically thinking of preventing SQL injection attacks here, so the script needs to sanctify any data that will be used in a query. The second concern is that legitimate records are being added to the database. Without authenticating the end-user submitting data to this PHP script, that's pretty much impossible to do.

The script will output plain text as its response.

1. Begin a new PHP script:

```
<?php
```

2. Add some minimal validation:

```
if (isset($_POST['departmentId'], $_POST['firstName'],
$_POST['lastName'], $_POST['email'], $_POST['phoneExt'],
$_POST['hireDate']) && ( ((int)$_POST['departmentId']) > 0 )
&& ( ((int)$_POST['phoneExt']) > 0 ) ) {
```

   The first part of this conditional confirms that six values are all present in **$_POST**: *departmentId*, *firstName*, *lastName*, *email*, *phoneExt*, and *hireDate*. The next two parts of this conditional confirm that the *departmentId* and *phoneExt*, when typecasted as integers, are greater than 0.

   There's much more you could, and probably should, do in a live script, but I don't want to get too bogged down in this side of things. But on a live script, I'd probably do the following:

   - Run the names and e-mail addresses through regular expressions
   - Confirm that the hire date is a valid date (and is maybe even within a certain number of days from today)
   - Check that the phone extension is within the allowed values (hypothetically between 100 and 500)
   - Test that the *departmentId* matches one of the values in the **departments** table.

3. Include the *mysql.inc.php* script and connect to the database:

```
require_once('mysql.inc.php');
$dbc = mysqli_connect(DB_HOST, DB_USER, DB_PASSWORD,
DB_NAME);
if ($dbc) {
```

4. Sanctify the provided information:

```
$firstName = mysqli_real_escape_string($dbc, trim($_POST['firstName']));
$lastName = mysqli_real_escape_string($dbc, trim($_POST['lastName']));
$email = mysqli_real_escape_string($dbc, trim($_POST['email']));
$hireDate = mysqli_real_escape_string($dbc, trim($_POST['hireDate']));
$departmentId = (int) $_POST['departmentId'];
$phoneExt = (int) $_POST['phoneExt'];
```

   To make the submitted data safe to use in a database query, all of the strings are run through the **mysqli_real_escape_string()** function and the two numbers are typecasted as integers. This is enough to prevent SQL injection attacks that would break the script and provide anything too revealing to a hacker.

5. Run the query:

```
$q = "INSERT INTO employees (departmentId, firstName, lastName, email, phoneExt, hireDate) VALUES ($departmentId, '$firstName', '$lastName', '$email', $phoneExt, '$hireDate')";
$r = mysqli_query($dbc, $q);
```

The query inserts the six pieces of information into the **employees** table as a new row.

6. Report upon the results:

```
if (mysqli_affected_rows($dbc) == 1) {
   echo 'The employee has been added.';
} else {
   echo 'The employee could not be added due to a system error.';
}
```

If one row was created for the new employee, then **mysqli_affected_rows( )** will return the value 1. In that case, a positive message is printed. If not, then a database error likely occurred and a message indicating such is printed. If you see this second message while testing the system, you'll need to debug the query to determine why it's not working properly.

7. Complete the script:

```
   } else {
      echo 'A server error occurred.';
   }
} else {
   echo 'This page has been accessed in error.';
}
?>
```

8. Save the script in your Web directory as *addEmployee.php*.

   You should save it in the *flex4ch08* folder created earlier.

9. If you want, test the PHP script by running it directly in your Web browser.

   As a simple test won't include posting data to the script, you should see the following message (**Figure 8.3**): *This page has been accessed in error.*

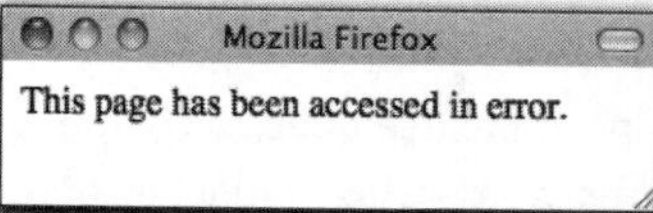

Figure 8.3

FLEX NETWORKING COMPONENTS

There are three Flex components used to perform client-server interactions: **HTTPService**, **WebService**, and **RemoteObject**. Which you'll use will depend upon the communication type supported by the server. As an analogy, think of the client-server communication like making a purchase: Many places take credit cards, some may only take cash; what you can use to pay will depend entirely upon what's accepted by the merchant. In other words, there's an agreed-upon medium involved with server communications, and it's the server that dictates the terms.

As a reminder, the use of components differs if you're using the Data/Services wizard in Flash Builder 4. The discussion of components is for historical and non-Flash Builder 4 benefit.

In non-layman's terms, the communication types are

- Representational State Transfer (REST)-style
- Web services (SOAP and WSDL)
- Remote Procedural Call (RPC)

The first thing you'll notice is that client-server communications are just filthy with acronyms. If it helps, I normally have to look these acronyms up as I can never remember their specific meanings myself (and it doesn't really matter).

REST-style services are simple, easy to use, and fairly efficient from a programming standpoint. You'll commonly use these in your Flex applications. The **HTTPService** component is used in Flex to perform REST-style requests. This protocol allows for the sending of data when the request is made, and the response can be in XML, JSON, or other plain-text formats. Data can be passed to the server during the request using either the POST or GET method.

Web services are a step up from REST services in terms of complexity. Web services use SOAP (Simple Object Access Protocol) as the means of communication, often returning WSDL (Web Services Description Language), which is based upon XML, to provide information about the service. If you really like acronyms, there's also UDDI (Universal Description, Discovery, and Integration), which is used to identify SOAP Web services. To perform SOAP requests, you use the Flex **WebService** component. Again, what communication methods you use will depend upon what the server supports, but you're probably least likely to use Web services.

All of the service components have been redefined in the Spark namespace.

Remote Procedural Calls (RPC) are a further step up from SOAP. RPC interactions will use special, often binary, formats, such as AMF. To perform RPC interactions, use the **RemoteObject** component. You'll get plenty of experience with RPC in Chapter 9, "Using Complex Services."

Over the next few pages you'll only work with the **HTTPService** class, as it's the easiest to use and perhaps the most common one. Unlike Web services and RPC, both covered in the next chapter, you won't even need to use extra libraries in either Flex or PHP to perform REST-style interactions.

THE HTTPSERVICE COMPONENT

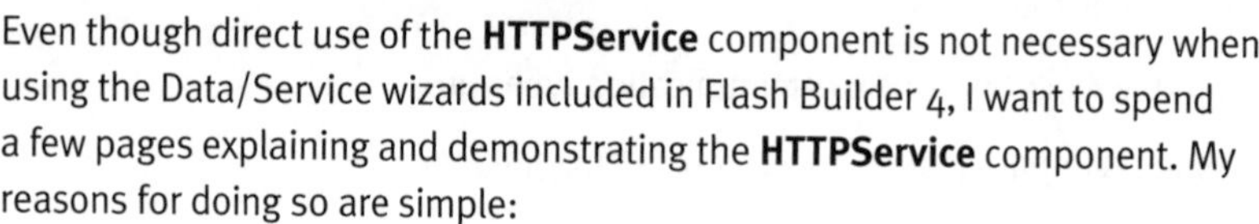

tip

Much of the explanation of the ***HTTPService*** component will also apply to the other service components discussed in Chapter 9.

Even though direct use of the **HTTPService** component is not necessary when using the Data/Service wizards included in Flash Builder 4, I want to spend a few pages explaining and demonstrating the **HTTPService** component. My reasons for doing so are simple:

- You may not be using Flash Builder 4.
- You may encounter older code that makes use of **HTTPService**.
- By understanding this approach to client-server interactions, you may appreciate the new Flash Builder 4 approach even more.
- Using **HTTPService** is remarkably simple.

Creating

To create an **HTTPService** component, you use the **HTTPService** tag, of course. As this is a non-visual component, you create it within the **Declarations** section:

tip

You can also create ***HTTPService*** instances using just Action-Script, if you prefer.

```
<fx:Declarations>
   <s:HTTPService />
</fx:Declarations>
```

As with any component, you customize the service by assigning values to its various properties. First, the **HTTPService** component should be assigned a unique **id** value, as you'll need to refer to the service elsewhere in the application. Second, the **url** property should be assigned the URL that is the server side of the communication. This would be your PHP script.

The **method** property indicates the type of request being made of the server. Generally, this will be either *GET* or *POST*. Which you use depends upon what the server-side script is expecting but, as a rule of thumb, GET requests are made to retrieve information, POST requests are made when the intent is to update the server. For example, you would GET a list of employees but POST the information for a new employee to be added to the database. The default value is GET. If you look at the PHP scripts already created, they're written to accept GET and POST values, accordingly.

tip

The ***HTTPService*** component can also be used to read in a static XML or plain-text file from a server.

At this point, the service component is just

<mx:HTTPService id="myService" url="http://www.example.com/somepage.php" method="GET" />

Next, there's the **resultFormat** property. Its value is used to set the processing of the returned server response. These formats largely correspond to those discussed in Chapter 7 and earlier:

- object
- array
- xml
- flashvars
- text
- e4x

By indicating to the Flash application the result format, the application will handle the response as that data type. For example, if XML is being returned by the server, you can have it be converted to an array, literal XML, or E4X (ECMAScript for XML). By default, the expected result format is a generic object.

tip

The ***HTTPService*** component also has a ***useProxy*** property that is assigned a Boolean value. Set this to true to use a proxy service.

A service that accesses the *getEmployees.php* script already defined would look like the following:

<mx:HTTPService id="getEmployeesService" url="http://*hostname*/flex4ch08/getEmployees.php" method="GET" resultFormat="e4x" />

A service that calls the *addEmployee.php* script would be defined as

<mx:HTTPService id="addEmployeeService" url="http://*hostname*/flex4ch08/addEmployee.php" method="POST" resultFormat="text" />

I've just used *hostname* in place of the actual hostname in both examples. You would need to replace this with *localhost*, *localhost:8888, www.yourdomain.com,* or whatever.

tip

The ***HTTPService***'s ***showBusyCursor*** property, when set to true, will change the cursor icon while a server request is occurring, thereby indicating to the user the behind-the-scenes action.

Invoking a Service

Just defining a service component does nothing but set the stage for later activity. A service is not actually called until you invoke the service's **send( )** method.

You'll want to call the **send( )** method after an event takes place, such as

- The user clicking a button
- A **DataGrid** or **AdvancedDataGrid** being fully rendered
- The application being completely created

You may think that a service ought to be automatically invoked once created, but by controlling the invocation of the service, you can dictate exactly when it should occur and, better yet, invoke the service multiple times in an application, as warranted.

For displaying all of the employees in a **DataGrid**, I would want to retrieve them from the server only after the **DataGrid** is ready:

```
<mx:DataGrid id="employeesDataGrid" creationComplete=
"getEmployeesService.send( )" />
```

The service call will be performed *asynchronously*, meaning it'll happen in the background. Both the application and the user can continue to perform other tasks while the server call and response are taking place.

Handling the Response

The **HTTPService** component's **result** property takes the name of the function that should be called when the server response is returned. This function applies when the client application successfully connects to the server and the server successfully replies; it does not necessarily mean that the server response was what you would expect it to be.

The function should be written so that it takes one argument of type **Event**. The specific event type is **ResultEvent**. You'll need to import that definition before using the object:

```
import mx.rpc.events.ResultEvent;
private function handleServiceResult(event:ResultEvent):void {
    // Do whatever.
}
```

The most important property in the **ResultEvent** object is **result**. This property reflects the data exactly as it is returned by the server. If the server returned just a bit of plain text, then **event.result** is a simple string. If the server returned XML, then **event.result** is XML. If the **HTTPService** component uses a **resultFormat** of *e4x*, then you can use the ECMAScript for XML capabilities built into ActionScript to work with the returned result. For example, say that the returned result is just the following:

```
<data>
   <count>14</count>
</data>
```

In this case, **event.result.data.count** has a value of 14. Or, because the returned data is in E4X format, which is easy to navigate, you could just use **event.result.count**.

As another example, say the returned result is an array of objects:

```
[{firstName:'John', lastName:'Doe', ext:324, department:'Human Resources'},
{firstName:'Jane', lastName:'Doe', ext:231, department:'Marketing'},
{firstName:'Samuel', lastName:'Smith', ext:212, department:'Marketing'},
{firstName:'Isabel', lastName:'Jackson', ext:102, department:'Accounting'}]
```

If the **resultFormat** is *array*, then the function can reference **event.result** to access the entire array, **event.result[0]** to access the first object in the array, and **event.result[3].ext** to access the **ext** value for the fourth item in the array (the value being 102).

Hopefully this aspect of the process does not seem to be more complicated than it is. Just remember that **event.result** is the data returned by the server, interpreted as the **resultFormat**. How you navigate within **event.result** depends upon the data returned and the **resultFormat**.

THE LASTRESULT PROPERTY

The **HTTPService** component has a **lastResult** property that is equivalent to the **ResultEvent** object's **result** property. However, **lastResult** is not assigned a value until after the result function executes. So, within the result event-handler function you can use **event.result** and outside of the function, after the result has been returned, you can use ***HTTPServiceComponentId*.lastResult**. This means that you could bind the **lastResult** property of a service as the data provider to a **DataGrid**:

```
<mx:DataGrid dataProvider="{getEmployeesService.lastResult.employee.
employees}"...>
```

Handling Response Errors

Whereas the **HTTPService** component's **response** property should be assigned the name of the function to call after the server responds, the **fault** property is assigned the function to call when the server call fails. This failure is not indicative of the server failing to return the result you expected, but rather a failure of the client to communicate with the server resource at all. This function should take an event object as its lone argument, specifically of type **FaultEvent**. Again, you'll need to import that definition first:

```
import mx.rpc.events.FaultEvent;
```

Within the function, you can access the error number in **event.fault.faultCode**. You can access the error message in **event.fault.faultString**.

Putting It All Together

tip

If you download the source code from the book's corresponding Web site (*www.dmcinsights.com/flex4/*), you'll find this example in the *Ch08/Ch08_01* folder.

tip

When using the ***HTTPService*** component, your Flex project does not need to be associated with a specific server type.

In the past several pages, I've walked through the fundamentals of using the **HTTPService** component. Now let's put that within the context of a Flex application so you can see it altogether. For this next example, you'll only create a **DataGrid** that displays every employee. The following example will do that, plus add a **DropDownList** for selecting which department's employees to return, and add a form for creating new employees.

1. Create a new project in Flash Builder or your alternative text editor or IDE.
2. Within the Declarations section, define the **HTTPService**:

```
<fx:Declarations>
    <s:HTTPService id="getEmployeesService" url="http://localhost
    /flex4ch08/getEmployees.php"
    method="GET" resultFormat="e4x"
    result="getEmployeesResult(event)" fault="serviceFault(event)" />
</fx:Declarations>
```

The **HTTPService** has an **id** of *getEmployeesService*. Its **url** is *http://localhost/flex4ch08/getEmployees.php*. You may need to change this based upon the particulars of your local environment. The service uses the GET method and parses the returned response as ECMAScript for XML. The **getEmployeesResult( )** function will be called when the server responds; **serviceFault( )** will be called upon error.

3. Within a **Script** block, import the two event definitions:

```
<fx:Script>
    <![CDATA[
        import mx.rpc.events.FaultEvent;
        import mx.rpc.events.ResultEvent;
```

These are the two types of event objects that will be received by the functions.

4. Create a bindable variable:

```
[Bindable]
private var employeesList:XMLList;
```

The **employeesList** variable will be used to store all of the employees. It needs to be bindable, as it'll be used as the data provider of the **DataGrid**. It's declared of type **XMLList** as it'll represent multiple employee records from the XML (and the **XMLList** data type is literally a list of XML records).

5. Define the **getEmployeesResult( )** function:

```
private function getEmployeesResult(event:ResultEvent):void {
    employeesList= event.result.employee;
}
```

This function takes one argument, of type **ResultEvent**, and returns nothing. Within the function, the returned result, found in **event.result**, needs to be assigned to the previously declared **employeesList** variable. The *getEmployees.php* script returns XML with a root node of *employees* and subnodes called *employee*. This means that **event.result.employees** is also XML, which cannot be directly assigned to **employeesList**, as **employeesList** is a variable of type **XMLList**. Therefore, **event.result.employee** is assigned using dot syntax.

6. Define the **serviceFault( )** function:

```
private function serviceFault(event:FaultEvent):void {
    trace(event.fault.message);
}
```

This function is called when a server error occurs. That should be unlikely in a live site, so for debugging purposes, I'm just outputting the error message to the console using **trace( )**. If you wanted, you could alternatively print a message in a **Label** that's visible to the end user (a generic error message, nothing too confusing or technically informative), or use an **Alert** window.

7. Complete the **Script** block:

```
    ]]>
</fx:Script>
```

8. Add a **Label** to the page to create a title:

```
<s:Label text="Manage Employees" horizontalCenter="0" top="10"
fontSize="36" fontFamily="Times New Roman" color="#362EDE"/>
```

This code is exactly the same as that used in earlier chapters.

9. Begin defining a **DataGrid**:

```
<mx:DataGrid id="employeesDG" width="85%" horizontalCenter="0"
top="45" creationComplete="getEmployeesService.send()"
dataProvider="{employeesList}">
```

The **DataGrid** invokes the **HTTPService**'s **send()** method once it's been completed. The **employeesList** variable is bound as the data provider. When the **DataGrid** is first created, **employeesList** is empty, so no records will be displayed. The server is then called and when it returns a result, the **employeesList** variable will be updated in the **getEmployeesResult()** function. At that point, since this **DataGrid** is watching for changes in that variable, the **DataGrid** will be populated with the new value of **employeesList**.

10. Define the **DataGrid**'s columns:

```
<mx:columns>
  <mx:DataGridColumn headerText="ID" dataField="id"/>
  <mx:DataGridColumn headerText="First Name" dataField=
  "firstName"/>
  <mx:DataGridColumn headerText="Last Name" dataField=
  "lastName"/>
  <mx:DataGridColumn headerText="Email" dataField="email"/>
  <mx:DataGridColumn headerText="Department" dataField=
  "departmentName"/>
  <mx:DataGridColumn headerText="Phone Ext." dataField=
  "phoneExt"/>
  <mx:DataGridColumn headerText="Hire Date" dataField=
  "hireDate"/>
</mx:columns>
```

For each column I'm setting the **headerText** and **dataField** properties. The latter values come from the names of the XML elements within each employee record.

tip

If you plan on formatting any data returned by a database (like the hire date), I would recommend doing so within the SQL query. It's always best to let the database do as much work as possible.

WEB VS FLASH CLIENT-SERVER INTERACTIONS

One thing to note about these Flash-based client-server interactions is how they differ from those with a standard Web page. If you have an HTML form that gets submitted to a server, and you're not using Ajax, the user will see the browser send that data to the server, await the response, and then refresh the page with the server response. With Rich Internet Applications, the same process is happening but entirely behind the scenes. In this particular case, ActionScript is used to dynamically update what the user sees in order to reflect the server response.

11. Complete the **DataGrid**:

</mx:DataGrid>

12. Save, run, and test the completed application (**Figure 8.4**).

Mozilla Firefox

Manage Employees

ID	First Name	Last Name	Email	Department	Phone Ext.	Hire Date
1	Liz	Lemon	ll@example.com	Human Resources	234	1992-05-13
2	Jack	Donaghy	jd@example.com	Accounting	130	1999-02-24
3	Pete	Hornberger	ph@example.com	Marketing	469	1997-10-28
4	Kenneth	Parcell	kp@example.com	Marketing	100	2006-08-02

Figure 8.4

To easily see the fault function in use, provide an invalid **url** value to **HTTPService**, then run the application in debug mode. You'll see the error message printed in the console (**Figure 8.5**).

```
Problems | Data/Services | Network Monitor | Console | Test Operation
Ch08_01 [Web Application] http://localhost:8888/Ch08_01-debug/Ch08_01.html
[SWF] /Ch08_01-debug/Ch08_01.swf - 370,463 bytes after decompression
[SWF] /Ch08_01-debug/Ch08_01.swf - 2,292,131 bytes after decompression
[SWF] /Ch08_01-debug/Ch08_01.swf - 441,686 bytes after decompression
[SWF] /Ch08_01-debug/Ch08_01.swf - 1,429,050 bytes after decompression
[SWF] /Ch08_01-debug/Ch08_01.swf - 323,414 bytes after decompression
faultCode:Server.Error.Request faultString:'HTTP request error' faultDetail:'Error: [IOErrorEvent type="ioError" bubbl
```

Figure 8.5

SENDING DATA TO A SERVER

Often enough, a server call will be used to just fetch information without providing any additional data to the server. For example, if you want to retrieve a full list of employees or access an RSS feed. Other times the client will need to send data along with the request. The data can be used to dictate what information is returned—just the employees in a certain department or just the stock price for a given stock—or be used to update the server's database, such as when the user completes and submits a form. In either case, all you need to do to send data to a server is add elements to the **HTTPService**'s **request** property:

```
<s:HTTPService...>
    <s:request>
    </s:request>
</s:HTTPservice>
```

Within the **request** tags, create a new element for each piece of data to be transmitted. The names of the elements will be entirely manufactured by you, but should be meaningful, should be restricted to just letters (and maybe numbers, if absolutely necessary), and cannot contain spaces or special characters. This next bit of code sends the value *ADBE* as the **symbol** value (that's Adobe's stock symbol):

```
<s:request>
    <symbol>ADBE</symbol>
</s:request>
```

In the corresponding PHP script that represents the server side of this equation, the value *ADBE* will be stored in the broad variable **$_REQUEST**, which represents all data sent to the script via the GET method, the POST method, or in a cookie. If you want to be more specific—and you really should, you would use **$_GET['symbol']** if the service uses the GET method and **$_POST['symbol']** if the service uses the POST method.

To dynamically assign the data to be passed to the server, you can use data binding. One option is to bind directly to the values of other components:

```
<s:request>
    <symbol>{symbolInput.text}</symbol>
</s:request>
```

Another option is to create a bindable variable, then use ActionScript to update that variable, when appropriate.

In either case, it's a good idea to use validators to inspect the data prior to invoking the service. There's no point in, say, telling the server to add a new employee when the user hasn't properly provided all of the information for adding a new employee. And, most importantly, remember that the server-side script is the critical point in the security here, as it protects the database. The server-side script must also validate and sanctify the data before using it in database queries (as the PHP scripts written earlier do).

tip

If you download the source code from the book's corresponding Web site (*www.dmcinsights.com/flex4/*), you'll find this example in the *Ch08/Ch08_02* folder.

With this in mind, let's update the Employees Management example so that two new features are added. First, a **DropDownList** will allow the user to view the employees in only a selected directory. Doing so requires sending the selected *departmentId* value to the *getEmployees.php* script. Second, a form will allow the user to add new employees. The application must validate the form data prior to sending it on to the *addEmployee.php* script. **Figure 8.6** shows the desired end result. You'll be adding about 100 lines of code to the earlier example, but I'll walk through the additions in detail. Because the new features involve interrelated code, I'm going to skip around among the MXML, ActionScript, and **Declarations** so you can best see how things tie together.

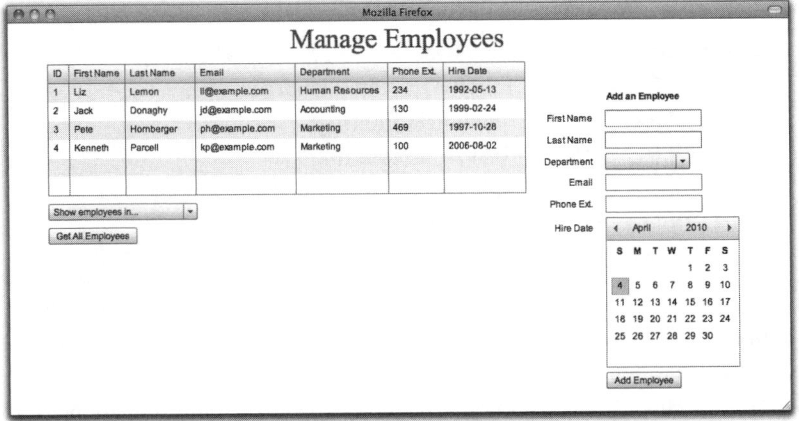

Figure 8.6

1. Open the previous **HTTPService** project in Flash Builder or your alternative text editor or IDE, if it is not already.

2. Wrap the **DataGrid** within a **VGroup** and an **HGroup**:

```
<s:HGroup width="90%" height="80%" verticalCenter="20"
horizontalCenter="0">
    <s:VGroup width="70%" gap="10">
        <mx:DataGrid id="employeesDB" width="100%"
    creationComplete="getEmployeesService.send()"
    dataProvider="{employeesList}">
```

   To achieve the desired layout, underneath the main title **Label**, everything will be placed within an **HGroup**: the **DataGrid** on the left, the form on the right. The **DataGrid**, the **DropDownList**, and the Button will all go within a **VGroup**. I've also changed the width of the **DataGrid**.

3. After the **DataGrid**, add a **DropDownList**:

```
<s:DropDownList id="getEmployeesDepartment" width="200"
dataProvider="{departmentsList}" prompt="Show employees in..."
change="getEmployeesService.send()" valueCommit=
"getEmployeesService.send()" />
```

   This **DropDownList** will display every department so that the end user can restrict the displayed employees to just that department. The data provider will be an **ArrayList** created in the **Declarations**. When either the **change** or **valueCommit** events occur, the **getEmployeesService**'s **send()** method will be invoked, thereby repopulating the **DataGrid**. The **change** event will be triggered when the user selects one of the departments. The need for the **valueCommit** event handler will be addressed in Step 6.

4. Create the **ArrayList** in the **Declarations**:

```
<s:ArrayList id="departmentsList">
    <fx:Object data="1" label="Human Resources" />
    <fx:Object data="2" label="Marketing" />
    <fx:Object data="3" label="Accounting" />
    <fx:Object data="4" label="Research and Development" />
    <fx:Object data="5" label="Sales" />
</s:ArrayList>
```

   Because the list of departments will be used twice in this application—for both retrieving employees and adding a new one, I'll define that list externally to any one component. I've defined the **ArrayList** as a series of generic objects. For each, the **label** is the visual value and the **data** corresponds to the primary key for that department from the database.

   Now, you may wonder why I'm not using an **HTTPService** to retrieve this information from the database. You could easily do so by creating a *getDepartments.php* script that works similarly to *getEmployees.php*. However, the departments in a company will change very rarely, so it'd be an unnecessary burden to make a service call for that information. Should the departments change, you'd just need to update this component, then recompile and redistribute the Flash application.

5. Change the **HTTPService** component so that the selected department is passed along to the server:

```
<s:HTTPService id="getEmployeesService" url="http://localhost:8888/
flex4ch08/getEmployees.php"
    method="GET" resultFormat="e4x"
    result="getEmployeesResult(event)" fault="serviceFault(event)">
<s:request>
    <departmentId>{getEmployeesDepartment.selectedItem.data}
    </departmentId>
</s:request>
</s:HTTPService>
```

   The selected department's ID value needs to be passed along to the PHP script under the name *departmentId*, so that's what I've named the tags within the **request** element. For that value, I'm binding to the **DropDown List**'s **selectedItem.data** property. Thus, if the user selects the first department listed, the **selectedItem** is the first object in the **departmentsList ArrayList**. The **data** attribute of that object will be a number like 1. So whenever this service is called, the current value of **getEmployeesDepartment.selectedItem.data** will be sent along to the server.

6. In the MXML, after the new **DropDownList**, add a **Button** and close the **VGroup**:

```
<s:Button label="Get All Employees" click=
"getEmployeesDepartment.selectedIndex = -1"
id="fetchSomeEmployeesButton"/>
</s:VGroup>
```

This **Button** comes into play should the user select a department to see a subsection of employees, then desire to see all the employees again. In that case, you don't want to send along a department ID to the PHP script. As the service automatically sends the currently selected department's ID to the PHP script, when this **Button** is clicked, the **Drop DownList**'s **selectedIndex** property needs to be assigned the value -1. (Remember that all events take ActionScript as their values, so no curly braces are necessary.) That simple step will reset the **DropDownList**. Unfortunately, that alone will not trigger a **change** event, as only user actions can count as a change. That is why the **DropDownList** also watches for the **valueCommit** event. That's the event that will be triggered when the **DropDownList**'s **selectedIndex** is changed programmatically here.

If you're keeping score at home, this means that the *getEmployees* service is being called after three different events:

- When the **DataGrid** is completely created.
- When the user selects a department from the **DropDownList**.
- When the user clicks the **Button**.

tip

In my opinion, it's the little things—*like making it easy for the user to re-display every employee—that makes for a quality user interface.*

7. Begin a **Form**:

```
<mx:Form width="30%">
   <s:Label id="addEmployeeLabel" color="#49B42C" fontSize="16"
   fontWeight="bold"/>
   <mx:FormHeading label="Add an Employee"/>
```

The form has a form heading, but do notice that I've added a blank **Label** at the top of the form, with a bit of formatting. It'll be used to report upon the result of adding a new employee.

8. Complete the **Form**:

```
   <mx:FormItem label="First Name">
      <s:TextInput id="employeeFirstName"/>
   </mx:FormItem>
   <mx:FormItem label="Last Name">
      <s:TextInput id="employeeLastName"/>
   </mx:FormItem>
```

code continues on next page

```
<mx:FormItem label="Department">
    <s:DropDownList id="employeeDepartment" dataProvider=
    "{departmentsList}" />
</mx:FormItem>
<mx:FormItem label="Email">
    <s:TextInput id="employeeEmail"/>
</mx:FormItem>
<mx:FormItem label="Phone Ext.">
    <s:TextInput id="employeePhoneExt"/>
</mx:FormItem>
<mx:FormItem label="Hire Date">
    <mx:DateChooser id="employeeHireDate"  />
</mx:FormItem>
<mx:FormItem>
    <s:Button label="Add Employee" id="addEmployeeButton"
    click="addEmployee()"/>
</mx:FormItem>
</mx:Form>
```

There's nothing revolutionary here; in fact, most of the code is identical to that in earlier chapters. The **DropDownList** here is also bound to the same **departmentsList** variable declared in Step 4. When the **Button** is clicked, the **addEmployees()** function will be called.

9. Complete the **HGroup**:

```
</s:HGroup>
```

10. Within the **Declarations**, create all the form validators:

```
<mx:StringValidator id="firstNameValidator" source=
"{employeeFirstName}" property="text" maxLength="20"
tooLongError="Please enter a valid first name." tooShortError="Please
enter a valid first name." enabled="{validatorsEnabled}" />
<mx:StringValidator id="lastNameValidator" source=
"{employeeLastName}" property="text" maxLength="40"
tooLongError="Please enter a valid last name." tooShortError="Please
enter a valid last name." enabled="{validatorsEnabled}" />
<mx:NumberValidator id="deptValidator" source=
"{employeeDepartment}" property="selectedIndex" minValue="0"
maxValue="4" lowerThanMinError="Please select a valid
department." exceedsMaxError="Please select a valid department."
enabled="{validatorsEnabled}" />
<mx:NumberValidator id="phoneValidator" source=
"{employeePhoneExt}" property="text" minValue="100"
```

```
maxValue="500" lowerThanMinError="The phone extension must be
between 100 and 500." exceedsMaxError="The phone extension must
be between 100 and 500." enabled="{validatorsEnabled}" />
<mx:EmailValidator id="emailValidator" source="{employeeEmail}"
property="text" enabled="{validatorsEnabled}" />
<mx:DateValidator id="hireDateValidator" source=
"{employeeHireDate}" property="selectedDate"
enabled="{validatorsEnabled}" />
```

The first four of these were first created and explained in Chapter 6, "Manipulating Data." They perform some validation on the first name, last name, department, and phone extension form elements. The next two validators are new to this version of the application, and apply to the e-mail address and the hire date. For the latter, the property being validated is the **DateChooser**'s **selectedDate**, which will be a **Date** object.

For each validator, I've bound the **enabled** property to a variable named **validatorsEnabled**. By doing so, I'll easily be able to turn all six validators on and off as needed. You'll see this in a few more steps.

11. Within the **Declarations**, create a formatter:

```
<mx:DateFormatter id="hireDateFormatter" formatString=
"YYYY-MM-DD" />
```

The hire date that's to be inserted into the database has to be in a specific format. The value selected by the user in the **DateChooser** will actually be a **Date** object, which isn't compatible with what the database will expect, let alone the PHP script. To convert the selected value from a **Date** object to an appropriate string, this formatter will be used.

12. Create a new **HTTPService** component:

```
<s:HTTPService id="addEmployeeService" url="http://localhost:
8888/flex4ch08/addEmployee.php"
method="POST" resultFormat="text"
result="addEmployeeResult(event)" fault="serviceFault(event)">
<s:request>
  <departmentId>{employeeDepartment.selectedItem.data}
  </departmentId>
  <firstName>{employeeFirstName.text}</firstName>
  <lastName>{employeeLastName.text}</lastName>
  <email>{employeeEmail.text}</email>
  <phoneExt>{employeePhoneExt.text}</phoneExt>
```

code continues on next page

```
<hireDate>{hireDateFormatter.format(employeeHireDate.
selectedDate)}
</hireDate>
</s:request>
</s:HTTPService>
```

This service calls the *addEmployee.php* script, using the POST method (remember that the PHP script expects all the data to be transmitted via POST). The returned result of the script will be text, so the **resultFormat** is assigned that here. Upon successful response, the **addEmployeeResult( )** function will be called. The already existing **serviceFault( )** function is used in case of failure.

The service must send six pieces of information to the PHP script. For four of these, it's the user-entered data, found within a **TextInput**'s **text** property. For the department, the data must be from the underlying objects in the **ArrayList** (the department needs to be a numeric value, not the department name string). For the **hireDate** value, it should be the **selectedDate** from the **DateChooser**, as formatted by the **DateFormatter**. Each element name here must exactly match those expected by the PHP script.

13. Within the **Script** block, import the **Validator** definition:

```
import mx.validators.Validator;
```

In order to perform the validation on the form, the application will need access to this definition.

14. Also within the **Script** block, create the **validatorsEnabled** variable:

```
[Bindable]
private var validatorsEnabled:Boolean = true;
```

This flag variable will be used to enable or disable all the validators in one fell swoop. It's initially set to true, so that the validators are all enabled. This variable must be bindable so that the validators respond to its changes.

15. Define the **addEmployee( )** function:

```
private function addEmployee( ):void {
  var vr:Array = Validator.validateAll([firstNameValidator,
lastNameValidator, deptValidator, emailValidator, phoneValidator,
hireDateValidator]);
  if (vr.length == 0) {
     addEmployeeService.send( );
  }
}
```

This function will be called when the user clicks the Add Employee button. Its purpose is to run all the validators, then invoke **addEmployeeService.send( )**. The use of **Validator.validateAll( )** is explained in Chapter 6. If it returns an empty array, it's safe to call the service (which will already have the associated values bound to its request parameters).

16. Begin defining the **addEmployeeResult( )** function:

```
private function addEmployeeResult(event:ResultEvent):void {
  addEmployeeLabel.text = event.result.toString( );
  getEmployeesService.send( );
```

This function will be called when the **addEmployeeService** result is returned. It should do three things: indicate to the user the server response, update the **DataGrid**, and reset the form. To do the first, assign to the **addEmployeeLabel**'s **text** property the server result. That result should be in plain text, but to be safe, the **toString( )** method is applied to it.

To update the **DataGrid**, just invoke the **getEmployeesService.send( )** method. The addition of an employee now counts as a fourth event that invokes this service call.

tip

Another way of handling the *addEmployee.php* response is to bind the ***text*** property of ***addEmployeeLabel*** to ***add EmployeeService.lastResult. toString( )***.

17. Reset the form:

```
validatorsEnabled = false;
employeeFirstName.text = '';
employeeLastName.text = '';
employeeDepartment.selectedIndex = -1;
employeeEmail.text = '';
employeePhoneExt.text = '';
employeeHireDate.selectedDate = null;
validatorsEnabled = true;
```

Much of this code was also used in Chapter 6. To reset the form, first every validator is disabled, so that no errors are displayed while the form is reset. To do that quickly, the **validatorsEnabled** variable is set to false. Then, each form **TextInput** is cleared of its text value. The **DropDownList** has its **selectedIndex** set to -1 and the **DateChooser** has its **selectedDate** set to **null**. Then the validators are re-enabled for the next employee to be added.

18. Complete the **addEmployeeResult( )** function:

```
}
```

19. Save, run, and test the completed application.

Figure 8.7 shows the result after successfully adding a new employee (two, actually).

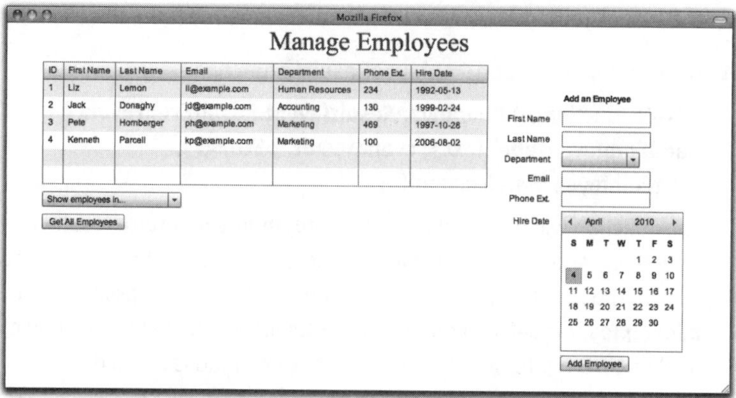

Figure 8.7

FLASH BUILDER DATA WIZARDS

tip

Flash Builder can automate interactions with a range of server-side technologies. In this book, I'm only using PHP.

tip

The Connect to XML process is really just a more specific Connect to HTTP wizard.

Over the previous 10+ pages, I discuss and demonstrate the **HTTPService** component in some detail: its properties, its events, and how you'll use it in an application. Those pages look at this component as if you were defining and using it from scratch. But if you're using Flash Builder for your Flex development, you should be aware of the wizards built into the application for auto-generating service components.

There are several similar wizards you can use to create the appropriate MXML and ActionScript for connecting to a server. For the purposes of this book, the wizards you might use are

- Connect to HTTP
- Connect to PHP
- Connect to Web Service
- Connect to XML

The generic Connect to Data/Service just brings up a prompt to let you select from the above. Over the next series of pages, I'll walk you through how to replicate the employees application primarily using Flash Builder's many wizards. The wizards will do a lot of the work for you, but the prompts and the generated result will be sufficiently different from that already discussed, so I want to cover these processes in some detail. In the next chapter, you'll use the wizards again, but without me going through all of the particulars so finely.

As a warning, the series of steps for using the wizards may make you think that this requires just as much time and effort as creating services from scratch (as in the previous sequences). That's a fair concern, but you'll have to keep in mind that this is a relatively simple example. As examples become more complex, the benefit of the wizards increases. Plus, the wizards will be doing behind-the-scenes things that improve the stability and security of the application.

To start, though, you'll need to create a new project and a bit of MXML yourself.

Creating a Client-Server Application

The first step is to create new Flex Project that identifies PHP as the server type. In the process, you'll establish the Web directory and URL to use for the services. You don't technically need to indicate the server type in this example, but it's still a useful addition.

1. Select File > New > Flex Project.
2. In the first window, enter *Ch08_03* as the Project name and select PHP as the Application server type, then click Next.

   When you select a value other than None/Other, the Finish button becomes disabled and the Next button will take you to a server configuration page.
3. On the Configure PHP Server page (**Figure 8.8**), start by entering the Web root.

tip

If you don't associate a server with a project when you create it, you an always make that association later using the Project > Properties menu item.

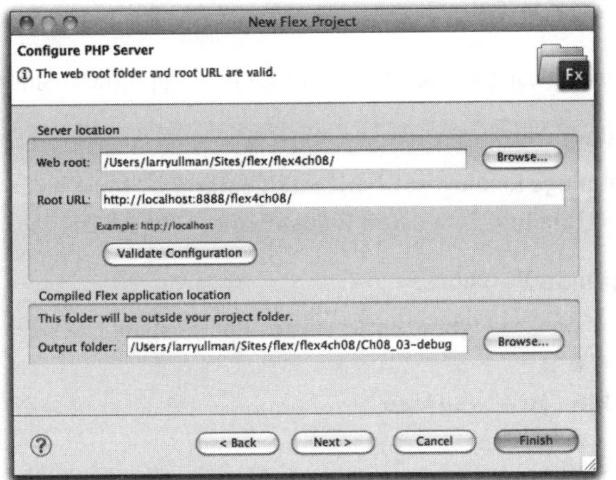

Figure 8.8

The Web root should be whatever your local environment uses for the Web root, plus the directory for this project: *flex4ch08*.

4. Next, enter the Root URL.

   The Root URL should be the primary URL for your local environment, plus the directory for this project.

5. Click Validate Configuration.

   When you click Validate Configuration, Flash Builder will confirm that both exist and that the Web server is running. You'll also notice (in Figure 8.8) that the output folder will be moved from the Flex project directory to the Web directory.

6. Click Finish.

   The generated MXML file at this point will look no different from those created for non-server applications.

Adding Some MXML

You may be surprised to see how much code the wizards will create for you, but in order to replicate the full application, some MXML will need to be added first.

1. In the **Declarations** block, define the **departmentsList** component:

```
<s:ArrayList id="departmentsList">
    <fx:Object data="1" label="Human Resources" />
    <fx:Object data="2" label="Marketing" />
    <fx:Object data="3" label="Accounting" />
    <fx:Object data="4" label="Research and Development" />
    <fx:Object data="5" label="Sales" />
</s:ArrayList>
```

   This component will be used as the data source for two drop-down menus.

2. Create the title **Label**:

```
<s:Label text="Manage Employees" horizontalCenter="0" top="10"
fontSize="36" fontFamily="Times New Roman" color="#362EDE"/>
```

3. Create an **HGroup** and a **VGroup**:

```
<s:HGroup width="90%" height="80%" verticalCenter="20"
horizontalCenter="0">
    <s:VGroup width="70%" gap="10">
    </s:VGroup>
</s:HGroup>
```

4. Within the **VGroup**, create a **DataGrid**:

```
<mx:DataGrid id="employeesDG" width="100%">
</mx:DataGrid>
```

   All I'm doing at this point is defining an empty **DataGrid**. It has an **id** property, but no **dataProvider** or columns. Those will all be dynamically determined by a wizard.

5. After the **DataGrid**, create a **DropDownList** and a **Button**:

```
<s:DropDownList id="getEmployeesDepartment" width="200"
dataProvider="{departmentsList}" prompt="Show employees in..." />
<s:Button label="Get All Employees" click="getEmployeesDepartment.
selectedIndex = -1" id="fetchSomeEmployeesButton"/>
```

   Both of these are exactly as in the other version of the application, except that no events handlers are declared for the **DropDownList**'s **change** and **valueCommit** events. This is because the service that should be called when those events occur has not yet been defined.

And that's it for now. You don't even need to define the form for adding new employees.

Creating Services

There are several ways to create a service using the wizards built into Flash Builder 4. You could simply select one of the options from the Data menu. Or you could click the Connect to Data/Service link in the Data/Services panel at the bottom of the workbench. Another option is, in Design mode, to right-click (Windows) or Control+click (Mac OS X) on the component that will use the service as its data provider (e.g., a **DataGrid**), then select Bind to Data. If you don't have any services defined, you'll be prompted to create a new one.

In the next series of steps, I'll walk through the wizards to create the two services: the first for fetching every employee and the second for adding a new employee.

1. Select Data > Connect to HTTP.

   Even though you'll be connecting to a PHP script in this example, select Connect to HTTP here. The Connect to PHP wizard assumes that you'll be using AMF to communicate with a PHP class (see Chapter 7), which is not the case with the two PHP scripts.

2. In the Configure HTTP Service window, in the operations section, use *fetchEmployees* as the operation name and set the URL as the full path to *getEmployees.php*.

3. Click the Add button just above the parameters section (just below the operations area).

tip

The data type associated with a parameter is for the benefit of the ActionScript code. The PHP script will not know of this parameter's type.

4. In the parameters section, enter a name of *departmentId*, a data type of *int*, and a parameter type of *GET*.

   This will be how the **departmentId** value gets passed to the script in the URL. The name and parameter type must match those expected by the PHP script.

5. Enter a meaningful value as the service name, such as *GetEmployeesService*.

   Do not use spaces or special characters in the service name. Conventionally, the service would be named using *UpperCamelCase*. **Figure 8.9** shows the completely filled-out window.

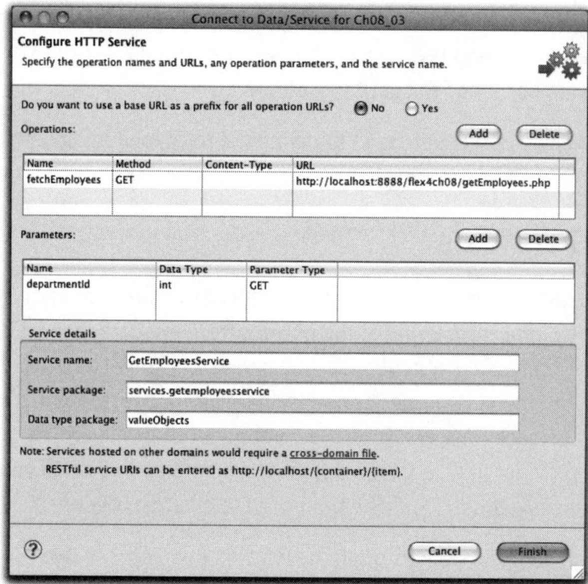

Figure 8.9

   The wizard will fill in some of the other fields based upon what you type above.

6. Click Finish.

   After a moment, you'll see that Flash Builder has added an item to the Data/Services panel at the bottom of the workbench. A services directory will also be created within your project. In that you'll see some automatically created ActionScript files.

To create the second service, repeat Steps 1-6, but fill out the Configure HTTP Service window as such (**Figure 8.10**):

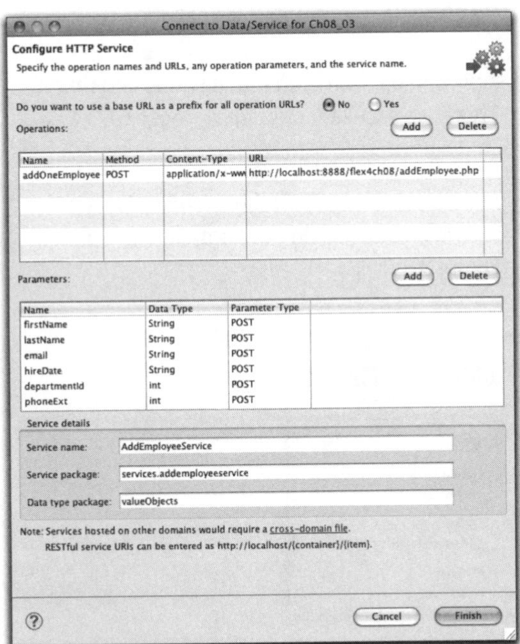

Figure 8.10

- Set the operation name to *addOneEmployee*.
- Set the operation method to *POST*.
- Set the operation URL to your *addEmployee.php* script.
- Add six parameters, all of type POST. The *firstName*, *lastName*, *email*, and *hireDate* should be of type *String*. The *departmentId* and *phoneExt* should be of type *int*. It does not matter in which order the parameters are listed.
- Enter *AddEmployeeService* as the service name.

tip

The hireDate parameter will be of type String because the value sent to the PHP script won't be a ***Date*** object but rather a ***Date*** object formatted as a string.

After a moment, you'll see that Flash Builder has added a second item to the Data/Services panel at the bottom of the workbench (**Figure 8.11**) and added another folder to the *src/services* directory (**Figure 8.12**):

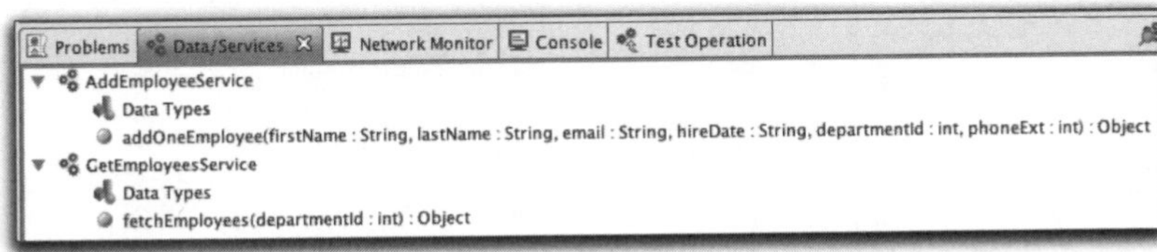

Figure 8.11

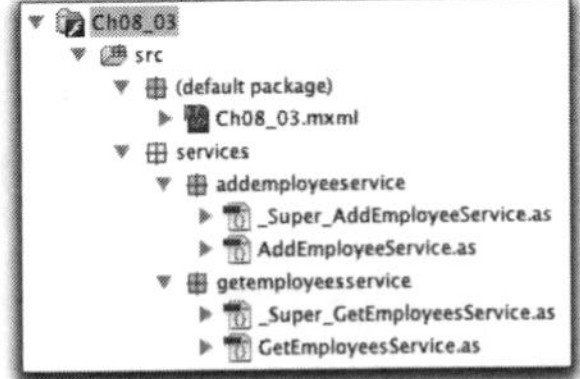

Figure 8.12

In the Data/Services panel, each operation is preceded by a silver circle, within its service.

Testing Services

You can test any established service to confirm both that it works and that it returns the result you expect. This is an excellent debugging tool and is well worth trying on any newly created service.

1. Right-click (Windows) or Control+click (Mac OS X) the *fetchEmployees* operation (listed under *GetEmployeesService* in the Data/Services panel), and select Test Operation (**Figure 8.13**).

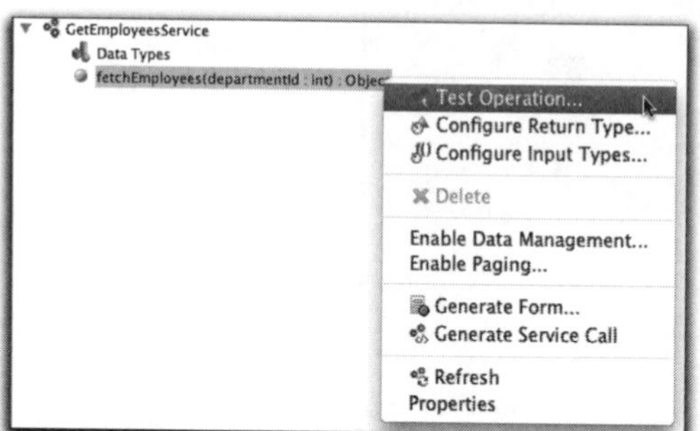

Figure 8.13

tip

If you click Raw View, you can see the actual, uninterpreted server result.

2. In the resulting window, click Test to see the results of running the service (**Figure 8.14**).

3. Enter a value for the *departmentId* parameter and click Test to see the new results (**Figure 8.15**).

   The results should just be limited to that department.

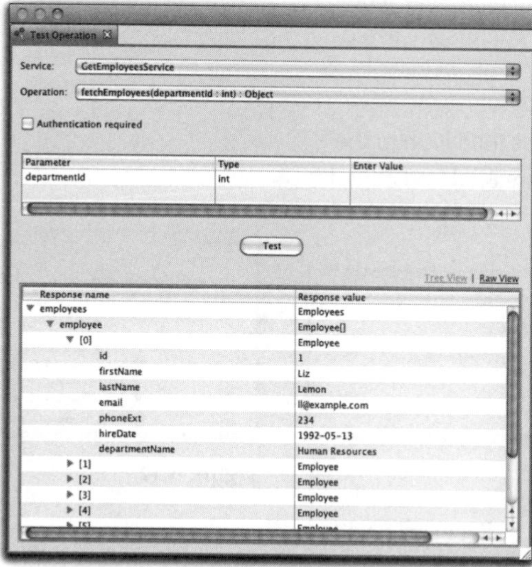

Figure 8.14

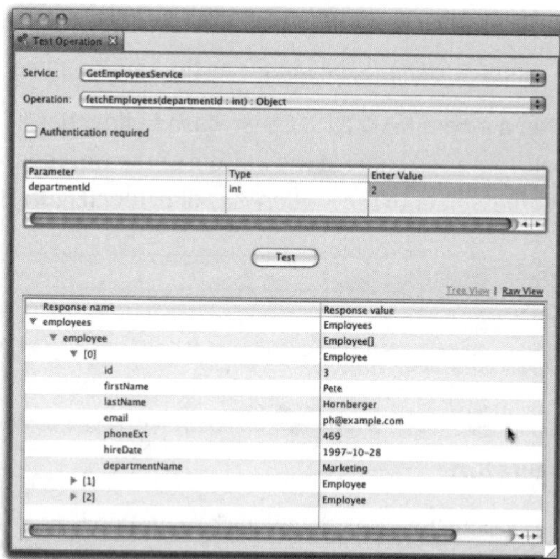

Figure 8.15

Unfortunately, as currently created, you can't test the *AddEmployeeService* because it returns plain text and the wizards only acknowledge (over HTTP) return responses of XML and JSON. So let's quickly edit that PHP script and adjust the service.

Making Changes

First, let's change the PHP script so that it outputs JSON instead of plain text. To do so, you'll only need to change each of the four uses of **echo** so that it "prints" JSON.

1. Open *addEmployee.php*.
2. Change the first **echo** statement (after the database insert worked) to read

   echo '{"message":"The employee has been added."}';

   Originally, the script just printed a simple text message for each individual possibility. Now the script will output some JSON data. JSON is just a JavaScript object, so to print JSON, merely print an object in the syntax **{"*property*":"*value*"}**. That's all that's happening here.

tip

When creating complex JSON data, it's best to use a converting function like ***JSON_encode()***, demonstrated in Chapter 7.

3. Repeat the change in Step 2 for the other three **echo** lines:

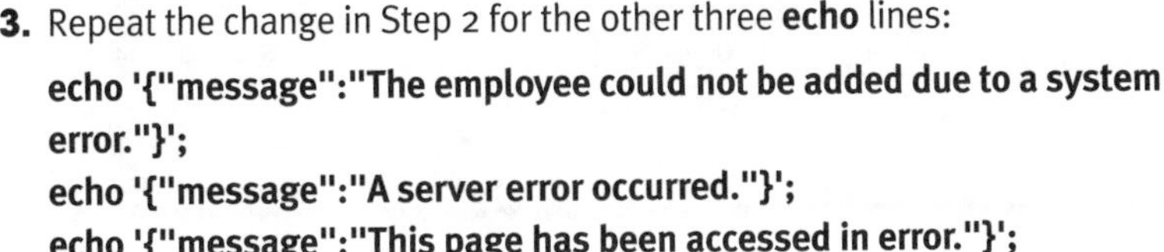

   echo '{"message":"The employee could not be added due to a system error."}';
   echo '{"message":"A server error occurred."}';
   echo '{"message":"This page has been accessed in error."}';

4. Save the script as *addEmployeeJSON.php*, in the same directory as the other PHP scripts.

Next, let's point the service to the new script.

1. Right-click (Windows) or Control+click (Mac OS X) the *AddEmployeeService* in the Data/Services pane.
2. Select Properties (**Figure 8.16**).

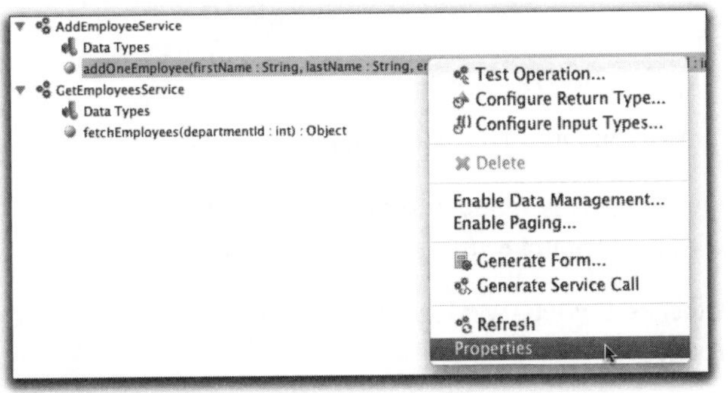

Figure 8.16

3. In the resulting window, change the *addOneEmployee* operation so that its URL now uses the JSON version of the PHP script.

   If the wizard drops all of the parameters (because of the URL change), you'll need to reenter those.

4. Click Finish.

You should now be able to test the operation using the steps already outlined. Fill out values for each parameter to see the result when a new employee is added (**Figure 8.17**). Fill out invalid values for each parameter to see the message *This page has been accessed in error.*

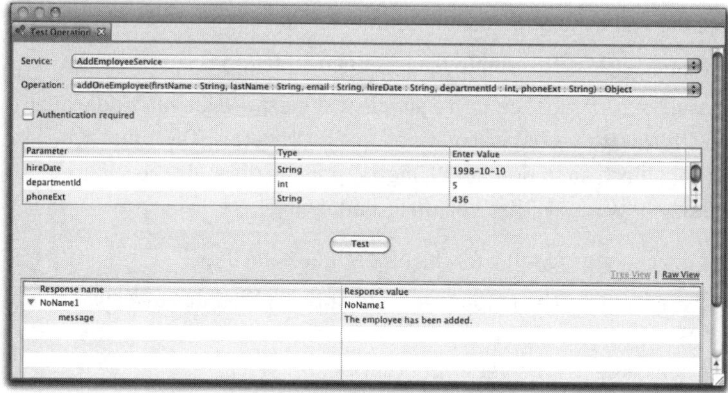

Figure 8.17

Configuring Services

Another wizard provided by Flash Builder is for configuring services. You can configure a service's *input* types and its *return* types. As you've already configured the input types (in the Configure HTTP Service window, see Figure 8.12), it's time to configure the return types.

1. Right-click (Windows) or Control+click (Mac OS X) an operation in the Data/Services panel.

   To start, use the *fetchEmployees* operation.

2. Select Configure Return Type in the contextual menu.

3. In the Configure Return Type window, select Auto-detect... (that's the default) and click Next (**Figure 8.18**).

4. In the Auto-Detect Return Type window, select Enter parameter... and click Next (**Figure 8.19**).

tip

If a service requires authentication, you can provide that information when you configure the return type. Just click the Authentication required box and you'll be prompted for the username and password.

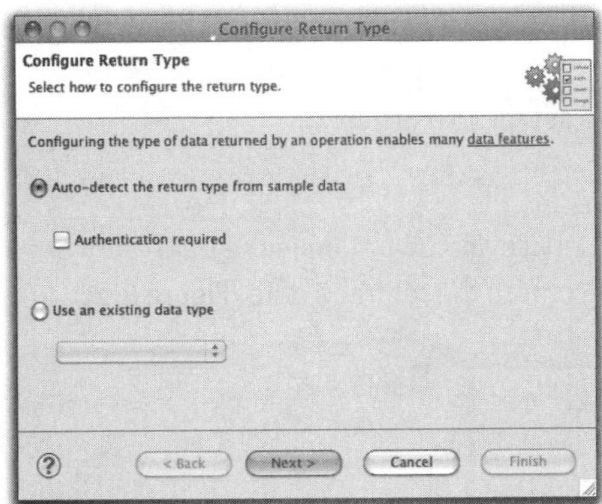

Figure 8.18

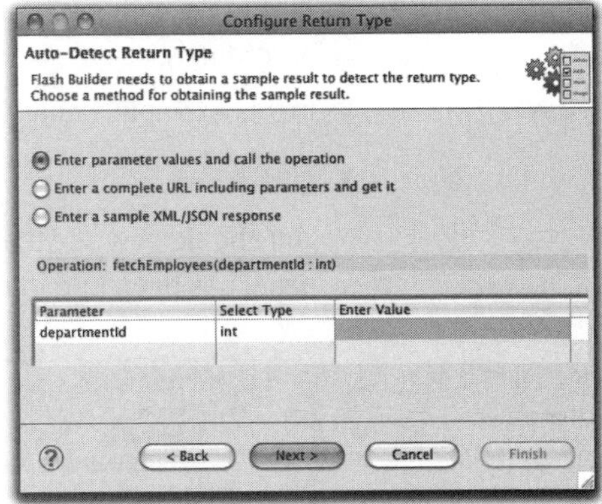

Figure 8.19

You can choose to enter a *departmentId* parameter or not. If you do, you just need to make sure it's a department that will return some employees.

After you click Next, the PHP script will be called and the returned result will be examined.

5. In the next window (**Figure 8.20**), change the *Select root* value to *employee*.

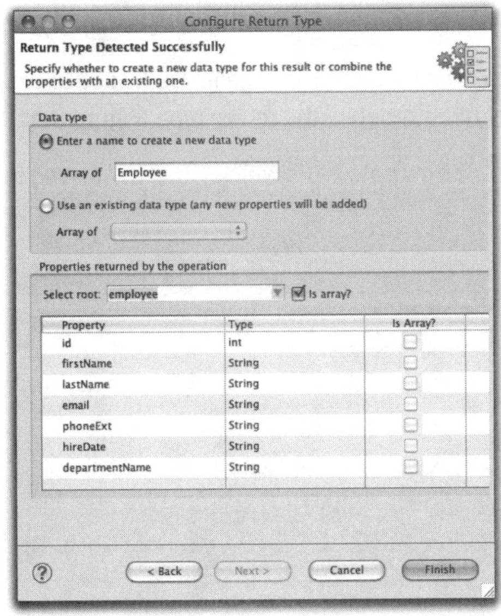

Figure 8.20

If you click the drop-down menu in the *Select root* area, you'll see the list of elements returned by the PHP script. Of those elements, the ones I'll want to use in this application is *employee*. When you select that from the list, the *Is array?* check box will automatically be selected, which is what you want as an array of employees will be returned. Also, the *Data type* value (at the top of the window) will change automatically.

If a service's return type isn't properly configured, you'll have a harder time binding that service call to components.

6. Also in the same window, use the properties section to set the data types accordingly.

   In this example, I only want to set the *id* as an *int*.

7. Click Finish.

   You should now see that the service and operation in the Data/Services panel has been updated to recognize the returned data (**Figure 8.21**).

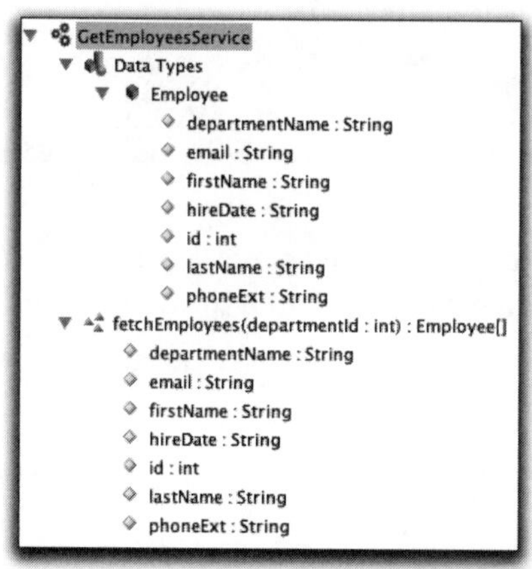

Figure 8.21

tip

When you configure the return type, Flash Builder creates a value object. A value object is a custom data type that reflects the information returned by the service. You'll learn more about this in the next chapter.

note

When you test or configure a service, you are actually running the PHP scripts. This means that each call to *addEmployee.php* could, if used properly, update the database.

Repeat Steps 1-7 for the *addOneEmployee* operation. Again, you'll need to enter lots of parameter values in order to auto-detect the return type (**Figure 8.22**).

On the last page, you would enter a new data type, which I named *Message* (**Figure 8.23**).

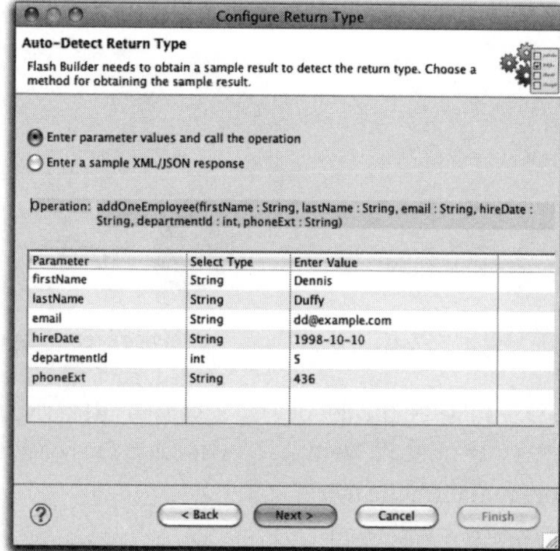

Figure 8.22

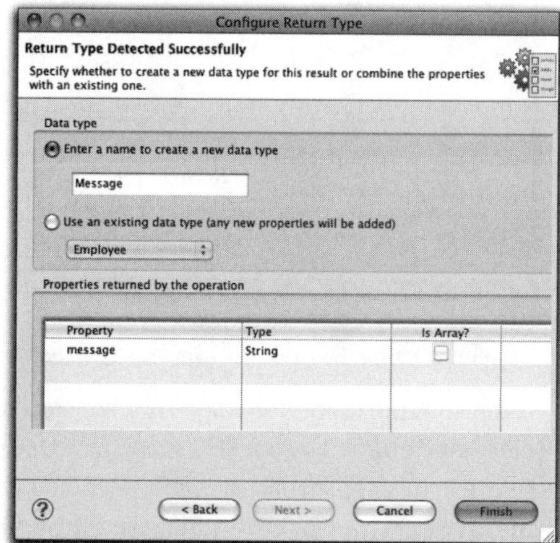

Figure 8.23

Using the Services

Now that the services have been created and configured, you can start using them in the application.

1. In Design mode, drag the *fetchEmployees* operation onto the **DataGrid**.

2. In the resulting window (**Figure 8.24**), confirm the Service, Operation, and Data provider.

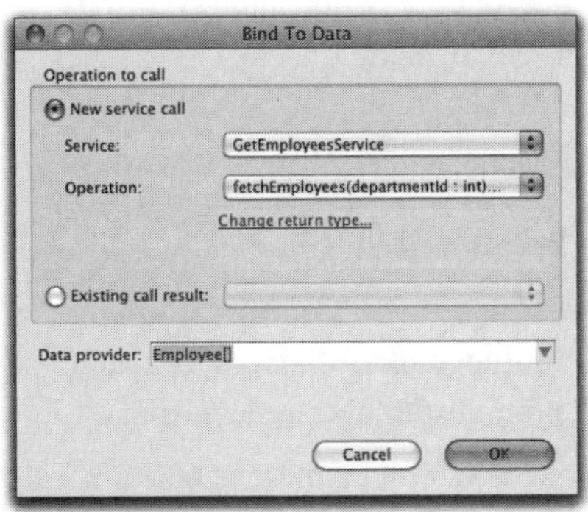

Figure 8.24

Having just configured the service, you should not need to adjust any of these. If you hadn't configured the return type, you could do so now.

3. Click OK.

   You should see the columns and column headings be automatically generated based upon the **Employee** data type. You'll also be taken to Source mode, with this code highlighted:

   fetchEmployeesResult.token = getEmployeesService.fetchEmployees(/*Enter value(s) for */ departmentId);

   That is the service call that populates the **DataGrid**. Because the operation expects one parameter (the *departmentId*) to be passed to the script, this call is written that way, too. The dummy code is added there as a placeholder for real code to be provided by you.

4. Replace the parenthetical with just 0:

   fetchEmployeesResult.token = getEmployeesService.fetchEmployees(0);

   The **fetchEmployees( )** method requires one argument (for the *departmentId*) but when the employees are first retrieved, they should all be retrieved. So I'm hard-coding the value 0 here.

   At this point you can even run the application to confirm that the **DataGrid** is being populated by the service call.

5. While still in Source mode, change the **DataGrid**'s column headings, if you want.

```
<mx:DataGridColumn headerText="ID" dataField="id"/>
<mx:DataGridColumn headerText="First Name"
dataField="firstName"/>
<mx:DataGridColumn headerText="Last Name" dataField="lastName"/>
<mx:DataGridColumn headerText="Email" dataField="email"/>
<mx:DataGridColumn headerText="Phone Ext" dataField="phoneExt"/>
<mx:DataGridColumn headerText="Hire Date" dataField="hireDate"/>
<mx:DataGridColumn headerText="Department"
dataField="departmentName"/>
```

   I changed *id* to *ID*, *firstName* to *First Name*, and so forth.

6. Add a **valueCommit** handler to the **DropDownList**:

```
<s:DropDownList id="getEmployeesDepartment" width="200"
dataProvider="{departmentsList}" valueCommit="employeesDG_
creationCompleteHandler(event)" prompt="Show employees in..." />
```

   The **valueCommit** event occurs when the Get All Employees button resets this **DropDownList**. In that event, every employee should be retrieved from the service. A function has already been defined for doing exactly that, so this event invokes the **employeesDG_creationCompleteHandler( )** function.

7. Add a **change** handler to the **DropDownList**:

```
<s:DropDownList id="getEmployeesDepartment" width="200"
dataProvider="{departmentsList}" change="getSomeEmployees(event)"
valueCommit="employeesDG_creationCompleteHandler(event)"
prompt="Show employees in..." />
```

   The **change** event occurs when the user selects a value in the **DropDown List**. In such a case, the application needs to fetch just a subset of the employees from the service. So a new event handler will be defined that does that.

8. In the **Script** block, define the **getSomeEmployees( )** function:

```
import spark.events.IndexChangeEvent;
private function getSomeEmployees(event:IndexChangeEvent):void {
    fetchEmployeesResult.token = getEmployeesService.
    fetchEmployees(event.target.selectedItem.data);
}
```

   This function calls the same **getEmployeesService.fetchEmployees( )** method, but this time the selected *departmentId* is passed along.

If you run the application as written now, the **DataGrid**, **DropDownList**, and **Button** components all work as they should, showing all or just some of the employees.

Generating Forms

The last thing I need to do is create the form for adding a new employee. I could add each item one at a time, then hook it to the *AddEmployeeService*, but there's another wizard that I can use instead. I'll show you how to use that, then finish tweaking the application to complete it.

1. Next, Right-click (Windows) or Control+click (Mac OS X), the *addOne Employee* operation and select Generate Form.
2. In the resulting window (**Figure 8.25**), deselect the *Make result form editable* option.

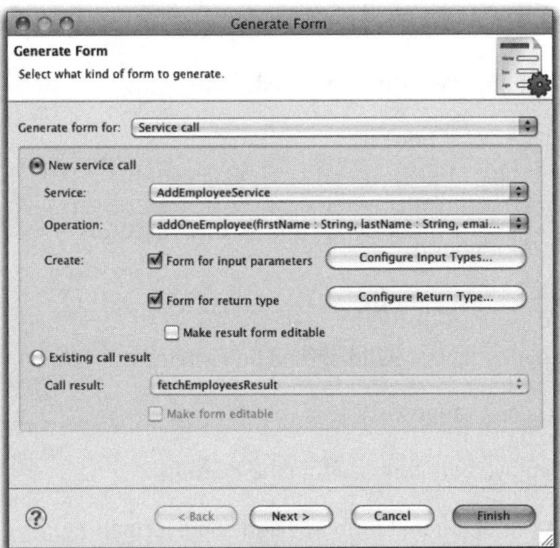

Figure 8.25

The Generate Form wizard can generate a form based upon a service call, a data type, or a master-detail combination (for example, the **DataGrid** could be the master for showing all records and a form would allow the user to edit the details of a specific record). In the wizard, you can select the service and operation (these will be preselected if you start this form from a service, as in Step 1). Then you can indicate what should be created. In this case, I want to create a form for the input parameters (i.e., the information to be sent to the service) and for the return type (the message returned by the service). I don't want that returned message to be editable, though.

tip

Chapter 9 explains the form generators in more detail.

3. Click Finish.

   The wizard will have created two forms: one for the input and one for the output. By default, it'll create these forms outside of any other container, so they'll overlap what you already created. If you move them to just inside the **HGroup**, you can better see what you have at this point (**Figure 8.26**).

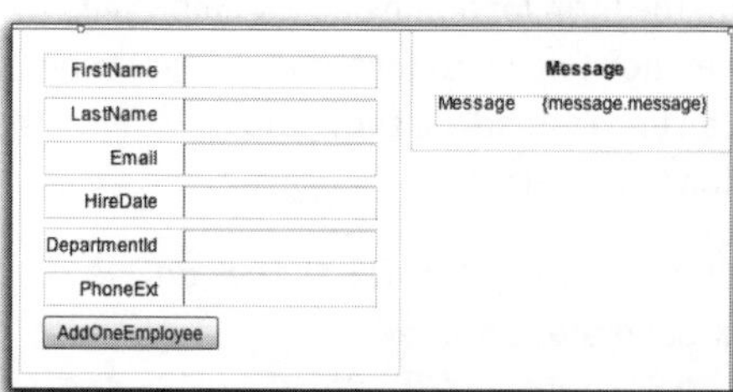

Figure 8.26

As auto-generated, the entered form data will be submitted to the *addEmployee.php* script, and that script's result will be assigned to the Message form (on the far right in Figure 8.26). But a few things need to be altered:

- The department input should be a **DropDownList**.
- The hire date should be a **DateChooser**.
- The form data must be validated.
- The hire date must be reformatted.
- Upon adding an employee, the form should be cleared.
- Upon adding an employee, the **DataGrid** should be updated.

I'll explain how to make these changes.

1. If you haven't already, move both forms within the **HGroup**.
2. Move the **Label** to the top of the first form and add some formatting:

   ```
   <s:Label id="messageLabel" text="{message.message}"
   color="#49B42C" fontSize="16" fontWeight="bold"/>
   ```

3. Delete what's remaining of the second form.
4. Just under the **Label**, add a **FormHeading**:

   ```
   <mx:FormHeading label="Add an Employee"/>
   ```

5. Change the department **TextInput** to a **DropDownList**:

   ```
   <s:DropDownList id="departmentIdInput" dataProvider=
   "{departmentsList}" />
   ```

I've also changed its name from *departmentIdTextInput* to just *departmentIdInput*.

6. Change the hire date **TextInput** to a **DateChooser**:

```
<mx:DateChooser id="hireDateInput"  />
```

Again, I've changed its name to *hireDateInput*.

7. Change the **Button**'s **label** property:

```
<s:Button label="Add Employee" id="button" click=
"button_clickHandler(event)"/>
```

8. Within the **Declarations** block, define the six validators:

```
<mx:StringValidator id="firstNameValidator" source=
"{firstNameTextInput}" property="text" maxLength="20"
tooLongError="Please enter a valid first name." tooShortError="Please
enter a valid first name." enabled="{validatorsEnabled}" />
<mx:StringValidator id="lastNameValidator" source=
"{lastNameTextInput}" property="text" maxLength="40"
tooLongError="Please enter a valid last name." tooShortError="Please
enter a valid last name." enabled="{validatorsEnabled}" />
<mx:NumberValidator id="deptValidator" source=
"{departmentIdInput}" property="selectedIndex"  minValue="0"
maxValue="4" lowerThanMinError="Please select a valid
department." exceedsMaxError="Please select a valid department."
enabled="{validatorsEnabled}" />
<mx:NumberValidator id="phoneValidator" source=
"{phoneExtTextInput}" property="text" minValue="100"
maxValue="500" lowerThanMinError="The phone extension must be
between 100 and 500." exceedsMaxError="The phone extension must be
between 100 and 500." enabled="{validatorsEnabled}" />
<mx:EmailValidator id="emailValidator" source="{emailTextInput}"
property="text" enabled="{validatorsEnabled}" />
<mx:DateValidator id="hireDateValidator" source="{hireDateInput}"
property="selectedDate" enabled="{validatorsEnabled}" />
```

These are all exactly the same as those created earlier in the chapter, but the **source** values have been updated to match the form inputs.

9. Define the formatter:

```
<mx:DateFormatter id="hireDateFormatter" formatString=
"YYYY-MM-DD" />
```

This is exactly the same as that defined earlier.

10. Within the **Script** block, import the **Validator** definition and create the **validatorsEnabled** variable:

```
import mx.validators.Validator;
[Bindable]
private var validatorsEnabled:Boolean = true;
```

In order to validate all the form data, you'll need to import this definition (see Chapter 6 for details).

11. Within the **button_clickHandler( )** function, invoke the validators:

```
private function button_clickHandler(event:MouseEvent):void
{
  var vr:Array = Validator.validateAll([firstNameValidator,
  lastNameValidator, deptValidator, emailValidator, phoneValidator,
  hireDateValidator]);
  if (vr.length == 0) {
```

This function is called when the Add Employee button is clicked. It must first validate the form data before trying to send it to the server. The validation code also comes from Chapter 6.

12. Update the **addOneEmployee( )** call to read:

```
addOneEmployeeResult.token = addEmployeeService.addOneEmployee
(firstNameTextInput.text,lastNameTextInput.text,emailTextInput.text,
hireDateFormatter.format(hireDateInput.selectedDate),
departmentIdInput.selectedItem.data,phoneExtTextInput.text);
```

This is mostly the code created by the wizard for sending the form data to the service. I've made two changes.

First, previously the code used **parseInt(departmentIdTextInput.text)** to take the **TextInput** value and turn it into an integer. But now the form element's name is *departmentIdInput* and its value is in **selectedItem.data**. That value is already an integer so you don't need to use **parseInt** (which turns a non-integer into an integer).

Second, the code previously used **hireDateTextInput.text** for that value. But now the element's name is *hireDateInput*, and I want to run its **selectedDate** value through the **hireDateFormatter**.

13. Reset the form:

```
  validatorsEnabled = false;
  firstNameTextInput.text = '';
  lastNameTextInput.text = '';
  departmentIdInput.selectedIndex = -1;
  emailTextInput.text = '';
```

```
    phoneExtTextInput.text = '';
    hireDateInput.selectedDate = null;
    validatorsEnabled = true;
}
```

This code also has been already explained earlier in the chapter. It's essentially the same except for the changes to the names of the form elements.

14. Update the **DataGrid**:

```
fetchEmployeesResult.token = getEmployeesService.
fetchEmployees(0);
```

This is just a replication of the code in the **employeesDG_creation CompleteHandler( )** functions.

And that's it! The entire application now works exactly as it had before, although with a bit more going on behind the scenes (**Figure 8.27**).

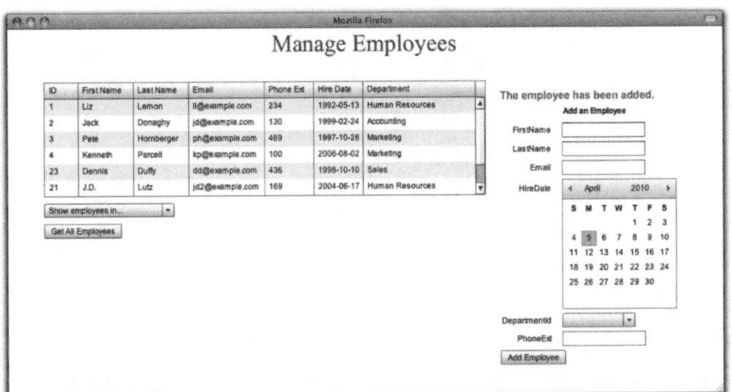

Figure 8.27

DEBUGGING PHP SCRIPTS

When a Flash application sends data to a PHP script, it can be that much more difficult to debug the problems that occur. One likely cause of complications may be that the application is not sending to the PHP script what you think it should be. As a simple debugging technique, you can write a PHP script containing just the following code:

```
foreach ($_REQUEST as $k => $v) {
    echo "$k: $v\n";
}
```

That code will print out each received key and value, one on each line. If you set your Flex to display the server response as plain text (like in a **RichText** component), you'll know for certain what information was provided to the server.

USING THE NETWORK MONITOR

Another benefit of using Flash Builder is its Network Monitor tool. You can use it to observe client-server interactions. By doing so, you can debug, profile, and improve your application. For example, you can see how long server calls take, and how they might be improved if you tweak what data is sent or returned.

1. With a project open, click the Enable Monitor icon in the Network Monitor panel (**Figure 8.28**).

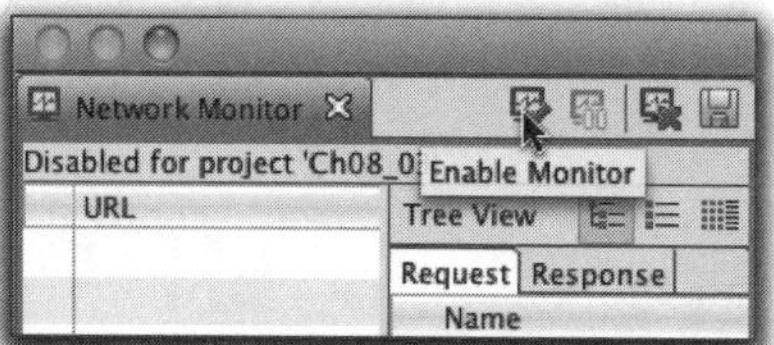

Figure 8.28

2. Run the application.
3. Experiment with the application so that it makes several server calls.
4. Close the application and return to Flash Builder.

   On the left side of the Network Monitor, you'll see a list of every server call, including the URL, the service type, the times (started, ended, elapsed), and the operation type (**Figure 8.29**).

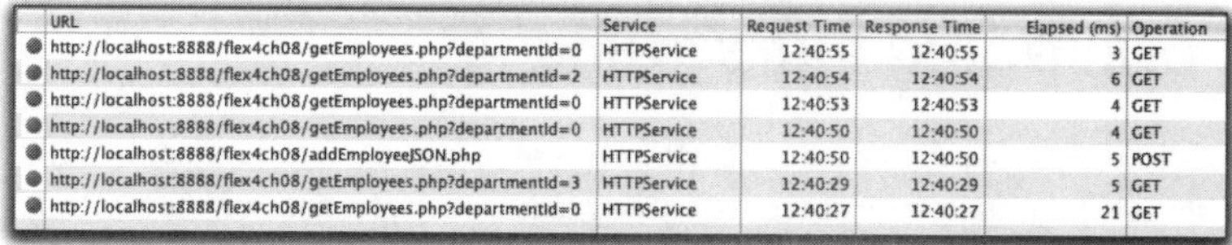

URL	Service	Request Time	Response Time	Elapsed (ms)	Operation
http://localhost:8888/flex4ch08/getEmployees.php?departmentId=0	HTTPService	12:40:55	12:40:55	3	GET
http://localhost:8888/flex4ch08/getEmployees.php?departmentId=2	HTTPService	12:40:54	12:40:54	6	GET
http://localhost:8888/flex4ch08/getEmployees.php?departmentId=0	HTTPService	12:40:53	12:40:53	4	GET
http://localhost:8888/flex4ch08/getEmployees.php?departmentId=0	HTTPService	12:40:50	12:40:50	4	GET
http://localhost:8888/flex4ch08/addEmployeeJSON.php	HTTPService	12:40:50	12:40:50	5	POST
http://localhost:8888/flex4ch08/getEmployees.php?departmentId=3	HTTPService	12:40:29	12:40:29	5	GET
http://localhost:8888/flex4ch08/getEmployees.php?departmentId=0	HTTPService	12:40:27	12:40:27	21	GET

Figure 8.29

5. Click a URL in the left-hand column to view the details in the right-hand side.

   You can view the details of the request or the response. **Figure 8.30** shows a request made when adding a new employee.

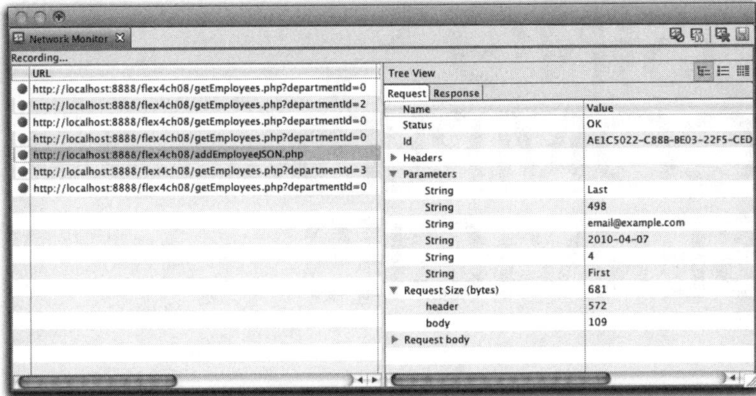

Figure 8.30

Figure 8.31 shows the response when fetching all of the employees.

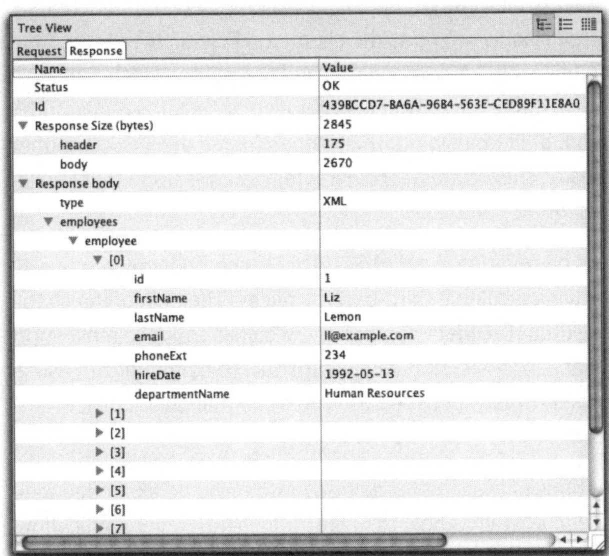

Figure 8.31

tip

You can click the icons on the far right to switch amongst Tree view, Raw view, and Hexadecimal view.

6. Disable the Network Monitor before exporting the application to be used on a live server!

   There's no need to include the extra code or overhead in the end product.

9 USING COMPLEX SERVICES

The previous chapter went through the basics of client-server interactions using Flex-generated Flash content as the client and PHP on the server. Those basics include the relevant Flex components and the built-in Flash Builder wizards for auto-generating code. That chapter also has a fairly real-world example application, built up using both methods (using the Flex components from scratch and using the wizards). This chapter expands upon that knowledge into the realm of "complex services."

The chapter begins by covering the **WebService** Flex component, along with two examples involving available third-party services. The bulk of the chapter will then utilize the **RemoteObject** component, which is truly the most sophisticated of the available options. And you'll learn how to communicate using AMF (Action Message Format) between the Flash client and your own PHP script on the server.

The final three sections of the chapter demonstrate new and expanded features in Flash Builder, as well as how to make your client-server applications more professional and secure.

CONNECTING TO WEB SERVICES

In Chapter 8, "Using Simple Services," I talk about the three broad types of services: REST-style, Web services (using SOAP and WSDL), and RPC. Chapter 8 exclusively used REST-style services, which were HTTP requests that returned plain text, JSON, or XML. The rest of this chapter will primarily focus on RPC, but briefly I want to demonstrate Web services first. As I also say in Chapter 8, which communication method you use depends almost entirely on what the server offers. Most third-party services offer either REST-style or RPC, and both of those are quite easy for you to create on your own. Setting up a Web service yourself is well beyond what I could cover in this chapter, and the fact is that only a small minority of available services seem to be currently using SOAP and WSDL. So I'll walk through this topic relatively quickly, using the services available at *www.webservicex.net*. I'll use a parallel structure as I do in Chapter 8, where I first look at the relevant Flex component in detail, then demonstrate the corresponding Flash Builder wizard. In the process, you'll see two different examples.

The WebService Component

The Flex component used to interact with Web services is the aptly named **WebService**. It has an **id** property, used to uniquely identify it, and a **wsdl** property, used to identify the server resource. This is equivalent to the **HTTPService**'s **url** property. You can also assign to the **WebService** component a value for its **fault** property. This should be the name of the function to call should the application fail to communicate with the server.

tip

Your fault handler doesn't have to do anything. But as long as you create one, errors will not be shown to the end user.

```
<s:WebService id="myWebService" wsdl="http://www.example.com/
something?wsdl" fault="serviceFault(event)">
</s:WebService>
```

Within the **WebService** tags, you place one or more **operation** elements. The **operation** tag has these key properties: **name**, **result**, **fault**, and **resultFormat**. The **name** value must correspond to the name of the operation as defined in the service itself. You do not just make up a name value! The **result** property is assigned the function to call when the service returns a response. The **fault** property is assigned the function to call upon a server error. For both **result** and **fault**, the **operation** values could be used to override the **WebService** values. In this next example, every operation uses the same fault handler but each has its own result handler:

```
<s:WebService id="myWebService" wsdl="http://www.example.com/
something" fault="serviceFault(event)">
<s:operation name="addEmployee" result="handleAddEmployee(event)" />
<s:operation name="updateEmployee" result="handleUpdateEmployee
(event)" />
</s:WebService>
```

tip

The ***WebService*** component, like ***HTTPService***, also has the ***showBusyCursor*** property for indicating the service is actively doing something.

To be clear, a single Web service may define multiple operations. You can think of this like an object-oriented class, where one class defines multiple methods. So a Web service for managing employees may have one operation for adding new employees, another operation for updating a single employee, a third for deleting a single employee, and a fourth for retrieving all the employees.

Unlike an **HTTPService**, which doesn't do anything until the **send()** method is called, when an application that defines a **WebService** runs, the simple declaration of a **WebService** has an effect. Specifically, the application will perform an **HTTPService** request of the Web service. The purpose of that request will be to load the service's WSDL document. This document provides all of the information needed to use the service. Once this has occurred, the **WebService** component will trigger a **load** event. You can use the **load** event to know when to invoke an operation, or you can call an operation in response to a user action.

To call an operation, use the ***serviceId.operationName()*** syntax. For example, to call the hypothetical *retrieveEmployees* operation after the *employeesService* has loaded, you would use the following:

```
<s:WebService id="employeesService" wsdl="http://www.example.com/
something?wsdl" fault="serviceFault(event)" load="employeesService.
retrieveEmployees()">
<s:operation name="retrieveEmployees" result="handleRetrieveEmployees
(event)" />
</s:WebService>
```

On the other hand, if you wanted to call the *addEmployee* operation after the user clicked a button, you would do this:

```
<s:Button label="Add Employee" click="employeesService.
addEmployee()" />
```

Many services will require that you send data when you perform the request. There are two ways you can do so. The first is to add **request** tags to the **operation** MXML, placing the values to be sent within appropriately named tags. For example, say you want to retrieve the employees in a specific department. That operation might be defined like so:

```
<s:operation name="retrieveEmployees" result="handleRetrieveEmployees
(event)">
   <s:request>
      <deptId>{deptList.selectedItem.data}</deptId>
   </s:request>
</s:operation>
```

As with the examples in Chapter 8, the names given to the tags in the request must match those values expected (i.e., required) by the service.

The second way to provide additional data to a service is to do so when calling the service:

```
<mx:DataGrid dataProvider="{employees}" creationComplete="employees
Service.retrieveEmployees(1)" />
```

If an operation takes multiple pieces of information, you just provide each value as if you were calling a function:

tip

The names of the request parameters and the order of the arguments in a method call can be found by looking at a service's description and documentation.

```
<s:Button label="Add Employee" click="employeesService.
addEmployee(firstName.text, lastname.text...)" />
```

Once you've made the operation call, you'll want to do something with the result. As with an **HTTPService** component, the **resultFormat** property dictates how the service result will be treated. The default is a generic object, but you can set this to *xml* or *e4x* instead.

The function called when the service responds should be defined so that it takes one argument of type **ResultEvent**. You'll need to import that definition:

```
import mx.rpc.events.ResultEvent;
private function handleAddEmployee(event:ResultEvent):void {
    // Do whatever.
}
```

Within the function you can use the **event's result** property to do whatever. Just be aware of the result format. For example, if you use the default format (a generic object), you can turn it into an **ArrayCollection** using the **as** keyword:

```
var info:ArrayCollection = event.result as ArrayCollection;
```

Or, if the result format is E4X, you can use it as an **XMLList** without conversion:

```
var info:XMLList = event.result;
```

Outside of the function, you can use the **lastResult** property of the operation to reference the returned value: ***serviceId.operationName*.lastResult**. You might do this to bind the returned result to a component.

The fault event handler needs to take one argument of type **FaultEvent**:

```
import mx.rpc.events.FaultEvent;

private function serviceFault(event:FaultEvent):void {
    // Do whatever.
}
```

Within the function, you can refer to the event's **message** property to see the detailed error. Or you can refer to **event.fault.faultDetail**, **event.fault.faultCode**, and **event.fault.faultString**, which are the individual pieces of the error message.

tip

Like pretty much any MXML component, you can also create, tweak, and use a ***WebService*** in just ActionScript.

tip

If you download the source code from the book's corresponding Web site (*www.dmcinsights.com/flex4/*), you'll find this example in the *Ch09/Ch09_01* folder.

tip

If you're using Flash Builder, you don't actually need to indicate a server type to use a ***WebService*** component.

Using the WebService Component

In this next application, I want to use the **WebService** Flex component and the *CurrencyConverter* service from *www. webservicex.net* so that the user can choose the currency to view his or her total in (**Figure 9.1**). The total is predefined as a constant, but it could be derived from a shopping cart. When the user selects other currencies from the **DropDownList**, the application will retrieve the conversation rate for that currency, perform the conversion, and even display the new total using currency-appropriate formatting (**Figure 9.2**).

Figure 9.1

Figure 9.2

1. Create a new Flex project in Flash Builder or your alternative text editor or IDE.
2. In the **Declarations** block, define the Web service:

```
<s:WebService id="currencyService" wsdl="http://www.webservicex.net/CurrencyConvertor.asmx?wsdl" showBusyCursor="true">
<s:operation name="ConversionRate" result="currencyResult(event)" />
</s:WebService>
```

   The **WebService** has an **id** of *currencyService* (the name given to a component can be any valid value; it's independent of the actual service name). The **wsdl** value is taken directly from the *www.webservicex.net* Web site. One operation is defined, named *ConversionRate*. When it returns its result, the **currencyResult( )** function will be called.

   To save time and space, I'm not creating a fault handler in this example, but you can add one, especially if you need to debug the client-server communications.

3. Also in the **Declarations**, create a **CurrencyFormatter**:

```
<mx:CurrencyFormatter id="currencyFormatter" precision="2" />
```

   I'll use this formatter to handle the displayed total so that it looks appropriate regardless of the total amount or the currency. It's created with the U.S.-centric defaults, plus a precision of two decimals.

4. Add a **DropDownList**:

```
<s:DropDownList id="currency" prompt="View total in..."
change="currency_changeHandler(event)" width="150" x="10" y="10">
<s:ArrayList>
<fx:Object data="AUD" label="Australian Dollars" />
```

```
<fx:Object data="GBP" label="British Pounds" />
<fx:Object data="EUR" label="Euros" />
</s:ArrayList>
</s:DropDownList>
```

The **DropDownList** uses an **ArrayList** defined inline as its data provider. Each element in the list is an object with **data** and **label** properties. The **data** property is the currency code. The **label** is what the user will see.

When the **DropDownList** changes, which is to say the user selects a new item, the **currency_changeHandler( )** function will be called.

5. Create two **Label**s:

```
<s:Label text="Total" fontWeight="bold"  y="15" x="170"/>
<s:Label id="totalLabel" text="{currencyFormatter.format(TOTAL)}"
y="15" x="205"/>
```

The first **Label** just creates the word *Total* in bold. The second will actually show the total. To start, it displays the formatted total (i.e., the value of the constant).

For simplicity's sake, I'm using absolute positioning to lay out the three elements.

6. In the **Script** block, import the necessary definitions:

```
import mx.rpc.events.ResultEvent;
import spark.events.IndexChangeEvent;
```

Two events will take place in this application: the user changing the **DropDownList**, which creates an **IndexChangeEvent**, and the service result being returned, creating a **ResultEvent**.

7. Create a constant to represent the total:

```
private const TOTAL:Number = 165.32;
```

8. Define the function that invokes the service:

```
private function currency_changeHandler(event:IndexChangeEvent):void {
    currencyService.ConversionRate('USD', event.target.selectedItem.data);
}
```

This function is called when the user changes the **DropDownList**. It needs to call the **ConversionRate** operation, sending it the two currency codes. The first should always be *USD*, for U.S. dollars. The second will be the **data** part of whichever object the user selected.

9. Start defining the function that handles the service result:

```
private function currencyResult(event:ResultEvent):void {
```

10. Adjust the **CurrencyFormatter** based upon the chosen currency:

```
if (currency.selectedItem.data == 'GBP') {
  currencyFormatter.alignSymbol = 'left';
  currencyFormatter.thousandsSeparatorTo = '.';
  currencyFormatter.decimalSeparatorTo = ',';
  currencyFormatter.currencySymbol = ' £';
} else if (currency.selectedItem.data == 'EUR') {
  currencyFormatter.alignSymbol = 'right';
  currencyFormatter.thousandsSeparatorTo = '.';
  currencyFormatter.decimalSeparatorTo = ',';
  currencyFormatter.currencySymbol = '€';
} else {
  currencyFormatter.alignSymbol = 'left';
  currencyFormatter.thousandsSeparatorTo = ',';
  currencyFormatter.decimalSeparatorTo = '.';
  currencyFormatter.currencySymbol = '$';
}
```

As an added touch, the **CurrencyFormatter** will be tweaked based upon the currency being displayed. If it's in British pounds or Euros, the thousands and decimal separators need to be changed, along with the currency symbol. The Euro symbol is also aligned to the right of the numeric value.

If the user opts for Euros first, then Australian dollars, I want to make sure that's formatted correctly, too, so the **else** clause comes into place then. It essentially resets the formatter to its original state.

11. Update the total **Label** and complete the function:

```
totalLabel.text = currencyFormatter.format(TOTAL * (event.result as Number));
```

The **totalLabel** component's **text** property should be assigned the formatted result of the calculation. To perform the calculation, the **TOTAL** constant is multiplied by the returned currency conversion rate. As the returned result will be a generic object, I cast it as a **Number** to make it usable in a mathematical operation without error or warning.

12. Save, run, and test the completed application.

If you download the source code from the book's corresponding Web site (*www.dmcinsights.com/flex4/*), you'll find this example in the *Ch09/Ch09_02* folder (although the point really is for you to run through the wizards yourself).

Using Flash Builder Wizards

To demonstrate how to use the Flash Builder wizards with a Web service, I'll create a different example, which also makes use of one of *www.webservicex.net*'s services. I personally like user interfaces that do some of the work for me (the end user), and one simple enough feature is for the user to enter his or her U.S. zip code and have his or her city and state automatically determined. The *GetInfoByZIP* operation of the *USZip* service will return the city, state, area code, and time zone for a given zip code (it also, redundantly, returns the zip code for that zip code). So let's create an application that performs a zip code lookup, letting Flash Builder do almost all of the work.

1. Create a new Flex Project in Flash Builder.

   Again, you don't actually have to indicate a server type here.

2. Select Data > Connect to Web Service.

3. In the first window for the wizard (**Figure 9.3**), enter *http://www.webservicex.net/uszip.asmx?wsdl* as the *WSDL URI*, then click Next.

   The wizard will automatically fill in the service name and package based upon the WSDL.

4. In the next window (**Figure 9.4**), select *USZipSoap* as the port and select the operations to use.

   These particular services are available using different *ports*, which is essentially a designation of the protocol to use. For this example, choose *USZipSoap*.

   This service has four operations, but only the *GetInfoByZIP* will be used in this application, so that's the only one that needs to be checked.

5. Click Finish.

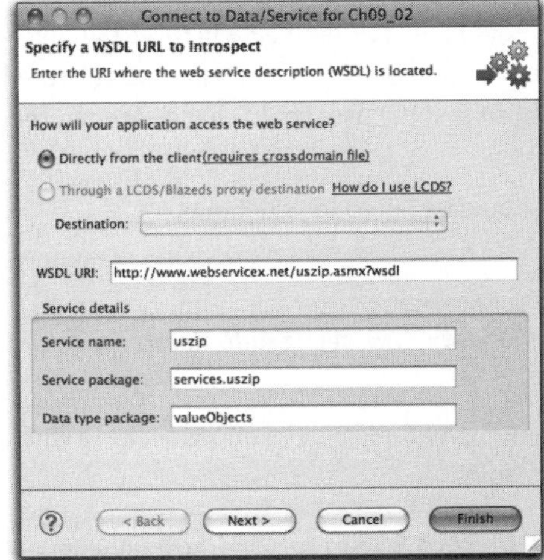

Figure 9.3

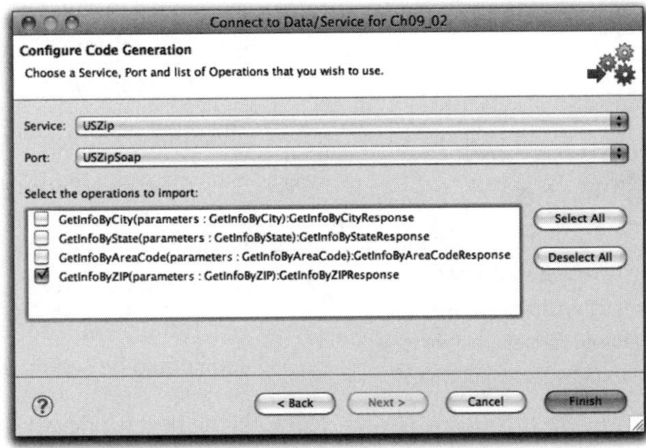

Figure 9.4

6. Right+click (Windows) or Control+click (Mac OS X) the *GetInfoByZIP* operation in the Data/Services panel and select *Generate Form* from the contextual menu.

7. In the Generate Form wizard (**Figure 9.5**), additionally check the *Create: Form for return type* option.

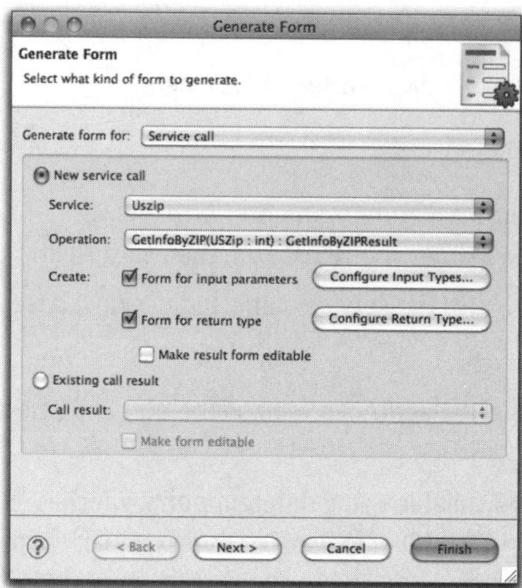

Figure 9.5

Since we're having Flash Builder do all the work, let's have it also automatically create the interface for displaying the returned results. This won't be checked for you, by default.

8. Deselect the *Make result form editable* option.

   There's no point in the user editing the returned data in this example, although if this was a live registration form, you could perhaps allow editing of the returned data form so that the user could change the returned city, if necessary.

   The other window options should be left to their defaults.

tip

In this case, you don't need to configure the input type, but you can click that button to see the configured input type, if you want.

9. Click Configure Return Type.

10. In the first Configure Return Type window, select *Auto-detect the return type...* and click Next.

    This is the default option. See Figure 8.18 if you're uncertain as to what you should be seeing at this point.

11. In the next window (**Figure 9.6**), enter a value for the *USZip* parameter and click Next.

To configure the return type, the service call needs to be made. As this call expects to receive a zip code, one needs to be passed along.

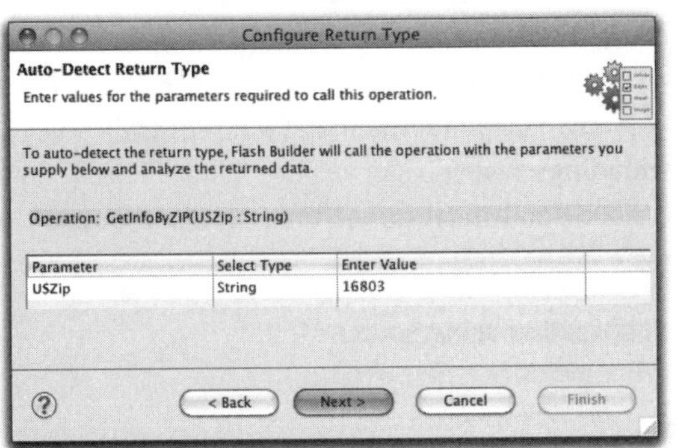

Figure 9.6

12. On the last Configure Return Type window (**Figure 9.7**), confirm the returned data and click Finish.

    You shouldn't need to do anything here, although you can rename this data type, if you'd like. You can also change the types of the returned data, if you want, like changing *ZIP* and *AREA_CODE* to number types.

13. Back in the Generate Form window (Figure 9.5), click Next.

14. On the final Generate Form window (**Figure 9.8**), confirm the settings and click Finish.

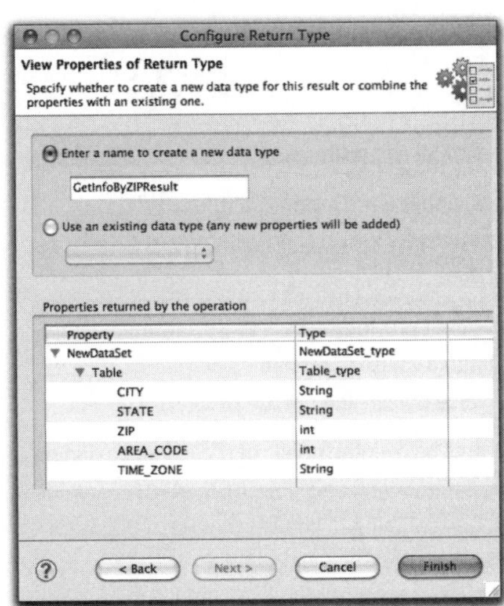

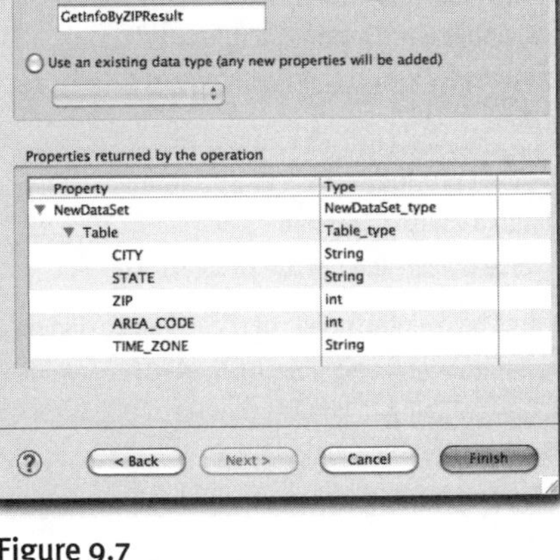

Figure 9.7

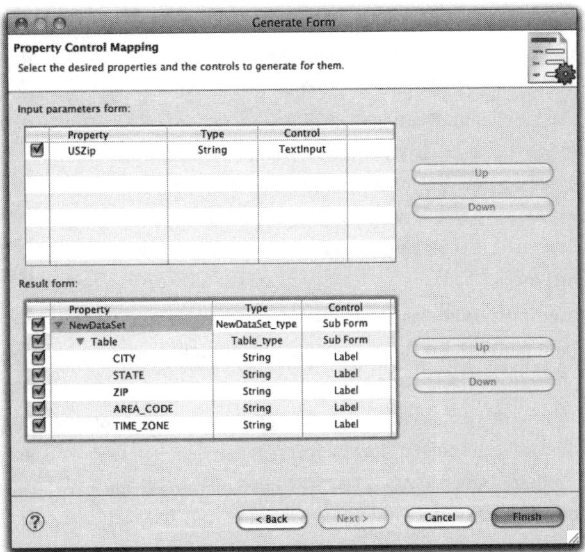

Figure 9.8

You'll see that for input parameters, there will be one item that takes a *USZip* using a **TextInput**. For the result form, there will be **Labels** for each returned value. Because the five pieces of information—*CITY*, *STATE*, *ZIP*, *AREA_CODE*, and *TIME_ZONE*—are returned inside of a *TABLE* inside of a *NewDataSet*, Flash Builder will create subforms for *TABLE* and *NewDataSet*. There's nothing you can do about that here, but those will really just end up being **FormHeadings** that you can easily edit out of the generated code. If you'd rather not display the returned time zone or area code, just deselect those boxes.

15. Add a layout to the application using Source Mode:

```
<s:layout>
  <s:VerticalLayout />
</s:layout>
```

The generated code will drop the two forms—for input and return data—on top of each other. Add the above code before the forms in order to correct this.

16. If necessary, remove the *as GetInfoByZIPResult* code from the following line:

```
<s:CallResponder id="GetInfoByZIPResult" result="getInfoByZIPResult
= GetInfoByZIPResult.lastResult as GetInfoByZIPResult"/>
```

BEHIND THE SCENES

When you use the Flash Builder wizards, you're still using the same **WebService** (or other) components, but Flash Builder is creating them entirely in ActionScript. In the U.S. zip code **WebService** example, Flash Builder creates a new ActionScript class called **Uszip**, which extends the **WebService** class. Then, instead of formally creating a **WebService** component in MXML, a **Uszip** instance is made:

```
<uszip:Uszip id="uszip" fault="Alert.show(event.
fault.faultString + '\n' + event.fault.faultDetail)"
showBusyCursor="true"/>
```

You can see in that code the assignation of the fault handler and the setting of the **showBusyCursor** property. In the *services/_Super_Uszip.as* file, the component's **wsdl** and **operation** properties are defined. If you need to tweak the default code, you should edit the **Uszip** ActionScript file (in this case), as the **_Super_Uszip.as** file may be automatically updated if you make later changes, like to the underlying data model.

Also in the MXML, a **CallResponder** object is created:

```
<s:CallResponder id="GetInfoByZIPResult"
result="getInfoByZIPResult = GetInfoByZIPResult.
lastResult"/>
```

This component provides access to the returned data, assigning it to a value object named *getInfoByZIPResult* (more on value objects later in the chapter).

All of this may be over the heads of those just beginning to learn Flex, ActionScript, and Object-Oriented Programming. But the important thing to know is that Flash Builder is just creating, largely using ActionScript, what you can also accomplish using MXML alone.

With the generated code, you may see that Flash Builder reports problems with the above (this was true using the first official release of Flash Builder, but may not be the case in later versions). The errors occur because the program isn't recognizing a data type named *GetInfoByZIPResult* (and that code is trying to cast the returned result to a variable of that type). Later in this chapter, you'll learn about *value objects*, which are involved here.

17. If you want, remove the following code from the return form:

```
<mx:FormHeading label="GetInfoByZIPResult"/>
<mx:HRule width="100%"/>
<mx:FormHeading label="NewDataSet_type"/>
<mx:HRule width="100%"/>
```

This is the extra information created because of the nested structure of the returned data.

18. If you want, edit the form item labels and the button's label.

For cosmetic reasons, you may want to change things from *CITY* to *City* and *AREA_CODE* to Area Code.

19. Save, run, and test the completed application (**Figure 9.9**).

After the application loads, you should wait a couple of seconds before clicking the button, in order to give the application time to load the WSDL.

To improve upon this application, you could add a **StringValidator** to confirm that a five-digit string is entered, prior to making the service request. It will have to be a string type, as zip codes can begin with 0.

Figure 9.9

GENERATING FORMS IN FLASH BUILDER

When you choose Generate Form from a contextual menu, you have the option of basing the generated form upon one of three models: *Service call*, *Master-Detail*, and *Data type*. If you select *Service call*, you can have up to two forms created: one for the data being sent to the service (the input) and another for the data returned from the service. If you right+click (Windows) or Control+click (Mac OS X) a service to bring up the contextual menu, this will be the selected option in the Generate Form window.

If you select *Master-Detail*, the master aspect is normally a list of data retrieved from a service. For example, the master might be a service-populated **DataGrid** or **List**, like the employees in a company. The detail form is then every input required to create or edit an individual record, like a specific employee. The form can be populated (for updating purposes) via either the selection of a record in the master component, or through another service call. You can start this process by right+clicking (Windows) or Control+clicking (Mac OS X) the master component, then selecting Generate Details Form.

If you select the *Data type* option, a form will be generated with inputs for every property in a complex data type. A complex data type in this meaning isn't an array or object, but rather a custom type like **GetInfoByZIPResult** that the Flash Builder wizards defined in order to represent the returned service data.

Between Chapter 8 and this chapter, you'll see examples of each of these uses of the Generate Form wizards.

SETTING UP THE LOCAL ENVIRONMENT

The last service type to demonstrate is Remote Procedure Call (RPC). As in the previous chapter, let's use our own computers as both the client and the server so that you can get the experience of writing both sides of the equation. If you have not already done so, see the instructions in Chapter 8 for installing and starting a Web server and database combination on your machine. You'll need to do that before proceeding.

RPC in Flash applications use AMF (Action Message Format) to communicate with the server. This is a binary format, which means that the PHP script needs extra libraries in order to participate. In Chapter 7, "Common Data Formats," I introduced the AMFPHP library (*www.amfphp.org*) for this purpose. You'll see another example using AMFPHP here. If you're using Flash Builder to create your services, it will install the Zend Framework (*http://framework.zend.com*) for you, so that your PHP scripts can make use of Zend AMF.

For the specific example, I'll set aside the employees-departments concept (which I think is a great practice example, but you can see plenty of those online already) and create a system for managing products, like those you would sell in an e-commerce site. For each product, there will be the following properties: *id*, *name*, *price*, and *inStock*. The *inStock* attribute will just be a *Yes/No*, indicating if the product is available. For each product, I want to be able to perform complete *CRUD*—Create, Retrieve, Update, and Delete—functionality in the Flash application.

Creating the Database

note

You can download the SQL, PHP, and Flex for this chapter from *www.DMCInsights.com/flex4/*.

The first step is to create and, if you want, populate the database. You will also be able populate the database from the Flash application, but if you pre-populate it, you'll know what queries and information are necessary for adding records and you'll be able to test the process for retrieving and displaying existing products.

1. Using phpMyAdmin, or another interface, create a new database or select an existing one.

   If you don't mind clutter, you can just create the table for this example in the *flex_practice* database used for Chapter 8's examples. If you'd rather keep things separate, create a new database, perhaps named *flex4ch09*.

2. Create a new table:

```
CREATE TABLE products (
id MEDIUMINT UNSIGNED NOT NULL AUTO_INCREMENT PRIMARY KEY,
name VARCHAR(60) NOT NULL,
price DECIMAL(7, 2) UNSIGNED NOT NULL,
inStock TINYINT(1) UNSIGNED NOT NULL DEFAULT 1,
UNIQUE (name)
);
```

   The **id** column will be the primary key. The **name** column will represent the product's name. It's limited to 60 characters and must be unique. The **price** is a real number with 2 decimal points, and it cannot be negative. The **inStock** column is simply a flag used to indicate if the product is in stock or not (i.e., can the user buy one?). The most efficient way of handling this is to use 0 for false/no and 1 for true/yes, so that column is defined as an unsigned tiny integer.

3. Add a few products to the table:

```
INSERT INTO products VALUES (NULL, 'Standard Widget', 19.95, 1);
INSERT INTO products VALUES (NULL, 'New, Improved Widget', 29.95, 1);
INSERT INTO products VALUES (NULL, 'Deluxe Widget', 49.95, 1);
INSERT INTO products VALUES (NULL, 'Super Deluxe Widget', 99.95, 0);
INSERT INTO products VALUES (NULL, 'Overpriced Widget', 199.95, 1);
```

If you wanted, you could now run some **SELECT**, **UPDATE**, and **DELETE** queries to test those as well.

Creating the PHP Script

In Chapter 7, I walk through an example PHP class to be used for remoting with AMF. I'll create another one here, and discuss it in some detail. This class will define all the functionality required to add, update, delete, and retrieve products from the database.

note

The PHP scripts can be found in the *Ch09/flex4ch09* folder, downloadable from *www.DMCInsights.com/flex4/*.

1. Begin a new PHP script:

```
<?php
```

2. Include the database information script:

```
require_once('mysql.inc.php');
```

   I'm going to use the same database connection script that the earlier examples (in the preceding chapter) used. Just make sure yours is in the same directory as this script and that it successfully connects to the correct database.

3. Begin defining the class:

```
class ProductsService {
    private $dbc;
```

This script will define a single PHP class called *ProductsService*. Conventionally one would use *UpperCamelCase* for class names, just as you would in ActionScript. The **$dbc** variable is internal to the class and will be used to store the database connection, which will be used by every class method.

4. Define the constructor:

```
public function __construct( ) {
    $this->dbc = @mysqli_connect(DB_HOST, DB_USER, DB_PASSWORD,
    DB_NAME);
}
```

The constructor uses the special name *__construct* (in PHP 5). It will automatically be called when an instance of this class is created. That will happen with every server call. The constructor creates a database connection and assigns it to the internal **$dbc** variable, available using the **$this->dbc** syntax. In OOP, **$this** is a special variable that represents the current object, so **$this->dbc** means this object's **$dbc** variable.

5. Define the **getAllProducts( )** method:

```
public function getAllProducts( ) {
    $data = array( );
    $q = 'SELECT * FROM products';
    $r = mysqli_query($this->dbc, $q);
    if (mysqli_num_rows($r) > 0) {
        while ($row = mysqli_fetch_array($r, MYSQLI_ASSOC)) {
            $data[] = $row;
        }
    }
    return $data;
} // End of getAllProducts( ) method.
```

This method selects everything from the **products** table and returns it as a multidimensional array. I walk through an explanation of this code in greater detail in Chapter 7.

6. Define the **createProduct( )** method:

```
public function createProduct($item){
    $name = mysqli_real_escape_string($this->dbc, trim($item['name']));
    $price = (float) $item['price'];
```

```
    $inStock = (int) $item['inStock'];
    $q = "INSERT INTO products VALUES (null, '$name', $price, $inStock)";
    $r = mysqli_query($this->dbc, $q);
    if (mysqli_affected_rows($this->dbc) == 1) {
        return mysqli_insert_id($this->dbc);
    }
    return null;
} // End of createProduct() method.
```

The **createProduct( )** method takes one argument, which will be a multidimensional array. The array should have three elements: the new product's name, price, and an *inStock* value. The values are then sanctified so that they're safe to be used in a database query. For the name value, a string, this means it's run through the **mysqli_real_escape_string( )** function. For the price, that value is typecasted to a floating point number (i.e., a real number). For the *inStock* value, it's typecasted as an integer. Of course, you could always do more here, like apply regular expressions on the product's name, confirm that the price is positive (although the database will enforce that), and ensure that the *inStock* value is either 0 or 1. But this minimal amount of work will sufficiently prevent any malicious uses of this script from breaking the database.

If the query works, in the sense that one row was created, the function returns the new record's primary key (the product ID). If the database query fails for some reason, the value **null** is returned (i.e., nothing). During the debugging process, you could return the MySQL error instead.

tip

The class's create and update methods could be written to take a single argument, as I define them, or multiple arguments (like one each for the name, price, and inStock values). Either approach is fine.

7. Define the **updateProduct( )** method:

```
public function updateProduct($item) {
    $id = (int) $item['id'];
    $name = mysqli_real_escape_string($this->dbc, trim($item['name']));
    $price = (float) $item['price'];
    $inStock = (int) $item['inStock'];
    $q = "UPDATE products SET name='$name', price=$price, inStock=
    $inStock WHERE id=$id";
    $r = mysqli_query($this->dbc, $q);
    if (mysqli_affected_rows($this->dbc) == 1) {
        return true;
    }
    return false;
} // End of updateProduct() method.
```

note

If the ***updateProduct()*** method is called using the current values for the product's name, price, and inStock properties, there will be no affected rows even if the query properly runs.

This method also takes one argument: an associative array. In this function, the associative array should have four elements, adding the product's ID to its name, price, and *inStock* values. To make the data safe to use in a query, the **$id** is typecast as an integer. Then, just as in the **createProduct()** method, the other three values are sanctified, too. Next, an **UPDATE** query is run. If one row is affected by the update, the Boolean value true is returned. Otherwise the value false is returned.

8. Define the **deleteProduct()** method:

```
public function deleteProduct($id) {
  $id = (int) $id;
  if ($id > 0) {
     $q = "DELETE FROM products WHERE id=$id";
     $r = mysqli_query($this->dbc, $q);
     if (mysqli_affected_rows($this->dbc) == 1) {
        return true;
     }
  }
  return false;
} // End of deleteProduct() method.
```

   This method takes one argument, the product's ID number, and deletes that record. If one row was deleted, the Boolean value true is returned. Otherwise the value false is returned.

9. Complete the class:

```
} // End of ProductsService class.
```

tip

You can test the PHP script using the AMFPHP Service Browser. See Chapter 7 for details.

10. Save the script as *ProductsService.php*.

   Three things to note here: First, I've omitted the closing PHP tag. I did this purposefully as any extraneous spaces after the closing PHP tag could taint the data returned by the script to the Flash client. Second, the name of the PHP file should be the same as the defined class, plus the *.php* extension. Third, you should save this script in the *flashservices/services* directory (when using AMFPHP).

USING RPC

Remote Procedure Calls (RPC) are the most sophisticated type of client-server interactions, providing tight client-server interactions and data transmitted in a concise, binary format. To use RPC with PHP, you'll need a third-party library like AMFPHP or Zend AMF. To use RPC within Flex, you'll use the **RemoteObject** component, which I'll discuss, then demonstrate, next.

The RemoteObject Component

The **RemoteObject** component is what you'll use in MXML for Remote Procedure Calls. Naturally it has an **id** property you'll want to use to create a unique identifier for the component. And it has the **showBusyCursor** property, if you'd like to indicate to the user when the service is active. The component's most important properties, however, are **destination, endpoint**, and **source**.

tip

I don't discuss this topic in the book, but Flash applications can make use of service configuration files, which are XML documents for defining available services.

The **destination** is an indicator of the type of service being called. For PHP scripts using the AMFPHP library, the value to use is *amfphp*. The **endpoint** is the URL to the service's *gateway*. Because AMF is the communication format, you cannot directly call the PHP script (the script itself does not understand AMF). Instead, you call a different script that acts as the agent. When using AMFPHP, this is *gateway.php*, found in the *flashservices* directory. The **source** is the name of the service to use. This would be the same as the PHP class name. So to use a hypothetical **EmployeesService** class via AMFPHP, the **RemoteObject** would start

```
<s:RemoteObject id="employeesService" destination="amfphp"
endpoint="http://domain/path/to/flashservices/gateway.php"
source="EmployeesService" showBusyCursor="true" />
```

That code assumes that the *EmployeesService.php* file is found within the AMFPHP's *flashservices/services* directory (which is AMFPHP's default location for services). If you placed the PHP script within a subdirectory of *flashservices/services*, your **source** value would be *subdirectoryName/EmployeesService*.

A single service will normally have multiple methods, such as **getAllProducts()**, **createProduct()**, and so forth. To define the methods associated with the **RemoteObject** component, use the **method** element. Each method's **name** property must exactly match the name of the method in the class (without the parentheses or arguments). Each method also has a **result** property, used to specify what function is called when the service method returns its response.

tip

You don't have to assign method elements to the ***RemoteObject*** component in MXML unless you want each method to use a unique result handler.

Building on an imaginary **EmployeesService**, you might have:

```
<s:RemoteObject id="employeesService" destination="amfphp"
endpoint="http://domain/path/to/flashservices/gateway.php"
source="EmployeesService" showBusyCursor="true">
    <s:method name="getAllEmployees" result="handleGetAllEmployees
    (event)" />
    <s:method name="updateEmployee" result="handleUpdateEmployee
    (event)" />
</s:RemoteObject>
```

You can also assign a **fault** property to either the methods or to the **RemoteObject** component as a whole. This will be the function that's called should a failure occur.

To invoke a service, call ***remoteObjectId.methodName( )***. You would do so when an event occurs, like a **DataGrid** or the application is created, or the user clicks a button:

```
<mx:DataGrid creationComplete="employeesService.getAllEmployees( )" />
<s:Button label="Update Employee" click="employeesService.
updateEmployee( )" />
```

Functions that handle a positive server result should take one argument of type **ResultEvent**. You can refer to the event object's **result** property to access the returned response. When using AMF, the data returned will be a generic object. As with most data, you can typecast it from one format to another:

tip

Later in the chapter you'll learn how to create and use value objects, so that the client and server are both using specifically typed data.

```
import mx.rpc.events.ResultEvent;
private function handleGetAllEmployees(event:ResultEvent):void {
    var employees:ArrayCollection = event.result as ArrayCollection;
    // Use employees.
}
```

Alternatively, you can bind to the **lastResult** property of the *method*:

```
<mx:DataGrid creationComplete="employeesService.getAllEmployees( )"
dataProvider="{employeesService.getAllEmployees.lastResult}"/>
```

note

Parentheses are used to invoke a method, but not to access its ***lastResult*** property.

There are two ways of passing data to a service method. The first is to use the **arguments** tags within the method's declaration:

```
<s:RemoteObject id="employeesService" destination="amfphp"
endpoint="http://domain/path/to/flashservices/gateway.php"
source="EmployeesService" showBusyCursor="true">
    <s:method name="getAllEmployees" result="handleGetAllEmployees
    (event)" />
    <s:method name="updateEmployee" result="handleUpdateEmployee
    (event)">
        <s:arguments>
            <id>{idVar}</id>
            <firstName>{firstName.text}</firstName>
            <lastName>{lastName.text}</lastName>
            <deptId>{dept.selectedItem.data}</deptId>
        </s:arguments>
    </s:method>
</s:RemoteObject>
```

The order of the arguments must exactly match the order of the parameters in the corresponding service method. So for the above code, the **update Employee( )** method in the PHP class should be defined like so:

```
public function updateEmployee($id, $firstName, $lastName, $deptId) {
    // Do whatever.
}
```

tip

The names of the arguments in the PHP function do not have to match the names of the arguments in the MXML code (because the names are irrelevant in function calls).

In the **ProductsService** PHP script, where the **createProduct( )** method is defined to take an associative array, you'd pass that as an array:

```
<s:method name="updateEmployee" result="handleUpdateEmployee
(event)">
    <s:arguments>
        <s:Array>
            <id>{idVar}</id>
            <firstName>{firstName.text}</firstName>
            <lastName>{lastName.text}</lastName>
            <deptId>{dept.selectedItem.data}</deptId>
        </s:Array>
    </s:arguments>
</s:method>
```

The second way to pass data to the server is to add the data as parameters when calling the method:

```
<s:Button label="Update Employee" click="employeesService.update
Employee(idVar, firstName.text, lastName.text, dept.selectedItem.data)" />
```

Finally, functions that handle a server fault should take one argument of type **FaultEvent**:

```
import mx.rpc.events.FaultEvent;
private function serviceFault(event:FaultEvent):void {
    // Do whatever.
}
```

Within the function, you can refer to **event.fault.faultDetail, event.fault. faultCode**, and **event.fault.faultString** properties. Or just use **event.message**, which is a combination of these other three.

 **tip**

AMFPHP is VERY slow with the Network Monitor enabled. The Network Monitor is great for debugging problems, but disable it to see how your application really performs.

 **tip**

If you download the source code from the book's corresponding Web site (*www.dmcinsights.com/flex4/*), you'll find this example in the *Ch09/Ch09_03* folder.

Using the RemoteObject Component

To use the **RemoteObject** component, let's develop an example that provides complete CRUD functionality through a Flash client. Thanks to a **DataGrid**, a **Form**, three **Button**s (**Figure 9.10**), plus a handful of functions, the user will be able to create, retrieve, update, and delete products stored in the database.

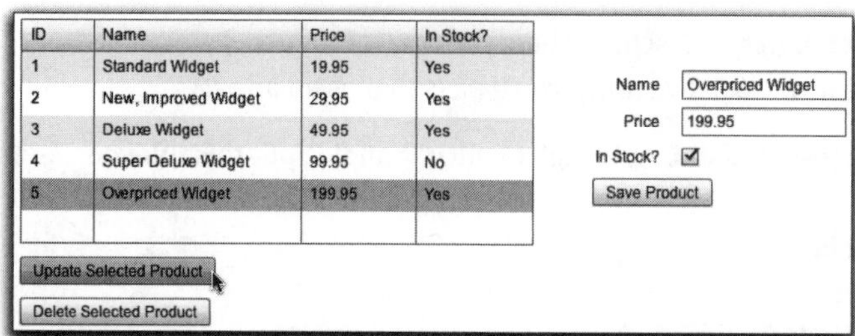

Figure 9.10

1. Create a new Flex project in Flash Builder or your alternative IDE or text editor.

   If using Flash Builder, you *do need* to select PHP as the server type, then provide a valid URL to the project's corresponding Web directory (say *flex4ch09*).

2. In a **Declarations** block, define the **RemoteObject**:

```
<fx:Declarations>
<s:RemoteObject id="productsService" destination="amfphp"
source="ProductsService" showBusyCursor="true"
fault="productsService_faultHandler(event)" endpoint="http://
localhost:8888/flex4ch09/flashservices/gateway.php">
   <s:method name="getAllProducts" />
   <s:method name="updateProduct" result="handleUpdateProduct
   (event)" />
   <s:method name="createProduct" result="handleCreateProduct
   (event)" />
   <s:method name="deleteProduct" result="handleDeleteProduct
   (event)" />
</s:RemoteObject>
```

   The **RemoteObject** uses the AMFPHP installation on my own local server as its **endpoint**. Make sure you change this value to be accurate for your local environment. The **destination** is *amfphp* and the **source** is *ProductsService*, which is the *ProductsService.php* script saved in the *flashservices/services* directory.

   Four methods are defined here, one for each method in the class. For three of the methods, a specific result handler is assigned. The **getAllProducts** method does not have an associated result handler as its results will be bound to a **DataGrid**.

3. Create two validators and complete the **Declarations** block:

```
<mx:NumberValidator id="priceValidator" minValue=".01"
source="{productPrice}" property="text" />
<mx:StringValidator id="nameValidator" minLength="3"
maxLength="60" source="{productName}" property="text" />
</fx:Declarations>
```

   These two validators will be used to validate new and updated products. The first guarantees a price of at least one cent. The second limits the length of the product's name to between 3 and 60 characters.

4. Create an **HGroup** and a **VGroup**:

```
<s:HGroup paddingLeft="10" paddingTop="10" gap="30" width="90%"
horizontalAlign="center">
    <s:VGroup gap="10">
    </s:VGroup>
</s:HGroup>
```

   I'll use these two containers to lay out the application.

5. Within the **VGroup**, create a **DataGrid**:

```
<mx:DataGrid id="productsDG" dataProvider="{productsService.
getAllProducts.lastResult}" creationComplete="productsService.
getAllProducts()">
    <mx:columns>
        <mx:DataGridColumn headerText="ID" dataField="id"/>
        <mx:DataGridColumn headerText="Name" dataField="name"/>
        <mx:DataGridColumn headerText="Price" dataField="price"/>
        <mx:DataGridColumn headerText="In Stock?" dataField=
        "inStock" labelFunction="inStockColumnLabeler"/>
    </mx:columns>
</mx:DataGrid>
```

   The **DataGrid** calls the **productsService.getAllProducts( )** service method once the **DataGrid** is complete. That call will fetch all of the current products so they can be displayed. The **DataGrid** has four columns. The **dataField** for each is assigned a value corresponding to the data returned by the service. The service returns a multidimensional array (see the PHP script), using the database column names as the keys. So here, I use those same database column names as the **dataField** properties.

For the *inStock* column, which should indicate whether or not the product is in stock, I want to use a label function. This is because the actual *inStock* value will just be 1 or 0. To make the displayed value more meaningful, a label function will convert those values into *Yes* and *No*.

6. After the **DataGrid**, add two buttons:

```
<s:Button label="Update Selected Product" id="updateButton"
click="updateButton_clickHandler(event)"/>
<s:Button label="Delete Selected Product" id="deleteButton"
click="deleteButton_clickHandler(event)"/>
```

The first **Button** starts the process for updating a selected product. The second will delete the selected product.

7. After the **VGroup**, define the **Form**:

```
<mx:Form>
    <s:Label id="messageLabel" color="#49B42C" fontSize="16"
    fontWeight="bold"/>
    <mx:FormItem label="Name">
        <s:TextInput id="productName"/>
    </mx:FormItem>
    <mx:FormItem label="Price">
        <s:TextInput id="productPrice"/>
    </mx:FormItem>
    <mx:FormItem label="In Stock?">
        <s:CheckBox id="productInStock"/>
    </mx:FormItem>
    <s:Button label="Save Product" id="saveButton" click=
    "saveButton_clickHandler(event)"/>
</mx:Form>
```

The form has a **Label**, which will be used to display messages, then three items, then a **Button**. When the **Button** is clicked, the **saveButton_click Handler( )** function will be called. I've chosen to label the **Button** as *Save Product*, as this one form will be used to both create new products and to save updates to existing ones.

8. In a **Script** block, import the required definitions:

```
import mx.rpc.events.FaultEvent;
import mx.rpc.events.ResultEvent;
import mx.validators.Validator;
```

The first two event definitions will be necessary for the **RemoteObject** result and fault handlers. The third definition is for validating the form.

9. Create a flag variable:

```
private var updateState:Boolean = false;
```

As the same form will be used to both add and update products, some technique needs to be devised for distinguishing between the two actions. That's the role of this variable. When an update is in progress, this variable will have a value of true. Otherwise, it will be false, the default value.

10. Define the label function:

```
private function inStockColumnLabeler(item:Object,
column:DataGridColumn):String {
  if (item.inStock == 1) {
     return 'Yes';
  } else {
     return 'No';
  }
}
```

Label functions must be defined so that they take one argument of type **Object**, which will be a row of data, and a second argument of type **DataGrid Column**, which will be the current column. The function must return a **String**. For this function, I want to return either *Yes* or *No*, indicating that the product is or is not in stock. So a conditional checks to see if **item.inStock** equals 1.

tip

For more on label functions, see Chapter 6, "Manipulating Data."

11. Define the fault handler:

```
private function productsService_faultHandler(event:FaultEvent):void {
}
```

As written, the fault handler does nothing, which isn't useful as a debugging tool but will prevent errors from being shown to the user. You can use the received event to reveal the problem in detail using **trace**, **Alert**, or whatever technique you prefer.

12. Define the **updateButton** handler:

```
private function updateButton_clickHandler(event:MouseEvent):void {
  if (productsDG.selectedIndex > -1) {
     productName.text = productsDG.selectedItem.name;
     productPrice.text = productsDG.selectedItem.price;
     if (productsDG.selectedItem.inStock == 1) {
        productInStock.selected = true;
     } else {
        productInStock.selected = false;
     }
     updateState = true;
  }
}
```

This function will be called when the user clicks the **updateButton**. First, it checks that an item was selected in the **DataGrid**. If so, the form is updated, setting the form's name and price inputs to the selected item's name and price values. If the selected item's *inStock* value equals 1, then the form's *inStock* check box is selected (i.e., checked). Otherwise, the box will be unchecked. Finally, the **updateState** flag variable is set to true, so that the system knows an update is occurring.

13. Define the **deleteButton** handler:

```
private function deleteButton_clickHandler(event:MouseEvent):void {
  if (productsDG.selectedIndex > -1) {
     productsService.deleteProduct(productsDG.selectedItem.id);
  }
}
```

Again, the first thing this function does is confirm that a product was selected. If so, the **productsService.deleteProduct( )** method is called, passing along the selected item's ID value.

14. Start defining the **saveButton** handler:

```
private function saveButton_clickHandler(event:MouseEvent):void {
  var vr:Array = Validator.validateAll([nameValidator, priceValidator]);
  if (vr.length == 0) {
     var item:Object = new Object( );
     item.name = productName.text;
     item.price = productPrice.text;
     if (productInStock.selected) {
        item.inStock = 1;
     } else {
        item.inStock = 0;
     }
```

The first step is to validate the form. If both tests passed (the name and price), a new object is created to store all the product information that will be passed to the PHP script. Then, the object's **name** and **price** properties are created and assigned values. Next, the object's **inStock** property is determined based upon whether or not the **inStock** check box is selected (i.e., checked).

15. Complete the **saveButton** handler:

```
     if (updateState) {
        item.id = productsDG.selectedItem.id;
        productsService.updateProduct(item);
```

```
        } else {
            productsService.createProduct(item);
        }
    }
}
```

At this point the data has been validated and either the **updateProduct( )** or the **createProduct( )** method needs to be called, based upon the value of the **updateState** flag variable. The update method call requires four pieces of information be passed, so an **id** property is assigned to the object first. The add product method call passes along three elements, as no ID value yet exists for new products.

tip

When using AMFPHP without value objects, the generic ActionScript object defined for creating and updating products will be received as an associative array in the corresponding PHP method.

16. Define the **updateProduct** result handler:

```
private function handleUpdateProduct(event:ResultEvent):void {
  messageLabel.text = 'The product has been updated.';
  productsService.getAllProducts( );
  updateState = false;
  clearForm( );
}
```

This function will be called when the service's **updateProduct** method returns a result. First, it creates a message indicating to the user that everything worked. Second, it updates the **DataGrid** by recalling the **getAllProducts** method. Third, it sets the flag variable **updateState** back to false, so that the next use of the form adds a new product (unless the user selects an existing product and clicks the update button again). Finally, the **clearForm( )** function is called. That function, to be defined in Step 19, will reset the form.

The function does not actually check the returned value to know for certain that the update worked. You could do so by adding a conditional checking the value of **event.result** against true and false.

tip

The application could be written for better performance by updating the values in the ***DataGrid*** for the selected product instead of re-fetching all of them from the database. The next example will demonstrate this.

17. Define the **deleteProduct** result handler:

```
private function handleDeleteProduct(event:ResultEvent):void {
  messageLabel.text = 'The product has been deleted.';
  productsService.getAllProducts( );
}
```

This function just presents a message and updates the **DataGrid**. It does not need to clear the form.

18. Define the **createProduct** result handler:

```
private function handleCreateProduct(event:ResultEvent):void {
  messageLabel.text = 'The product (#' + event.result + ') has been
  added.';
  productsService.getAllProducts( );
  clearForm( );
}
```

This function creates a message, fetches all the products for the **DataGrid**, and clears the form. For the message itself, the returned primary key for the newly created product is included in the message.

19. Define the **clearForm( )** function:

```
private function clearForm( ):void {
  priceValidator.enabled = false;
  nameValidator.enabled = false;
  productName.text = '';
  productPrice.text = '';
  productInStock.selected = false;
  priceValidator.enabled = true;
  nameValidator.enabled = true;
}
```

Since two events—the adding and updating of a product—mandate that the form be cleared, I decided to put that process in a separate function. First, the two validators are disabled. Then the three form elements are reset. Then the validators are re-enabled.

20. Save, run, and test the completed application.

Figure 9.11 shows the result after updating one product, deleting another, then adding a new one.

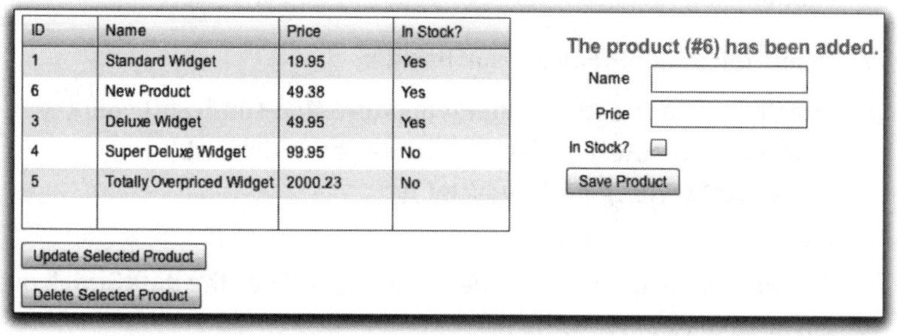

ID	Name	Price	In Stock?
1	Standard Widget	19.95	Yes
6	New Product	49.38	Yes
3	Deluxe Widget	49.95	Yes
4	Super Deluxe Widget	99.95	No
5	Totally Overpriced Widget	2000.23	No

Update Selected Product

Delete Selected Product

The product (#6) has been added.

Name

Price

In Stock?

Save Product

Figure 9.11

DATA MANAGEMENT IN FLASH BUILDER

In this chapter and the last, I've been repeatedly using a parallel structure: First I discuss a service-related Flex component and create an example using it (which would work in any development environment), then I create a similar example primarily using Flash Builder's service-related wizards. By doing so, you're learning how to develop without Flash Builder (should you choose) and getting a sense of the larger picture, with slight variations on how things can be done. Let's now create CRUD functionality for the products this same way. Here, though, we're going to use Flash Builder's *data management* support to do a lot of the work. I'll also use the Zend Framework for the AMF support, as an alternative solution. This means some slight changes are required to the PHP script first.

Updating the PHP Script

One difference between Zend AMF and AMFPHP is that AMFPHP will pass an ActionScript object to the PHP script as an associative array (unless a value object has been defined), but Zend AMF will pass an ActionScript object to the PHP script as a generic object. So let's quickly update the PHP script accordingly. While we're at it, I'm going to make some changes to how the *inStock* value will be returned in the client and tweak the return value of the **updateProduct()** method.

tip

When a Flash application shows an error about "channels disconnect," that most likely means there's a problem with the service (i.e., the PHP script).

1. Open *ProductsServices.php* in your PHP text editor or IDE.

2. In the **createProduct()** method, change instances of **$item['*something*']** to **$item->*something***:

   ```
   $name = mysqli_real_escape_string($this->dbc, trim($item->name));
   $price = (float) $item->price;
   $inStock = (int) $item->inStock;
   ```

   These three lines need to be changed to treat **$item** as an object instead of an array.

3. Repeat Step 2 for the **updateProduct()** method:

   ```
   $id = (int) $item->id;
   $name = mysqli_real_escape_string($this->dbc, trim($item->name));
   $price = (float) $item->price;
   $inStock = (int) $item->inStock;
   ```

   The code is the same as in Step 2, with the addition of a line for the product's ID.

4. Also in the **updateProduct()** method, return the item instead of the value true:

```
if (mysqli_affected_rows($this->dbc) == 1) {
    return $item;
}
```

In the previous version of this script, the Boolean true was returned if the update was made. However, to use data management, the method will need to return the updated item instead (i.e., the method returns the object it receives).

5. Within the **while** loop in the **getAllProducts()** method, change the *inStock* value to a Boolean:

```
while ($row = mysqli_fetch_array($r, MYSQLI_ASSOC)) {
    $row['inStock'] = ($row['inStock'] == 1) ? true : false;
    $data[ ] = $row;
}
```

As you'll shortly see, this version of the application will allow the user to edit products within the **DataGrid**. It wouldn't make as much sense for the user to set the *inStock* value to 0 or 1, so I'll use a check box instead. Towards that end, the Flex code will be easier to manage if I turn the *inStock* value into a Boolean, which is what is happening here. The first line within the **while** loop assigns a new value to **$row['inStock']** using the ternary operator. This is just a much shorter version of:

```
if ($row['inStock'] == 1) {
    $row['inStock'] = true;
} else {
    $row['inStock'] = false;
}
```

Then, the entire row of data is assigned to the **$data** array as it was before.

6. In the **updateProduct()** method, change the assignment to the **$inStock** variable to

```
$inStock = ($item->inStock == true) ? 1 : 0;
```

Just as Step 4 changes this script so that *inStock* is sent out as a Boolean, it'll come back as a Boolean, too. But the database expects it to be a tiny integer, so again the ternary operator is used to make that switch. If the incoming *inStock* value equals true, then **$inStock** is assigned the value 1; otherwise, **$inStock** is assigned 0.

7. Make the same change in the **createProduct()** method:

```
$inStock = ($item->inStock == true) ? 1 : 0;
```

8. Save this updated *ProductsService.php* script to a new folder in your Web directory.

   The *ProductsService.php* file in the *flashservices/services* directory is available when using AMFPHP. As I want to use Zend Framework this time, I'll just copy the file to my Web directory, or a subdirectory like *flex4ch09*.

tip

If you download the source code from the book's corresponding Web site (*www.dmcinsights.com/flex4/*), you'll find this example in the *Ch09/Ch09_04* folder.

tip

Flash Builder can even generate a complete PHP script for you, providing CRUD functionality for a database table. Just click the link in the Select PHP Class window to start that process.

Establishing the Service

The second step in this process is to create and configure the PHP service within Flash Builder.

1. Create a new Flex Project in Flash Builder.

   You do need to indicate that PHP is the server type and provide a valid Web root and root URL for the server (**Figure 9.12**).

2. Select Data > Connect to PHP.

3. In the first window for the wizard, click Browse.

4. Use the Select PHP Class window to select the *ProductsService.php* script.

   When you return to the Connect to Data/Service window, you'll see that the service name and other values will have been filled in for you (**Figure 9.13**).

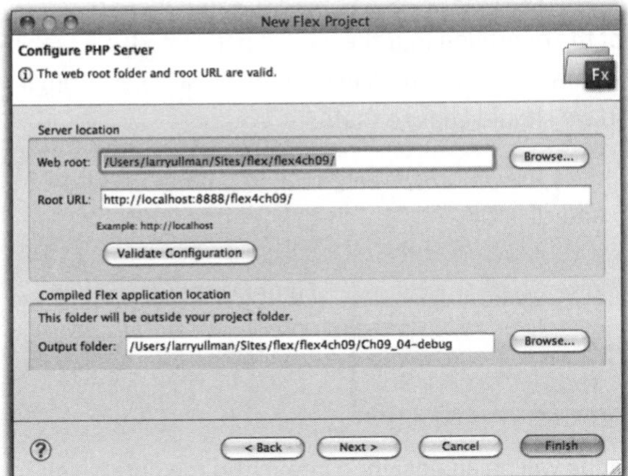

Figure 9.12

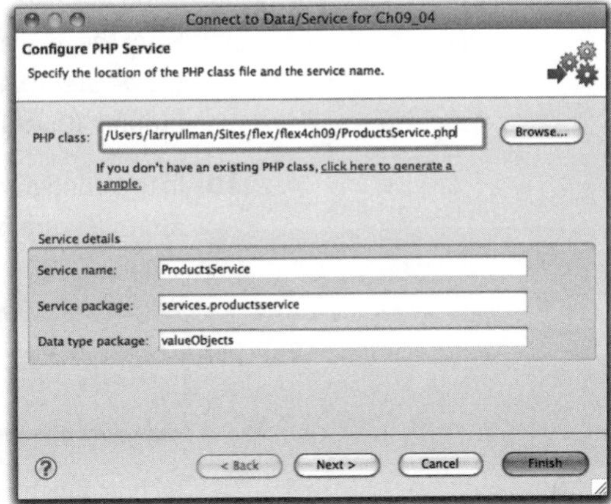

Figure 9.13

5. Click Next.

6. At the Install Zend AMF prompt, click OK.

   Flash Builder will automatically install the Zend Framework for you so that the application can use Zend AMF. This may be an outdated version of the framework, however, so see the sidebar "Customizing the Zend Framework Installation," on page 41.

Note that you'll only see this prompt if the Zend Framework isn't already installed and available to this project.

7. Click OK at the prompt indicating that the framework was installed.

   You may also be prompted that a newer version of the framework is available.

8. Click Finish in the window that displays the service's operations (**Figure 9.14**).

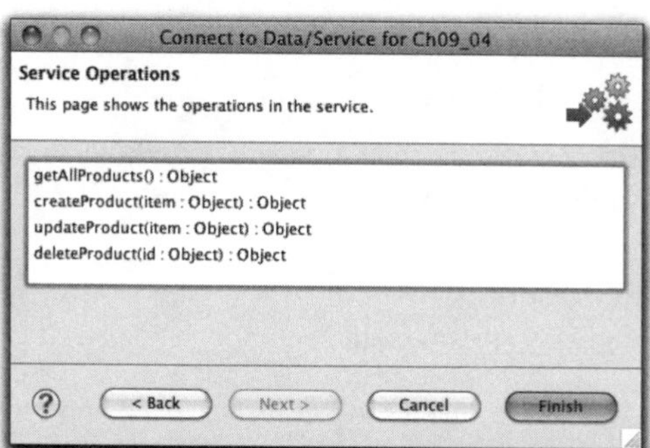

Figure 9.14

9. In the Data/Services panel, right+click (Windows) or Control+click (Mac OS X) the *deleteProduct* operation and select *Configure Input Types*.

   From the analysis of the operation that the wizard performed, it'll look like the *deleteProduct* operation takes an object, when it just takes a single product ID value, so we should change that.

10. In the Configure Input Types window, change the **id** parameter's type to *String* (**Figure 9.15**) and click OK.

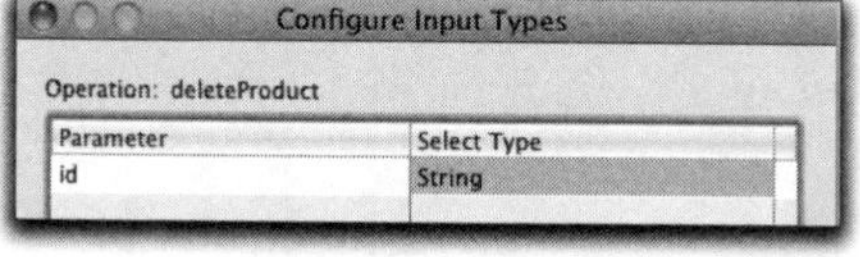

Figure 9.15

Technically the **id** value will be an unsigned integer (in the database), but as PHP is weakly typed, it'll receive the data as a string.

note

Select String, not String[ ] as the id type. String[ ] means an array of strings.

11. In the Data/Services panel, right+click (Windows) or Control+click (Mac OS X) the *getAllProducts* operation and select *Configure Return Type*.

    In order to facilitate some of the later steps, let's now identify the type of data being used in this application: products.

12. In the first Configure Return Type window, select *Auto-detect...* (the default option) and click Next.

13. In the final Configure Return Type window, change the name of the type to *Product* (**Figure 9.16**) and click Finish.

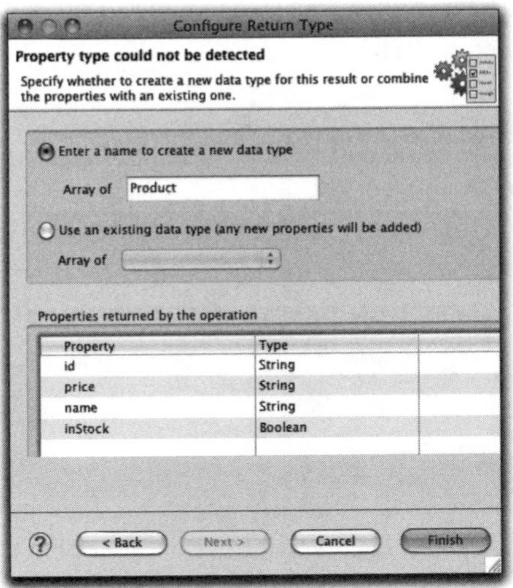

Figure 9.16

14. In the Data/Services panel, right+click (Windows) or Control+click (Mac OS X) the *Product* data type and select *Enable Data Management* (**Figure 9.17**).

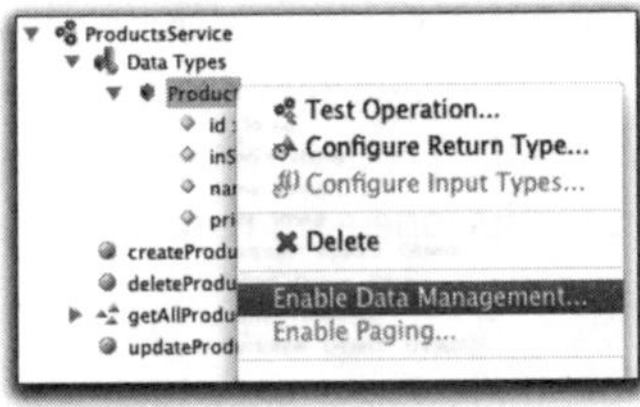

Figure 9.17

15. In the first Data Management window, check the **id** box (**Figure 9.18**) and click Next.

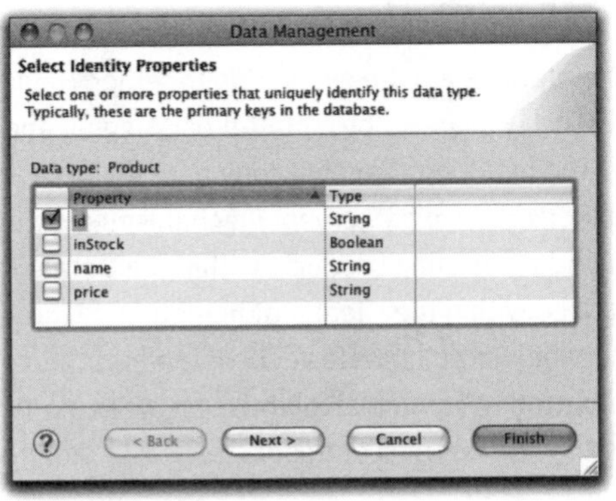

Figure 9.18

This first prompt is asking you to identify the primary key for each product so it knows which property to use for deleting and updating records.

16. In the second Data Management window, select the proper service for each action (**Figure 9.19**), then click Finish.

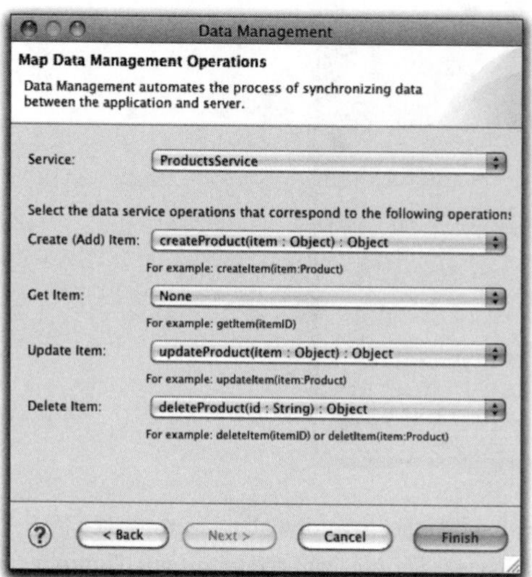

Figure 9.19

Here you're associating the service operations with CRUD actions. The PHP class does not define a method that retrieves a single record, so you can leave the *Get Item* drop-down at *None*. If you did define such a method, it'd just take a primary key value as its lone argument, then select the corresponding record from the database, and return it.

And that's it for configuring the service. Behind-the-scenes, Flash Builder will have created several ActionScript files representing the service and the **Product** data type.

Creating the Flash Client

Now it's time to create the user interface and tie everything together. Having already configured the service, this will largely be a matter of dragging and dropping within Design mode. The resulting client will look and behave a little differently, thanks to Flash Builder's *data management* mechanism (**Figure 9.20**). The user will be able to update existing products within the **DataGrid**. But the changes will be memorized within the client, not immediately transferred to the server. Then, once the user has performed all the updates required, he or she can click a button to commit all of those changes at once. This approach greatly reduces the number of client-server requests required.

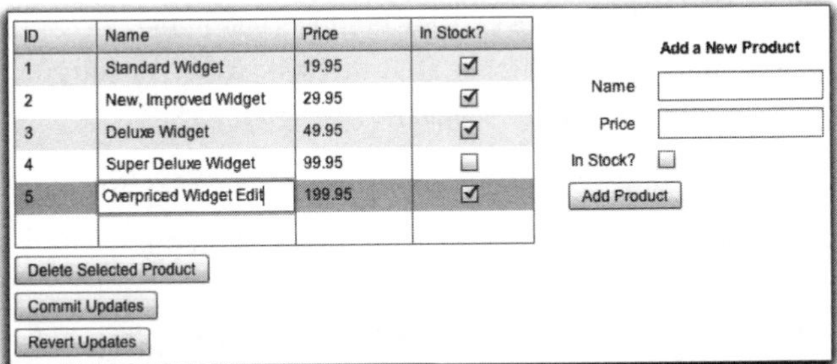

Figure 9.20

tip

With data management enabled, you can set a service to automatically commit all changes, if you prefer.

In this specific example, only the updates will fall under the data management approach. The act of adding or deleting products will be immediately recorded on the server. However, to further reduce the number of server calls, when products are added or deleted, those changes will also be reflected in the **DataGrid** without re-retrieving all of the products.

1. In Design mode, add an **HGroup**, then a **VGroup** within that.
2. Add a **DataGrid** within the **VGroup**.
3. Drag the *getAllProducts( )* operation from the Data/Services panel onto the **DataGrid**.
4. In the Bind To Data window, check the settings (**Figure 9.21**) and click OK.

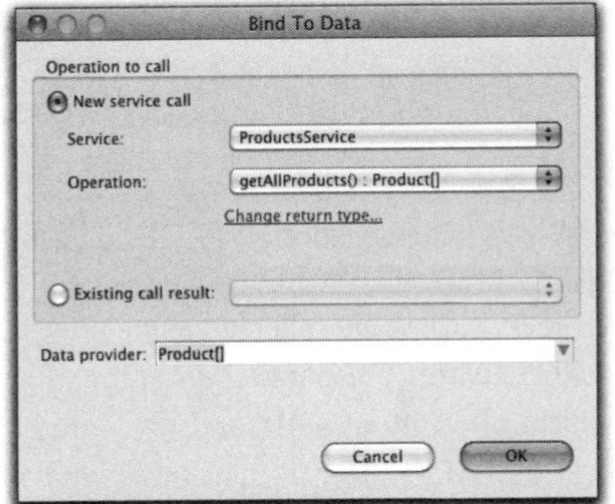

Figure 9.21

The window should already have *New service call* selected, using the *ProductsService* service and the *getAllProducts( )* operation. The data provider should already have a value of *Product[ ]* (because the service has already been configured to recognize the returned data type).

5. Switch over to Source mode and make the **DataGrid** editable:

```
<mx:DataGrid id="dataGrid" creationComplete="dataGrid_
creationCompleteHandler(event)" dataProvider="{getAllProductsResult.
lastResult}" editable="true">
```

The user is going to be able to update existing products within the **DataGrid**, so it needs to be made editable. Only this last property needs to be added; the rest will have automatically been generated.

6. Change the **DataGrid**'s first three columns so they are defined like so:

```
<mx:DataGridColumn headerText="ID" dataField="id" editable=
"false"/>
<mx:DataGridColumn headerText="Name" dataField="name"/>
<mx:DataGridColumn headerText="Price" dataField="price"/>
```

Largely, this is just a matter of changing the **headerText** values. However, the **id** column is being set as non-editable, as one should never change a primary key value.

tip

You can also configure a ***DataGrid***'s columns in Design mode by clicking the Configure Columns button in the Properties panel (with the ***DataGrid*** selected).

7. Update the *inStock* column so that it's defined like so:

```
<mx:DataGridColumn headerText="In Stock?" dataField="inStock"
rendererIsEditor="true" editorDataField="selected">
    <mx:itemRenderer>
        <fx:Component>
        <s:MXDataGridItemRenderer>
        <s:Group horizontalCenter="0">
            <s:CheckBox selected="{data.inStock}" />
        </s:Group>
        </s:MXDataGridItemRenderer>
        </fx:Component>
    </mx:itemRenderer>
</mx:DataGridColumn>
```

There's a bit of new information here, so I'll explain it in some detail. First, for the general concept of using item renderers or item editors, see Chapter 6. Here, the primary goal is to have the *inStock* value reflected using a check box (checked if the item is in stock). So within the **itemRenderer** tags, there's a **Component** element (which is how **itemRenderers** are created inline). Within those are **MXDataGridItemRenderer** tags, as that's what's being created here: an item renderer for an MX **DataGrid**. Within those tags is the actual item renderer: a **CheckBox** wrapped inside of a **Group** (so that the **CheckBox** is centered horizontally). For the **CheckBox**, its **selected** value will be based upon **data.inStock**. Within an item renderer, **data** is a special object that represents the current information being displayed. Its **inStock** property will be whatever the PHP script returned for each row. So, if a product in the database has an *inStock* value of 1, then the PHP script will return the Boolean true for that product, and that Boolean value will be used as the value of the selected property, thereby checking or not checking the box accordingly.

Within the column defintion, the **rendererIsEditor** property is set to true, so that the same component—the **CheckBox**—will both display the *inStock* status and allow the user to edit its status. Second, the **editor-DataField** property is assigned **selected**, which is to say that the value of the item editor's **selected** property (i.e., the **CheckBox**'s **selected** property) will be used for the item's value.

At this point, two fourths of the CRUD functionality—retrieve and update—has been implemented just using the **DataGrid**.

8. In the Data/Services panel, right+click (Windows) or Control+click (Mac OS X) the **Product** data type and select *Generate Form*.

   To create a form for adding new products, let's have the wizard base the generated form on the known data type.

9. In the Generate Form window, make sure that *Data type* is selected in the drop-down list, the *Data type* is *Product*, and the *Make form editable* box is checked (**Figure 9.22**), then click Next.

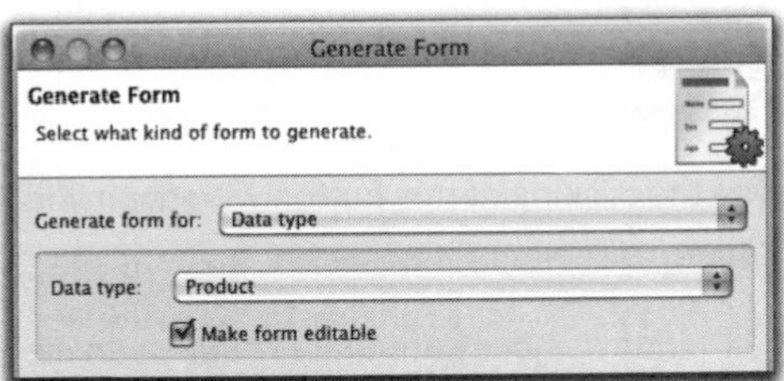

Figure 9.22

10. In the second Generate Form window, deselect the check box next to the *id* property (**Figure 9.23**), then click Finish.

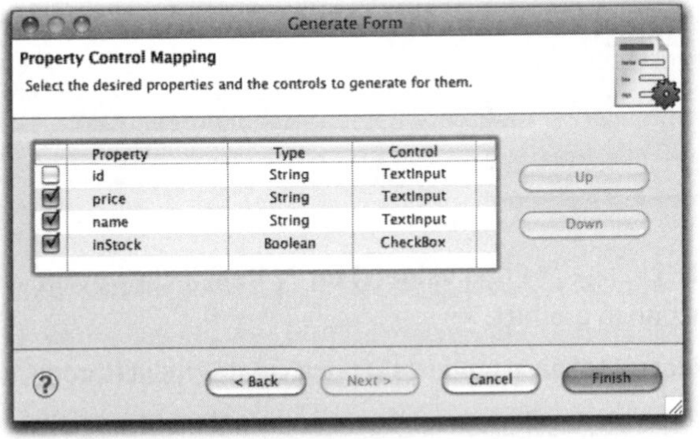

Figure 9.23

The *id* will be automatically created by the database, so the user shouldn't enter that. You'll notice that since the *inStock* property is a Boolean, its control will automatically be set as a **CheckBox**.

11. Customize the generated form.

    I did the following:

    - Moved the form so that it was within the **HGroup** but not the **VGroup** (thereby putting it to the right of the **DataGrid**).
    - Changed the *inStock* label.
    - Added a form heading.
    - Swapped the order of the price and name form items.
    - Changed the label of the **Button** to *Add Product*.

12. In Design mode, select the Add Product button (by clicking it once), then click the "lightning bolt plus" icon found to the right of the *On click* box in the Properties panel.

13. In the context menu that appears (**Figure 9.24**), select *Generate Service Call*.

Figure 9.24

    The next step is to associate the clicking of this button with the invocation of the *createProduct* operation.

14. In the Generate Service Call window, make sure that *ProductsService* is the selected *Service* and *createProduct* is the selected *Operation*, then click OK (**Figure 9.25**).

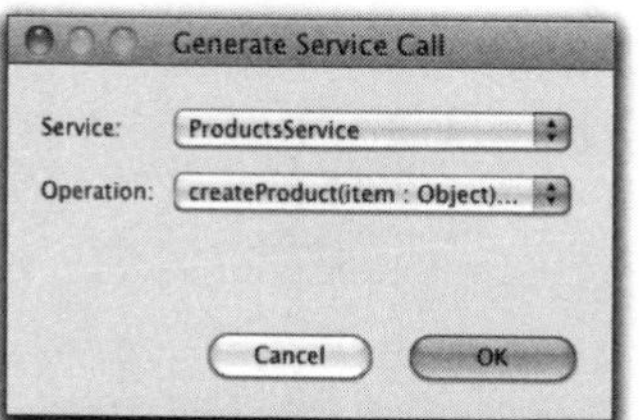

Figure 9.25

15. In Source mode, change **/* Enter value(s) for */ item** in the **button_click Handler( )** function to **product**:

    createProductResult.token = productsService.createProduct(product);

    The previous three steps will create a line of code in the **button_click Handler( )** function, which is the function called when the Add Product button is clicked. The purpose of the line is to call the *createProduct* operation. However, the generated code will use */* Enter value(s) for*

/item as the argument to the service call. You'll need to replace that temporary code with the actual code for submitting the new product to the server. Fortunately, the function already creates a **product** variable using these previous three lines:

```
product.price = priceTextInput.text;
product.name = nameTextInput.text;
product.inStock = inStockCheckBox.selected;
```

So the only thing left to do is provide the **product** variable to the service call.

16. Add this line to the **button_clickHandler( )** function, after the service call, so that the new product is added to the **DataGrid**:

```
dataGrid.dataProvider.addItem(product);
```

In the earlier products example, after a product was added, all of the products were re-retrieved from the database. Here is a more efficient route, not requiring another server call. To manipulate what's displayed in a **DataGrid**, you can reference the **DataGrid**'s **dataProvider** property. Here, the **addItem( )** method is called on the **dataGrid.dataProvider** property, providing this method with the new product. In other words, this code is saying "add this object to whatever is the data source for the **DataGrid**."

As you'll see when you run the example, one interesting thing is that the product added to the **DataGrid** will also include the newly created ID number, as this line occurs after the call to the **createProduct** service, and that service returns the new primary key value.

tip

For the sake of expediency, I am assuming that the service calls work. On a real-world application, I'd update the ***DataGrid*** and clear the form in a function called after the service call returned a positive result.

17. As the last line in the **button_clickHandler( )** function, reset the form and the product:

```
product = new Product( );
```

In the previous version of this example, and in similar examples in this book, I had to reset the form by updating the value of each of the inputs. In this case, the form itself is tied to the **product** variable, so the act of turning **product** into a new, empty **Product** object will effectively reset the form.

tip

To save a few steps, I have not implemented the validators in this example, but you could easily apply the appropriate parts of the other example here in order to validate the user-supplied data.

The complete **button_clickHandler( )** function should now look like this:

```
protected function button_clickHandler(event:MouseEvent):void
{
  product.price = priceTextInput.text;
  product.name = nameTextInput.text;
  product.inStock = inStockCheckBox.selected;
  createProductResult.token = productsService.createProduct(product);
  dataGrid.dataProvider.addItem(product);
  product = new Product( );
}
```

18. In Design mode, drag a **Button** component just underneath the **DataGrid**.

    This button will be used to delete products.

19. Drag the *deleteProduct* operation onto the new **Button**.

    Dragging an operation onto a **Button** is a simple way to associate the clicking of that button with the execution of that operation.

20. In the newly created **Button** click handler (in Source mode, to which you'll automatically be taken), change the code from

    ```
    deleteProductResult.token = productsService.deleteProduct(/*Enter
    value(s) for */ id);
    ```

    to

    ```
    if (dataGrid.selectedIndex > -1) {
      deleteProductResult.token = productsService.deleteProduct(dataGrid.
      selectedItem.id);
    }
    ```

    This code says that as long as one item in the **DataGrid** is selected, call the *deleteProduct* operation, passing along the selected item's product ID value.

21. Change the **Button**'s label to *Delete Selected Product*.

22. In Design mode, add another **Button**, just below the delete button.

23. Select the newest button, if it's not already, then click the "lightning bolt plus" icon found to the right of the *On click* box in the Properties panel (as in Figure 9.24).

24. In the contextual menu that appears, select *Generate Event Handler*.

    The next step is to associate the clicking of this button with the commitment of all the updates.

25. In the newly defined event handler (in Source mode, to which you'll again automatically be taken), change the function's body to be

    ```
    productsService.commit( );
    ```

    As the user updates the list of products using the **DataGrid**, the data management tool will track all of the changes. In order to enact all of those changes, the **commit( )** method must be called on the service, which is what's happening here.

26. Change the **Button**'s label to *Commit Updates*.

27. Repeat Steps 22-24 to add another **Button** with another event handler.

28. Change the new event handler's function body to be

    productsService.revertChanges( );

    This method call will undo all of the changes made in the **DataGrid** since the previous **commit( )** call.

29. Change the **Button**'s label to *Revert Updates*.

30. Save, run, and test the complete application.

CUSTOMIZING THE ZEND FRAMEWORK INSTALLATION

When using Flash Builder, it will automatically install the Zend Framework in your project's server directory. You should plan on customizing this installation to make it more current and secure. To start, download the latest version of the Zend Framework from *http://framework.zend.com*. Then expand the downloaded file (it'll be compressed as a ZIP originally). Move the *library* folder to your Web server, preferably outside of the Web directory.

Next, you'll need to tell the server's **gateway.php** script application where to find the Zend Framework. To do so, open *amf_config.ini*, found in the project's exported files or in its debug directory, in any text editor or IDE. (The *gateway.php* script will also be in the project's exported files and its debug directory.) Remove the semicolon from before *zend_path* and assign to this parameter the absolute location of the Zend Framework directory:

zend_path = /*path*/*to*/library/

You do not quote this value.

DATA PAGING

By default, a function like **getAllProducts( )** or **getEmployees( )** is set to return every record from the database. When you're just getting started, with maybe only a couple of dozen of records, this isn't a problem, even though the Flex component—a **DataGrid** or **List**, perhaps—will only display a few at a time. But as the datasets become larger, into the thousands of records, you absolutely don't want to return all of the information with each request. Instead, you can add *paging* to your application, where only a subset of records are fetched with each service call. To do so, two additional methods must be added to the PHP script that is the service. Then you use Flash Builder to add paging to the component that displays the records.

Updating the PHP Script

You must first define two new methods in your PHP class: **count( )** and **get*Things*_paged( )**. For the latter, *Things* should be replaced with the class name or something else meaningful: **getProducts_paged( )** or **getEmployees_paged( )**.

The **count( )** function should just return a number indicating how many total records exist. You can achieve this using the following:

```
public function count() {
    $q = 'SELECT COUNT(*) FROM products';
    $r = mysqli_query($this->dbc, $q);
    $data = mysqli_fetch_array($r, MYSQLI_NUM);
    return $data[0];
}
```

The **count( )** method is used by the Flex application to know how many total "pages" of records exist. For example, if there are 904 records in the database and 20 at a time are being fetched, then there are 46 "pages" (with only four records on the last "page").

The **get*Things*_paged( )** method needs to take two arguments. The first is a number indicating where in the result set to start retrieving from. The second argument is the number of items to fetch:

```
public function getProducts_paged($start, $num) {
}
```

This function would then only differ from a **getAllProducts( )** function in that its query would apply a **LIMIT** clause (when using MySQL):

```
$q = "SELECT * FROM products LIMIT $start, $num";
```

The complete **getProducts_paged( )** method would look like the following:

tip

You can also create a ***get*Things*_pagedFiltered()*** function that pages a restricted result set, like only the employees within a specific department.

```
public function getProducts_paged($start, $num) {
    $data = array();
    $start = (int) $start;
    $num = (int) $num;
    $q = "SELECT * FROM products LIMIT $start, $num";
    $r = mysqli_query($this->dbc, $q);
    if (mysqli_num_rows($r) > 0) {
        while ($row = mysqli_fetch_array($r, MYSQLI_ASSOC)) {
            $data[] = $row;
        }
    }
    return $data;
}
```

Updating the Flash Client

Once the PHP script has been written to support paging, you can tell the Flex application to use it. If you haven't yet added the service to the project, you would do that first. If you've already created the service in Flash Builder, you can just right+click (Windows) or Control+click (Mac OS X) the service in the Data/Services panel and select Refresh from the contextual menu. The new methods should then be recognized. You'll also need to configure the operation's return and input types (which you've seen many times over by now). Then...

1. Right+click (Windows) or Control+click (Mac OS X) the *getProducts_paged* operation in the Data/Services panel.
2. Select *Enable Paging* from the contextual menu.
3. In the first Enable Paging window, make sure the *id* property is checked as the primary key, then click Next.
4. In the second Enable Paging window, enter a number for the Page size (**Figure 9.26**).

tip

The default page size is 20 records, should you not provide a number in the Enable Paging window.

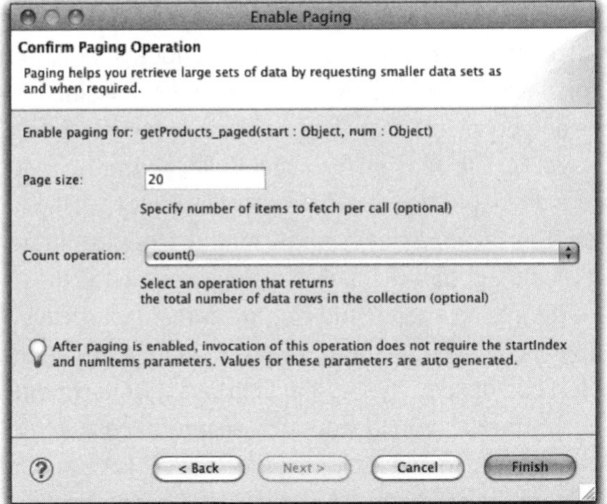

Figure 9.26

tip

Paging can work with any of the service components: ***HTTPService***, ***WebService***, or ***RemoteObject***.

This is the number of items to retrieve per request. It corresponds to the second argument in the PHP script's **getProducts_paged( )** method.

5. Also in that same window, make sure the **count( )** method is selected for the *Count* operation.
6. Click Finish.

tip

You can also page a ***List***, if your application uses a server-driven one.

7. Bind the paging method to the **DataGrid**.

   To do so, you can just drag the *getProducts_paged* operation onto a **DataGrid**. If the **DataGrid** is already bound to an existing operation, you'll be prompted about changing the binding.

8. When you scroll through the **DataGrid**, the rows will be fetched and displayed one "page" at a time.

CREATING VALUE OBJECTS

PHP is a weakly typed language, which means that variables aren't strictly tied to any one data type. You don't define a variable's type when it's created in PHP, and you can assign values of other types to a variable without errors (i.e., assign a numeric value to a string). This is both a strength and a weakness of the language. On the plus side, it makes PHP easier to learn and program in. On the other hand, it allows for bugs and careless programming. ActionScript, conversely, is a strongly typed language: Each variable is declared to be of a certain type, can only be assigned that kind of value, and can only be used as that data type (for example, you couldn't perform multiplication using a string, which you can do in PHP). Again, this has its benefits and costs.

When using Flex and PHP together, which is to say ActionScript and PHP, the weak-type/strong-type distinction can be an issue. Data on the one side of the equation has restrictions and behaviors that the same data, when received on the other side, will not have. For this reason, the Flash Builder wizards want you to configure the return and input types of different calls prior to using the data in an application. This is *client-side typing*: creating a representation of the server data in the client. Through client-side typing, you can tell the application that a service returns an integer and a string or that a particular operation takes one string and one number. But object-oriented applications actually use more complex, custom data types, like **Employee**, **Department**, **Product**, **User**, and so forth. The Flash Builder wizards also turn these into custom data types in ActionScript, known as *value objects* (VO). For example, after you create and configure the products service in Flash Builder, Flash Builder creates a *valueObjects/Product.as* file that defines the **Product** data type. Then the application can create new objects of that type, just as it would a new object of type **String**.

Using value objects results in smarter code, that's easier to comprehend and less likely to have bugs. When using Flash Builder, value objects also provide for code hinting, as the object becomes a new known type. In a fully fledged application, whether you're using Flash Builder or not, you should define and use value objects. But you can expand upon the concept by creating a corresponding object in the server. These are known as data transfer objects (DTO).

By defining a new PHP data type, the PHP service can return objects of that type. The client will then receive objects of the matching type, creating a more tightly coupled data transfer. And, when the client sends a custom object back to the server, it'll be recognized in PHP as such.

Updating the PHP Code

To start, you should create a PHP script that defines the new object. With the products example, that PHP script would start with a representation of every property found in a product, which is to say every column from the database. For each product property, you'd declare a public variable:

```
<?php // File name Product.php
class Product {
    public $id;
    public $name;
    public $price;
    public $inStock;
}
?>
```

tip

People often use VO in the class name to indicate it'll be used as a value object. (I don't, however.)

All that code does is define a **Product** class that contains four public variables. When you make a new object of type **Product**, that object would then have **$obj->id**, **$obj->name**, and so forth (using PHP's OOP syntax).

The PHP class could also define methods. In the Flash Builder products example, I hacked two of the methods to convert the *inStock* values between Booleans and unsigned integers. Class methods could do that instead:

```
public function inStockToBoolean() {
    return ($this->inStock == 1) ? true : false;
}
public function inStockToInt() {
    return ($this->inStock == true) ? 1 : 0;
}
```

For the data type association to be made between the PHP and the ActionScript, the PHP class needs to indicate the associated ActionScript value object definition. To do so, add this code to the class:

```
var $_explicitType = 'ext.domain.valueObjects.Product';
```

You must use **$_explicitType** here. The value assigned to it will need to match the resource in the client. For this I recommend using the reverse-domain scheme. So a value of *com.dmcinsights.valueObjects.Product* would refer to the *Product.as* file found within the Flex project's *src/com/dmcinsights/valueObjects* directory.

The PHP script that is the service would also need to be updated to return an array of **Product** objects. For example, the **getAllProducts( )** method would have this as its **while** loop:

```
while ($row = mysqli_fetch_array($r, MYSQLI_ASSOC)) {
    $obj = new Product( );
    $obj->id = $row['id'];
    $obj->name = $row['name'];
    $obj->price = $row['price'];
    $obj->inStock = $row['inStock'];
    $data[] = $obj;
}
```

The other methods, such as **createProduct( )**, would need to be written so they accept an object:

tip

Without having a server-side data transfer object definition, AMFPHP turns client objects into associative arrays; Zend AMF turns client objects into generic objects.

```
public function createProduct($product) {
    $name = mysqli_real_escape_string($this->dbc, trim($product->name));
    $price = (float) $product->price;
    $inStock = $product->inStockToInt( );
    // And so forth.
```

On that penultimate line you can see how one would be able to call a PHP class method on the received object, because it is of a known type.

Of course, the PHP script would need access to the **Product** definition first, so the PHP service script would begin like so:

```
<?php
require_once('mysql.inc.php');
require_once('path/to/Product.php');
class ProductsService {
```

tip

Remember that AMFPHP comes with a browser you can use to test your PHP services.

Where you store *Product.php* depends upon the AMF library in use. With Zend AMF, it really doesn't matter; you can put both *Product.php* and *Products Service.php* in the same directory. With AMFPHP, the *Product.php* file needs to be placed within *flashservices/services/vo*, while *ProductsService.php* goes within just *flashservices/services*.

Updating the Flex Client

tip

If using Flash Builder, select File > New > ActionScript Class to easily generate a class within a package.

The next step is to create a companion file in ActionScript that defines the **Product** data type. In Chapter 3, "ActionScript You Need to Know," I discuss external ActionScript files, packages, and classes. To start, you should define the **Product** class as part of a package, so the *Product.as* file stored in *src/com/dmcinsights* would begin with the following:

```
package com.dmcinsights {
```

Next, you need to use *metadata* to make the association between this object definition and the one on the server:

[RemoteClass(alias="*path.to.*Product")]

This is just the other side of the **$_explicitType** code in the PHP class. So if you have *Product.php* stored in the *flashservices/services/vo* directory, where AMFPHP uses *flashservices/services/vo* as the root directory for value object files, you would just use

[RemoteClass(alias="Product")]

If you placed *Product.php* in *flashservices/services/vo/com/dmcinsights*, you would use

[RemoteClass(alias="com.dmcinsights.Product")]

Next, you define the class. The class just needs to declare a variable for each property in the object:

```
public class Product {
    public var id:int;
    public var name:String;
    public var price:Number;
    public var inStock:Boolean;
}
```

note

The inStock variable in the ActionScript code could be an unsigned integer or a Boolean, depending upon which version of the ***ProductsService*** PHP script you're using.

The names of the variables within this class must match those in the PHP class!

A common and easy trick is to make the entire class bindable so that objects of that type can be bound to other components. To do that, just put the metadata **[Bindable]** before the class definition.

The complete *Products.as* file might therefore be the following:

```
package com.dmcinsights {
    [RemoteClass(alias="Product")]
    [Bindable]
    public class Product {
        public var id:int;
        public var name:String;
        public var price:Number;
        public var inStock:Boolean;
    }
}
```

To use the **Product** type in your Flex application, you must first import the definition:

```
import com.dmcinsights.valueObjects.Product;
```

Then you can create new objects of that type:

```
var product:Product = new Product();
product.price = priceTextInput.text;
product.name = nameTextInput.text;
product.inStock = inStockCheckBox.selected;
productsService.createProduct(product);
```

tip

There are tools available online that will auto-generate PHP and ActionScript value object code for you.

That code sends a **Product** object to the PHP script, where it'll be received as a **Product** object! If you have a PHP method like **getProductById()** that returns a single **Product**, it can be received as a **Product** object in Flex:

```
var product:Product = event.result;
```

ADDING AUTHENTICATION

tip

Flash Builder can internally store, for a development session, authentication credentials used to test services. These credentials will not be built into the exported application, however.

I try to be as mindful as I can of security whenever I write books (while simultaneously not overwhelming the reader): For the most part, you cannot be too careful. In the services developed in this chapter, and in Chapter 8, there is a glaring security hole: As it stands, PHP scripts exist on the server that can manipulate a database without any user authentication whatsoever. This is not good. Real-world services not intended for public use should implement authentication and authorization. In the next couple of pages, I'll explain a few of the options for implementing authentication and authorization. As any one of these options would require pages and pages to fully develop, I'll focus on the fundamental theories and code required by each, without walking through all the gritty details.

Using .htaccess

The Apache Web server uses *.htaccess* files to configure how the server runs. One thing you can do with an *.htaccess* file is restrict access to an entire directory to an authenticated user. That code might look like this at its most basic:

```
AuthType Basic
AuthName "Password Required"
AuthUserFile /www/passwords/password.file
```

Normally the username-password combinations are stored in special text files on the server. When you attempt to access a protected directory, you'll be presented with a prompt for inputting your username and password (**Figure 9.27**). For the remainder of the browser session, you'll then be able to access the contents of that directory.

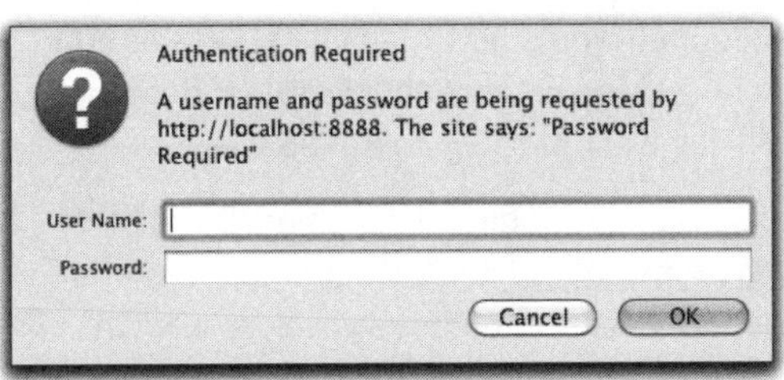

Figure 9.27

Of course, a Flash client can't "see" that prompt, let alone "type" in it, but there is a workaround: You can pass the username and password in the request by changing the server URL to *http://username:password@services.example.com*.

This will work, but you probably don't want to hard-code your credentials into the client application. First of all, if you change the access information, you'll need to recompile the application. Second, Flex applications can easily be decompiled, allowing someone to see the underlying code, thereby making the security measure meaningless.

An alternative, then, would be to use two **TextInput**s to take the username and password information from the user, then to programmatically add that to the service URL. This would require manipulating the service component in ActionScript:

```
serviceName.url = 'http://' + usernameTextInput.text
serviceName.url += ':' + passwordTextInput;
serviceName.url += '@services.example.com';
```

That code assumes that an MXML **HTTPService** component with an **id** of *serviceName* exists. If you wanted to create one in ActionScript, you'd just start with

```
var service:HttpService = new HttpService( );
```

Using PHP Sessions

The *.htaccess* approach works if you're using Apache, can create or edit *.htaccess* files, and want to restrict access to an entire directory. But if all of those don't apply to you, or if you want to restrict access based upon the specific user or user type, you'll need to implement the authorization within PHP. This isn't as hard as one might initially think.

To start, you'd just need to create a PHP login script that expects a username and password to be posted to it. This would be exactly like an HTML login page, without all of the HTML. The username and password would be validated, probably against a database, and, if correct, a new session would be started and whatever variables required would be stored in that session. The Flash client again would need to take the username and password from the client, then send those to the PHP login script using an **HTTPService**.

When the PHP script creates the session, by default the session ID will be sent to the client in a cookie. Every request from the client to the server will automatically include that session ID, because that's how cookies work in a browser-server dynamic. In fact, if you are using the Network Monitor in Flash Builder, you can see that the PHP session cookie is part of each request, regardless of the request type (**Figure 9.28**).

Figure 9.28

When using sessions, you could then write checks into your PHP scripts so that certain actions can only be taken by authorized users:

```
public function deleteProduct($id) {
    if (isset($_SESSION['usertype']) && ($_SESSION['usertype'] ==
    'admin')) {
        // Proceed
    } else {
        return null;
    }
}
```

Generally speaking one shouldn't pollute a class file with secondary code like this, so you could make it cleaner by creating an **authorized()** method that performs the security check based upon the desired action:

```
public function deleteProduct($id) {
    if ($this->authorized('delete')) {
        // Proceed
    } else {
        return null;
    }
}
```

That **authorized()** method might be defined like this:

```
public function authorized($action) {
    // Check for the user type:
    if (isset($_SESSION['usertype'])) {
        $usertype = $_SESSION['usertype'];
    } else {
        return false; // Invalid if no session variable!
    }
```

```
    // Create allowed actions by user type:
    $allowed['admin'] = array('create', 'retrieve', 'update', 'delete');
    $allowed['yogi'] = array('create', 'retrieve', 'update');
    $allowed['user'] = array('retrieve');
    // Validate the action/user:
    if (in_array($action, $allowed[$usertype])) {
        return true;
    } else {
        return false;
    }
} // End of method.
```

AN HTML-BASED ALTERNATIVE

Ryan Stewart, an Adobe evangelist and the tech reviewer for this book, wrote up an example on his blog (*http://blog.digitalbackcountry.com*) that presents an alternative way to authenticate users. His argument is that users expect certain things, such as their browser remembering usernames and passwords for them, which cannot easily be done within Flash. His solution is to use a standard HTML page for the login process, then have the PHP script authenticate the user, start a session, and redirect the user to the Flash content. See his blog for the full code.

Using PHP Tokens

If you don't want to go the full session route, you can use *tokens* instead. This is essentially the same premise as a session without formally using sessions. The process goes like this:

1. The Flash client sends the access credentials to a PHP script via a service.
2. The PHP script validates the credentials and creates a unique identifier.

   You can create a unique identifier by applying PHP's **md5()** or **sha1()** function to any piece of data, like the current timestamp or a random number. The unique identifier will act as a representation of the authenticated user, so it would need to be stored on the server somehow, probably in a database.
3. The PHP script returns the identifier (i.e., the token) to the Flash client.
4. The Flash client stores the token in a local variable, then includes that token in every request of the server.

5. The PHP script would then validate the received token against the database prior to taking any actions.

   As with my sessions example, you could create a special class method expressly for this purpose.

FINDING SERVICES

Most of the client-server examples in this book require user-defined services. With a limited amount of space, I wanted to be certain that you could adequately create both the client and server sides of these interactions. But of course, there are tons of third-party services out there, which I could still only touch upon even if I dedicated a whole book to them. So how would you find and learn how to use these third-party services?

To start, all of the big Web sites that you already may use—Google, Amazon, Twitter, Ebay, Yahoo!, Flickr, Wikipedia, etc.—provide services. If you search their sites or just Google, for example, "Amazon web services," you'll find all the resources you need. Most of these sites only provide services to registered users, meaning you'll need to pass along an ID in your requests. Some of these large sites also have ActionScript-specific libraries you can use (MapQuest, for one, provides this).

The quality of a service depends upon the quality of its documentation, and most of the above examples provide more than sufficient information for how to use their services. All you really need to know, though, is what URI to use, what parameters are expected (names and types), and what should be returned (names and types). If you search "Flex" plus whatever service, you'll likely find existing tutorials on how to use Google Maps, Yahoo!'s Upcoming service, Amazon's Simple Storage Service, and so forth.

Some services do exist but aren't well documented, like the iTunes store, which has an underrepresented WebObjects service (WebObjects is an Apple server-side technology). If you really need to use under-documented services, my best recommendation is to practice testing and using the service thoroughly before getting too far along developing the client application. There's no use in getting too far along before you're certain that a service will do the job.

DEPLOYING CLIENT-SERVER APPLICATIONS

When it's time to deploy your client-server application, there are a few steps you should take ahead of time. First, make sure you change the URLs of the services from their local values to their proper online ones (i.e., from *http://localhost* to *http://www.example.com*). You can, of course, make the use of the service more secure by using a Secure Socket Layer connection (i.e., https). While thinking about the server, you'll need to check that it has the additional libraries, such as AMFPHP or Zend AMF, installed, when necessary. If using AMFPHP, remove its browser feature (because you don't want just anyone to be able to browse through your services).

Second, be certain to implement authentication if the service is not meant for public use. This would also be a good time to make sure that the service is not vulnerable to attacks. In other words, double-check that you have thoroughly validated and sanctified all data provided to the service. If you used prototyped PHP code created by Flash Builder, go through that with extra care.

Finally, before going to export the project from Flash Builder, disable the network monitor if you had enabled it for the project.

PART THREE
Application Development

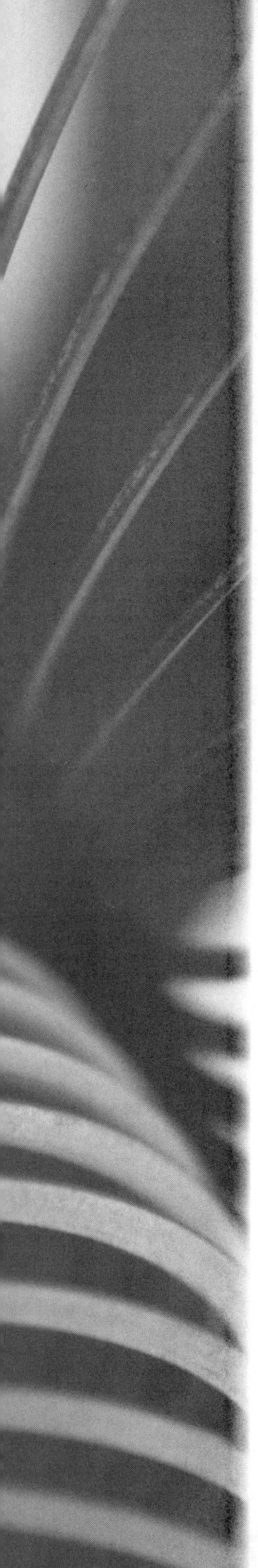

10 CREATING CUSTOM CODE

Real-world development of Flex applications inevitably involves creating custom code. Instead of relying solely upon the predefined MXML components and ActionScript classes, you can easily create your own user interface controls, events, formatters, and validators. By using custom code you can better organize your projects and make them easier to maintain. Custom code can also be easily reused from one project to another.

Creating custom components is not as daunting as you might worry it would be, but the chapter does include a little bit more about Object-Oriented Programming (OOP), which you'll need to know. Before and after that section, you'll learn how to create both simple and more complex custom components. The chapter finishes with discussions of custom events, formatters, validators, and editors. And, you'll also be given some recommendations as to where you can go to access the custom work other people have already created.

SIMPLE CUSTOM COMPONENTS

There are many reasons you might create custom components. For example, a custom component could be as simple as a **DropDownList** that's prepopulated with a list of countries. A custom component could also be as elaborate as a template for displaying information about a product—its name, price, description, image, etc., plus a button that, when clicked, adds that product to a shopping cart. Used like so, a custom component is similar to an item renderer used with a **List** (see Chapter 6, "Manipulating Data"). Creating custom components that are strictly visual, without any extra logic, is quite simple, and I'll start by demonstrating that concept.

Creating Custom Components

Custom components can be created using MXML, ActionScript, or a combination thereof. I'll start with MXML, as it's easiest to understand.

To create a custom MXML component, create a new MXML file with a unique, meaningful name. In the MXML file, place whatever combination of MXML, ActionScript, and so forth, you need. And that's it! As a very trivial example, say you wanted to create a custom **Button** used as a submit button for forms. This is really just a **Button** with a default **label** of *Submit*. To do that, you would create a file named *SubmitButton.mxml*. The file would contain the following:

```
<?xml version="1.0" encoding="utf-8"?>
<s:Button xmlns:fx="http://ns.adobe.com/mxml/2009"
        xmlns:s="library://ns.adobe.com/flex/spark"
        xmlns:mx="library://ns.adobe.com/flex/mx"
        label="Submit">
</s:Button>
```

tip

The custom component's name is the name of the MXML file without the extension.

This is just a **Button**, with a **label** property, plus the namespace and XML declarations.

tip

You would never create a custom component based upon the ***Application*** tag, as each Flex program can only have one ***Application*** instance and that's what the primary MXML file is.

You would save this MXML file in your project's directory so that it's available to use. You might store the file in a *components* directory or in *com/example/components* (replacing *com* and *example* with a representation of your organization). The important thing is that you organize your custom components in a way that still makes it clear what the file's purpose is. Also, conventionally if a custom component is just an extension of one MXML component, you would use that MXML component's name in the filename, as in *SubmitButton*.

Again, that's all there is to it. If you take those steps, you'll have created your own custom component of type **SubmitButton**.

tip

If you download the source code from the book's corresponding Web site (*www.dmcinsights.com/flex4/*), you'll find this example in the *Ch10/Ch10_01* folder.

To really hammer the point home, let's create the departments **DropDownList** as a custom component.

1. Create a new project in Flash Builder or your alternative IDE or text editor.
2. Create a new MXML file named *DepartmentsDropDownList.mxml*, to be stored in the *src/components* directory.

tip

You can add style properties to custom components in their definition, if you want, or allow the application to style the components. See Chapter 13, "Improving the Appearance," for more on styling.

If you're using Flash Builder, select File > New > MXML Component. In the prompt (**Figure 10.1**), enter *components* as the package, *DepartmentsDrop DownList* as the name, and base it upon the **DropDownList** component.

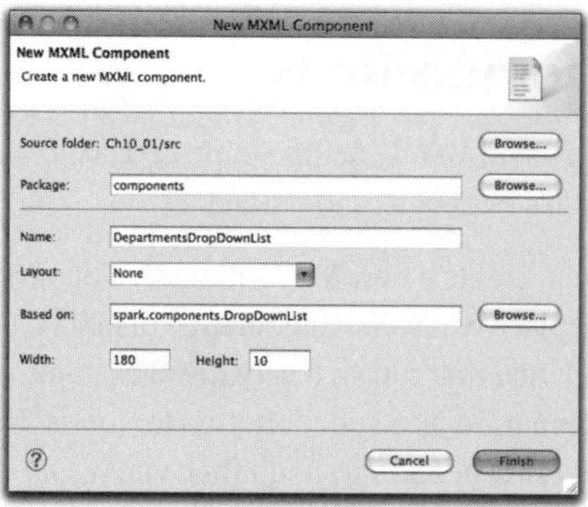

Figure 10.1

If you're not using Flash Builder, you'll need to add this code to the file:

```
<?xml version="1.0" encoding="utf-8"?>
<s:DropDownList xmlns:fx="http://ns.adobe.com/mxml/2009"
   xmlns:s="library://ns.adobe.com/flex/spark"
   xmlns:mx="library://ns.adobe.com/flex/mx" width="180"
   height="10">
</s:DropDownList>
```

3. Before the closing tag, add an **ArrayList**:

```
<s:ArrayList>
   <fx:Object data="1" label="Human Resources" />
   <fx:Object data="2" label="Marketing" />
   <fx:Object data="3" label="Accounting" />
   <fx:Object data="4" label="Research and Development" />
   <fx:Object data="5" label="Sales" />
</s:ArrayList>
```

This will be the data that populates the **DropDownList**. The actual values come from an example in Chapter 8, "Using Simple Services."

4. Save the file.

tip

In this chapter, the focus will really be on customizing existing components to suit your needs, but you can create entirely new components from scratch, if need be.

Using Custom Components

Once you've defined a custom component, you can use it in your Flex application. The first thing you'll need to do is create a namespace for the component. You do so in your opening **Application** tag, just as you declare the *fx*, *s*, and *mx* namespaces. For example, if you define your custom components in the *components* directory (also called the *components* package), you might use

```
<s:Application xmlns:fx="http://ns.adobe.com/mxml/2009"
    xmlns:s="library://ns.adobe.com/flex/spark"
    xmlns:mx="library://ns.adobe.com/flex/mx"
    xmlns:cx="components.*">
```

Now *cx* is an alias for everything defined in that directory/package.

You don't have to use cx as the component alias but something short makes the most sense.

Next, use the component as you would any predefined Flex component. For the **SubmitButton**, that would be

```
<cx:SubmitButton id="mySubmitButton" click="doThis()" />
```

That will create a **SubmitButton** component in the application. Because **SubmitButton** extends **Button**, it has all the properties and methods of **Button**. You can assign an **id** to the component, set **x** and **y** properties, add event listeners, whatever.

Let's use the **DepartmentsDropDownList** component in an application:

If you download the source code from the book's corresponding Web site (*www.dmcinsights.com/flex4/*), you'll also find this code as part of the *Ch10/Ch10_01* project.

1. Open the previous project in Flash Builder or your alternative IDE or text editor, if it is not already.
2. In the primary application MXML file, add the namespace for your custom component:

   ```
   <s:Application xmlns:fx="http://ns.adobe.com/mxml/2009"
       xmlns:s="library://ns.adobe.com/flex/spark"
       xmlns:mx="library://ns.adobe.com/flex/mx"
       xmlns:cx="components.*">
   ```

   If you stored the *DepartmentsDropDownList.mxml* file in a *com/example/components* directory, you would need to use **xmlns:cx="com.example.components.*"** in the **Application** tag instead.
3. In the application, use the custom component:

   ```
   <cx:DepartmentsDropDownList id="dept" x="10" y="10" />
   ```

   I'm going to give the component an **id** value that will be used by the application.
4. Create a **Label** bound to the custom component:

   ```
   <s:Label text="{dept.selectedItem.label}" x="200" y="15" />
   ```

   Just so that you see how custom components are used just like built-in components, this **Label** will reflect the currently selected item in the **DepartmentsDropDownList**, through data binding. Because each item in the list is an object, you need to refer to **selectedItem.label** to get to something meaningful.

5. Save, run, and test the completed application (**Figure 10.2**).

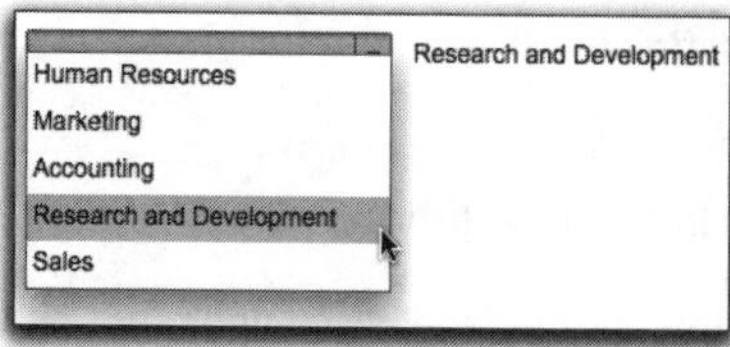

Figure 10.2

Creating More Complex Components

 **tip**

When you base a custom component on a container, such as ***Form***, it's called a composite component, as it'll be made up of multiple components.

The pages thus far discuss and demonstrate only very simple custom components that extend a single MXML component. But you can make your custom components as complex as you need. Here, let's create a login form as its own component, consisting of a form with a heading, two text inputs, and a button. To try this quickly, we'll just add the new component to the existing project.

1. Open the previous project in Flash Builder or your alternative IDE or text editor, if it is not already.

2. Create a new MXML file named *LoginForm.mxml*, to be stored in the *src/components* directory.

   If you're using Flash Builder, select File > New > MXML Component. In the prompt, enter *components* as the package, *LoginForm* as the name, and base it upon the **Form** component.

   If you're not using Flash Builder, you'll need to add the following code to the file:

```
<?xml version="1.0" encoding="utf-8"?>
<mx:Form xmlns:fx="http://ns.adobe.com/mxml/2009"
   xmlns:s="library://ns.adobe.com/flex/spark"
   xmlns:mx="library://ns.adobe.com/flex/mx" width="300"
   height="200">
</mx:Form>
```

 **tip**

If you download the source code from the book's corresponding Web site (*www.dmcinsights.com/flex4/*), you'll also find this code as part of the *Ch10/Ch10_01* project.

3. Before the closing tag, add the form contents:

```
<mx:FormHeading label="Login Form"/>
<mx:FormItem label="Email Address">
   <s:TextInput id="emailInput"/>
</mx:FormItem>
<mx:FormItem label="Password">
   <s:TextInput id="passwordInput"/><s:Label text="(Between 6-20
   characters)" />
</mx:FormItem>
```

 **tip**

If you want the entered password to be hidden, set the ***displayAsPassword*** property to true in the password ***TextInput***.

```
<mx:FormItem>
    <s:Button label="Login" id="loginButton"/>
</mx:FormItem>
```

The form contains two **TextInput**s and a **Button**.

4. Add two validators:

```
<fx:Declarations>
    <mx:EmailValidator id="emailValidator" source="{emailInput}"
    property="text" trigger="{loginButton}" triggerEvent="click" />
    <mx:StringValidator id="passwordValidator" source=
    "{passwordInput}" property="text" trigger="{loginButton}"
    triggerEvent="click" minLength="6" maxLength="20" />
</fx:Declarations>
```

These two validators will validate the two form inputs when the login button is clicked.

5. Save the file.

6. In the main MXML file, add an instance of the following new **LoginForm** component:

```
<cx:LoginForm id="loginForm" x="10" y="30" />
```

Again, this is all you need to do to use the custom component.

7. If you want to tie in to the **LoginForm** component, change the **Label** to

```
<s:Label text="{loginForm.passwordInput.text}" x="200" y="15" />
```

Instead of having the **Label** reflect the selected department, it'll show the typed password. This has no practical purpose; it just demonstrates how the primary application file can tap into the custom component.

8. Save, run, and test the completed application.

Figure 10.3 shows the application (with the no-longer-necessary **Drop DownList**) and how the password is immediately reflected by the **Label**. Figure 10.3 also shows the active validators.

Figure 10.4 shows a properly validated result.

tip

In Source mode, Flash Builder can perform code hinting for your custom components.

tip

In Design mode, Flash Builder will list your custom components in the Components panel.

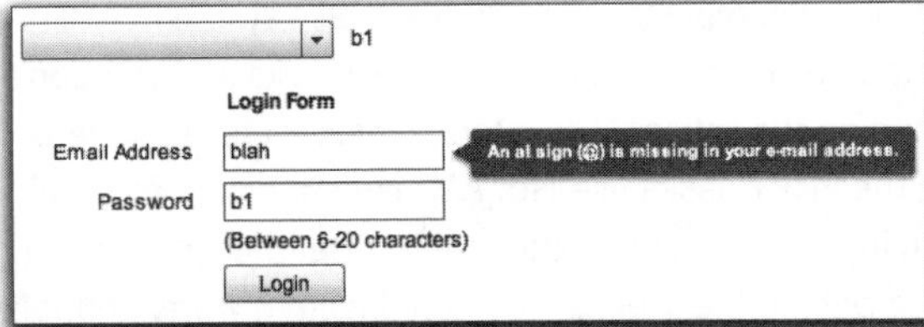

Figure 10.3

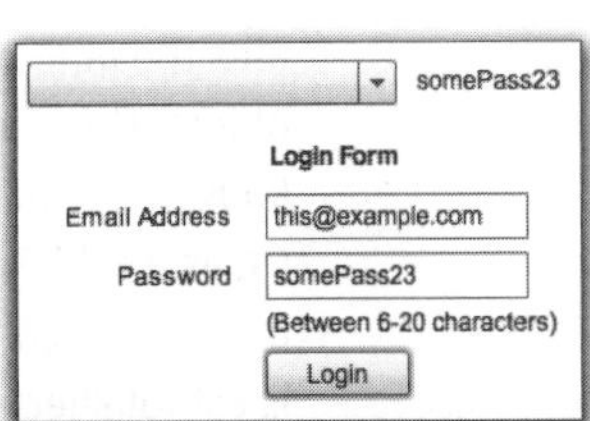

Figure 10.4

A WEE BIT MORE OOP

In Chapter 3, "ActionScript You Need to Know," I highlight key aspects of Object-Oriented Programming. Mostly it was a matter of explaining the basic terms and syntax. One subject I glossed over was *access modifier keywords*: *public*, *private*, and *protected*. In that chapter I just recommend you use the private modifier when you create variables and functions, which is what I've done throughout this book. But when you start creating custom code, always using private will not work. It's time to actually explain what these terms mean.

OOP is as much, if not more, about theory than it is syntax. Two parts of OOP design are *inheritance* and *encapsulation*. Inheritance is the act of creating one class that is an extension of another, creating a parent-child relationship (or *superclass* and *subclass* or *base* class and *derived* class). When inheritance occurs, the child class will inherit attributes and functionality defined in the parent. The child class can take this further, by updating or expanding the inherited qualities. To use an example, in a sidebar on inheritance in Chapter 3, I talk about how one might create a base class called **Pet**, which would define basic behavior common to pets—eating, sleeping, playing, etc.—as well as basic attributes—name, age, whatever:

```
public class Pet {
    // Variables, aka properties.
    // Functions, aka methods.
}
```

A specific **Pet** might be a **Dog** or **Cat**, so the **Dog** and **Cat** classes extend **Pet**:

```
public class Dog extends Pet {
}
```

Even without any additional code, the **Dog** class would already have the variables and functions defined within **Pet**. Assuming, that is, that the right access modifiers were used. And I'll get to that in a minute, but first, encapsulation...

A class should be designed so that it defines all the functionality and properties needed to completely represent a thing. For example, the **Array** class creates the ability to add, remove, replace, and retrieve values stored in an array object. There are methods you can call to perform these tasks and you don't know what happens behind the scenes. The internal logic is encapsulated. Or, as a PHP example, the PHP classes used for AMF communications require a database connection in order to perform the queries. But that connection is established and used behind the scenes; you don't need to worry about it (moreover, you can't touch the connection) outside of the class.

All of this gets us back to access modifiers. By using the keywords **public**, **protected**, and **private**, you are controlling the availability of a class's functions and variables (aka its *members*). Here is exactly what they mean:

- A *public* member is accessible anywhere.
- A *protected* member is only accessible through the class or through derived classes.
- A *private* member is only accessible through the class.

tip

ActionScript also has the ***internal*** and ***static*** access modifiers. An internal member is available within the same package. Static members are used without class instances.

In terms of a Flex application, when you create *SomeProject* with its *Some Project.mxml* primary MXML file, the application itself will be an instance of the **SomeProject** class (and the **SomeProject** class is just a custom **Application** component). The **SomeProject** object makes use of many other classes, such as **TextInput** or **Group**. Each of these classes needs to be public in order for that to be possible.

Those classes have properties, such as the **TextInput's text** and **id**, that the **SomeProject** object needs to access, so those are defined as public within the **TextInput** class definition. If **SomeProject** creates an object of type **Array**, it may need to call that class's **push( )** method to add a new item to the array, so **push( )** must be defined as public, too.

On the other hand, the **TextInput** and other classes have protected and private members, too. In **TextInput**, there is the **measure( )** method that determines the size of the component. It's a protected method, meaning that it's used internally by the **TextInput** class and cannot be called outside of that class (it's also inherited by classes that extend **TextInput**).

When it comes to creating your own code, you'll need to choose the proper access modifier for the variables and functions based upon the realms in which those members should be accessible. For variables and functions defined using ActionScript in the primary MXML file, I've been using private throughout the book. That makes sense as the variable or function would not be used outside of the *SomeProject.mxml* file and the **SomeProject** class will not be extended. When you create custom components, you can't just use private across the board.

tip

OOP theory says that classes should be loosely coupled, meaning their functionality is not tightly tied to other classes.

If you take the *Ch10_01* project, it uses two custom components: **Departments DropDownList** and **LoginForm**. This is possible because both of those classes are also public. However, if you were to create variables and functions within **Script** tags in either of those components, the ability to access those from *Ch10_01.mxml* would depend upon their access modifiers. I'll demonstrate this in the next example.

USING ACTIONSCRIPT IN COMPONENTS

The custom **LoginForm** component, while a fine start, isn't great from an OOP standpoint. Here are three quick reasons why:

1. It requires knowledge of the **id**s of the two **TextInput**s to access their values.
2. The entered e-mail address and password values are available (through the **TextInput**s, even if they don't pass the validation, see Figure 10.3).
3. The password's size requirements are written into the component. To change the requirements, you'd need to change the component itself.

tip

If you download the source code from the book's corresponding Web site (*www.dmcinsights.com/flex4/*), you'll find this example in the *Ch10/Ch10_02* folder.

In short, the **LoginForm** class is poorly encapsulated. To fix this, let's add some public and private members to the custom component. To do so, I'm going to create this as a new project, so that the new ideas don't get muddled with those used in the earlier project.

1. Create a new project in Flash Builder or your alternative IDE or text editor.
2. Create a new MXML file named *LoginForm.mxml*, to be stored in the *src/components* directory.

   If you're using Flash Builder, select File > New > MXML Component. In the prompt, enter *components* as the package, *LoginForm* as the name, and base it upon the **Form** component.

   If you're not using Flash Builder, you'll need to add the following code to the file:

```
<?xml version="1.0" encoding="utf-8"?>
<mx:Form xmlns:fx="http://ns.adobe.com/mxml/2009"
   xmlns:s="library://ns.adobe.com/flex/spark"
   xmlns:mx="library://ns.adobe.com/flex/mx" width="300"
   height="175">
</mx:Form>
```

3. Within a **Script** block, import the **Validator** class:

```
<fx:Script>
   <![CDATA[
   import mx.validators.Validator;
```

4. Create two public, bound variables:

```
[Bindable]
public var passwordMinLength:uint = 1;
[Bindable]
public var passwordMaxLength:uint = 100;
```

These two variables will be used to dynamically change the password's length requirements. Both are bindable, as they'll be bound within the password validator, and have default values.

5. Create two public variables:

```
public var email:String = null;
public var password:String = null;
```

These variables will be used to store the submitted and validated e-mail and password values. Both are initialized as empty strings.

6. Define a function for handling the login button click:

```
private function handleLogin(event:MouseEvent):void {
    var vr:Array = Validator.validateAll([emailValidator, passwordValidator]);
    if (vr.length == 0) {
        email = emailInput.text;
        password = passwordInput.text;
    }
}
```

In this version of the form, the inputs will be validated when the user clicks the login button. In this function that handles that event, the **Validator. validateAll( )** method is called to perform the validations. If the returned array has a length of 0, both tests passed.

If both validation tests passed, the **TextInput** values are assigned to the public variables. This function is marked as private, as it should not be available outside of the class itself.

7. Complete the **Script** block:

```
    ]]>
</fx:Script>
```

8. Add the form contents:

```
<mx:FormHeading label="Login Form"/>
<mx:FormItem label="Email Address">
    <s:TextInput id="emailInput"/>
</mx:FormItem>
<mx:FormItem label="Password">
    <s:TextInput id="passwordInput"/><s:Label text="(Between
    {passwordMinLength}-{passwordMaxLength} characters)" />
</mx:FormItem>
<mx:FormItem>
    <s:Button label="Login" id="loginButton" click=
    "handleLogin(event)"/>
</mx:FormItem>
```

The form is written exactly as it was before except that the **Label** text after the password now uses the values from the two public, bindable variables to indicate the password's length requirements. Also, the **Button** now calls the **handleLogin( )** function when it's clicked.

9. Add two validators:

```
<fx:Declarations>
  <mx:EmailValidator id="emailValidator" source="{emailInput}"
  property="text" trigger="{loginButton}" triggerEvent="click" />
  <mx:StringValidator id="passwordValidator" source=
  "{passwordInput}" property="text" trigger="{loginButton}"
  triggerEvent="click" minLength="{passwordMinLength}"
  maxLength="{passwordMaxLength}" />
</fx:Declarations>
```

These two validators are again defined as they were before except that the **minLength** and **maxLength** properties of the **StringValidator** will come from variables.

10. Save the file.

GETTER AND SETTER METHODS

Fully encapsulated classes often deny any direct access to the class's variables (aka attributes), making them all private or protected. Instead, the class creates public "getter" and "setter" methods through which one can retrieve or assign a variable's value. For example, consider the following:

```
public function set passwordMinLength(value:uint):void {
    passwordMinLength = value;
}
public function get email( ):String {
    return email;
}
```

Note that in ActionScript, these functions are written using the keywords **set** and **get**, followed by a space. For the primary MXML file to then set the minimum password length, it would still just use the following:

```
<cx:LoginForm passwordMinLength="6" />
```

And for the primary MXML file to access the submitted e-mail address, it would refer to **loginFormId.email**.

In both cases, even though it looks like the MXML is referencing properties, behind the scenes the applicable methods will be called.

Besides creating better encapsulation, another benefit of using getter and setter methods is they allow you to add validation and formatting to the input and output.

11. In the main MXML file, add the component's namespace:

```
<s:Application xmlns:fx="http://ns.adobe.com/mxml/2009"
  xmlns:s="library://ns.adobe.com/flex/spark"
  xmlns:mx="library://ns.adobe.com/flex/mx"
  xmlns:cx="components.*">
```

The abbreviation *cx* will represent classes defined in the *components* directory (or package).

12. Add an instance of the following new **LoginForm** component:

```
<cx:LoginForm id="loginForm" x="10" y="10"
passwordMinLength="2" passwordMaxLength="4"/>
```

The component is created as it was before, but now it has two new properties: **passwordMinLength** and **passwordMaxLength**. Values assigned to these properties in the component instance will be assigned to the variables in the **LoginForm** class.

13. Create a **Button** and a **Label** for retrieving the form data:

```
<s:Button label="Check Info" x="10" y="175" click="checkLabel.text =
'Email: ' + loginForm.email + ' Password: ' + loginForm.password"  />
<s:Label id="checkLabel" x="100" y="180" />
```

The last thing we need to do is access the e-mail and password values from the login form, just to confirm that the process worked. To do so, I'm adding this button that, when clicked, posts that information in a corresponding **Label**. The validated e-mail and password values are available through the **email** and **password** properties of the **LoginForm** component.

14. Save, run, and test the completed application.

Figure 10.5 shows the application and the values of the e-mail and password prior to validation.

Figure 10.6 shows a properly validated result.

tip

Change the ***passwordMinLength*** and ***passwordMaxLength*** properties in the ***LoginForm*** component, and then rerun the application to see the effect.

Login Form
Email Address this is no good!
Password ;alfkjlskadjf
(Between 2-4 characters)
This string is longer than the maximum allowed length. This must be less than 4 characters long.
Login
Check Info Email: null Password: null

Figure 10.5

Login Form
Email Address test@example.com
Password 1234
(Between 2-4 characters)
Login
Check Info Email: test@example.com Password: 1234

Figure 10.6

CUSTOM EVENTS

The custom **LoginForm** component is pretty good at this state: It creates the form, validates the submitted data, allows the validation to be slightly customized, and then sets up the public e-mail and password variables for use as properties through component instances. However, as it stands, there's still a two-step process:

1. The user clicks the login button.
2. Another button must be clicked to retrieve the validated data.

It'd clearly be better if the action taken on the login button were to be reflected in the primary application window (which is where the program would likely authenticate the supplied information). However, you cannot add event listeners in the primary application file to the login button in the custom component without knowing the button's **id** value. And even if you did go that route, it'd again be a case of poor encapsulation. The solution is to use a custom event.

tip

The primary application file can automatically watch for events on a custom component's top component, such as ***Form*** in the ***LoginForm*** component. But to catch events from subcomponents, like the login ***Button***, custom events are required.

The principle behind a custom event is that the custom component creates its own event that is triggered when appropriate. The primary application file, on the instance of the custom component, would watch for and handle that custom event type.

To start, you'll need to add a piece of *metadata* to the custom component's MXML file, declaring your intended custom event. That syntax is

```
<fx:Metadata>
[Event(name="eventTypeName", type="flash.events.Event")]
</fx:Metadata>
```

Metadata is a directive to the compiler indicating your intentions. You've frequently seen the **[Bindable]** metadata directive, and **[Event]** is another (although here it's being declared within MXML, not ActionScript). In total layman's terms, the above code says to the compiler, "Don't freak out when you see an event of type *eventTypeName*; I know what I'm doing."

tip

Custom events are required by composite custom components. With simple custom components, such as a ***SubmitButton*** or ***DepartmentsDropDownList***, the custom component inherits and can use all the same events as the parent component.

The *eventTypeName* needs to be something unique and meaningful. The event type is the class of event that will be created, such as a generic **Event**.

Once you've declared the intent to use a new event type, you can, when appropriate, create an event of that type. To do so, create a new **Event** object, providing it with the name of the event type:

```
var eventObject:Event = new Event('eventTypeName');
```

To trigger that event, you need to call the **dispatchEvent( )** function:

```
dispatchEvent(eventObject);
```

You can combine these two lines into one, for brevity:

```
dispatchEvent(new Event('eventTypeName'));
```

Thanks to this **dispatchEvent( )** call, the entire custom component will send out an **eventTypeName** event; you just need to watch for this new event type on the instance of the custom component:

```
<cx:SomeCustomComponent eventTypeName="handleEvent(event)" />
```

Let's update the previous example using this information.

1. Open the previous project in Flash Builder or your alternative IDE or text editor, if it is not already.
2. Within *LoginForm.mxml*, add a Metadata block:

   ```
   <fx:Metadata>
      [Event(name="loginButtonClick", type="flash.events.Event")]
   </fx:Metadata>
   ```

   The event's name is *loginButtonClick* and it's of type **flash.events.Event**.
3. Within the **handleLogin( )** function, after assigning values to the e-mail and password variables, dispatch the event:

   ```
   dispatchEvent(new Event('loginButtonClick'));
   ```

   You would want to do this only after the validation has passed and the values have been assigned to **email** and **password** (as the primary MXML file will use this event as an indicator that it's safe to access those values).
4. Save the *LoginForm.mxml* file.
5. In the main MXML file, add a **loginButtonClick** event handler to the instance of the **LoginForm** component:

   ```
   <cx:LoginForm id="loginForm" x="10" y="10" passwordMinLength="8"
   passwordMaxLength="12" loginButtonClick="loginButtonClickHandler
   (event)" />
   ```

   Now the application will watch for **loginButtonClick** events on this component. When one occurs, the **loginButtonClickHandler( )** function will be called. I've also changed the password requirements, for variety.
6. Drop the Check Info button as it's no longer required.

tip

If you download the source code from the book's corresponding Web site (*www.dmcinsights.com/flex4/*), you'll also find this code as part of the Ch10/Ch10_02 project.

tip

To be more precise, the ***loginButtonClick*** event could be of type ***MouseEvent***.

7. Define the **loginButtonClickHandler( )** function:

```
<fx:Script>
<![CDATA[
private function loginButtonClickHandler(event:Event):void {
    checkLabel.text = 'Email: ' + loginForm.email + ' Password: ' +
loginForm.password;
}
]]>
</fx:Script>
```

This function just updates the **Label**, as the earlier button had done.

8. Save, run, and test the completed application.

Figure 10.7 shows the application with invalid data.

Figure 10.8 shows a properly validated result, with the automatically updated **Label**.

Login Form
Email Address this won't work!
Password abc
(Between 8-12 characters)
This string is shorter than the minimum allowed length. This must be at least 8 characters long.
Login

Figure 10.7

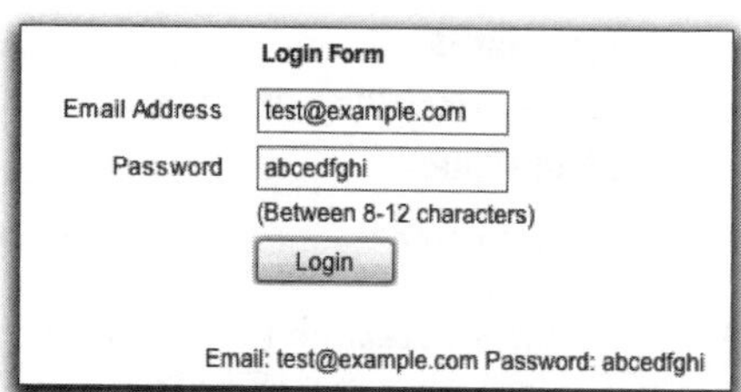

Figure 10.8

EXTENDING THE EVENT CLASS

An even better improvement on the **LoginForm** component would be to have it pass the validated e-mail and password values along in the custom event object. To do so you'll need to use ActionScript to extend the **Event** class. In the extended class, you would add the required properties (those two variables). Then you would assign the values—the e-mail address and password—to those properties before sending the event. The handler that watches for that event type could then access the e-mail address and password without directly referring to the instance of the custom component. As you might be able to tell, this involves a bit more complex OOP, which is why I don't demonstrate it here.

CREATING A CUSTOM EDITOR

The last type of custom code to discuss is the custom editor. In Chapter 6, I describe how one can use an existing Flex component as an item editor in a **DataGrid**. For example, you could use a **NumericStepper** instead of the default **TextInput**. In Chapter 9, "Using Complex Services," I use a check box to edit a product's *inStock* property. In some cases, though, dropping in a simple component as an editor won't work. For example, in Chapter 9 I had to change how the **inStock** property was represented from a small number (0/1) to a Boolean in order to use a check box. If I didn't want to (or couldn't) make that change in the PHP code but still wanted to use a check box, I could make a custom component to use instead. Such a component would start with a container and a check box:

```
<?xml version="1.0" encoding="utf-8"?>
<mx:Box xmlns:fx="http://ns.adobe.com/mxml/2009"
        xmlns:s="library://ns.adobe.com/flex/spark"
        xmlns:mx="library://ns.adobe.com/flex/mx">
   <s:CheckBox id="inStockCheckBox" />
</mx:Box>
```

Then I would need to use ActionScript to check or uncheck the box based upon the incoming *inStock* value (remember that the **data** object is how information is passed to item renderers and the like):

```
if (data.inStock == 1) {
   inStockCheckBox.selected = true;
} else {
   inStockCheckBox.selected = false;
}
```

The ActionScript would also need to create a public variable that would be used to reflect (back to the **DataGrid**) the *inStock* status:

```
if (inStockCheckBox.selected) {
   inStockValue = 1;
} else {
   inStockValue = 0;
}
```

Of course, those two conditionals would be written within functions called when the component is created and when the check box's **selected** status changes.

Or as another example, Part 2 of the book had several employee-department examples. In one version in Chapter 6, the employees were displayed in a

DataGrid and were editable inline. Logically, you'd want to be able to edit the employee's department using the same **DropDownList** you'd use to add a new one (**Figure 10.9**). In the next series of steps I'll explain how one would do that.

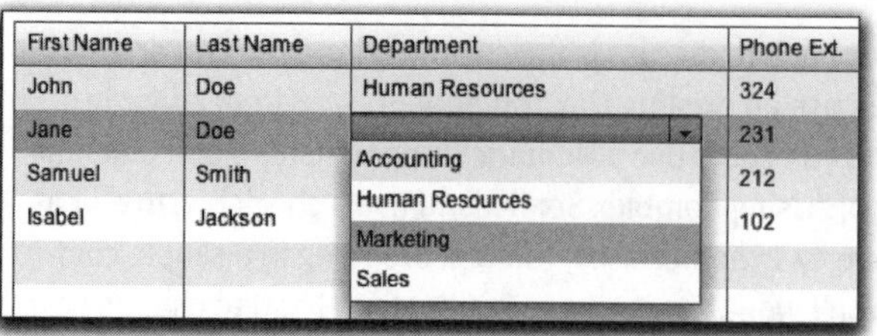

Figure 10.9

tip

If you download the source code from the book's corresponding Web site (*www.dmcinsights.com/flex4/*), you'll find this example in the *Ch10/Ch10_03* folder.

1. Create a new project in Flash Builder or your alternative IDE or text editor.
2. Create a new MXML file named *DepartmentEditor.mxml*, to be stored in the *src/components* directory.

   If you're using Flash Builder, select File > New > MXML Component. In the prompt, enter *components* as the package, *DepartmentEditor* as the name, and base it upon the **Box** component.

   If you're not using Flash Builder, you'll need to add the following code to the file:

```
<?xml version="1.0" encoding="utf-8"?>
<mx:Box xmlns:fx="http://ns.adobe.com/mxml/2009"
        xmlns:s="library://ns.adobe.com/flex/spark"
        xmlns:mx="library://ns.adobe.com/flex/mx" width="200"
       height="15">
</mx:Box>
```

   This will be a composite component, whose root tag is a **Box** and that contains a **DropDownList**. This is a bit technical, but the reason for this is that a custom editor component must implement the **mx.core.IDataRenderer** class. Only a handful of components do implement that class, and most are defined in Halo, not Spark. So I'm using **Box** as the primary element, not **DropDownList**.

tip

You can actually use any component as a custom editor, even if it doesn't implement ***IDataRenderer***, but doing so requires extra OOP code.

3. Add a **dataChange** event handler to the opening **Box** tag:

```
<mx:Box xmlns:fx="http://ns.adobe.com/mxml/2009"
        xmlns:s="library://ns.adobe.com/flex/spark"
        xmlns:mx="library://ns.adobe.com/flex/mx" width="200"
       height="15" dataChange="init()">
```

   The custom editor must do some setup when it's created. That setup will take place in the **init()** function. With many components, you could perform setup when a **creationComplete** event occurs. However, with custom editors, the same editor instance will be reused from one edited record to the next, so its **creationComplete** event may only occur once. The proper event to watch for, then, is **dataChange**.

As explained in Chapter 6, the **data** object is how a particular record is passed to a custom editor or renderer. If a user goes to edit multiple employees in the **DataGrid**, the same instance of this **DepartmentEditor** will be reused for each, but the data provided to the editor will change each time, triggering a **dataChange** event, which is when the setup will be performed.

4. Within the **Script** section, import the **IndexChangeEvent** class:

```
<fx:Script>
<![CDATA[
import spark.events.IndexChangeEvent;
```

   The **DropDownList** triggers events of this type, so its definition must be imported.

5. Create one public, bound variable:

```
[Bindable]
public var dept:String;
```

   This variable will be used to pass the selected department back to the **DataGrid**.

6. Define the **init( )** function:

```
private function init( ):void {
    dept = data.department;
}
```

   This function is called whenever the **dataChange** event occurs. It assigns to the **dept** variable the value of the current department (coming from the **DataGrid** record). This is necessary so that the current department value doesn't get lost if the user fails to make a selection using the **DropDownList**.

USING THIRD-PARTY CUSTOM CODE

Another benefit of custom code is that instead of creating your own, you can use some of the wonderful custom components that others have already created. A search online will turn up scads of commercial and free options, but you may want to start with the open source FlexLib Project (*http://code.google.com/p/flexlib/*). Also online is RIAForge (*www.riaforge.org*), a Rich Internet Application variant on SourceForge. Finally, the Tour de Flex application also lists and demonstrates some of the most popular custom components around.

7. Define a function for handling the **DropDownList** change event:

```
private function departmentHandler(event:IndexChangeEvent):void {
  dept = event.currentTarget.selectedItem;
}
```

This function assigns to the **dept** variable whatever value was selected in the **DropDownList**.

8. Complete the **Script** block:

```
]]>
</fx:Script>
```

9. Add the **DropDownList**:

```
<s:DropDownList selectedItem="{dept}" change="departmentHandler
(event)">
  <s:ArrayList>
      <fx:String>Accounting</fx:String>
      <fx:String>Human Resources</fx:String>
      <fx:String>Marketing</fx:String>
      <fx:String>Sales</fx:String>
  </s:ArrayList>
</s:DropDownList>
```

The **DropDownList** uses an **ArrayList** of strings as its data provider. The **DropDownList**'s **selectedItem** property is bound to the **dept** variable. When the **DropDownList**'s **change** event occurs, the **department Handler( )** function is called.

tip

The ***DropDownList***'s ***selectedItem*** property could also be bound to ***data.department***.

10. Save the file.

11. In the main MXML file, create the data source:

```
<fx:Script>
<![CDATA[
import mx.collections.ArrayCollection;
[Bindable]
private var employees:ArrayCollection = new ArrayCollection([{firstName:
'John', lastName:'Doe', ext:324, department:'Human Resources'},
{firstName:'Jane', lastName:'Doe', ext:231, department:'Marketing'},
{firstName:'Samuel', lastName:'Smith', ext:212,
department:'Marketing'},
{firstName:'Isabel', lastName:'Jackson', ext:102,
department:'Accounting'}]);
]]>
</fx:Script>
```

The data source for the **DataGrid** will be these four employees represented by an **ArrayCollection**.

12. Create a **DataGrid** instance:

```
<mx:DataGrid width="100%" id="employeesDG"
dataProvider="{employees}" editable="true" x="10" y="10">
  <mx:columns>
    <mx:DataGridColumn headerText="First Name"
    dataField="firstName"/>
    <mx:DataGridColumn headerText="Last Name"
    dataField="lastName"/>
    <mx:DataGridColumn headerText="Department"
    dataField="department" editorDataField="dept" width="200"
    itemEditor="components.DepartmentEditor" />
    <mx:DataGridColumn headerText="Phone Ext." dataField="ext"/>
  </mx:columns>
</mx:DataGrid>
```

The **DataGrid** uses the **employees** variable as its data provider. The entire **DataGrid** is set to be editable. For each of the four columns, the **headerText** and **dataField** properties are assigned. For the department column, the **itemEditor** property is assigned the value of **components.DepartmentEditor**, which is the full package reference of the component just created. As I mention in Chapter 6, when using custom editors, you must always provide full package references (so *components.DepartmentEditor* or *mx.controls.NumericStepper*, not just *Department Editor* or *NumericStepper*).

The **editorDataField** property has a value of *dept*. This is to say that the value returned by the custom editor to the **DataGrid** will be stored in a **dept** variable.

13. Save, run, and test the completed application.

CUSTOM FORMATTERS AND VALIDATORS

If the built-in Flex formatters and validators cannot suit your needs, even with their many adjustable properties, you can create your own custom formatters and validators. In order to do so, you'll need to use ActionScript and more OOP.

A custom formatter can extend either the **Formatter** base class or one of the specific **Formatter** classes, such as **NumberFormatter**. The custom formatter must function like the others, meaning it must have a **format()** method that takes one argument—the data to be formatted, as a generic **Object**—and returns a **String**. Within the **format()** method, the actual formatting takes place. Formatters, by convention, return an empty string if the formatting fails. They also assign to their **error** property a message indicating the problem. Your custom formatter should take these steps, too.

A custom validator can extend either the **Validator** base class or one of the specific **Validator** classes, such as **StringValidator**. The custom validator must have a **doValidation()** method. This method must take one argument, of generic type **Object**, and return an array.

For examples of these, see the Adobe documentation.

11 IMPROVING THE USER EXPERIENCE

In this chapter you'll learn about a hodgepodge of ways you can improve the user's experience with your Flash application. The first part of the chapter covers ways to make a Flex-based application behave more like a desktop application, using menus and virtual pages of content. Then you'll see the flipside of the equation: ways to make Flash interact better with the browser. By the chapter's conclusion, you'll have multiple methods for making your programs more dynamic and professional, while still being backwards compatible for the browser environment. Along the way, you'll also develop one real-world application that integrates most of these techniques.

ESTABLISHING MENUS

Flex defines three components used to create menus: **Menu** (**Figure 11.1**), **MenuBar** (**Figure 11.2**), and **PopUpMenuButton** (**Figure 11.3**). Although they are all similar in purpose, they differ slightly in how they are used.

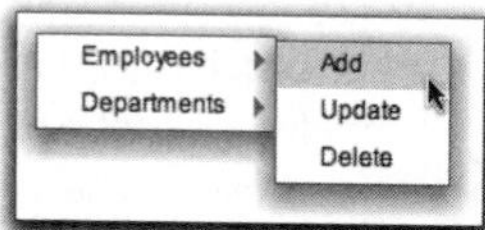

Figure 11.1

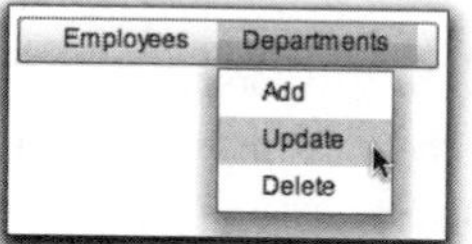

Figure 11.2

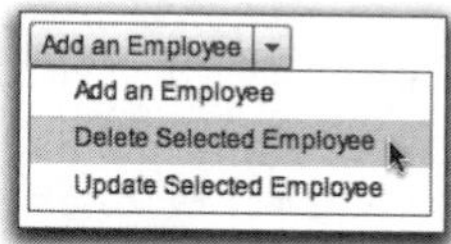

Figure 11.3

The **Menu** control can only be created and manipulated using ActionScript (there is no MXML tag for it). Normally you would create a **Menu** upon a user action, such as clicking a button, and the menu disappears once the user makes a selection, clicks outside of the menu, or presses Escape. To create a **Menu** control in ActionScript, call the **Menu.createMenu()** method. Its first argument is the parent container for the menu. You can use **null** or **this**, to refer to the application as a whole, or have the menu appear relative to a specific container by using that component's **id**. The second argument is the data provider and the third is a Boolean for whether or not the root node of the data source should be displayed.

```
import mx.controls.Menu;
var someMenu:Menu = Menu.createMenu(null, menuData);
```

That code creates the **Menu** but does not actually display it in the application. To do that, call the **show()** method on the **Menu** object, indicating the x and y location for the menu's upper-left corner:

```
someMenu.show(5,5);
```

tip

You can also call the ***hide()*** method on a ***Menu*** object to make it disappear programmatically.

The **MenuBar** control, shown in Figure 11.2, is a permanent horizontal menu bar. It can be created in MXML (or in ActionScript, of course). Its **dataProvider** property dictates the menu options:

```
<mx:MenuBar id="someMenu" dataProvider="{menuData}" />
```

The **PopUpMenuButton**, shown in Figure 11.3, is a two-part control, with a primary button on the left and a pop-up button on the right. The primary button will display the current selection from the pop-up menu. By default, this will be the first option when the component is initially created. When the main button is clicked, the effect is as if the user selected that same option from the menu again. Unlike the **Menu** and **MenuBar** controls, the list of options in a **PopUpMenuButton** is one-dimensional. But like the **MenuBar**, the **dataProvider** property dictates the menu options:

note

The three menu components are all defined in the Halo namespace.

```
<mx:PopUpMenuButton id="someMenu" dataProvider="{menuData}" />
```

Menu Data

Like the components that display data—**DropDownList, Tree, List, DataGrid,** among others, the **dataProvider** property is used to populate the **MenuBar** and **PopUpMenuButton** controls. For the **MenuBar**, the data would be hierarchical in nature, and most likely represented as XML, an **XMLList**, an **XMLList Collection**, or an **ArrayCollection**. For the **PopUpMenuButton**, the data would not be hierarchical and can be as simple as an array.

tip

If the menu options might change dynamically during the use of the application, use an ***XMLListCollection*** or an ***ArrayCollection*** as the data source.

As with the data-driven components, you can define the data source in ActionScript, in an MXML component (in the **Declarations** section) or within the menu component itself. Here's one way to create a **PopUpMenuButton** (this code was used to create what you see in Figure 11.3):

```
<fx:Script>
<![CDATA[
[Bindable]
private var menuData:Array = ['Add an Employee', 'Delete Selected
Employee', 'Update Selected Employee'];
]]>
</fx:Script>
<mx:PopUpMenuButton dataProvider="{menuData}" />
```

And here's a **MenuBar** (see Figure 11.2):

```
<fx:Declarations>
<fx:XML id="menuXML" format="e4x"><menus>
    <menu label="Employees">
        <menuItem label="Add" />
        <menuItem label="Update" />
        <menuItem label="Delete" />
    </menu>
    <menu label="Departments">
        <menuItem label="List" />
        <menuItem label="Add" />
        <menuItem label="Update" />
    </menu>
</menus></fx:XML>
</fx:Declarations>
<mx:MenuBar dataProvider="{menuXML}" labelField="@label"
showRoot="false"/>
```

With an XML data source, the names of the elements in the XML can be anything, but you might as well make them obviously meaningful. Also, if you're using XML as the data provider, you'll most likely want to set the menu component's **showRoot** property to false, as in the above.

No matter how you're creating the menu data—as an **ArrayCollection** or as XML—you can associate different properties with each menu item. The above bit of XML uses the made-up *label* attribute and then the **MenuBar**'s **labelField** property is told to use the **@label** attribute for the menu item labels.

The next most important property to give menu items is **type**. The possible values are *normal*, *check*, *radio*, and *separator*. A normal menu item is just that. A check menu item toggles back and forth between checked and unchecked. The radio menu items are organized in groups, allowing the user to only select one from that group (groups are created using the **groupName** property). A separator item creates a horizontal line. **Figure 11.4** shows this XML as a **Menu**, with one of the menu items already selected:

```
<fx:XML id="formattingMenu" format="e4x">
<menus>
   <menu label="Font Color">
      <menuItem label="red" type="radio" groupName="colors" />
      <menuItem label="yellow" type="radio" groupName="colors" />
      <menuItem label="blue" type="radio" groupName="colors" />
   </menu>
   <menu label="Font Size">
      <menuItem label="Small" type="radio" groupName="sizes" />
      <menuItem label="Medium" type="radio" groupName="sizes" />
      <menuItem label="Large" type="radio" groupName="sizes" />
   </menu>
</menus>
</fx:XML>
```

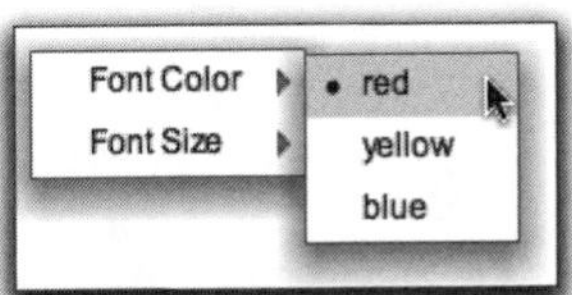

Figure 11.4

Other properties you can give your menu items include **enabled** and **toggled**. If **enabled** is assigned a value of false, that item will be disabled. If **toggled** is assigned a value of true, that item will initially be selected.

The normal type of menu item can have an **icon** property used to associate an icon with it. The value must be the name of a class that represents the image file. To do that, you use an **Embed** metadata directive:

```
[Embed(source='path/to/image.ext')]
[Bindable]
private var iconImage:Class;
```

The variable itself is of generic type **Class** and it will be a reference to the embedded image. To use the variable with the menu, provide the variable as the **icon** property's value. You can use this same technique to apply custom **radioIcon** and **checkedIcon** images.

tip

There's no point for a separator menu item type to have a ***label*** property, as no label will be displayed.

The menu component's **labelField** property is used to indicate which part of the data source is to be used as the displayed text, as you've already seen. You can also use the **labelFunction** property to assign a function whose returned text will be used for the menu label, just like using item renderer functions (discussed in Chapter 6, "Manipulating Data").

Menu Events

Because menus have various behaviors, there are several types of menu events that can be triggered. The **Menu** and **MenuBar** controls share the same events. To start, there's **change**, which is when a new menu selection is made. The **itemClick** event is triggered when the user clicks a normal, check, or radio item, but not a separator, disabled item, or an item that generates a submenu. The **itemRollOver** and **itemRollOut** events occur when the mouse goes over or leaves a menu item. The **menuShow** and **menuHide** events occur when a menu or submenu opens or closes. All of these events are defined in **mx.events.MenuEvent**.

The **PopUpMenuButton** control is actually an extension of the **PopUpButton**, so its events are a bit different. The **PopUpMenuButton** contains two elements: the main button, which is on the left side of the control, and the pop-up button on the right. The main button will display the currently selected menu item and triggers a **MouseEvent click** event when clicked. The pop-up button triggers **MenuEvent change** and **itemClick** events.

Depending upon the menu control and the type of event, the **event** object received by the listener will have one or more of the following properties:

- **item**, the item from the data provider associated with the event
- **index**, the index of the trigger menu item
- **label**, the label of the trigger menu item
- **menu**, the menu control itself

The **item** property is the most important of these and how you use it will depend upon the underlying data type. If the data is a collection of objects, you might use **event.item.*property*** to gather information about the specific item selected. If the data collection is XML, you would use **event.item.@*attribute***.

Starting the Example

Over the course of this chapter you'll continue to build up one Flex application. The example will be tragically self-serving but will do a great job of making practical use of the information being covered. The application will have a menu at the top, organized by topic, through which the user can select one of my books. For the selected book, its description, table of contents, and theoretically more will be available (**Figure 11.5**). While I'll concede that you probably don't have a list of your own books that you'd like to present, this fundamental approach to making information readily available will be usable in many situations you do have. To start, let's create the menu.

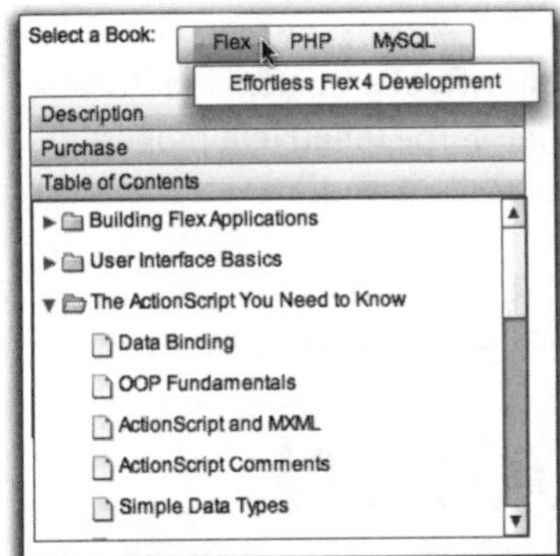

Figure 11.5

tip

If you download the source code from the book's corresponding Web site (*www.dmcinsights.com/flex4/*), you'll find this example in the *Ch11/Ch11_01* folder.

1. Create a new project in Flash Builder or your alternative IDE or text editor.

2. In the **Declarations** section, create the menu data as XML:

```
<fx:Declarations>
<fx:XML id="booksXML" format="e4x">
<subjects>
   <subject label="Flex"><book label="Effortless Flex 4 Development"
   id="flex" /></subject>
   <subject label="PHP">
      <book label="PHP for the Web" id="php" />
      <book label="PHP 6 and MySQL 5 for Dynamic Web Sites"
      id="phpmysql" />
      <book label="PHP 5 Advanced" id="phpadv" />
   </subject>
   <subject label="MySQL">
      <book label="MySQL" id="mysql" />
      <book label="PHP 6 and MySQL 5 for Dynamic Web Sites"
      id="phpmysql" />
   </subject>
</subjects>
</fx:XML>
</fx:Declarations>
```

This data will be used to populate the menus. There are three subjects: Flex, PHP, and MySQL. Within each are listed the books that cover that topic. For each book, there's both a **label**—the book's title—and an **id**. The **id** will be used later in the application.

3. Create a **Label** and a **MenuBar**:

```
<s:Label text="Select a Book:" top="10" left="10"/>
<mx:MenuBar dataProvider="{booksXML}" showRoot="false"
labelField="@label" top="10" left="100"/>
```

The **Label** just acts like a prompt. The **MenuBar** creates the menu itself. Its **dataProvider** points to the XML data. The **showRoot** property is set to false, so that the initial level displays the three topics. The **labelField** property indicates which attribute in the XML should be displayed.

4. Save the file.

   You can run it if you want, although it doesn't do much at this point.

ADDING NAVIGATION

In a Web site, navigation is a matter of having links that take the browser to other HTML pages. But a Flash application behaves more like a desktop application, without obvious pages. Still, by using navigator containers you can create virtual pages in order to hide and show parts of your content as warranted.

tip

The Spark ***NavigatorContent*** is the only Spark container that can go in a Halo navigator container and that is the only way it can be used.

Creating "pages" in Flex is a matter of placing the content within specific containers. An interface element will then control which of the containers is on display. There are three Halo components used to add navigation: **Accordion**, **TabNavigator**, and the **ViewStack**. At the time of this writing, these components have not been implemented in Spark, although they are sure to be in the future. Further, the immediate children of a Halo navigation component can only be either other Halo components or the Spark **NavigatorContent** container, so you can't just use a Spark **Group**, for example, as the content provider.

The Accordion and TabNavigator

The **Accordion** container creates a vertical series of panels with a header bar across the top of each (see Figure 11.5). Clicking that title bar displays that panel, thereby hiding the others. The **TabNavigator** container displays the pages as a series of tabs (**Figure 11.6**). Clicking a tab shows that content. For both containers, you create the pages by placing other containers within the opening and closing tags. The **label** property of each navigation container's children will be used as the text on the navigation control:

```
<mx:TabNavigator>
    <mx:VBox id="vbox1" label="Heading One">
        <s:Label text="This is the content for page one." />
    </mx:VBox>
    <mx:VBox id="vbox2" label="Heading Two">
        <s:Label text="This is the content for page two." />
    </mx:VBox>
    <mx:VBox id="vbox3" label="Heading Three">
        <s:Label text="This is the content for page three." />
    </mx:VBox>
</mx:TabNavigator>
```

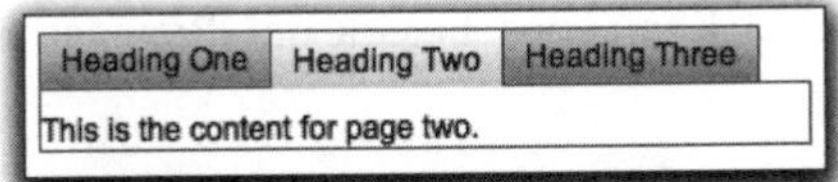

Figure 11.6

For the **Accordion** you can size the overall component using its **width** and **height** properties, or set its **resizeToContent** property to true so that it resizes accordingly for each child. By default, the **TabNavigator** will initially be sized to fit the contents of the first container. The navigator will not resize when other tabs are selected. You can fix the size of the entire component using the **TabNavigator**'s **height** and **width** properties. For both containers, the layout and positioning of elements within each child container will be determined by the individual container.

Both containers have **selectedChild** and **selectedIndex** properties that can be used to get or set the currently selected content provider. The **selectedChild** value will be the **id** of the child, such as *vbox1* above. The **selectedIndex** goes from 0 to the number of children minus one.

The **Accordion** and **TabNavigator** will both trigger a **change** event when the user clicks to go to another panel. You can use this event, along with the **selectedChild** and **selectedIndex** properties to take whatever action in response to the new selection.

The ViewStack and Navigation Button Components

Unlike the **Accordion** and the **TabNavigator**, the **ViewStack** is an empty navigation container that does not have a predefined navigation interface. Like the others, you create multiple children within it, but you'll need to use another component, or set of components to provide navigation. Most commonly, you would use one of the following for that purpose:

- **ButtonBar** (Spark)
- **TabBar** (Spark)
- **LinkBar** (Halo)

Figure 11.7 shows how each of these appears by default. The **ButtonBar** creates a row of horizontal or vertical **Button**s. The **TabBar** creates a row of tabs. The **LinkBar** is similar to the **ButtonBar** except that it creates text links (technically, **LinkButton**s).

Figure 11.7

To use these controls, provide the **ViewStack** component as the **dataProvider**:

```
<s:TabBar dataProvider="{vs}" />
<mx:ViewStack id="vs">
   <mx:VBox id="vbox1" label="Heading One">
      <s:Label text="This is the content for page one." />
   </mx:VBox>
   <mx:VBox id="vbox2" label="Heading Two">
      <s:Label text="This is the content for page two." />
   </mx:VBox>
   <mx:VBox id="vbox3" label="Heading Three">
      <s:Label text="This is the content for page three." />
   </mx:VBox>
</mx:ViewStack>
```

The **ButtonBar** and **TabBar** controls trigger **change** events (of type **Index ChangeEvent**) when used. For the **LinkBar**, you'll want to watch for **itemClick** events. Note that you don't need to add any code to make the navigation controls apply to the **ViewStack**; that will happen automatically through the **dataProvider** association.

Adding to the Example

tip

If you download the source code from the book's corresponding Web site (*www.dmcinsights.com/flex4/*), you'll find this example in the *Ch11/Ch11_02* folder.

Let's use this new information to add an **Accordion** to the work in progress. The **Accordion** will have three children for each book: a description, information on purchasing the title, and the table of contents. To reduce clutter in the MXML file, most of the data will be retrieved from plain text and XML files. More importantly, the contents displayed in the **Accordion** will dynamically change based upon the book being selected. In order to pull that off, a bit more code and explanation will be required. Although I normally try to discuss the MXML and ActionScript code separately in steps like these, here I'm going to sequence the steps by application concept, so I'll go back and forth between MXML and ActionScript.

1. Open the previous project in Flash Builder or your alternative IDE or text editor, if it is not already.

2. Add the **Accordion**:

   ```
   <mx:Accordion id="bookInfo" width="300" height="200" left="10"
   top="50">
   </mx:Accordion>
   ```

   The **Accordion** has an **id** of *bookInfo* and is sized and positioned using fixed values.

3. Within the **Accordion**, add three **NavigatorContent** containers:

```
<s:NavigatorContent label="Description" width="100%"
height="100%">
    <s:TextArea textFlow="{bookDescription}" editable="false"
    width="100%" height="100%" />
</s:NavigatorContent>
<s:NavigatorContent label="Purchase" width="100%" height="100%" />
<s:NavigatorContent id="tocNavigator" label="Table of Contents"
width="100%" height="100%" />
```

It's best to use Spark components when you can, so I'm using Spark **NavigatorContent** containers as the children of the **Accordion**. Each is sized to 100% of the width and height of the **Accordion**. For the first container, the content itself will be represented by a **TextArea**. The text it actually displays will be bound to the **bookDescription** variable. This is assigned to the **textFlow** property, which is where the displayed text goes in a **TextArea** (see Chapter 2, "User Interface Basics," for more).

The second container will theoretically display purchasing information, but I'm not going to actually implement that here. The third child will display the table of contents as a **Tree**. The table of contents for each book will be in XML format, so a **Tree** is a good choice. However, a **Tree** cannot be dynamically updated, so we'll need to use some ActionScript to create it for each book. For that reason, this is also the only container to have an **id** value.

4. In the project folder, add *assets/contents* and *assets/descriptions* folders.

Text files placed in these two directories will be used by the application.

5. In the **Declarations**, add the table of contents for each book:

```
<fx:XML id="flexTOC" source="../assets/contents/flex.xml"
format="e4x" />
<fx:XML id="phpTOC" source="../assets/contents/php.xml"
format="e4x" />
<fx:XML id="phpmysqlTOC" source="../assets/contents/phpmysql.
xml" format="e4x" />
<fx:XML id="phpadvTOC" source="../assets/contents/phpadv.xml"
format="e4x" />
<fx:XML id="mysqlTOC" source="../assets/contents/mysql.xml"
format="e4x" />
```

As I said, I want to store as much data as I can outside of the application, so the table of contents for each book is being stored in separate XML files within the *assets/contents* directory. By using the **fx:XML** component, you can easily represent external XML in an MXML component. This approach is discussed in Chapter 5, "Displaying Data."

6. Create the XML file for each book.

   You should probably just download the code from the book's Web site for this. In short, though, each XML file has the following structure:

```
<?xml version="1.0" encoding="utf-8"?>
<contents>
    <chapter number="1" title="Building Flex Applications">
        <section title="A Survey of the Land" />
        MORE SECTIONS
    </chapter>
    MORE CHAPTERS
</contents>
```

   The files are all stored in the *assets/contents* directory, with the names *flex.xml*, *php.xml*, and so forth.

7. In the **Declarations**, add the description of each book:

```
<fx:String id="flexDescription" source="../assets/descriptions/
flex.txt" />
<fx:String id="phpDescription" source="../assets/descriptions/
php.txt" />
<fx:String id="phpmysqlDescription" source="../assets/descriptions/
phpmysql.txt" />
<fx:String id="phpadvDescription" source="../assets/descriptions/
phpadv.txt" />
<fx:String id="mysqlDescription" source="../assets/descriptions/
mysql.txt" />
```

   This is the same principle as that for the table of contents, but each book's description will be in **String** format instead. The **fx:String** component also has a **source** property that allows you to use a text filename for the string's value.

8. Create the text file for each book.

   Again, you should probably just download the code from the book's Web site for this. These text files are kept quite simple, however:

```
This is the description of "Effortless Flex 4 Development".
This is another paragraph.
```

   The files are all stored in the *assets/descriptions* directory, with the names *flex.txt*, *php.txt*, and so forth.

9. In a **Script** block, create the **bookDescription** variable:

```
import flashx.textLayout.elements.TextFlow;
[Bindable]
private var bookDescription:TextFlow;
```

The new Spark **TextArea** component can display text using the new Text Layout Framework (discussed in Chapter 2). That's a good thing, but it makes assigning text to the control dynamically a bit more challenging. The text itself needs to be represented as a **TextFlow** object, so that definition is first imported and then the variable is declared of that type.

10. Create a variable to represent the current book selection:

```
private var selection:String;
```

This variable will be used globally by the application to reflect the current book being displayed. It's a string that does not need to be bound.

11. Create a variable to represent the table of contents:

```
import mx.controls.Tree;
private var tocTree:Tree;
```

As I said, the **Tree** control is limited in that its data provider cannot be changed dynamically when created in MXML. So instead, I'll create one in ActionScript.

12. Have the application call a function when it's created:

```
<s:Application xmlns:fx="http://ns.adobe.com/mxml/2009"
    xmlns:s="library://ns.adobe.com/flex/spark"
    xmlns:mx="library://ns.adobe.com/flex/mx"
creationComplete="init()">
```

The **init()** function will perform some of the setup.

13. Define the **init()** function:

```
private function init():void {
    tocTree = new Tree();
    tocTree.width = 300;
    tocTree.height = 400;
    tocTree.showRoot = false;
    tocTree.labelField = '@title';
    tocNavigator.addElement(tocTree);
}
```

For now, this function sets the defaults on the table of contents **Tree**. The last two properties are based upon what's known about the underlying XML data. Then the **Tree** is added to the table of contents **NavigatorContent** container. However, at this point there's no assigned **dataProvider**.

14. Have the **MenuBar** call a function when its items are clicked:

```
<mx:MenuBar dataProvider="{booksXML}" showRoot="false"
labelField="@label" top="10" left="100" itemClick=
"handleMenuItemClick(event)"/>
```

The **handleMenuItemClick( )** function will handle the user's interactions with the **MenuBar**.

15. Define the **handleMenuItemClick( )** function:

```
import mx.events.MenuEvent;
private function handleMenuItemClick(event:MenuEvent):void {
  if (event.item.@id != null) {
      selection = event.item.@id;
      updateBookInfo( );
  }
}
```

This function retrieves the **id** attribute from the original **booksXML** and assigns it to the **selection** variable. Then it calls the **updateBookInfo( )** function, which will actually update the **Accordion**.

Because this function receives a **MenuEvent**, that class definition is imported first.

16. Start defining the **updateBookInfo( )** function:

```
private function updateBookInfo( ):void {
  var description:String;
  var toc:XML;
  switch (selection) {
```

This function needs to update what's displayed within the containers of the **Accordion**. For now, that's just the description and table of contents. Two variables will be used to represent that content. A **switch** conditional will assign values to those based upon the currently selected book.

17. Complete the **switch**:

```
case 'flex':
    toc = flexTOC;
    description = flexDescription;
    break;
case 'php':
    toc = phpTOC;
    description = phpDescription;
    break;
```

```
  case 'phpadv':
    toc = phpadvTOC;
    description = phpadvDescription;
    break;
  case 'phpmysql':
    toc = phpmysqlTOC;
    description = phpmysqlDescription;
    break;
  case 'mysql':
    toc = mysqlTOC;
    description = mysqlDescription;
    break;
}
```

For each case, the appropriate table of contents XML will be assigned to the **toc** variable and the appropriate book description string will be assigned to **description**.

18. Set the **dataProvider** for the **Tree**:

```
tocTree.dataProvider = toc;
```

At this point in the function, **toc** is XML data. Just assign that as the **Tree**'s **dataProvider** and the **Tree** will now reflect the table of contents.

19. Update the **bookDescription** variable:

```
bookDescription = TextFlowUtil.importFromString(description,
WhiteSpaceCollapse.PRESERVE);
```

This is entirely new information but isn't that complicated if you follow the syntax properly. What needs to happen is the string stored in the plain text files needs to be converted to a **TextFlow** object so it's usable in a **Text Area**. To do that, the **TextFlowUtil** class's **importFromString( )** method is invoked. Its first argument is the string itself, assigned to **description** in the **switch**. The second argument dictates how white space is handled. If you want it preserved, so that paragraphs and line breaks are maintained, use the **WhiteSpaceCollapse.PRESERVE** constant. To use the method and the constant, you'll also need to import the following two classes:

```
import spark.utils.TextFlowUtil;
import flashx.textLayout.formats.WhiteSpaceCollapse;
```

20. Select the first **Accordion** child and complete the function:

```
  bookInfo.selectedIndex = 0;
}
```

If the user changed books, I want to revert the **Accordion** back to the first child (the description).

21. Save, run, and test the completed application.

    Figure 11.8 shows the result after selecting this Flex book from the menu.

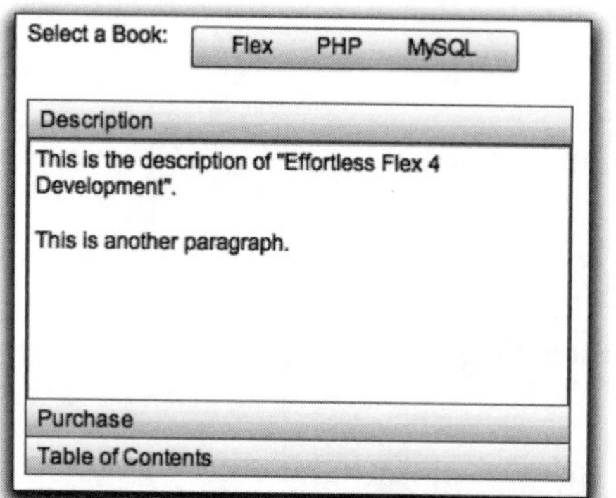

Figure 11.8

USING VIEW STATES

note

How view states work has changed significantly in Flex 4 from earlier versions of Flex.

View states are a way to change an application—its appearance and/or its content—in response to user actions. It's something you've already seen quite frequently: As just one example, buttons look different in their default state, when the user mouses over them, and when the user clicks them.

Creating View States

View states are created by first declaring, in your application or within a specific component, what states exist. To do so, you assign to the **states** property two or more **State** instances:

```
<s:states>
    <s:State name="default" />
    <s:State name="loggedIn" />
</s:states>
```

tip

The default state will be the first state listed, regardless of its name.

You should note that the outer **states** tag is in lowercase as this is a property of the parent component. The parent could be the application itself, a container, or a custom component.

Using View States

Once you've established what states exist, you customize the various *components* to change their properties as needed in different states. When you create an application, every component you define will exist with the set properties in the default state. For example, the following **Button** will be enabled, visible, and have the *Change States* label in every application state:

```
<s:Button label="Change States" />
```

tip

Components, like the ***Button***, will often have their own states that are separate from the application's states.

For each component in an application, you can customize it for the various states by using any of the following:

- The ***property.stateName*** syntax
- **includeIn**
- **excludeFrom**

For example, if you have a **Button** whose label should change based upon the state, you would define its default label and its label in a different state:

```
<s:Button label="Login" label.loggedIn="Logout" />
```

tip

To clear a property value in a state, set its value to ***@Clear()***: ***color.stateName="@Clear()"***.

You can use the ***property.stateName*** approach to set properties such as **label** or **enabled**, stylistic properties like the colors used, and even to change event listeners:

```
<s:Button label="Login" label.loggedIn="Logout" click=
"handleLogin(event)" click.loggedIn="handleLogout(event)" />
```

The **includeIn** and **excludeFrom** properties of a component dictate the states in which the component is visible and active. You can use one or the other, but not both:

```
<mx:Form id="loginForm" excludeFrom="loggedIn">
<!-- Form elements. -->
</mx:Form>
```

If you want to list multiple include or exclude states, separate each name by a comma:

```
<mx:Form id="loginForm" includeIn="default,loggedOut">
<!-- Form elements. -->
</mx:Form>
```

tip

You can use ***includeIn*** and ***excludeFrom*** on every visual component except for ***Application***.

Another way of using **includeIn** and **excludeFrom** are to use state groups. The **States** tag has a **stateGroups** property that can be used to group states together. You can then more easily use this group name for the **includeIn** or **excludeFrom** values:

```
<s:State name="default" />
<s:State name="show" stateGroups="products" />
<s:State name="cart" stateGroups="products" />
<s:State name="list" stateGroups="products" />
```

You can even place the same state in multiple groups, by separating each with a comma:

```
<s:State name="default" />
<s:State name="show" stateGroups="products" />
<s:State name="cart" stateGroups="products,ordering" />
```

WHEN TO CREATE COMPONENTS

By default, Flex will create new components required by a view state when the components are required. For example, if your application switches from stateA to stateB, and a **Button** only exists in stateB, it'll be created when the view state switch occurs. If you have a component that might take a little time to create, and you don't want that to be apparent to the end user, you can assign the value *immediate* to the component's **itemCreationPolicy** property:

```
<mx:DataGrid dataProvider="{someData}" itemCreationPolicy="immediate">
```

Now the component will be created when the application loads and be immediately available when the state changes.

View State Events

When the view state changes, four events are triggered: **enterState**, **exitState**, **currentStateChanging**, and **currentStateChange**. You can watch for the first two events on the **State** elements:

```
<s:State name="loggedIn" enterState="prepLogin(event)" />
```

The second two events are triggered by the component whose state is changing.

View States and Custom Components

Figure 11.9

Effortless Flex 4 Development

Written by Larry Ullman
Published 2010

Figure 11.10

Custom components, covered in Chapter 10, "Creating Custom Code," can have their own states. Just define the states as a property of the custom component's root tag. For example, say that you create a **BookInfoGroup** custom component that would show the book's cover in one state and the book's information in another (**Figures 11.9** and **11.10**). Such a component would have two states:

```
<?xml version="1.0" encoding="utf-8"?>
<s:VGroup xmlns:fx="http://ns.adobe.com/mxml/2009"
   xmlns:s="library://ns.adobe.com/flex/spark"
   xmlns:mx="library://ns.adobe.com/flex/mx">
   <s:states>
      <s:State name="default" />
      <s:State name="info" />
   </s:states>
</s:VGroup>
```

Within the **VGroup**, you might have an **Image** that appears in one state and a **RichText** that appears in the other:

```
<mx:Image source="@Embed('../assets/coverSmall.png')" includeIn=
"default" />
<s:RichText includeIn="info" width="123" height="150">
    <s:textFlow>
        <s:TextFlow>
            <s:div><s:span fontSize="16">Effortless Flex 4 Development
            </s:span><s:br />
                <s:p>Written by Larry Ullman<s:br />Published 2010</s:p>
            </s:div>
        </s:TextFlow>
    </s:textFlow>
</s:RichText>
```

When you create an instance of that custom component (in the primary application MXML), you can set the component's state using its **currentState** property. In this code, the **BookInfoGroup** component's state is changed when the user mouses over it or mouses out:

```
<cx:BookInfoGroup id="book" mouseOver="book.currentState = 'info'"
mouseOut="book.currentState = 'default'" />
```

tip

You can also use view states within item renderers to change how items are rendered based upon the user's actions.

View States in Flash Builder

If you're using Flash Builder for your Flex development, it has some of its own tools for creating and using view states, most of which are apparent in Design mode. For starters, there's the States panel (**Figure 11.11**) that lets you add, edit, and delete states for the application as a whole or for individual components. When you click the button to add a new state, you're presented with a simple interface for naming and defining it (**Figure 11.12**).

Figure 11.11

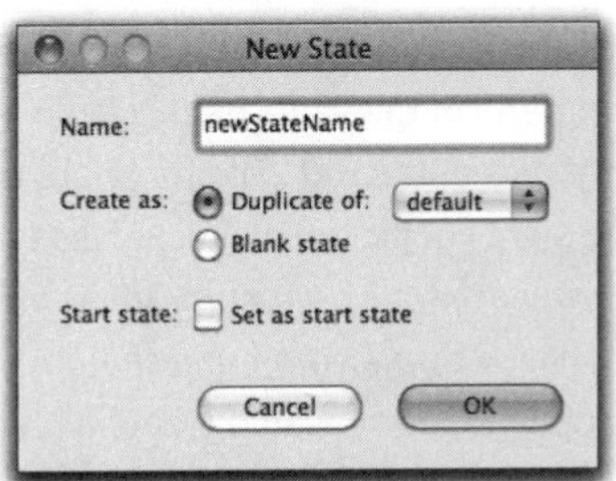

Figure 11.12

Second, when you have more than one state, the Common area of the Properties panel will let you select in which states the selected component will be available (**Figure 11.13**). Finally, you can use the State drop-down at the top of the Design mode window to select which state to view (**Figure 11.14**). By switching states there, you can see how the application or specific component looks in each existing state. If you use the State drop-down in Source mode, components that are inactive in the selected state will appear in grey.

Figure 11.13

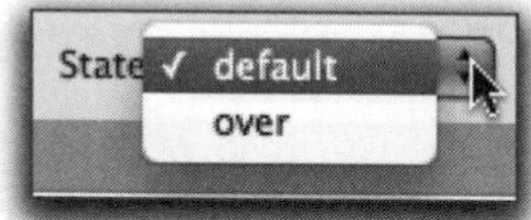

Figure 11.14

ADDING DEEP LINKING

A Flash application behaves more like a desktop application than an HTML page in many ways. Just one example is that by using navigational elements and view states, what users see—what "page" they are on—can change without making an obvious server request, reloading the page, or going to a new HTML page. This is a great thing in terms of the user experience but it also means that you lose the ability to bookmark the "page," share it, or navigate the application using the browser's back and forward buttons (which would be a habit for most users). A solution is to use *deep linking*: a way to tie a Flash application's current setup to a unique URL.

Deep linking works by literally changing the URL so that the browser treats different Flash compositions as if they were different pages (or, technically, different parts of the same page). To do so, you use ActionScript to update the *fragment* part of the URL. The fragment comes at the very end of a URL, after a pound sign. For example, if your Flash application is run through the page *http://www.example.com/something.html*, the deeply linked URLs would be *http://www.example.com/something.html#identifier*. For each notable page in the application you would create a unique identifier. With unique identifiers, the browser will record each "page" as a separate record in its history. The Flash application can then check for a fragment when the browser's URL changes in order to establish what content should be shown.

tip

Deep linking replaces an older approach using the ***HistoryManager*** class.

tip

The URL fragment is also known as the anchor, as it anchors the browser to a specific spot on the page.

tip

Deep linking requires that JavaScript be enabled and requires a supported browser, such as Internet Explorer 6 and greater (Windows), Safari (Mac OS X), or Firefox (Windows, Mac).

Setting Up the HTML Page

The first thing you'll need to do to allow for deep linking is set up the HTML page. Along with the HTML page itself and the Flash SWF application, you'll need to provide the following files:

- *history.css*
- *history.js*
- *historyFrame.html*

Flash Builder will automatically generate these for you and samples are also included in the Flex SDK. The recommendation is to create a directory called *history*, in the same folder as the HTML page that includes the Flash application. Those three files would then be stored in the *history* folder.

The HTML page needs to include the CSS and the JavaScript at some point:

```
<link rel="stylesheet" type="text/css" href="history/history.css" />
<script src="history/history.js" language="javascript" />
```

Again, if you're using Flash Builder, the outputted HTML wrapper for the Flash application will do this automatically. If you're not using Flash Builder, you'll need to add this code to the HTML wrapper yourself.

Using the BrowserManager

The **BrowserManager** is the ActionScript class that's used to communicate with the JavaScript running in the browser. You'll first need to import three classes:

```
import mx.managers.BrowserManager;
import mx.managers.IBrowserManager;
import mx.events.BrowserChangeEvent;
```

The **BrowserManager** class defines the functionality you'll need. It returns an object of type **IBrowserManager** that you'll use to interact with the browser. The **BrowserChangeEvent** is what the application should watch for in order to adjust the Flash to the URL.

To start, you'll want to create an instance of the **BrowserManager** in a function called when the application loads:

```
private var browserManager:IBrowserManager;
private function init( ):void {
    browserManager = BrowserManager.getInstance( );
}
```

After getting the **BrowserManager** instance, the application should initialize it:

browserManager.init( );

The **BrowserManager**'s **init( )** method takes two optional arguments: The first is the fragment and the second is the title to be associated with that fragment. If you want to initialize the manager for the opening status with a custom title, you could do the following:

browserManager.init('', 'Welcome to This Thing!');

Your application needs to pay attention to the user's actions in order to decide when to create "bookmarks" for the current arrangement of elements. At those times, you use the **setFragment( )** method to create a specific URL fragment:

browserManager.setFragment('*name=value*');

The *name* and *value* values should be something both meaningful yet brief, such as *id=X* (where X is a significant number) or *dept=Accounting*.

You can add multiple pieces of information to the fragment, too, separating each by an ampersand:

browserManager.setFragment('product=35&page=details');

In order to associate a custom title with the bookmark, call the **setTitle( )** method *prior to* calling **setFragment( )**:

browserManager.setTitle('Fancy Widget Details');
browserManager.setFragment('product=35&page=details');

The **BrowserManager** has three events you might listen for: **browserURLChange**, **urlChange**, and **applicationURLChange**. The **browserURLChange** event is the most important of these. It will be triggered when the user clicks the back or forward buttons. It will also be triggered when the user manually changes the URL in the address bar and presses Return/Enter (although this is less common). An **applicationURLChange** event occurs when the URL is changed programmatically (e.g., when you invoke the **setFragment( )** method). A **urlChange** event is triggered when either of the other two events occur.

tip

If your application uses states, you can use the ***BrowserManager*** to reflect the current state in the URL fragment.

With this in mind, you should add an event listener for the **browserURLChange** event so that the application can watch for, and respond to, user actions:

browserManager.addEventListener(BrowserChangeEvent.BROWSER_URL_CHANGE, handleURLChange);

Reading the URL

Part of the deep-linking process is setting new URL fragments (and titles) for different application pages. The second part is reading in a URL fragment and adjusting the Flash application accordingly. This is something the application would do when **browserURLChange** events occur. Here's the start of that event handler:

```
private function handleURLChange(event:BrowserChangeEvent):void {
}
```

Within the function, you would need to parse the **BrowserManager**'s **fragment** property. That's easily done using the **URLUtil** class's **stringToObject( )** method, which converts a string to an object. It's defined in **mx.utils.URLUtil**, so that must be imported first:

```
import mx.utils.URLUtil;
private function handleURLChange(event:BrowserChangeEvent):void {
    var fragment:Object = URLUtil.stringToObject(browserManager.fragment);
}
```

If the fragment would have multiple pieces of information separated by an ampersand, as in *product=35&page=details*, you should indicate the separator to the **stringToObject( )** method:

```
var fragment:Object = URLUtil.stringToObject(browserManager.fragment, '&');
```

tip

The default separator for the ***stringToObject( )*** method is a semicolon.

At this point, assuming the fragment *product=35&page=details*, **fragment.product** has a value of 35 and **fragment.page** has a value of *details*. You can use that information to adjust the Flash application. You'll see an example of this shortly.

Watching for **browserURLChange** events will allow the application to respond to the back and forward browser buttons, but you should also examine the URL fragment when the application first loads to see if it should have any initial page settings. This would be the case should the user come directly to a page, such as *something.html#product=35&page=details* from a bookmark, a link in an e-mail, or a link on another HTML page. To address this possibility, you should also parse the URL for its fragment when the application first loads.

Completing the Example

tip

If you download the source code from the book's corresponding Web site (*www.dmcinsights.com/flex4/*), you'll find this example in the *Ch11/Ch11_03* folder.

Let's wrap up the ongoing example by adding deep-linking functionality so that the selected book and current page of the **Accordion** are both noted. By doing so, users will be able to bookmark, for example, a specific book's table of contents, and they can use their back and forward buttons to navigate their history.

1. Open the previous project in Flash Builder or your alternative IDE or text editor, if it is not already.

2. Import the necessary classes and create a new variable:

   ```
   import mx.managers.BrowserManager;
   import mx.managers.IBrowserManager;
   import mx.events.BrowserChangeEvent;
   import mx.utils.URLUtil;
   private var browserManager:IBrowserManager;
   ```

   The four classes are required to provide deep-linking functionality. The **browserManager** variable will be used to access the **BrowserManager** instance anywhere in the application (it must be declared outside of any function for that to be possible).

3. Within the **init( )** function, set up the **BrowserManager**:

   ```
   browserManager = BrowserManager.getInstance( );
   browserManager.addEventListener(BrowserChangeEvent.BROWSER_
   URL_CHANGE, handleURLChange);
   browserManager.init( );
   ```

   First, the **BrowserManager** instance is fetched. Then an event listener is added to the object, so that when a **browserURLChange** event occurs, the **handleURLChange** function is called.

4. Finally (still in the **init( )** function), call the **handleURLChange( )** function:

   ```
   handleURLChange(new BrowserChangeEvent('BrowserChangeEvent'));
   ```

   The **handleURLChange( )** function will be written so that it responds to **browserURLChange** events. When those occur, that function will parse the fragment of the URL and set the stage accordingly. This should also be done when the application first loads, so the function should be called in the **init( )** function. However, the **handleURLChange( )** function expects to receive one argument of type **BrowserChangeEvent**, so a new, dummy **Browser ChangeEvent** should be created and passed along in this function call.

5. Add **setTitle( )** and **setFragment( )** method calls to the **handleMenuItem Click( )** function:

```
private function handleMenuItemClick(event:MenuEvent):void {
    if (event.item.@id != null) {
        selection = event.item.@id;
        updateBookInfo( );
        browserManager.setTitle(event.item.@label);
        browserManager.setFragment('id='+selection);
    }
}
```

   To make the selection of a book be its own URL, the **setTitle( )** and **setFragment( )** methods need to be invoked in this function, which is called when menu items are selected. For the title, I want to use the book's title. Since **event.item** refers to the underlying XML used to populate the **MenuBar**, **event.item.@label** will be, for example, *Effortless Flex 4 Development*. For the fragment, I want to use the syntax *id=XXX*, where *XXX* is the **id** attribute from the XML, which has already been assigned to **selection**.

6. Add a **change** event handler to the **Accordion**:

```
<mx:Accordion id="bookInfo" width="300" height="200" left="10"
top="50" change="handleBookInfoChange(event)">
```

   To record which **Accordion** child is being displayed, an event handler has to watch for changes on this component.

7. Define the **handleBookInfoChange( )** function:

```
import mx.events.IndexChangedEvent;
private function handleBookInfoChange(event:IndexChangedEvent):void {
    browserManager.setTitle(booksXML.subject.book.(@id==selection).
    @label + '::' + event.target.selectedChild.label);
    browserManager.setFragment('id='+selection+'&a='+event.
    newIndex);
}
```

   This function is called when the user clicks the **Accordion** to change which child container is in view. All this function has to do is create a new fragment (and title) to reflect the change. For the title, I want to use the book's title plus the name of the **Accordion** child, resulting in, for example, *Effortless Flex 4 Development Table of Contents*. To find the book's title, I'll need to drill down into the original **booksXML** to find the **@label** value for the **book** element that has an **id** attribute equal to **selection**. This is just using E4X to find something within XML. For the second part of the title, I want the **label** property from the selected **Accordion** child, available through **event.target.selectedChild** (because the event target in this function is the **Accordion**).

For the fragment, the selected **Accordion** index should be appended to the *id*, resulting in *id=XXX&a=Y*. When the **Accordion**'s **change** event occurs, the **event** object's **newIndex** property reflects the currently selected item's index.

8. Begin defining the **handleURLChange( )** function:

```
private function handleURLChange(event:BrowserChangeEvent):void {
    var fragment:Object = URLUtil.stringToObject(browserManager.
    fragment, '&');
```

This function is called when the application is first loaded or when the browser's URL changes. It needs to parse the fragment section of the URL and set up the application. To start, it calls the **URLUtil.stringToObject( )** method to create an object from the URL fragment.

9. If there is a new fragment *id*, change the selected book:

```
if (fragment.id && (selection != fragment.id)) {
    selection = fragment.id;
    updateBookInfo( );
}
```

The first part of the conditional checks for a **fragment.id** value. There would not be one if the application were loaded without any fragments. The second part of the conditional checks if the **fragment.id** value is not the same as the current selection. If so, **selection** is assigned this new value and the **updateBookInfo( )** function, which changes the data in the **Accordion** containers, is called. This conditional ensures that the **Accordion** is only updated if the user's action requests a new book's information (as opposed to just a different page in the **Accordion** for the same book).

10. If there is a **fragment.a** property, change the **Accordion** selection:

```
if (fragment.a) {
    bookInfo.selectedIndex = fragment.a;
}
```

The **a** property of the fragment would reflect the viewed **Accordion** child. If it exists, that child of the **Accordion** should be selected.

11. Complete the **handleURLChange( )** function:

```
}
```

12. Save, run, and test the completed application.

Figure 11.15 shows the browser after selecting a book from the menu. **Figure 11.16** shows the browser after changing the **Accordion**. Make note of the URL and browser title in both images.

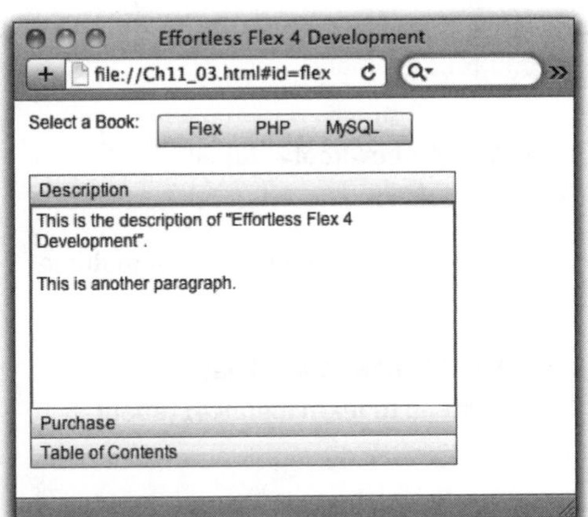

Figure 11.15

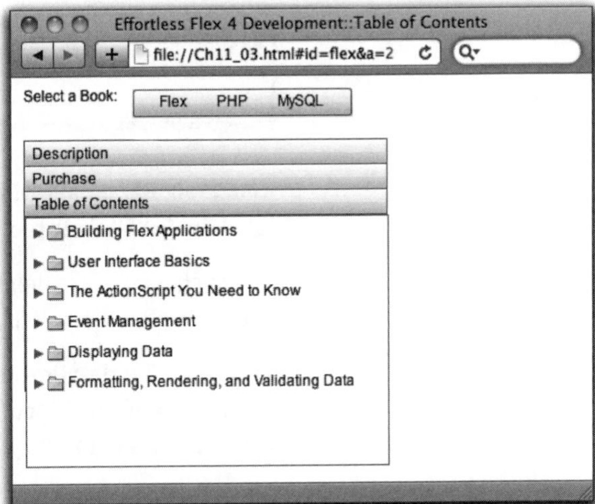

Figure 11.16

CUSTOMIZING THE CURSOR

In a Flex application you can even manipulate the user interface to the point of customizing the cursor. Through the **CursorManager**, you can replace the default cursor with a JPEG, GIF, PNG, or SVG file. You can also use a Sprite object or SWF for that purpose. By default, the Flash application will use the system cursor, whatever the user has that set to be. There's also a default busy cursor, which is an animated clock.

To change the cursor, you'll need to create a variable reference to the image file:

```
[Embed(source="../assets/cursor.jpg")]
private var myCursor:Class;
```

Then provide that variable to the **setCursor()** method:

```
CursorManager.setCursor(myCursor);
```

You can establish a custom busy cursor using the **setBusyCursor()** method:

```
CursorManager.setBusyCursor(myBusyCursor);
```

The busy cursor is used by the Image, SWFLoader, and Web services components to indicate they're processing.

MORE ON TOOLTIPS

In Chapter 2, I introduce the **ToolTip**, which is a simple way to provide some visual cues to users as they interact with your application (**Figure 11.17**):

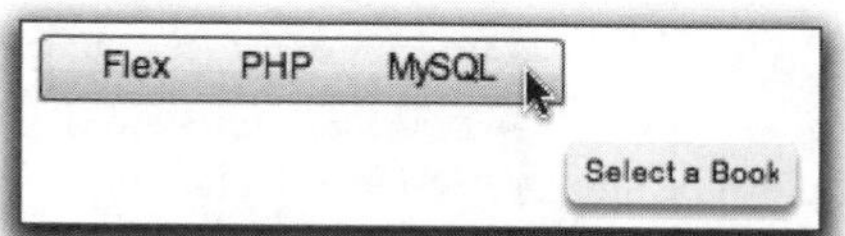

Figure 11.17

```
<mx:MenuBar dataProvider="{booksXML}" showRoot="false"
labelField="@label" toolTip="Select a Book"/>
```

In that chapter, I also mention that you can display your tip text over multiple lines using the **
** entity:

```
<mx:MenuBar dataProvider="{booksXML}" showRoot="false"
labelField="@label" toolTip="Use this menu to learn more&#13about
any of Larry's books." />
```

When setting a **ToolTip** using ActionScript, you can use the newline character (**\n**) instead:

```
menuBarId.toolTip = "Use this menu to learn more\nabout any of Larry's
books.";
```

Through the **ToolTipManager**, there are other ways you can manipulate how **ToolTip**s work in Flex. To access the **ToolTipManager**, you'll need to import its class definition in your ActionScript code:

```
import mx.managers.ToolTipManager;
```

Once you've done that, you can set **ToolTip** behavior through the manager. This next line disables **ToolTip**s entirely:

```
ToolTipManager.enabled = false;
```

There are three time-related settings when it comes to **ToolTip**s: **showDelay**, **hideDelay**, and **scrubDelay**. The **showDelay** setting is how long the user must mouse over a component before its **ToolTip** is displayed. The default value is 500 milliseconds, which is half a second (all these settings use milliseconds). You can change this to your liking, although you wouldn't want to set this delay too low or else **ToolTip**s will be consistently appearing.

The **hideDelay** is really how long the **ToolTip** is displayed while the mouse is over the component (i.e., it's the delay until the tip is hidden). By default, the **ToolTip** will be shown for ten seconds (10,000 milliseconds) or until the mouse leaves the component, whichever comes first. If you set the **hideDelay** to 0, the tip will not be shown; set to *Infinity*, the tip will remain until the mouse leaves the component.

The **scrubDelay** is kind of tricky as it's affected by the **showDelay**. If a user mouses over component A, that **ToolTip** will be shown after **showDelay** milliseconds. If the user then moves the mouse over component B within **scrubDelay** milliseconds, component B's **ToolTip** will be shown immediately, instead of after **showDelay** milliseconds.

tip

Error messages generated by validators are actually custom ToolTips.

PROMOTING ACCESSIBILITIES

Along with supporting the ability to use the browser's back and forward buttons, and the browser's bookmarks, Flash applications should also be aware of accessibility issues. A properly designed Web page is still usable by visually impaired users. By default, accessibility features are enabled in Flex applications, such as the use of ToolTips to indicate to screen readers the role of interface elements. That's a good start, but you can take accessibility much further. The Adobe documentation has lots of information regarding accessibility, from good design policies to specifics on how individual components support accessibility to using ActionScript to even further improve the accessibility of your application.

tip

In Chapter 13, "Improving the Appearance," you'll see how to stylize ToolTips.

12 ALERTS AND POP-UPS

All of the examples in the book up to this point have taken place entirely within the primary application window. There are many times, though, when you have the need to create secondary windows, be they very basic notifications or closer in style and functionality to the primary application window. Doing either in Flex is a snap. In this chapter you'll first learn about **Alert**, used to create notifications with very little user interface. You'll also see how to customize the **Alert** to make it as useful as possible. The second part of the chapter walks through creating and customizing secondary windows that can pop up separately from the primary window.

WORKING WITH ALERTS

The **Alert** class defines the ability to create, manipulate, and reference basic pop-up windows (**Figure 12.1**). Like the JavaScript **Alert**, a Flex **Alert** can only relate basic information and take a minimal amount of user response. Also like the JavaScript **Alert**, the Flex **Alert** can easily be annoying if used too often!

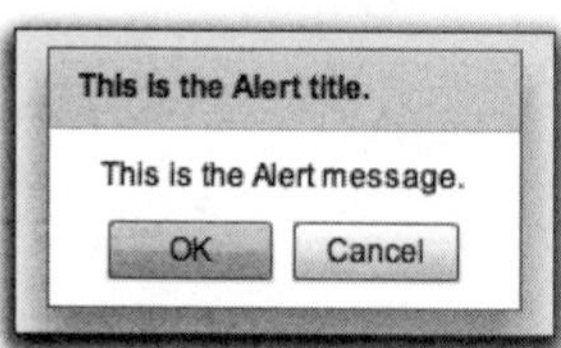

Figure 12.1

Creating a Basic Alert

An **Alert** will only ever be referenced using ActionScript, so you must first import that class definition within your **Script** tags:

```
<fx:Script>
<![CDATA[
import mx.controls.Alert;
]]>
</fx:Script>
```

The **Alert** method that creates the notification window is **show( )**. Its first argument is the most important—the text message that should be displayed (**Figure 12.2**):

```
Alert.show('Oh, hello!');
```

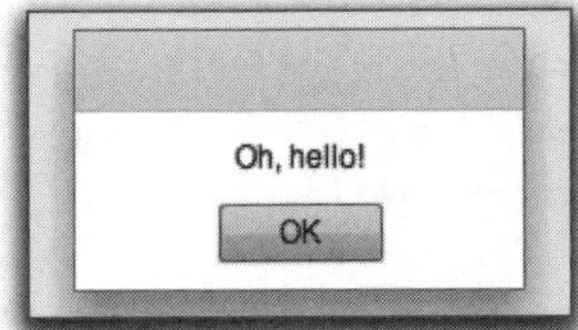

Figure 12.2

When it comes to debugging applications, **Alert** can be one of your best friends, as you can use it to indicate the progress of the app:

```
Alert.show('Now in the button click event handler.');
```

Or you can use it to display the value of a variable:

```
Alert.show('The value of someVar is ' + someVar.toString( ));
```

Unless you're using **Alert** for debugging purposes, you probably don't want that empty area at the top of the notification, which is where the **Alert**'s title goes (compare Figure 12.2 with Figure 12.1). To provide a title, use the second argument to the **show( )** method:

```
Alert.show('The record has been updated.', 'Status');
```

Before going any further, there are two quick things you should know about **Alert**s. First, an **Alert** is *modal*, which means that it keeps all of the user focus while it exists. In other words, from the time the **Alert** appears to the time the user clicks one of its buttons (or presses an appropriate key), the user cannot interact with the primary application window. Second, and this may sound contradictory, the application continues to run while the **Alert** exists. After the **Alert.show( )**, if there are any other statements, those will continue to be executed. And, for that matter, the application will still be able to handle non-user events and respond accordingly.

note

If you create multiple ***Alert***s at once, the last created ***Alert*** will have the current focus (i.e., appear on top of the others).

tip

If you don't set an ***Alert***'s size, it'll automatically be sized to display its contents.

note

Alert buttons can only appear in the order OK, Yes, No, Cancel, regardless of how they are ordered as the third argument to the ***show()*** method.

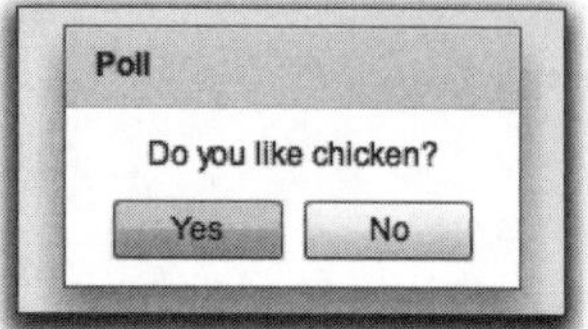

Figure 12.3

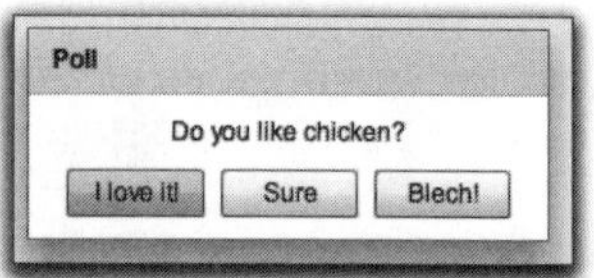

Figure 12.4

note

Changing the labels via the ***Alert*** class changes them for every ***Alert*** created by an application.

tip

You can change the sizes of the buttons using the ***Alert.buttonHeight*** and ***Alert.buttonWidth*** properties.

Customizing the Look

The **Alert** is restricted as to what it can display—you can't create a form within it or add any other MXML components, but that doesn't mean there's nothing you can do. For starters, you can set the **Alert**'s **height** and **width** properties. To do so, start by assigning the **Alert.show( )** call to a new variable:

```
var myAlert:Alert = Alert.show('message');
myAlert.height = 300;
myAlert.width = 300;
```

Now you might think this process is backwards—creating an **Alert**, then customizing it, but this is the way it works. You need an object to reference before setting its properties. But rest assured that the properties you set will take effect fast enough to be unnoticeable to the user.

You can do a lot more customization by adjusting the buttons that are displayed (discussed next) or by styling the **Alert** (styling is covered in the next chapter).

The Alert Buttons

By default, an **Alert** only creates one button with a label of *OK*, but it can have up to four buttons, whose default labels are *OK*, *Yes*, *No*, and *Cancel*. To indicate which buttons should be present, you use the **Alert.show( )** method's third argument, providing it with the corresponding constants, each separated by a | (the "pipe" character). The following **Alert** will only have *Yes* and *No* buttons (**Figure 12.3**):

```
Alert.show('Do you like chicken?', 'Poll', Alert.YES|Alert.NO);
```

You can change the displayed text on the buttons using the **cancelLabel**, **noLabel**, **okLabel**, and **yesLabel** properties on the **Alert** class itself (**Figure 12.4**):

```
Alert.okLabel = 'I love it!';
Alert.yesLabel = 'Sure';
Alert.noLabel = 'Blech!';
Alert.show('Do you like chicken?', 'Poll', Alert.OK|Alert.YES|Alert.NO);
```

Because you can't change the order of the displayed buttons, I just used the first three button options and changed their labels to what I needed.

The **Alert**'s default button is that which will be virtually clicked if the user presses Enter or Return. This button is also highlighted to indicate its status (see the *I love it!* button in Figure 12.4). The default button is *OK* (or *Yes*, if there is no *OK* option); the Escape key will trigger the *Cancel* or *No* button.

You can identify the default button, that which is virtually clicked if the user presses Enter or Return via the seventh argument to **show( )**. I haven't gotten to arguments four through six yet, so just use *this*, *null*, and *null* for those values until I explain them fully (**Figure 12.5**):

```
Alert.okLabel = 'I love it!';
Alert.yesLabel = 'Sure';
Alert.noLabel = 'Blech!';
Alert.show('Do you like chicken?', 'Poll', Alert.OK|Alert.YES|Alert.NO, this,
null, null, Alert.YES);
```

Figure 12.5

Handling Alert Events

When you have more than one button, you'll want the application to react differently based upon which button the user selected (by either clicking or pressing Enter/Return or Escape). The fifth argument to **Alert.show( )** is where you can identify an event handler. However, the fourth argument hasn't yet been discussed. This is where you identify the parent of the **Alert**. For this argument, use the special keyword **this**, which refers to the current object (i.e., the primary application window):

```
Alert.show('message', 'title', Alert.OK, this, alertListener);
```

As you can see in that line, you also need to name what buttons should exist, even if only using the single default button, because you can't skip any arguments.

When the user closes that **Alert** by clicking a button or using the keyboard, the **alertListener( )** function will be called. It needs to be defined so that it takes an argument of type **CloseEvent**:

```
import mx.events.CloseEvent;
private function alertListener(event:CloseEvent):void {
    // Do whatever.
}
```

Within the function, the event object's **detail** property reflects the selected button:

```
if (event.detail == Alert.YES) {
    // Do this.
} else if (event.detail == Alert.NO) {
    // Do this instead.
}
```

tip

If you download the source code from the book's corresponding Web site (*www.dmcinsights.com/flex4/*), you'll find this example in the *Ch12/Ch12_01* folder.

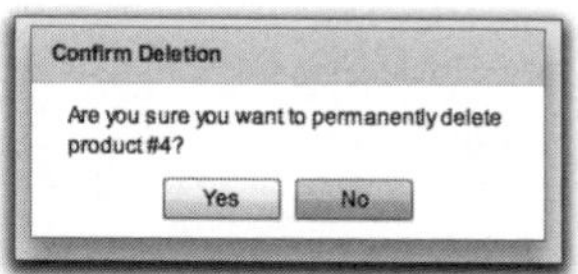

Figure 12.6

Putting It Together

To demonstrate a reasonable use of an Alert (for non-debugging purposes), I want to return to the *Ch09_03* example. In it, the selection of a record in the **DataGrid** and the clicking of the *Delete* button immediately removed the record. It'd be better to give the user a chance to reconsider before making that deletion. Let's update that example accordingly.

1. Open the project in Flash Builder or your alternative IDE or text editor.
2. Within the **Script** tags, import the **Alert** definition:

   ```
   import mx.controls.Alert;
   ```

3. Change the body of the **deleteButton_clickHandler( )** function to

   ```
   if (productsDG.selectedIndex > -1) {
       Alert.show('Are you sure you want to permanently delete product #' +
       productsDG.selectedItem.id +'?', 'Confirm Deletion', Alert.YES|Alert.
       NO, this, deleteAlertHandler, null, Alert.No);
   }
   ```

   Previously, the function checked that a product was selected, and then called the delete operation. Now it'll prompt the user instead. The prompt shows the product number and has *Yes* and *No* buttons, with *No* being the default as an extra precaution (**Figure 12.6**). When the user clicks a button or presses the right key, the **deleteAlertHandler( )** function will be called.

4. Define the **deleteAlertHandler( )** function:

   ```
   private function deleteAlertHandler(event:CloseEvent):void {
       if (event.detail == Alert.YES) {
           productsService.deleteProduct(productsDG.selectedItem.id);
       }
   }
   ```

   This function is called when the user clicks either **Alert** button, or presses Enter/Return or Escape. It confirms that the *Yes* button was selected and, if so, invokes the *deleteProduct* operation. It does not do anything if the user selected *No*, although you could easily do something in that case (such as notify the user that the product was not deleted).

5. Add the **CloseEvent** definition to the **Script** section:

   ```
   import mx.events.CloseEvent;
   ```

   This is necessary as the **deleteAlertHandler( )** takes an argument of type **CloseEvent**.

6. Save, run, and test the completed application.

Adding an Image

As I said, there's not much you can do with the contents of an Alert, but it is possible to add a single graphic to it using the sixth argument to the **show()** method. To start, you need to create an ActionScript variable that will represent the image. The variable needs to be bindable and use the **Embed** metadata to associate the image file:

```
[Embed(source='path/to/image.ext')]
[Bindable]
private var alertImage:Class;
```

The variable itself is of generic type **Class** and it will be a reference to the embedded image. To use the variable with the **Alert**, provide the variable as the **show()** method's sixth argument:

```
Alert.show('message', 'title', mx.controls.Alert.OK, this, null, alertImage);
```

Figure 12.7 shows the result of the following code:

```
[Embed(source='../assets/coverSmall.png')]
[Bindable]
private var alertImage:Class;
Alert.show('Do you like the cover?', 'Poll', Alert.YES|Alert.NO, this, null,
alertImage);
```

Figure 12.7

CREATING POP-UP WINDOWS

If you need to create more elaborate pop-up windows, for example, to display a form or a chart of information, you'll need to use a combination of the **TitleWindow** MXML component and the **PopUpManager** ActionScript class.

The TitleWindow Component

When you create a pop-up window for a Web page using JavaScript, the pop-up itself will be another HTML page. In Flex, the pop-up itself will be another MXML page, but instead of using **Application** or **ApplicationWindow** as the root element, it will use **TitleWindow**. **TitleWindow** is an extension of the **Panel**, intended to be used as a pop-up window. It has a title bar and a main content area. The title bar will also contain an X button for the user to close the window (**Figure 12.8**).

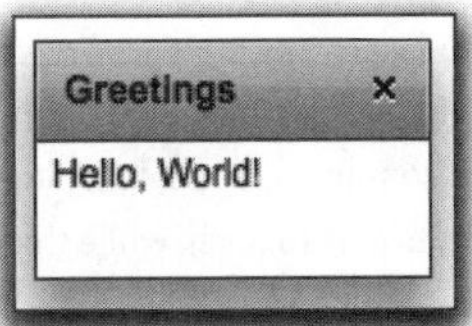

Figure 12.8

note

An entire application can only have one ***Application*** component.

tip

You can create a pop-up window entirely in ActionScript, without using MXML, but doing so is less common.

tip

If you really want to change the overall appearance, you can create a custom skin for the ***TitleWindow*** component (see Chapter 13, "Improving the Appearance").

tip

The ***TitleWindow***, like the ***Panel***, can have a control bar at the bottom of the window.

tip

As with the ***Alert***, the main application continues to run, listening to events and so forth, while the pop-up window is open.

The pop-up up shown in Figure 12.8 is generated by the following code:

```
<?xml version="1.0" encoding="utf-8"?>
<s:TitleWindow xmlns:fx="http://ns.adobe.com/mxml/2009"
   xmlns:s="library://ns.adobe.com/flex/spark"
   xmlns:mx="library://ns.adobe.com/flex/mx" width="130" height="75"
   title="Greetings">
   <s:Label x="5" y="5" text="Hello, World!"/>
</s:TitleWindow>
```

The **TitleWindow** component has many properties you'll want to use, such as **width**, **height**, and **title** in the above. You can position the window relative to the Flash application using the **x** and **y** properties. You can even rotate the window, if you want to do something unusual.

Between the root **TitleWindow** tags, you can put pretty much anything you want, just like you would within a **Panel**. This includes everything from other MXML components to the layout classes. You can also place ActionScript, CSS, declarations, and so forth, as you would within the primary application window or a custom component.

The PopUpManager

Just as the ActionScript **Alert** class is used to create an alert, the ActionScript **PopUpManager** is used to create the pop-up window that consists of the created MXML file. To create a pop-up window, you must first import the **PopUpManager** class:

```
import mx.managers.PopUpManager;
```

Then you call **PopUpManager.createPopUp( )**. The method's first argument is the pop-up window's parent. You can normally use the special **this** keyword, which is the current object (i.e., the main application window). The second argument is the class name to be used as the pop-up window's source. This could be the name of the MXML file, without the extension, or the name of a custom component:

```
PopUpManager.createPopUp(this, SomePage);
```

Unlike the **Alert** prompts, which are always modal, you can use the third argument in **createPopUp( )** to dictate whether or not the pop-up window is modal. Its default value is false.

Closing the Window

By default the **TitleWindow** container creates an X button in the upper-right corner of the window (see Figure 12.8). This X is intended to be used to close the window, in keeping with common user interface conventions. But in order for that to happen, you'll need to add some functionality via ActionScript.

The button, when clicked, triggers a **close** event automatically, so one option is to listen for that event on the **TitleWindow**:

```
<s:TitleWindow xmlns:fx="http://ns.adobe.com/mxml/2009"
    xmlns:s="library://ns.adobe.com/flex/spark"
    xmlns:mx="library://ns.adobe.com/flex/mx"
    close="closeHandler(event)">
```

The event listener should be written to take an event object of type **CloseEvent**:

```
import mx.events.CloseEvent;
private function closeHandler(event:CloseEvent):void {
}
```

Within the function, call the **PopUpManager**'s **removePopUp()** method, providing it with the window to close. In the current **TitleWindow**, that would be **this**:

```
PopUpManager.removePopUp(this);
```

The **TitleWindow** will need to have imported the **PopUpManager** definition, of course:

```
import mx.managers.PopUpManager;
```

An alternate way to close the window is to create your own button that, when clicked, closes the window. For that functionality, you'd just need to create a click handler for the button that invokes **removePopUp()**. Logically, you'd probably want to get rid of the default close button. To do so, you could use a custom component or create a skin for the **TitleWindow** component (see Chapter 13). Or you could just set the visibility of the close button to false. Here's a complete solution (**Figure 12.9**):

```
<?xml version="1.0" encoding="utf-8"?>
<s:TitleWindow xmlns:fx="http://ns.adobe.com/mxml/2009"
    xmlns:s="library://ns.adobe.com/flex/spark"
    xmlns:mx="library://ns.adobe.com/flex/mx" width="130" height="75"
    initialize="init()">
<fx:Script>
<![CDATA[
import mx.events.*;
import mx.managers.PopUpManager;
private function init():void {
    this.closeButton.visible = false;
}
```

code continues on next page

tip

In OOP, ***this*** is a special keyword that refers to the current object. Its exact value will change upon the context but its meaning is consistent.

tip

The pop-up window can respond to other events, such as the user clicking within the window, the user moving the window, and so forth.

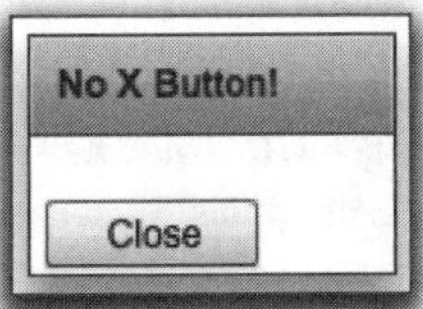

Figure 12.9

```
private function closeWindow(event:MouseEvent):void {
    PopUpManager.removePopUp(this);
}
]]>
</fx:Script>
<s:Button x="5" y="20" label="Close" click="closeWindow(event)" />
</s:TitleWindow>
```

A third way to close the pop-up window is from the primary window. To do so, create a variable when you call the **createPopUp( )** method:

```
// Outside of any function:
private var infoWindow:TitleWindow;
// Inside a function:
infoWindow = PopUpManager.createPopUp(this, Info) as TitleWindow;
```

The variable type needs to match the kind of window created, in this case **TitleWindow**. The **createPopUp( )** method returns a generic object, so the **as** keyword is used to typecast the returned object as a **TitleWindow**.

Then, when appropriate, do the following:

```
PopUpManager:removePopUp(infoWindow);
```

CUSTOM BEHAVIORS

If you create a variable to reference a pop-up window, there are other ways you can manipulate the pop-up. For example, the **centerPopUp( )** method will center the pop-up window within the Flash application:

```
var window:TitleWindow = PopUpManager.
createPopUp(this, SomePage);
PopUpManager.centerPopUp(window);
```

You can also dynamically change the window's title:

```
window.title = 'Updated Title';
```

And you can change any of the window's styling on the fly:

```
window.setStyle('backgroundColor', 'yellow');
```

tip

If you download the source code from the book's corresponding Web site (*www.dmcinsights.com/flex4/*), you'll find this example in the *Ch12/Ch12_02* folder.

Putting It Together

In Chapter 9, "Using Complex Services," I mentioned several ways of adding authentication to the client-server processes. One recommendation is to take the user credentials in a form, then using those credentials for authentication purposes on the server. As you'd only want to do this once per user session, it makes sense to create a separate interface in which this would occur. In this next example, I'll create the shell of this process. It'll be expanded upon slightly in the last section of this chapter.

1. Create a new project in Flash Builder or your alternative IDE or text editor.

   For this demonstration, I won't actually tie it to a server-side script, so it doesn't matter whether you indicate a server type (in Flash Builder) or not.

2. Create a new MXML file named *LoginWindow.mxml*, to be stored in the *src/components* directory.

   If you're using Flash Builder, select File > New > MXML Component. In the prompt (**Figure 12.10**), enter *components* as the package, *LoginWindow* as the name, and base it upon the **TitleWindow** component.

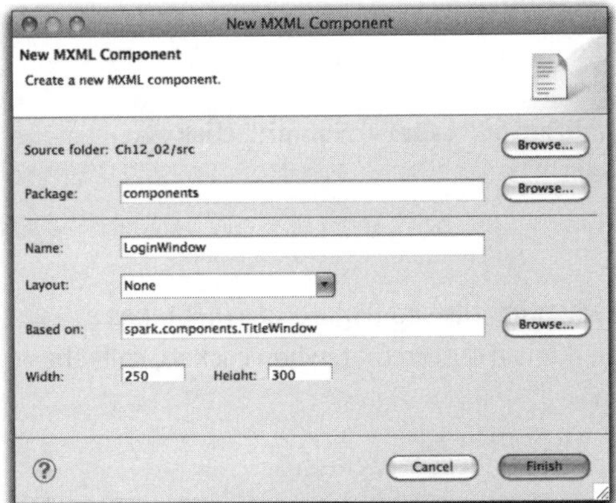

Figure 12.10

   If you're not using Flash Builder, you'll need to add the basic code:

```
<?xml version="1.0" encoding="utf-8"?>
<s:TitleWindow xmlns:fx="http://ns.adobe.com/mxml/2009"
   xmlns:s="library://ns.adobe.com/flex/spark"
   xmlns:mx="library://ns.adobe.com/flex/mx" width="250"
   height="300">
</s:TitleWindow>
```

3. If you want, add **title**, **x**, and **y** properties to the opening **TitleWindow** tag:

```
<s:TitleWindow xmlns:fx="http://ns.adobe.com/mxml/2009"
   xmlns:s="library://ns.adobe.com/flex/spark"
   xmlns:mx="library://ns.adobe.com/flex/mx" width="250"
   height="300" x="50" y="50" title="Login Form">
```

4. Add a close event handler to the opening **TitleWindow** tag:

```
<s:TitleWindow xmlns:fx="http://ns.adobe.com/mxml/2009"
   xmlns:s="library://ns.adobe.com/flex/spark"
   xmlns:mx="library://ns.adobe.com/flex/mx" width="250"
   height="300"
   x="50" y="50" title="Login Form" close="closeHandler(event)">
```

When this window is closed by clicking the X button, the **closeHandler( )** function will be called.

5. Within the body of the **TitleWindow**, create a form:

```
<mx:Form horizontalCenter="0" top="10">
    <mx:FormHeading label="Enter Credentials"/>
    <mx:FormItem label="Username">
        <s:TextInput id="username"/>
    </mx:FormItem>
    <mx:FormItem label="Password">
        <s:TextInput id="password"/>
    </mx:FormItem>
    <mx:FormItem>
        <s:Button id="submitButton" label="Submit" click=
        "submitHandler(event)"/>
    </mx:FormItem>
</mx:Form>
```

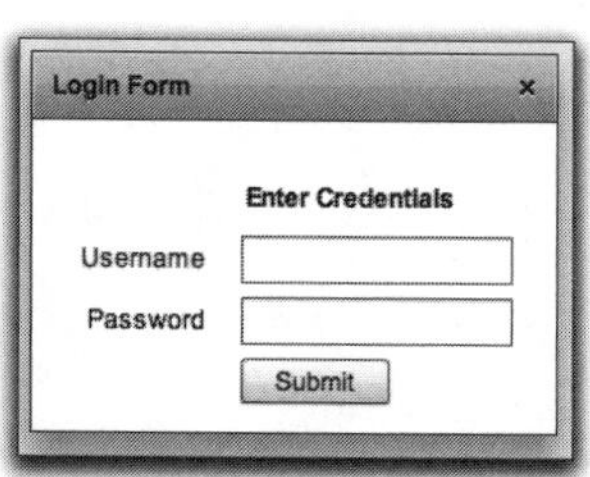

Figure 12.11

The form is what the user will primarily see (**Figure 12.11**). It takes a username and a password. It has a button that, when clicked, calls the **submitHandler( )** function.

6. Within the **Script** tags, import the necessary classes:

```
<fx:Script>
<![CDATA[
import mx.managers.PopUpManager;
import mx.controls.Alert;
```

This page will have two key events—a **CloseEvent** and a **MouseEvent**, so I first import **mx.events.***. The page will also make use of **PopUpManager**, to close this window, and **Alert**, in case of invalid credentials.

7. Define the **closeHandler( )** function:

```
private function closeHandler(event:CloseEvent):void {
    PopUpManager.removePopUp(this);
}
```

8. Define the **submitHandler( )** function:

```
private function submitHandler(event:MouseEvent):void {
    if ((username.text == 'test') && (password.text == 'test') ) {
        PopUpManager.removePopUp(this);
    } else {
        Alert.show('Invalid credentials! Please try again.', 'Error');
    }
}
```

This function is called when the submit button is clicked. Its purpose is to validate the user-submitted credentials. Normally this would be done using a server call, but to save time and space, I'll just check against static values. When the user submits *test/test*, the window will be closed. In a few pages you'll see how to update the primary application to reflect the proper authentication.

If the user does not submit valid credentials, they'll see an **Alert** message (**Figure 12.12**).

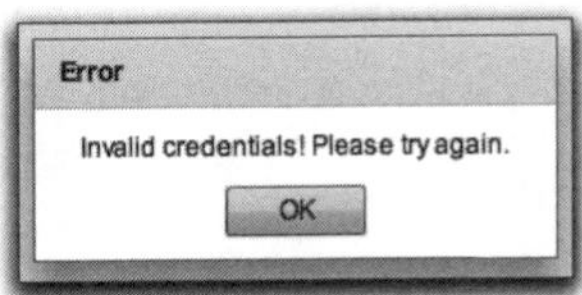

Figure 12.12

9. Complete the **Script** block:

```
]]>
</fx:Script>
```

10. In the primary application MXML file, create a **Button**:

```
<s:Button x="10" y="10" label="Login" click=
"loginButtonHandler(event)"/>
```

11. In a **Script** block, import the class definitions:

```
<fx:Script>
<![CDATA[
import mx.managers.PopUpManager;
import components.LoginWindow;
```

The **loginButtonHandler( )** function will create the pop-up window, so it needs access to the **PopUpManager**. The window's source will be the *components/LoginWindow.mxml* file, so that definition needs to be available, too.

12. Define the **loginButtonHandler( )** function:

```
private function loginButtonHandler(event:MouseEvent):void {
  PopUpManager.createPopUp(this, LoginWindow, true);
}
```

Because the credentials will be necessary for the rest of the application to use the service (in theory), I've made the window modal, by setting its third argument to true. By doing so, the user cannot ignore the login window and just return to the primary application window.

13. Save, run, and test the completed application.

Click the login button to launch the pop-up, then enter invalid and valid credentials to see the results.

COMMUNICATING BETWEEN WINDOWS

There's one more thing you need to know in order to fully use pop-up windows: how to communicate between the primary application window and a pop-up window. In the login example, some method needs to be in place to let the primary application window know that the user has successfully validated his or her credentials. There are two easy ways to accomplish this: using events or using variables.

Using Events on Other Windows

Event listeners can be created in many ways. One route, discussed in Chapter 4, "Event Management," is to use ActionScript's **addEventListener()** method. Its syntax is ***object*.addEventListener(*event*, *eventHandler*)**. You can use this method to add an event listener in the primary application window that watches for an event in the pop-up window. Start by creating a variable that will be a reference to the pop-up window:

```
private var login:TitleWindow;
```

tip

For related information on passing data between two components, see Chapter 10, "Creating Custom Code."

Next, in the function that is called when the login button is clicked, assign the creation of the pop-up window to this variable:

```
login = PopUpManager.createPopUp(this, LoginWindow, true);
```

Next, treat **login** like an associative array so that you can access its children components. In this case, the event listener must be added to the button with an **id** of *submitButton*:

```
login['submitButton'].addEventListener(MouseEvent.click,
handleSubmitButton);
```

All of this code is in the primary application file, including the definition of the **handleSubmitButton()** function. That function can access the form values by again referencing the **login** variable:

```
private function handleSubmitButton(event:MouseEvent):void {
    if ((login['username'].text == 'test') && (login['password'].text ==
    'test') ) {
        // Etc.
```

tip

You can also add a close event listener to the pop-up window from the primary application window.

By just making these few changes, the pop-up window can create the user interface but all of the logic can go in the primary application window. In a fully realized application, the **handleSubmitButton()** function would call the service operation that performs the validation. If that server-side validation process returned a token that needed to be passed along in subsequent requests, it could be stored in a local variable within the primary application window.

Using Variables

The second way to communicate between two windows is to use variables. However, the variables must be public! By definition, a private variable is only available within that same class, so a separate class, such as **TitleWindow**, couldn't "see" the **private** variables in the primary application file (and vice versa). This is all explained in more detail in the *A Wee Bit More OOP* section of Chapter 10.

Using the login example, if you wanted to retain all of the validation logic within the pop-up window, you could create a variable used to represent the validation status:

```
public var validUser:Boolean = false; // In LoginWindow.mxml
```

Then the **submitHandler( )** method would set **validUser** equal to true, when appropriate.

Looking at the primary application file, you would again want to create a reference to the pop-up window when it's created:

```
private var login:TitleWindow;
private function loginButtonHandler(event:MouseEvent):void {
    login = PopUpManager.createPopUp(this, LoginWindow, true);
}
```

Now, after the login window has validated the user, set **validUser** to true, and closed the window, the primary application could check the status by referring to **login.validUser**.

You can also pass data from the primary application window to the pop-up window by assigning a value to one of the pop-up window's public variables:

```
login.someVar = 123;
```

If you'd like to refer to one of the primary application window's public variables from the pop-up window, there's the special **parentApplication** object. For example, if the primary application window has this variable:

```
public var token:String = null;
```

Then the pop-up window could assign a new value (like the authentication token returned by the server call) in the following way:

```
parentApplication.token = event.result; // Or whatever.
```

tip

You can refer to components in other windows just as easily as you can variables.

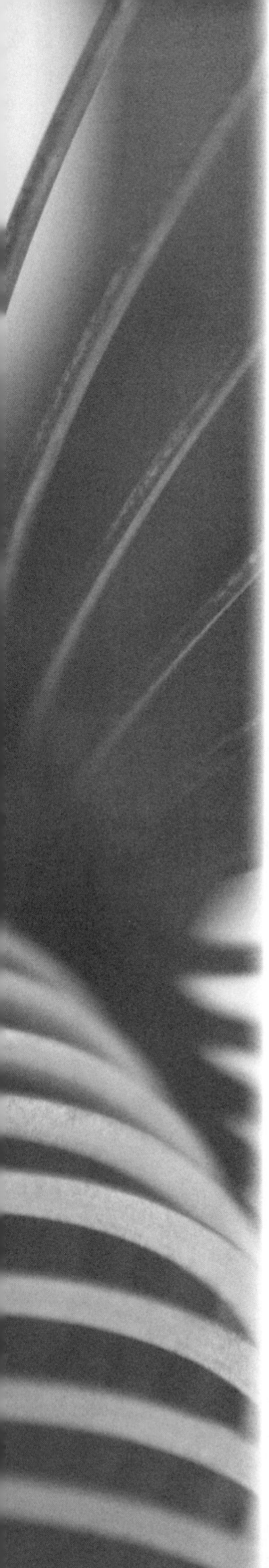

13 IMPROVING THE APPEARANCE

Flex, and especially Flex 4, make improving the appearance of an application quite easy. Primarily through styles and skins, you can customize the whole user interface to your liking.

The chapter begins with an introduction to creating graphics using MXML. In itself, just being able to draw a rectangle or circle in an application doesn't seem that significant, but when coupled with the concept of skins, you can dramatically change the application's appearance.

The second subject in the chapter is styling applications using Cascading Style Sheets (CSS). If you've used CSS in a Web page, you'll have no problems with applying CSS to Flex apps.

Next, you'll learn how to *skin* applications. Skinning goes well beyond what can be accomplished using just style sheets, and is an improved capability in Flex 4.

After that, the chapter walks through using fonts in an application. The options here range from just choosing from the common fonts that most browsers have installed to embedding your own.

The chapter ends with a quick discussion of themes. Themes are just a combination of these other elements, packaged together to create a new and complete aesthetic for your applications.

CREATING GRAPHICS

You can easily add graphical elements to your Flex application by using the **Image** tag or embedding them through CSS. But you can also add graphics to an application using MXML alone. There are three basic kinds of shapes you can create: lines, ellipses, and rectangles. Although you wouldn't likely want to go this route to create elaborate designs, using MXML is a practical option for creating simple graphics.

Before getting into the specifics, I want to point out three quick things:

1. As with almost everything in Flex, you can create graphics and manipulate using MXML or ActionScript. I'll only demonstrate the MXML here.

2. If you're already using the Adobe Creative Suite, or part thereof, you should look into the FXG (Flash XML Graphics) format. Thanks to support for FXG, you can create graphics in Illustrator, Photoshop, Flash Catalyst, and the like, and then export them in the FXG format for easy use in a Flex application.

3. On my most creative and inspired day, my graphic design skills qualify as poor. And, this is a black-and-white book. What I'm saying is pay attention to the code but don't expect to be visually wowed by my examples. Undoubtedly you can do better with the concepts taught here.

Stroking Graphics

I could start by talking about how to create the basic shapes, but because the shapes you create have no color without taking some steps (i.e., they aren't visible), I'll get to the actual shapes last. First, you should know about *stroking* a graphic, which is the term for drawing in a line, including the outline of a shape. There are three classes for creating a stroke: **SolidColorStroke**, **LinearGradientStroke**, and **RadialGradientStroke**.

SolidColorStroke creates a solid line. Its key properties are

- **color**, the actual color of the line (as a six-digit hexadecimal number)
- **weight**, the thickness in pixels
- **alpha**, the transparency (on a scale from 0.0, transparent, to 1.0, opaque)
- **caps**, how the ends are formatted (*round*, *none*, *square*)
- **joints**, how the corners are formatted (*round*, *bevel*, *miter*)

To create a blue stroke that's 2 pixels thick, fully opaque (the default), with rounded corners, you would use

```
<s:SolidColorStroke color="#0000FF" weight="2" joints="round" />
```

A **LinearGradientStroke** is exactly the same as a **SolidColorStroke** except that it transitions linearly from one color to one or more others. The **Radial GradientStroke** transitions radially from one color to one or more others (i.e., like from the inside of a circle to the outside, in arcs).

To create any kind of gradient, you must add two or more **GradientEntry** tags to the component. **GradientEntry** has **color**, **alpha**, and **ratio** properties. The **ratio** is used to control the gradient. To it you assign a value from 0.0 to 1.0. This value indicates at what point in the graphic should this gradient color reach its full saturation. For example, to evenly change from one color to another, you would use 0 and 1:

```
<s:LinearGradientStroke weight="5">
   <s:GradientEntry color="#000000" ratio="0" />
   <s:GradientEntry color="#FFFFFF" ratio="1" />
</s:LinearGradientStroke>
```

Figure 13.1

Or say you want to create a line that goes from green to yellow to red to indicate warning levels (green is fine, yellow is caution, and red is danger). Perhaps the first 80 percent of the line should be green, the next 15 percent yellowish, and the last 5 percent red. Here's how that would be represented (**Figure 13.1**, which is much less impressive in grayscale):

```
<s:LinearGradientStroke weight="10">
   <s:GradientEntry color="green" ratio="0" />
   <s:GradientEntry color="yellow" ratio=".95" />
   <s:GradientEntry color="red" ratio="1" />
</s:LinearGradientStroke>
```

The line starts with full green 0 percent of the way through, and gradually changes to full yellow at the 95 percent mark, with red being at 100 percent.

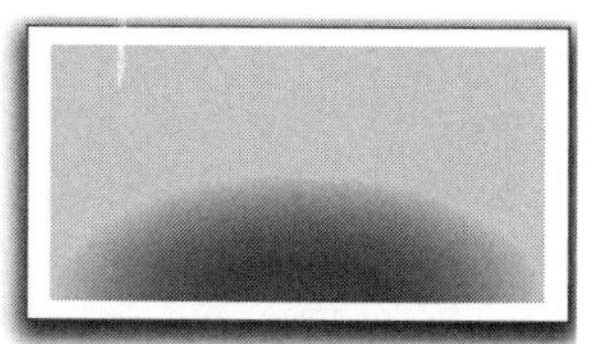

Figure 13.2

A **RadialGradientStroke** works the same way, except that it radiates out from the center. Two or more **GradientEntry** elements are used to control the colors involved (**Figure 13.2**):

```
<s:RadialGradientStroke weight="10">
   <s:GradientEntry color="#FF0000" ratio=".35" />
   <s:GradientEntry color="#FFFF00" ratio="1" />
</s:RadialGradientStroke>
```

When using gradients, there are a number of other properties that affect how the gradient is created, such as **interpolationMethod**, **rotation**, **scaleX**, **spreadMethod**, and more (but you really don't need to see five more pages on just gradients).

Filling Graphics

A line is made visible by stroking it, but rectangles and ellipses can also be colored by filling them in. For these two shapes you can use stroking and filling either individually, or both together. The fill options are **SolidColor**, **Linear Gradient**, **RadialGradient**, and **BitmapFill**. The first three are like the stroke versions but apply to the interior of the whole shape, not to just the shape's line. The **SolidColor** class has **color** and **alpha** properties:

```
<s:SolidColor color="#00FF00" alpha=".4" />
```

tip

You cannot use a fill for a line shape.

The **LinearGradient** and **RadialGradient** classes again use **GradientEntry** tags to assign the gradient colors. Here's a linear gradient from red to purple, equally spaced:

```
<s:LinearGradient>
    <s:GradientEntry color="#FF0000" ratio="0" />
    <s:GradientEntry color="#800080" ratio="1" />
</s:LinearGradient>
```

BitmapFill uses bitmap data (i.e., an image file) instead of a color. Its **source** property is where you would embed the image file. Its **fillMode** property is used to decide how the image is presented in the available area. Its possible values are *clip* (clip the image to fit), *scale*, and *repeat*. **Figure 13.3** shows an ellipse filled with repeating images. Here is part of that code:

Figure 13.3

```
<s:BitmapFill source="@Embed('../assets/logo3.png')" fillMode="repeat" />
```

Basic Shapes

As I already said, the basic shapes you can create in MXML are the rectangle, ellipse, and line. From the rectangle, you can create a square; from the ellipse, a circle; from several lines, pretty much anything. Each has **x** and **y** properties, to position the shape absolutely within its container. For the rectangle, the **x** and **y** values are for the upper-left corner of the rectangle. For an ellipse, the **x** and **y** values are for the upper-left corner of an imaginary box drawn around the ellipse, just big enough to contain it. For a line, the **x** and **y** values are the starting point of the line. All three shapes have **width** and **height** properties, used to size them. Here's a rectangle, a circle, and a line:

```
<s:Rect x="10" y="10" width="50" height="75" />
<s:Ellipse x="75" y="10" width="25" height="25" />
<s:Line x="110" y="10" width="25" height="5" />
```

Note that because none of these shapes have strokes or fills, they would not be visible in a Flex application as is. To provide a stroke or fill, use those tags within each component, then the appropriate stroke or fill class within those.

Figure 13.4

Here's a rectangle with a dark green border and a light green fill, a circle with a **BitmapFill**, and a line with a linear gradient (**Figure 13.4**):

```
<s:Rect x="10" y="10" width="50" height="75">
    <s:fill>
        <s:SolidColor color="#CCFB5D" alpha=".4" />
    </s:fill>
    <s:stroke>
        <s:SolidColorStroke color="#A0C544" weight="3" />
    </s:stroke>
</s:Rect>
<s:Ellipse x="75" y="10" width="50" height="50">
    <s:fill>
        <s:BitmapFill source="@Embed('../assets/logo3.png')"
        fillMode="scale" />
    </s:fill>
</s:Ellipse>
<s:Line x="145" y="20" width="150" height="10">
    <s:stroke>
        <s:LinearGradientStroke weight="15">
            <s:GradientEntry color="#FBB117" ratio="0" />
            <s:GradientEntry color="#C35817" ratio="1" />
        </s:LinearGradientStroke>
    </s:stroke>
</s:Line>
```

(I know, I know: My design skills are breathtaking.)

For lines, you can use the **x**, **y**, **width**, and **height** properties to size them, or use **xFrom**, **yFrom**, **xTo**, and **yTo**, which may be more intuitive.

Figure 13.5

All three shapes also have the **rotation** property. This is a value from 0 to 360 to turn the shape clockwise (rotation values of 90 and 270 are equivalent to swapping the shape's height and width for rectangles and ellipses).

A rectangle can be given rounded corners by setting **radiusX** and **radiusY** values (**Figure 13.5**). You can also round any individual corner by using **bottomLeftRadiusX**, **bottomLeftRadiusY**, **bottomRightRadiusX**, **bottomRightRadiusY**, and so forth.

tip

You can also create paths in MXML, which are a series of points that can be stroked to create a line or custom shape.

```
<s:Rect x="10" y="10" width="100" height="75" radiusX="20"
radiusY="20">
    <s:stroke>
        <s:SolidColorStroke color="#A0C544" weight="3" />
    </s:stroke>
</s:Rect>
```

The last thing to know is that if you create multiple graphics that overlap each other, they'll be drawn on the screen in the order they appear in your MXML (or are created in ActionScript). Whichever graphic is created last will be on top of the others.

tip

You can use the ***fx:Library*** and ***fx:Definition*** tags to define custom graphics to be used in an application.

A Simple Example

As a simple example of using the graphic-generating MXML, let's quickly create the image you see in **Figure 13.6**.

Figure 13.6

1. Create a new Flex project using Flash Builder or your own development tools.
2. Start by creating a filled rectangle:

```
<s:Rect x="100" y="100" width="500" height="300" radiusX="25"
radiusY="25">
    <s:fill>
        <s:LinearGradient rotation="35">
            <s:GradientEntry color="#4A7494" ratio="0" />
            <s:GradientEntry color="#66B0BA" ratio=".33" />
            <s:GradientEntry color="#83E3D8" ratio=".66" />
        </s:LinearGradient>
    </s:fill>
</s:Rect>
```

This rectangle's top-left corner is at 100, 100, and it has a width of 500 pixels and a height of 300. I've rounded every corner, too. The rectangle is filled with a linear gradient, consisting of three colors. The whole gradient is rotated slightly.

3. Add two lines:

```
<s:Line xFrom="110" yFrom="110" xTo="110" yTo="393">
    <s:stroke>
        <s:SolidColorStroke color="#E9E2CC" weight="5" />
    </s:stroke>
</s:Line>
<s:Line xFrom="110" yFrom="110" xTo="593" yTo="110">
    <s:stroke>
        <s:SolidColorStroke color="#E9E2CC" weight="5" />
    </s:stroke>
</s:Line>
```

These two tan-gray lines begin inside the top-left corner of the rectangle and go horizontally and vertically to the ends of the box. I experimented with the **yTo** and **xTo** values to get them to end just right.

tip

If you download the source code from the book's corresponding Web site (*www.dmcinsights.com/flex4/*), you'll find this example in the *Ch13/Ch13_01* folder.

4. Create a stroked rectangle:

```
<s:Rect x="100" y="100" width="500" height="300" radiusX="25"
radiusY="25">
    <s:stroke>
        <s:SolidColorStroke color="#161DD3" weight="4" />
    </s:stroke>
</s:Rect>
```

This rectangle is sized exactly the same as that in Step 2, but only contains a **stroke** property, no **fill**. By adding this outlined rectangle on top of the existing rectangle, it'll cover the ends of the two lines.

5. Add a circle:

```
<s:Ellipse x="75" y="75" width="75" height="75">
    <s:fill>
        <s:SolidColor color="#E9E2CC" />
    </s:fill>
</s:Ellipse>
```

The circle is the same color as the two lines and covers the upper-left corner of the rectangle.

6. Change the application's background color by adding **backgroundColor="#2B4161"** to the opening **Application** tag.

7. Save, run, and test the completed application.

tip

If you add a ***Label*** positioned over the rectangles, the text will appear above the graphics.

STYLING APPLICATIONS

CSS can be used in Flex applications exactly as it is in HTML pages. By defining CSS rules, you can adjust the appearance of elements, including the fonts used; the font sizes, styles, and colors; spacing; and more. In Flex 4, how components are defined makes skinning more appropriate for many cosmetic changes, but CSS still has its place in Flex applications, if, at the very least, for simple alterations or to customize older, Halo components, which cannot be skinned as easily.

CSS styling can be applied to components in many ways:

- Inline, within the MXML
- Within **Style** tags
- In an external style sheet
- Dynamically, using ActionScript

Again, this is all very similar to how HTML works (except using JavaScript instead of ActionScript).

tip

When styling within MXML, you can use bound variables for the values of the styles.

I've used a few examples of inline styling throughout the book. It's easy to implement for individual components:

```
<s:Label text="This is some text." fontFamily="Georgia" fontSize="18"
color="#300D0D" textAlign="center" />
```

tip

The Properties panel in Flash Builder has a Styles section where you can customize the look of individual components.

There are two problems with inline styling. First, you end up intertwining your presentation with your content. That's not a functional problem, but as your applications become more complex, separating out your code as much as possible is best. Second, and more important, styling on a case-by-case basis is inefficient when attempting to create a cohesive look. For this reason, applications normally use CSS that's external to the component MXML.

Basic CSS Syntax

As with CSS for a Web page, the basic CSS syntax is

***selector* { *rules* }**

The *selector* can be a specific component type, a specific style name, or an individual component. If you want to create some style rules for the entire application, you can use the special **global** keyword:

global { *rules* }

tip

In the Flash Builder Appearance panel, you can set global styles using a graphical interface.

To select one particular component, you would preface the component's **id** value with the pound sign:

#someThing { *rules* }

Many components in Flex have the **styleName** property, which can be used to associate a style class with that component. If you have

```
<s:Label text="This is some text." styleName="caption" />
```

then you would select components with that style using

.caption { *rules* }

You can even assign multiple styles to the same component by separating each with a space:

```
<s:Label text="This is some text." styleName="caption codeFont" />
```

To apply style rules to an entire type of component—every **Button** in an application or every **Label**, you would refer to the component itself:

Button { *rules* }
Label { *rules* }

However, as of Flex 4, many components have both an older Halo version and a newer Spark version; how you use styles and skins with each differs. To style a specific family of components, first import the namespaces, providing representative abbreviations for them:

tip

The abbreviations s and mx are commonly used for these namespaces, but you can use anything.

@namespace s "library://ns.adobe.com/flex/spark"
@namespace mx "library://ns.adobe.com/flex/ms"

Now you can be explicit about the component to style using the ***namespace|component*** syntax (that's the "pipe" character in between):

s|Button { *rules* }

To apply the same rules to different component types, separate them using commas:

note

If you separate two components by a space, you're narrowing the selection. If you separate two components by a comma, the selection is broader.

s|Button, s|Label { *rules* }

Selectors can be combined to help narrow the selections. This next code selects only **Label**s found within **Forms**:

s|Form s|Label { *rules* }

This is known as a *descendent selector*, as you're selecting the child of a particular parent.

You can also select just components with a specific class. This next code selects only **Label**s with a *header* style name:

s|Labels.header { *rules* }

If you're using states (see Chapter 11, "Improving the User Experience"), you can use pseudo selectors, in which rules are applied to specific component states.

tip

To style the application's ***ToolTip***s, use ***mx|ToolTip*** as the selector.

This selector applies to a **Button** in its down state:

s|Button:down { *rules* }

This selector applies to an **Image** in its over state:

mx|Image:over { *rules* }

tip

To style validation errors, use ***.errorTip*** as the selector.

The rules part of this syntax consists of one or more *property:value* pairs, each terminated by a semicolon. The available properties will depend upon the component(s) involved, but they include things like **color**, **fontFamily**, **fontSize**, **fontStyle**, **fontWeight**, **chromeColor**, **selectionColor**, **borderStyle**, **borderColor**, and so forth. You'll want to check the documentation for the components to see what styles are available. If you're using Flash Builder, it will provide a list of possible style properties via code hinting in the MXML (**Figure 13.7**).

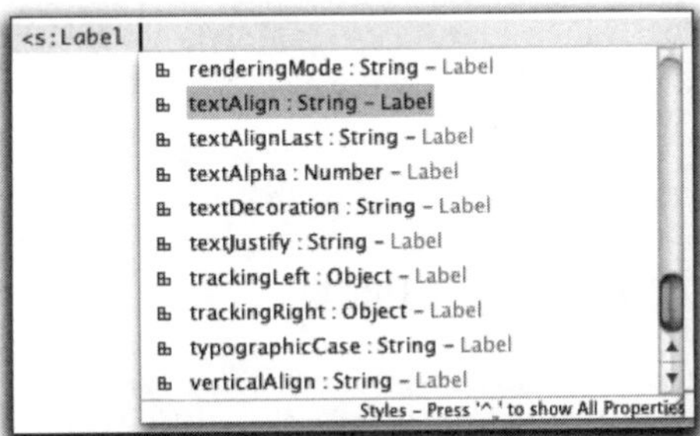

Figure 13.7

The values you use will obviously depend upon the property, but I'll explain a few rules about CSS values.

First, the default unit of measurement will be pixels, so you don't have to include *px* or *pixels* to set, say, the font size:

```
s|Label { fontSize: 15; }
```

Colors are represented using the pound sign followed by six hexadecimal digits. Sixteen colors can be represented using these case-insensitive strings: *aqua, black, blue, fuchsia, gray, green, lime, maroon, navy, olive, purple, red, silver, teal, white,* and *yellow.*

tip

Properties in CSS can be referred to using either camelcase *or hyphens. This means that both* fontSize and font-size will work. In MXML and ActionScript, you can only use the camelcase syntax.

Some properties expect an array of values. There is no CSS array data type, so just separate the multiple values by commas:

```
mx|Tree { alternatingItemColors: navy, gray; }
```

For all of these rules, you should notice that you don't quote any of the values used, even when they are strings.

If the value of a property is to be an asset, like a media file, use the **Embed** directive:

```
s|Panel { backgroundImage: Embed('../assets/watermark.png'); }
```

tip

The ***fontSize*** property can also be assigned xx-small, x-small, small, medium, large, x-large, or xx-large. What these mean in terms of actual font sizes will depend upon the browser in use.

All of your CSS code is added to an application in one of two places: within **Style** tags in the MXML file or in a separate CSS file. To do the former, you would just have the following:

```
<fx:Style>
/* Actual CSS */
</fx:Style>
```

tip

Behind the scenes, Flex uses two *default.css* files for basic formatting of applications and components.

tip

You can load a CSS script at runtime if it's first converted to a SWC file.

To use an external CSS file, you still use the **Style** tag, but use its **source** property to point to the file:

<fx:Style source="*/path/to/something*.css" />

You should only use the **source** property to include an external style sheet in the primary MXML file. Including external CSS pages this way in secondary MXML files can lead to problems.

> **SELECTING A CUSTOM COMPONENT**
>
> When using custom components in an application (see Chapter 10, "Creating Custom Code") you can style those as well. You can do this using CSS, ActionScript, and MXML within the component's definition files. Or you can style the component from the main style sheet or style section in your application's primary MXML. In that case, you'll need to first create a namespace reference for the custom component. If you have all your custom components defined in the *src/components* directory, then you would use
>
> **@namespace cx "components.*"**
>
> Now you can style the components using this syntax:
>
> **cx|*CustomComponentName* { *rules* }**

Creating Styles in Flash Builder

If you're using Flash Builder, the Styles section of the Properties panel is where you set the most common rules. By doing so, you'll be adding inline styling to the component's MXML. But you can also use this interface to begin defining the proper CSS code. Here's how:

1. Using the Properties panel, completely style a selected component as you want it to look.
2. On the Properties panel, click the Convert to CSS button.
3. In the New Style Rule window (**Figure 13.8**), select the style sheet where the rule should be defined.

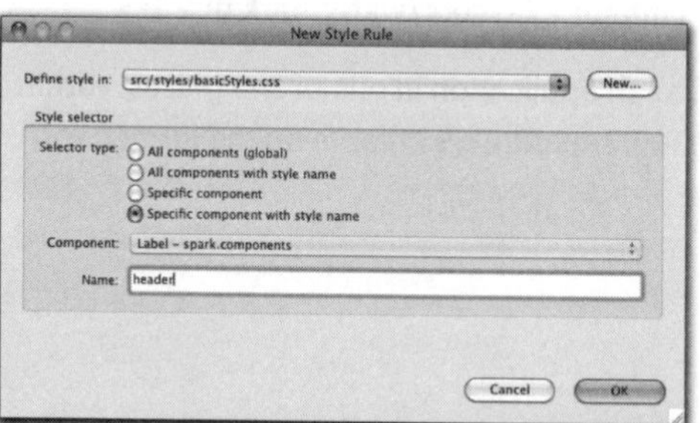

Figure 13.8

Click New if you have not yet created a primary CSS document for the application. Then, in the New CSS File window (**Figure 13.9**), identify a CSS package and filename (without the extension).

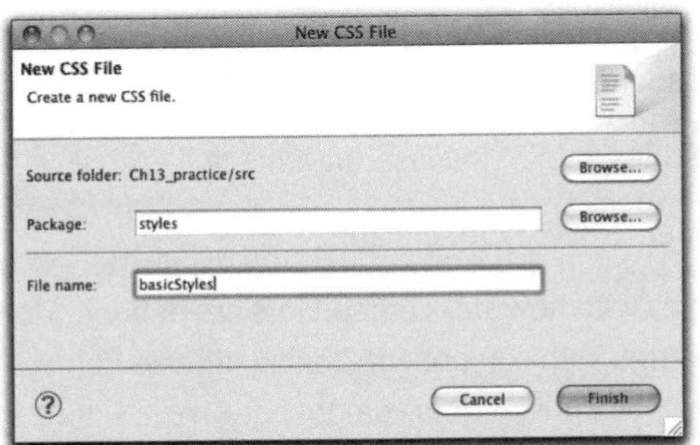

Figure 13.9

4. In the New Style Rule window, choose a selector type.
5. If you selected one of the two *...with style name* options in Step 4, provide a name for this style.
6. Click OK to complete the process.

Once you've created a CSS file for an application, other rules you add can be written to it (it'll be listed as an option in the New Style Rule window). Also, you can easily apply defined style rules to components using the Style section of the Properties panel (**Figure 13.10**).

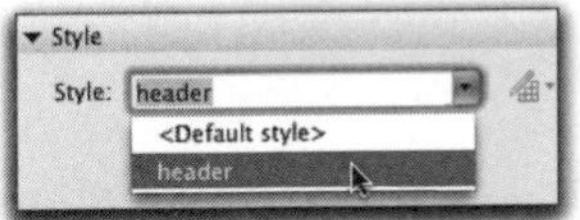

Figure 13.10

tip

As with using Dreamweaver to create a Web page, Flash Builder shows the effect of CSS styling in Design mode.

Understanding CSS Inheritance

Inheritance comes into play in two ways when using CSS in Flex. First of all, by definition, the styling rules in Cascading Style Sheets cascade down through an application, from general rules to specific ones. What this means is that you might first define rules that apply to the entire application:

```
global {
    fontSize: 12;
    fontFamily: Georgia;
}
```

Then you might create customized rules for specific parts of the application:

```
s|Button {
    fontFamily: Arial;
}
```

In a case like this, the **Button** will use a **fontSize** of 12 but a **fontFamily** of Arial. The **Button** rules first inherit the rules from the global selector, and then override any rules that get defined new values. That's the basic premise of CSS inheritance, but the actual particulars can be tricky, as there are lots of possible combinations.

Generally speaking, note the following:

- Inline styling will take precedence over anything set in CSS.
- If you have two applicable rules in CSS, the last rule wins.
- *Class* selectors take precedence over *type* selectors.

Inheritance also comes into play with how Flex components are defined. Flex has a strong hierarchical structure, with component Z being derived from component Y, which in turn may be derived from component X. As a simple and obvious example, the **HGroup** and **VGroup** components are children of **Group**. What this means in terms of your CSS is that any rules that apply to **Group** also apply to any component derived from **Group**. I'm using **Group** in particular here because *lots* of components inherit from **Group**, making it particularly impactful should you style the **Group** component.

As a good rule, never apply style rules to the ***Group*** component.

There are many inheritances that may not be obvious to you. For example, scrollbars are derived from **Button**; if you style a **Button** you're also styling **Scroller**s. Or, a **Button** contains a **Label** (the **Label** is the component that actually shows the **Button**'s text). And the **HSlider** and **VSlider** components are made up of **Button**s and **Label**s.

Despite the fact that components are inherited from one another, not all properties can be inherited. Generally speaking, color and text styling is inherited. If you look at the Adobe documentation, you'll see it say *Yes* for *CSS Inheritance* if a particular property can be inherited.

Finally, two selectors come into play with inheritance. If you set style rules on the **Application** component, those rules will apply to all *inheritable* properties. Conversely, the **global** selector's rules will be applied to all components, whether or not they can inherit the particular property.

The ***getStyle()*** method can be called on a component to get its current settings. It takes one argument, the property whose value you want to retrieve, such as ***myLabel.getStyle('fontSize')***.

Changing Styles Using ActionScript

Another way you can adjust styling is using ActionScript. You might logically do so in response to an event, such as a user action. To affect the styling of a component, apply the **setStyle()** method to the component. The syntax is ***componentId*.setStyle(*property*, *value*);**

Here is an example:

```
myPanel.setStyle('alpha', 0.5);
```

When using ActionScript for this purpose, you must quote the property name, and the values if they are strings. One gotcha when it comes to using **setStyle()** is that you cannot use the *#XXXXXX* syntax for color values. Instead you use *0x* in lieu of the number sign:

```
myLabel.setStyle('backgroundColor', 0x736AFF);
```

The most important thing you should know about **setStyle()** is that you should avoid using it, if at all possible. Just as data binding is great to have but can easily be overused, **setStyle()** is an expensive operation, in terms of computer resources. It should only be used when no other option exists.

tip

Remember that you can change the styling of components in response to some user actions by applying rules to the various states.

SKINNING APPLICATIONS

The *skin* of a component is the combination of those things that give the component its visual appearance. For example, a **Button**'s default skin includes the graphic, the graphic's color, some text, and the text's color. But **Button**s also have states: *normal*, *disabled*, *over* (when the cursor is over it), and *down* (when the **Button** is being clicked. So the **Button**'s state also dictates how the **Button** looks at each of these stages. Using CSS, MXML, and ActionScript you can change the skin of a component and even of the application as a whole.

An important thing to know up front about skins is that they can't be applied to every component. First of all, Halo components (those in the *mx* namespace) have their skins built in, so the look of those components is tightly integrated with the functionality. It doesn't mean you can't change their looks; you just can't do so easily by skinning. In this chapter I'm only going to discuss the skinning of Spark components.

Second, some components even in Spark are specifically designed not to be skinnable. These include **Group** and **DataGroup**. If you need to skin components with the same functionality, you would turn to **SkinnableContainer** and **SkinnableDataContainer**, accordingly.

Skins can come from many places. Obviously Flex ships with default skins for the components already. But you can download free and commercial skins from various Web sites, if you are graphically incompetent, such as I am. Or, you can create your own, as you'll learn about here.

How Skins Are Written

A skin starts off as a separate MXML file, like when you create a custom component, which means the first line must be the XML declaration:

```
<?xml version="1.0" encoding="utf-8"?>
```

Next, a skin's root tag should be **SparkSkin**. In that tag, declare the namespaces so that you can use the various Flex components:

```
<s:SparkSkin xmlns:fx="http://ns.adobe.com/mxml/2009"
   xmlns:s="library://ns.adobe.com/flex/spark"
   xmlns:mx="library://ns.adobe.com/flex/mx">
```

You may also see skins written using **Skin** as the root class. **SparkSkin** is just a specific extension of **Skin**. This root tag—**Skin** or **SparkSkin**—has its own properties you can set, adjusting the size and other attributes of the whole skin.

The next step is to add, within a **Metadata** section, an indication of what component type is being skinned. Use the **HostComponent** flag, providing it with a full package reference for the component. For example, to skin a **Button**, start with the following:

```
<fx:Metadata>
<![CDATA[
   [HostComponent('spark.components.Button')]
]]>
</fx:Metadata>
```

This metadata is optional, but it's best to include it so that potential bugs might be caught during the compilation process.

Next, you need to identify the states that might apply. Every skin needs at least two states: *normal* and *disabled*. For a **Button**, the normal state is *up*, but you would also likely have *over* and *down* states:

```
<s:states>
   <s:State name="up" />
   <s:State name="down" />
   <s:State name="over" />
   <s:State name="disabled" />
</s:states>
```

tip

If you use Flash Builder's wizard to create a new skin (File > New > MXML Skin), the resulting code will indicate the contract elements in a section of comments.

After that, you can create the elements that make up the skin. This is the trickiest part, and the reason why many tutorials talk about creating a "contract." This is just to say that when you go to use, say, a **Button** in a Flex application, Flex assumes that the **Button** has certain elements and capabilities. If you create a new skin for the **Button**, it must still honor that contract (i.e., meet those expectations). To find out what's expected of a component, check out the ActionScript reference for it. In the documentation, you'll see two key sections when it comes to skinning: *Skin Parts* and *Skin States* (**Figure 13.11**). As you can see in the figure, a **Button** has a skin part named *labelDisplay* of type **TextBase**, but that it's not required. A **NumericStepper** has three skin parts: a **Button** named *decrementButton*, another **Button** named *incrementButton*, and a **TextInput** named *textDisplay*. This last element is required.

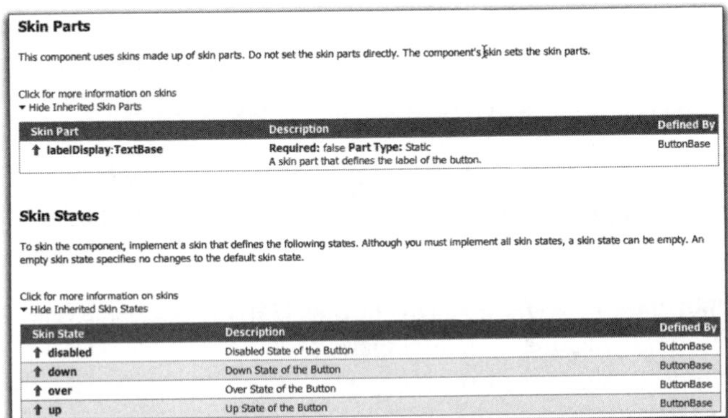

Skin Parts

This component uses skins made up of skin parts. Do not set the skin parts directly. The component's skin sets the skin parts.

Click for more information on skins
▾ Hide Inherited Skin Parts

Skin Part	Description	Defined By
↑ **labelDisplay:TextBase**	**Required:** false **Part Type:** Static A skin part that defines the label of the button.	ButtonBase

Skin States

To skin the component, implement a skin that defines the following states. Although you must implement all skin states, a skin state can be empty. An empty skin state specifies no changes to the default skin state.

Click for more information on skins
▾ Hide Inherited Skin States

Skin State	Description	Defined By
↑ **disabled**	Disabled State of the Button	ButtonBase
↑ **down**	Down State of the Button	ButtonBase
↑ **over**	Over State of the Button	ButtonBase
↑ **up**	Up State of the Button	ButtonBase

Figure 13.11

Normally you would place the elements in the skin using **BasicLayout**, which is absolute positioning. Absolute positioning is relative to the component's container, so if you're skinning a **Panel** that will be placed within a **VGroup** in the application, the **Panel**'s positioning will be absolute to that **VGroup** in that instance. With **BasicLayout**, you can also use constraint-based layout, to position the skin relative to its parent.

Skinning States

Before walking through some examples of making your own skins, let's take a deeper look at skinning states. The MXML file needs to identify the states that the component should recognize. Logically, the component will look different in each state. At the very least, a disabled component is normally shown as dimmed and a **Button** looks different when it's clicked (i.e., in its down state) than when it's not.

To make changes based upon the state, use the ***property.state*** syntax. For example, a **Button**, in its default skin, is just a rounded rectangle. Its fill is a gradient made up of two colors. In the *over* and *down* states, the gradient colors change:

```
<s:LinearGradient rotation="90">
   <s:GradientEntry color="0xFFFFFF"
      color.over="0xBBBDBD"
      color.down="0xAAAAAA"
      alpha="0.85" />
   <s:GradientEntry color="0xD8D8D8"
      color.over="0x9FA0A1"
      color.down="0x929496"
      alpha="0.85" />
</s:LinearGradient>
```

As another example, if you had a graphic and you wanted to change its appearance when the user mouses over it, you could increase its line weight:

```
<s:SolidColorStroke color="#7F38EC" weight="2" weight.over="5"/>
```

As already stated, a component is normally dimmed when in its *disabled* state. To maintain that effect, you can change the **alpha** property (the level of transparency) on the root element:

```
<s:SparkSkin xmlns:fx="http://ns.adobe.com/mxml/2009"
   xmlns:s="library://ns.adobe.com/flex/spark"
   xmlns:mx="library://ns.adobe.com/flex/mx"
   alpha.disabled="0.5">
```

State changes can apply to more than just the cosmetics; you can alter most properties during state changes, such as the **label** of a **Button**:

```
<s:Button id="thumb" label="move me" label.down="moving" />
```

tip

You can show and hide a component, without affecting the layout, by changing its alpha (to 0) or visible (to false) property.

One caveat about altering properties based upon the state is that some changes may affect the sizing or layout of the other elements in the skin.

Finally, if you want to create components only in certain states, use the **includeIn** property:

```
<s:Rect id="hldownstroke1" left="1" right="1" top="1" bottom="1"
radiusX="2" includeIn="down">
```

If you want an element to exist in most states, use **excludeFrom** to indicate when it shouldn't exist:

```
<s:Rect id="highlightStroke" left="1" right="1" top="1" bottom="1"
radiusX="2" excludeFrom="down">
```

Both of those examples are taken right from the default **Button** skin.

Creating Your Own Skins

There are two ways you can create your own skins: Start writing them from scratch or copy an existing skin and edit it as needed. In time, taking the second route would be best, but when you're just getting started, the amount of code in the framework skins can be daunting.

If you are *not* using Flash Builder...

1. Create a new MXML file in your text editor or IDE.
2. Add the code for the skin.

   You'll see two specific examples shortly.

3. Save the file as *ComponentNameSkin.mxml*.

   Skins are named using the *ComponentNameSkin.mxml* format, such as *ApplicationSkin.mxml* or *PanelSkin.mxml*. If you have multiple skins for the same component type, you'll need to expand upon this naming scheme.

   You should place your skins in their own, logical directory, such as *src/skins* or *src/com/example/skins*.

If you *are* using Flash Builder...

1. Select File > New > MXML Skin.
2. At the prompt (**Figure 13.12**), do the following:
   - Enter the package name, such as *skins* or *com.example.skins*.
   - Enter the skin name, such as *ButtonSkin*.
   - Select the *HostComponent*. Start typing to use code hinting to find the component, or click Browse.
   - Decide whether to start with a copy of the default skin or not. I'd recommend not, when just starting.
3. Click Finish.

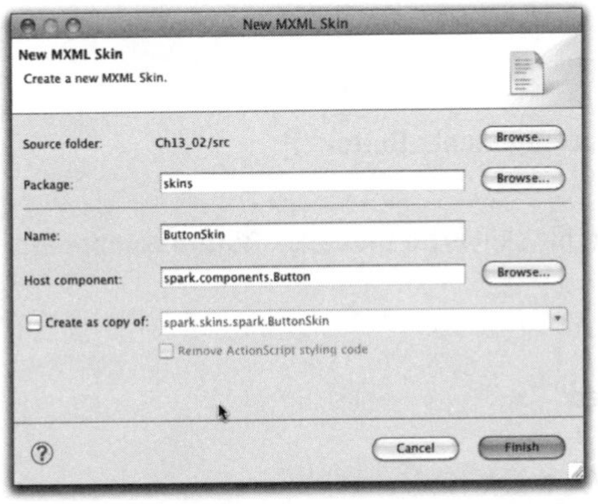

Figure 13.12

Skinning a Button

For the first example of creating your own skin, let's make a **Button** that includes a small image, displays a border on mouseover, and changes color when clicked. To make the states even more obvious, at least in **Figures 13.13**, **13.14**, and **13.15**, the **Button** text will change at each point.

Figure 13.13

Figure 13.14

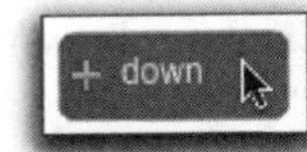

Figure 13.15

tip

If you download the source code from the book's corresponding Web site (*www.dmcinsights.com/flex4/*), you'll find this example in the *Ch13/Ch13_02* folder.

1. Create a new MXML file project using Flash Builder or your own development tools.
2. Create a new MXML file for the skin.

   If you're using Flash Builder, start by selecting File > New > MXML Skin.
3. Begin with the XML declaration:

```
<?xml version="1.0" encoding="utf-8"?>
```

   Some of this code, including this line, will be automatically created for you if you use Flash Builder to create the skin template.
4. Add the **SparkSkin** tag:

```
<s:SparkSkin xmlns:fx="http://ns.adobe.com/mxml/2009"
   xmlns:s="library://ns.adobe.com/flex/spark"
   xmlns:mx="library://ns.adobe.com/flex/mx"
   minHeight="35" minWidth="85" alpha.disabled=".5">
```

   The **SparkSkin** tag identifies the three namespaces. It also establishes a minimum height and width, so that the **Button** component (in the application) cannot be made smaller than the size required to display this skin's graphics.

   The root tag also indicates that during the *disabled* state, the entire skin should be at half transparency.
5. Add the metadata:

```
<fx:Metadata>
   [HostComponent("spark.components.Button")]
</fx:Metadata>
```

   The metadata indicates that this skin is for the Spark **Button component**.
6. Identify the states:

```
<s:states>
   <s:State name="disabled" />
   <s:State name="down" />
   <s:State name="over" />
   <s:State name="up" />
</s:states>
```

   Buttons have four states.
7. Begin a rectangle:

```
<s:Rect left="2" top="2" width="80" height="30" radiusX="5"
radiusY="5">
   <s:stroke>
      <s:SolidColorStroke color="#306EFF" weight="3" alpha="0"
      alpha.over="1" />
   </s:stroke>
```

The rectangle begins 2 pixels in from the left and top, and is 80 pixels wide and 30 pixels tall. The corners are rounded slightly. A solid color stroke is added to the rectangle. However, its **alpha** property is initially 0, meaning it'll be transparent. On the *over* state, the **alpha** is set to 1, making it visible.

8. Add the fill:

```
<s:fill>
  <s:LinearGradient rotation="235">
    <s:GradientEntry color="#6D7B8D" ratio=".33" color.down=
    "#893BFF" />
    <s:GradientEntry color="#646D7E" ratio=".66" color.down=
    "#893BFF" />
    <s:GradientEntry color="#657393" ratio="1" color.down=
    "#893BFF" />
  </s:LinearGradient>
</s:fill>
```

The rectangle will be filled with a linear gradient, involving three colors. For each **GradientEntry**, during the *down* state, the color is set to the same value, thereby changing the entire rectangle to a solid color.

9. Complete the rectangle:

```
</s:Rect>
```

10. Add an image:

```
<mx:Image source="@Embed('../assets/plus.png')" x="5" y="10" />
```

The image is named *plus.png* (it's a simple plus sign) and is stored in the *assets* directory. Its top, left corner is at 5, 10, placing it vertically centered on the left side of the rectangle.

11. Add a **Label**:

```
<s:Label id="labelDisplay" x="25" y="12" text.over="over"
text.down="down" color="#FFFFFF" />
```

The **Label** will be positioned to the right of the image. It has an **id** of *labelDisplay*, per the **Button** Skin Parts documentation. This means that when a **Button** is created in the application that uses this skin, whatever value is provided for the **Button**'s **label** property will be used for this **Label**'s **text** property.

On the *over* state, the **Button**'s **text** is changed to the word "over" and on the *down* state to "down." This is mostly just to make the states most apparent in the earlier images.

12. Complete the root element:

```
</s:SparkSkin>
```

13. Save the file as *ButtonSkin.mxml*.

    You should save it in a separate directory, like *src/skins* or *src/com/example/skins* (changing *com* and *example* to reflect your domain).

    After you create another skin (next), you'll see how to use this new **Button** skin.

tip

If you download the source code from the book's corresponding Web site (*www.dmcinsights.com/flex4/*), you'll also find this example in the *Ch13/Ch13_02* folder.

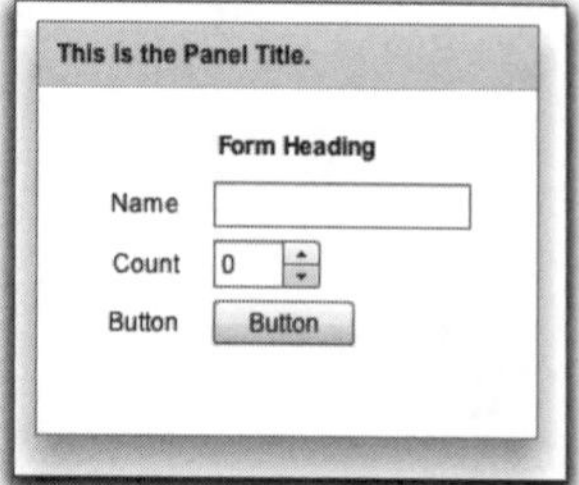

Figure 13.16

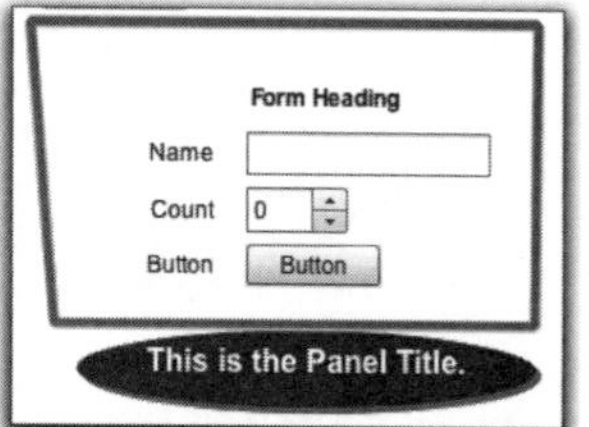

Figure 13.17

Skinning a Panel

To provide a fuller sense of what it means to skin components, let's create a skin for a different type: the **Panel**. A **Panel** has a title area at the top on a gray background, and a content area beneath on white. There's also a slight shadow for the whole component (**Figure 13.16**). Let's skin the **Panel** so that it uses an odd outline for the content, with the title in an ellipse below that (**Figure 13.17**).

1. Add another MXML file to the existing project.

   This will be *PanelSkin.mxml*, the new skin definition.

2. Create the XML declaration and the root tag:

```
<?xml version="1.0" encoding="utf-8"?>
<s:SparkSkin xmlns:fx="http://ns.adobe.com/mxml/2009"
      xmlns:s="library://ns.adobe.com/flex/spark"
      xmlns:mx="library://ns.adobe.com/flex/mx" alpha.disabled=".5">
```

   Again, I've changed the transparency of the whole skin in the *disabled* state.

3. Add the metadata:

```
<fx:Metadata>
   [HostComponent("spark.components.Panel")]
</fx:Metadata>
```

   This time the *HostComponent* is the Spark **Panel**.

4. Add the states:

```
<s:states>
   <s:State name="disabled" />
   <s:State name="normal" />
</s:states>
```

   This **Panel** only recognizes the two default states.

5. Add an outlined rectangle:

```
<s:Rect horizontalCenter="0" top="2" height="80%" width="90%"
rotationX="10">
    <s:stroke>
        <s:SolidColorStroke color="#401F13" alpha=".7" weight="5"
        joints="bevel" />
    </s:stroke>
</s:Rect>
```

   The rectangle just has a stroke property, no fill. I'm using relative positioning to place and size the rectangle.

6. Add two ellipses:

```
<s:Ellipse height="20%" width="80%" bottom="2"
horizontalCenter="-2">
    <s:fill>
        <s:SolidColor color="#736F6E" />
    </s:fill>
</s:Ellipse>
<s:Ellipse height="20%" width="80%" bottom="5"
horizontalCenter="-5">
    <s:fill>
        <s:SolidColor color="#401F13" />
    </s:fill>
</s:Ellipse>
```

   The first ellipse will act as the shadow of the second. To accomplish that effect, it's just moved three pixels. Both ellipses use relative positioning from the bottom of the parent.

7. Add a **Group**:

```
<s:Group id="contentGroup" width="80%" horizontalCenter="0"
top="10" />
```

   If you look at the documentation for the **Panel** (under the Skin Parts section), you'll see that a **Panel** can contain a **Group** element with an **id** of *contentGroup*. This represents the main content area for the **Panel** (the bottom of the **Panel** in its default skin). The **Group** is positioned to appear within the rectangle.

8. Add a **Label**:

```
<s:Label id="titleDisplay" horizontalCenter="-5" bottom="20"
color="#FFFFFF" fontSize="16" fontWeight="bold" />
```

   A **Label** with an **id** of *titleDisplay* is how the **Panel**'s title is displayed. It's positioned to appear on top of the ellipses.

9. Close the root tag:

```
</s:SparkSkin>
```

10. Save the file as *PanelSkin.mxml*.

You should save it in the same directory as *ButtonSkin.mxml*.

Using Skins

Once you've created a skin, you can apply it to your components. A direct way of doing so is to use the component's **skinClass** property:

```
<s:Panel skinClass="path.to.SkinClassName" />
```

You'll need to provide the complete path to the MXML file, minus the *.mxml* extension. If you placed the MXML file in the *skins* directory (or package), then *skins.SkinClassName* will work. If you placed the MXML file in *com.example.skins*, then you would use

```
<s:Panel skinClass="com.example.skins.SkinClassName" />
```

This code is equivalent to styling an individual component. If you have multiple components of a certain type in an application and you'd like the same skin to be applied to all, you're better off setting the skin in CSS. To do so, assign a value to the component's **skinClass** property. For the value, use **ClassReference('*path.to.SkinName*')**:

```
s|Panel {
    skinClass: ClassReference('skins.SkinName');
}
```

tip

As with most styles, you can set the skin on the fly using ActionScript, but you probably shouldn't.

However, because of the way inheritance can muddle the end result (because components inherit from many different classes), you're better off using class selectors when applying skins via CSS:

```
.skinnedPanel {
    skinClass: ClassReference('skins.SkinName');
}
```

tip

If a custom skin contains components that should also be skinned, you'll need to identify the custom skin on those components within the primary skin.

To use the **Button** and **Panel** skins just created, the *Ch13_02.mxml* file uses this code:

```
<s:Button x="10" y="10" label="Add This" skinClass="skins.ButtonSkin" />
<s:Panel x="10" y="50" width="500" height="400" skinClass=
"skins.PanelSkin" title="This is the Panel Title.">
</s:Panel>
```

As you can see in Figure 13.17 (and in the MXML file available from the book's corresponding Web site), I dropped a form in between the **Panel** tags in order to place some content within the rectangle.

WORKING WITH FONTS

Another way you can affect the look of an application is by controlling the fonts. To start, CSS has the **fontFamily** property, which dictates what font should be used:

```
global {
    fontFamily: Arial;
}
```

You can also provide a list of fonts for the value, in which case the first font from the list that is available on the user's browser will be selected:

```
global {
    fontFamily: Arial, Verdana, Helvetica;
}
```

Alternative solutions are to use *device* fonts or *embedded* fonts.

Using Device Fonts

A device font is a generic way to reference a font type. The three possible values are

- *_sans*, sans-serif, such as Arial
- *_serif*, serif font, such as Times Roman
- *_typewriter*, a monospaced font, such as Courier

If what you really want to ensure is that a sans-serif font is used, you can provide the names of specific sans-serif fonts, then end this list with *_sans*:

```
global {
    fontFamily: Arial, Helvetica, '_sans';
}
```

Essentially this means the following: Use Arial, if you can; if not, use Helvetica, if you can; if not, use whatever sans-serif font is available. As these device fonts aren't actual font names, they must be quoted in your CSS.

tip

There may be a slight performance hit if the Flash Player has to use the device font, in that the player will need to identify what font that is on the user's computer.

tip

You can also embed fonts using ActionScript. See the Adobe documentation for examples.

note

Some fonts have licenses dictating the conditions in which you can distribute them with an application.

Embedding Fonts

An alternative to relying upon the user-provided fonts is to embed fonts into the Flash application. You can embed these font types:

- TrueType (*.ttf*)
- OpenType (*.otf*)
- TrueType Collections (*.ttc*)
- Mac Data Fork Fonts (*.dfont*)
- Mac Data Fork TrueType Suitcases (no extension)

By embedding fonts, you're guaranteeing that the font you choose will be used. Also, embedded fonts can look nicer as they take advantage of anti-aliasing. On the other hand, embedding fonts increases the size of the application and you may have to take extra steps to ensure that the embedded font is handled properly, especially by the older Halo components. For example, the MX **Button** control uses the bold version of a font for its label, whereas the Spark **Button** uses the normal weight of the font.

To embed a font in an application, use the CSS *@font-face* declaration, creating an alias for the embedded font:

```
@font-face {
    src: url('/path/to/font.ttf');
    fontFamily: someFont;
}
```

If the font will be used in other styles and weights—italic, bold, etc., you'll need to also define aliases for those cases:

```
@font-face {
    src: url('/path/to/font-bold.ttf');
    fontFamily: someFont;
    fontWeight: bold;
}
```

In both cases, the **fontFamily** is given the same name. If the font is used in the application in normal weight, the first version of the font will be used:

```
<s:Label text="Embedded!" />
```

If it's used in bold weight, the second declaration applies:

```
<s:Label text="Embedded!" fontFamily="someFont" fontWeight="bold" />
```

If a font might be used in normal weight, bold weight, italic style, and in bold-italic, you would need four declarations: one for each possibility.

To use the embedded font in your CSS, you just refer to the alias where appropriate:

```
s|Label {
    fontFamily: someFont;
}
```

tip

If you have an embedded font that's not handled properly specifically by MX controls, see the Adobe documentation for the fix.

USING THEMES

A theme is a combination of CSS and skins used to give an application a complete, coherent look. The default theme in Flex 4 is *Spark*. In Flex 3, the default theme was *Halo*, but even Flex 3 (i.e., *MX* namespace) components in Flex 4 now use the Spark theme for consistency.

Although a theme can consist of just a CSS file, a theme is normally created in a SWC format, which will wrap together the CSS code plus all of the assets required, like the images, fonts, and MXML skin files. You can create your own themes, using the CSS and skinning information already presented, download free ones available online, or purchase commercial themes. The Flex SDK and Flash Builder both ship with a few themes, too.

To change a theme when using Flash Builder, do the following:

1. In Design mode, access the Appearance panel (**Figure 13.18**).

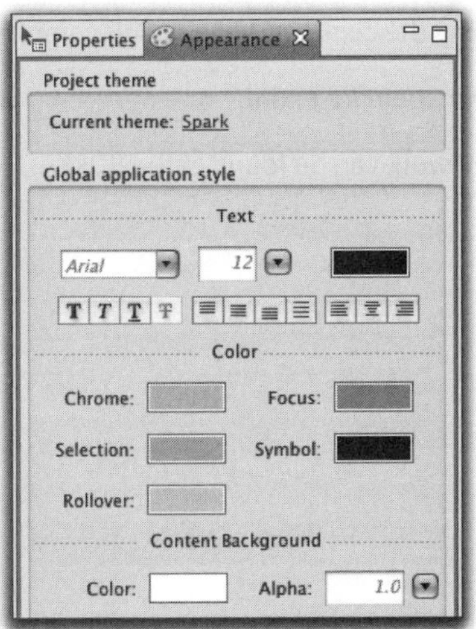

Figure 13.8

2. Under *Project theme*, click the current theme's name.

3. Use the Select project theme window (**Figure 13.19**) to preview and select a new theme.

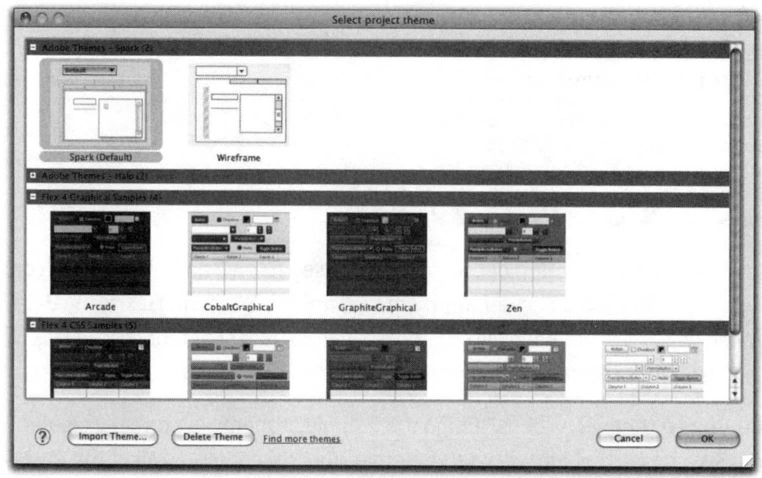

Figure 13.19

As you can see in that figure, you can also use this window to import a theme you've created or downloaded, or click the link to be taken online to view more themes.

tip

You can also select the theme in Flash Builder by going to Project > Properties > Flex Theme.

4. Click OK.

tip

To see how to create your own themes (i.e., as SWC files), see the Using Flex 4 Adobe documentation.

To change the theme if you're not using Flash Builder, you identify the theme to use as a compilation argument when using the command-line *mxmlc* compiler:

mxmlc -theme *path/to/theme*.swc *ApplicationFile*.mxml

The themes that come with the Flex framework can be found in the SDK's *frameworks/themes* directory.

INDEX

SYMBOLS

A

B

C

D

G

H

J

K

L

M

N

O

P

Q

R

S

W